The 9 Guideline Principles to Enact Change

A Legislator's Memoir from the Outhouse to State House

The 9 Guideline Principles to Enact Change
A Legislator's Memoir from Outhouse to State House

Don Brown

REBELL BOOKS

Copyright © Donald Brown, 2024

Trade paper ISBN: 9798327646230

E-book

1st edition July 2024

Printed in the United States of America

All Rights Reserved

No part of this publication may be reproduced, stored in a retrieval system or transmitted in any form or by any means, electronic, mechanical, photocopying, recording or otherwise, without prior written permission of both the copyright owner and the above publisher.

Genre: 1: Political Science   2: Memoir & Biography

REBELL BOOKS, LLC

Atlanta GA

Dedication

This book is dedicated to my beloved wife and life partner of over 45 years, Diane Brown. Her unwavering love, support, and companionship have been the foundation of my life, and I cannot imagine my journey without her by my side.

I also dedicate this book to our precious daughter, Lori Callista Brown Field, a true gift from God. Finally, I dedicate this work to our grandchildren, Christopher Brantley, Callista Grace, Addalyn Reese, and Grayson James Field. They are my hope for the future and the next generation, embodying the promise of a brighter tomorrow.

Don

ACKNOWLEDGEMENTS

This book would never have come to fruition without the encouragement and unwavering support of my dear friend Chuck Lawson. A respected State Farm agent in our hometown, Chuck was not only known for his professional integrity but also revered as a community leader. His engagement in various clubs and social groups, coupled with his role as a steadfast promoter of good governance, established him as a voice of reason within our community.

The journey toward writing this book began after the special legislative session of January 2007. Chuck was the one who suggested that I write not simply to critique those who promoted House Bill 1A, but to provide alternative perspectives on solving public policy challenges. He strongly felt that the expansion of government's role in the Florida property insurance market by House Bill 1A—a political solution to a political problem—made the underlying issues even more complex, and that this story needed to be told.

We spent hours mapping out the approach, with Chuck advocating for a narrative that was both instructive and engaging. He believed that employing a lighter tone, sprinkled with humor and illustrations, would make the complex content more accessible. He often highlighted the importance of understanding the sequence of choice and consequence, famously noting, "First there are choices, then decisions, and finally the consequences. You can hide from reality, but you cannot hide from the consequences of hiding from reality."

As life's responsibilities temporarily slowed down my progress, the project was shelved, awaiting a time when the pace of life would permit me to return to it. Recently, inspired to complete my initial vision, I returned to the unfinished work. After six dedicated months, the result is what you hold in your hands—a compilation of true stories representing a lifetime of learning. Many of life's lessons were obvious; many more were less obvious, often learned through the tough teachers of trial and error, and the inevitable consequences of choices and decisions.

Reflecting on my experiences and the conversations with Chuck, I am reminded of a personal conviction I have always held and am now more convinced of than ever: "I have always been told and am now convinced that one of the least painful ways to learn life's lessons is to study and learn from the mistakes of others." This belief has not only shaped the narratives within these pages but has also guided my approach to sharing the collective wisdom gleaned from decades of public service.

With Chuck's wisdom and my experiences as a Florida legislator, this book aims to share insights from what I describe as the "Florida Grand Experiment." Learning from Florida's missteps could spare you considerable hardship.

To Chuck Lawson, thank you for being the catalyst and the conscience of this endeavor. Your wisdom has not only shaped this narrative but also enriched my life immeasurably.

Endorsement by Leslie Waters

Currently: Mayor, Seminole, FL

Former: Florida House of Representatives 1998-2006

Speaker pro tempore 2004-2006

When I first picked up Don Brown's book, "The 9 Guideline Principles to Enact Constructive Change: A Legislator's Memoir from the Outhouse to Statehouse." I anticipated a compelling read. This book is a heartfelt journey, a tapestry of life lessons, legislative insights, and poignant reflections, all woven together with Don's humor and authenticity.

Growing up in a small rural community, Don paints a picture of a simpler time filled with profound lessons. The stories of his childhood, like the whimsical escapade with "The Wart" and the endearing mischief involving "Peanut," serve as powerful metaphors for resilience, humility, and the influence of family. These narratives highlight the significant role our upbringing plays in shaping our worldview and character.

During my time in the Florida House of Representatives, I witnessed firsthand the unique blend of wit, wisdom, and unwavering principles that Don brought to his legislative career. Serving with him from 2000 to 2006, I saw his steadfast commitment to his guiding principles of less government, lower taxes, personal responsibility, individual freedom, and stronger families. These were the bedrock of his legislative actions and decisions.

One memorable moment was his encounter with Chairman Brummer. Don's ability to stand his ground with dignity and humor was a testament to his character. He approached each legislative battle with a clear sense of purpose, whether working alongside Governor Jeb Bush on legal reform or expressing his disappointment over House Bill 1A with Speaker Marco Rubio. His recounting of these events in the book makes the reader feel as if they were right there in the chambers, witnessing history unfold.

Don's work on insurance reform, especially after the devastating 2004 and 2005 hurricane seasons, showcased his deep understanding of the issues and dedication to protecting Florida's homeowners. His essays on the Florida homeowners insurance market should be required reading for current and future legislators. Don's mantra of correctly identifying the problem before attempting to solve it is a wake-up call for all involved in public policy.

What makes this book truly remarkable are the personal stories and reflections. The heartfelt recounting of his adventures on the shrimping boat, Polly Ann, with his father, Dewey Brown, offers a glimpse into the life lessons learned on Choctawhatchee Bay. These experiences taught Don about perseverance, responsibility, and the unbreakable bond between father and son.

Faith plays a central role in Don's life, beautifully captured in this book. From the prayers that led to the mysterious disappearance of a childhood wart to the profound spiritual lessons from his mother, Velma Brown, Don's journey of faith is deeply inspiring.

"From Roots to Realization" is more than just a memoir; it is a heartfelt testament to the values that Don Brown holds dear. It is a book that entertains, educates, and inspires, urging us all to reflect on our principles and the legacy we wish to leave behind. Don's humor, wisdom, and unwavering commitment to his principles shine through every page, making this a must-read for anyone interested in leadership, public policy, and the enduring power of faith and family.

Leslie Waters
Mayor, Seminole, FL
Speaker pro tempore 2004-2006

Endorsement By Scott Johnson, AAI, CAE

First a point of personal privilege. Don Brown has proven himself to be the consummate lawmaker. Technically proficient, particularly with respect to Florida's most pressing problems such as its petulant weather, and…strategically competent with the rules of parliament and politics. The combination has proven devastating for a few detractors, and both serendipitous and immensely valuable for the 22.9 million residents of America's third most populous state. He is, most of all, to me, an independent insurance agent, a proven courageous defender of fairness and the truest of friends.

You'll find this work by Don teeming with home spun philosophies applied to massive and complex social problems. It is a world class lesson in decision making, for lawmakers and lobbyists, and for anyone pondering what is just and how to achieve justice against overwhelming odds.

Opening chapters spin tales of the simplest human endeavors juxtaposed against life in Don's small town of DeFuniak Springs. These parables are the foundation for his public life and his guiding principles that road mapped reform for Florida's "Hurricane Crisis." Simplicity, discipline, safety and security for Florida citizens and unrelenting devotion to truth--hallmarks of Don Browns' amazing legislative career.

But…it's more than that!

I garnered much from the style of his prose. I was moved to rethink Florida's trek since Hurricane Andrew and the 04/05 storms and the legislative aftermath of both. I further believe that, in the future, we should contrast some contemporary approaches with his well-established "Guiding Principles" provided in the appendix-- even the slightest erosion of which, in my opinion, could lead Florida further from the scientific and rational message and inexorably closer to short term solutions more likely to dissolve in the sand.

Far from hyperbole, Don's message is testament to the value of history. Even if you were absent when we suffered eight landfalls in 16 months (04/05) you are now dealing with the misdirections spawned to reshape the future. Don Brown was there though. This book puts you there too.

I found these pages oozing with confidence and determination. Like when this "Country Boy" from an obscure Panhandle District 5 was first elected during the Bush/Gore hanging chad fiasco. Or like grabbing the legislative sword against a cauldron of nay sayers (leaders), to oversee the repeal of Florida's Joint and Several Liability doctrine. In typical fashion he was warned it couldn't be done. I was there when it *was* done…by Don Brown. And, like his public service generally, it was accomplished, despite the odds and without a thought of personal reward.

It's so well written and crawling with life that I want to read Don's book to you like a bedtime story. But that wouldn't be right, would it? You'd lose impact and the motivation to delve.

You've got to read it yourself to know what's here and how to apply Don Brown's lessons to your own life and circumstance.

I enthusiastically recommend his book confident you'll find it to be more than just a good read…

…You'll find it to be an adventure well worth taking with lessons that extend beyond the mere act of making laws.

Endorsement by Tom Feeney

I first met Don Brown over 25 years ago when I was an elected member of the Florida House of Representatives. As a Philadelphia-born lawyer who had carpetbagged to Orlando, I found myself forming an unlikely friendship with this "Tom Sawyer" type country boy from DeFuniak Springs in Florida's panhandle.

One of my earliest encounters with Don was when I, as part of the Republican House leadership, tried to persuade him to postpone his ambition of being elected to the Florida House. We had successfully convinced a sitting Democratic legislator to switch parties, and we wanted to send a message that we would support new Republicans, even if it meant asking existing ones to temporarily delay their plans. Don, ever humble yet principled and determined, was unimpressed by our scheme but after considerable persuasion he graciously acquiesced for the next two years.

When Don was finally elected to the House, I had already become the Speaker. I admired his humility, sense of humor, and perseverance. What I didn't fully appreciate at the time was the steel-trap mind, free-market philosophy, and expertise in insurance policy that lay behind his folksy charm.

As part-time citizen legislators, we brought diverse backgrounds and professions to the table during our 60-day legislative sessions, establishing laws and policies that govern America's third-largest state. For most of us, the intricacies of Florida's precarious property and casualty insurance market remained an insolvable mystery. However, Don's expertise enriched our policymaking process immensely.

In Don's book "The 9 Guideline Principles to Enact Constructive Change: A Legislator's Memoir from Outhouse to Statehouse," Don explains the futility of well-intentioned populist efforts to counteract the laws of economics when managing catastrophic events in a state with more flood risk than any other. Legislators hoping to artificially subsidize risk have tried to override economic principles, as though they could successfully outlaw hurricanes or reverse the laws of gravity.

Don once asked me a rhetorical question that I initially thought was a trick: "How much will it cost Floridians if Florida has a '50 billion hurricane?" The answer, of course, is that Floridians will need to find a way to pay $50 billion, one way or another. The point is, you have no control over hurricanes, but you can limit the damage they cause by building smarter and stronger. The most creative gimmicks to finance catastrophe risk with borrowing may appear tempting at first but you still must pay the bill. There is no magic, if you want to reduce homeowners' insurance premiums in Florida, you must reduce losses by building smarter and stronger.

On a lighter note, throughout this book, Don memorializes his wonderful childhood family memories and seamlessly transitions from cracker wisdom to economic philosophy. His lessons learned from his parents, neighbors, and even magnolia trees inspired his incredible leadership as one of Florida's foremost insurance risk policy experts. Don always focused on addressing the real problems, not just the symptoms. Much credit should go to Diane, Don's wife. She may have been born with a hole in her heart, but her heart is so enormous, fifty holes would not suppress her passion for and love of life. Don and Diane symptomize a family of servant leaders and the benefits of citizen legislative leadership.

I recommend this book to anyone who cares about Florida and its history. If I were miraculously to become Florida's House Speaker again, I would request that every member read Don's book. His chapters on the enormously risky and complex insurance market are a must-have resource. More importantly, I would want all members to enjoy reading about Don's journey in his "Outhouse to Statehouse."

On a personal note, I am struck by how this cheerful panhandle boy engaged a "Philadelphia lawyer" and taught me about the imperatives of fair market insurance and the horrible consequences of letting short-term political expediency override common-sense planning and risk management. Even more valuable are the lessons Don taught me about servant leadership, sacrifice, principle, and humility. If, like me, you meet your "betters" in life, they may come from DeFuniak Springs, Florida, and they may impart wisdom that will stay with you forever.

Endorsement by Jeb Bush
Currently: Chairman, Finback Investment Partners LLC
Former: Governor of the State of Florida 1998-2006

"For six of my eight years as Governor, I had the opportunity to serve with Don Brown. He was always prepared, served with collegiality and good humor and was principled centered.

His book, "The 9 Guideline Principles to Enact Constructive Change: A Legislator's Memoir from the Outhouse to Statehouse" describes Don's journey from small businessman to State representative. The book also describes Don's efforts to apply sound, conservative principles to address Florida's property insurance crisis. Equally important, Don's book is a primer for current legislators to do the right thing to bring stability to insurance rates and lessen government's involvement and the liability that eventually will be passed on to Florida's families.

We need more Don Browns serving at every level of our political system."
Jeb Bush

Chairman, Finback Investment Partners LLC

Endorsement by
Dr. Jack Nicholson

Don Brown's perspective of the Florida Insurance Market has been developed over the past thirty plus years. He has seen the insurance and reinsurance market develop and change over time and has been one of the key leaders involving its evolution. Don has been an agent who has dealt with consumer/policyholder concerns at the grass root level. His experience as a state representative and chair of the insurance committee has heightened his view of the workings of insurers, reinsurers, insurance regulation, and the legislative environment in Florida.

Don Brown is a member of the Advisory Council for the Florida Hurricane Catastrophe Fund as well as a member of the Florida Building Commission where he has had a role in building and strengthening state programs. Service as a consultant and lobbyist has acquainted Don with a broad perspective of the reinsurance markets and capital markets that are essential to any viable insurance market's overall success.

Most importantly, Don's book is a constructive attempt to not only explain the structure and history of the Florida insurance market, but to critique it in a way that only someone with his perspective and background can do. I have worked closely with Don over the last 20 years in discussing numerous issues, problems, proposed reforms, legislation, and the need for responsible and practical ways to strengthen the system in the future.

Don's book is well written, organized, and thought out. It is an excellent read for those in the insurance industry, in government, or for those seeking knowledge about the workings of the insurance system in Florida and its evolution.

Dr. Jack E. Nicholson is President and Consultant for Catastrophe Risk Consulting, LLC. Dr. Nicholson was the Chief Operating Officer for the Florida Hurricane

Catastrophe Fund for over 21 years and also served as a research faculty member and Director of the Florida Catastrophic Storm Risk Management Center at Florida State University.

Foreword By Dennis Ross

Let me tell you about a man who seems to have been crafted by God with a rather unique recipe. Picture this: a dash of Billy Graham's evangelistic zeal, a good dose of Jeff Foxworthy's down-home humor, a solid measure of Ronald Reagan's integrity and statesmanship, and just for a kick, a pinch of Southern charm that might remind you of a redneck joke or two. This man is none other than my friend and mentor, Don Brown. Don holds a distinctive place not just in my heart but also in the annals of Florida's legislative history.

As you delve into "From the Outhouse to the State House," you'll come to see the many facets of Don. You'll discover his religious conviction that echoes Billy Graham's fervor and the way he brings that same passion to everything he speaks and does. I can't count the number of times during our days in the legislature when I wondered if we were in the middle of a policy debate or listening to a Sunday sermon!

Don's storytelling is nothing short of captivating. He brings a chapter like "Roots to Realization" to life, almost as if you're stepping right into a scene from "Tom Sawyer." Knowing Don for over twenty years, I've seen how he can spin a simple chat into a Southern tale that leaves everyone a bit wiser and much more entertained.

Take, for example, the story he tells, a story I personally witnessed, in chapter nine while in debate with his Democrat colleague Jack Seiler. He made his point on the floor of the Florida House of Representatives using the elimination of two of his three fingers only to leave the middle finger remaining. The legislative chamber erupted with laughter. That's Don for you – never ordinary, always memorable.

Don is a true statesman through and through. He embodies what the 19th-century theologian James Freeman Clarke meant when he said, "A politician thinks of the next election. A statesman, of the next generation." Like Ronald Reagan, Don has always had his eyes on what's best for the next generation.

During a crucial debate on the High-Speed Rail Authority Bill, which I was sponsoring, Don faced a tough choice. Despite his personal reservations and potential political fallout back home, he whispered to me that he'd sacrifice his vote if I needed it to pass the bill. That's the kind of man he is—ready to put his career on the line for a friend. Luckily, we passed the bill without needing to compromise his stand, and he could record a 'No' vote.

Don's influence on my career has been profound, warning me against those who talk a good game about the greater good but act out of self-interest. His stories in this book aren't just tales; they are life lessons on principled leadership. The controversy around House Bill 1A, for example, shows how we stood by our principles, facing ostracism from our party but earning respect from our constituents—a testament to the value of standing firm in one's beliefs.

Above all, Don is a man of deep wisdom and patience, particularly about risk management and insurance, advocating for market-based solutions over government interventions. His experiences lend a credible voice to what truly benefits the state of Florida.

While you might enjoy Don's candid narration of his life and political escapades, I challenge you to also draw from his wisdom. Let it inspire you to prioritize the greater good in your own life. I know I am better for having Don in my life, and I believe you'll feel the same after reading his story.

Table of Contents

Introduction 1

Part 1: Personal Foundations and Early Insights 5

Chapter 1: Reflective Beginnings: Paths of Resilience and Gratitude 6

Chapter 2: Under the Magnolia: Lessons from a Rural Upbringing.............. 12

Chapter 3: From Roots to Realization: A Tale of Family, Faith, and Discovery 25

Chapter 4: 'Til The Storm Passed By.. 41

Part 2: Professional Beginnings and Political Ascent 53

Chapter 5: Transformative Echoes: A Journey Through Leadership and Legacy in DeMolay.. 54

Chapter 6: My Political Career - Early Education and Influences 66

Chapter 7: My Political Career - Professional and Political Beginnings............ 71

Part 3: Legislative Career and Major Themes 80

Chapter 8: My Political Career - State Representative Career – Personal Challenges and Reflections.. 81

Chapter 9: My Political Career - Legislative Achievements and Battles 90

Chapter 10: My Political Career - Conclusion and Reflections on Leadership 112

Chapter 11: From Roots to Realization - Bridging Youthful Lessons and Professional Wisdom.. 123

Part 4: Essays on Insurance and Public Policy 127

Chapter 12: Introduction to the Chapters on Insurance................................. 128

Chapter 13: Introduction to the Chapters on Insurance: The Evolution of Insurance: From Ancient Practices to Modern Risk Management 135

Chapter 14: Navigating Florida's Insurance Market: Challenges and Opportunities 141

The 9 Guiding Principles for Insurance Legislation 150

Chapter 15: The Key to Reducing Florida Homeowners' Insurance Premiums:- Reduce Losses! 156

Chapter 16: Code Plus: Elevating Florida's Defense Against Hurricanes Through Enhanced Building Standards.. 164

Chapter 17: Risk vs. Uncertainty: Insights from Dr. Frank H. Knight........... 181

Part 4: Essays on Insurance and Public Policy 194

Chapter 18: Storms and Stability: Crafting Equitable Strategies in Residential Property Insurance 195

Chapter 19: The Price of Paradise: Unmasking the True Cost of Living in Hurricane-Prone Florida 207

Part 4: Essays on Insurance and Public Policy 220

Chapter 20: Risk Management in the Face of Florida's Catastrophe Hurricane Exposure 221

Chapter 21: The Joseph Principle: Navigating the Storms of Florida's Property Insurance Market 229

Chapter 22: Hurricane Models: Imperfect Yet Indispensable Tools in Risk Management 240

Chapter 23: Gambling vs Insurance 248

Chapter 24: The Comedy of Stubborn Human Behavior: 257

Chapter 25: Citizens Property Insurance Company: The Big Gamble 266

Chapter 26: Citizens Assessments... 273

Chapter 27: Economic Recovery Post Canterbury Earthquake in New Zealand Versus Japan... 277

Chapter 28: Ellsberg, Knight, and the Florida Investor: A Tale of Risk and Uncertainty 285

Chapter 29: Florida's Shifting Paradigms: Navigating Through the Storms of Change 292

Chapter 30: Beyond the Storm: How Reinsurance Protects Florida's Homeowners... 300

Chapter 31: Navigating the Complexities of Florida's Property Insurance Market 315

Chapter 32: Behavioral Economics and Decision Making Under Uncertainty: A Comprehensive Analysis 325

Chapter 33: The History of Florida Hurricanes: The Apex of Catastrophe 332

Chapter 34: Navigating the Storm - Synthesizing Florida's Insurance Landscape 359

Chapter 35: From Roots to Realization: Honoring the Influential Figures of My Legislative Journey 366

Chapter 36: My Steadfast, Loving Wife 413

Part 5: Concluding Reflections and Tributes 429

Chapter 37: Brad Drake – My Righthand Man 430

Part 6: Media Relations 436

Chapter 38: Introduction to Media Interactions 437

Chapter 39: Balancing Act: Navigating Insurance, Environment, and The Economy in Florida's High-Risk Waters 440

Chapter 40: Northwest Florida Daily News 02.11.2007 Guest Column By Don Brown Can Florida afford "affordable" insurance? 444

Chapter 41: The Walton Sun Editorial Opinion 02.2007 Don Brown voted correctly on the Florida Insurance Bill 448

Chapter 42: Principle Over Politics: The Story of Two Lawmakers Stand Against Insurance Reform 450

Chapter 43: DeFuniak Herald Breeze Editor's Comment 02.2007 No Insurance Against Sore Winners 458

Chapter 44: Brown: Crist is a 'Classic Demagogue' 460

Chapter 45: Former Rep. Brown Speaks to State Farm Agents, Criticizes Gov. Crist 462

Chapter 46: Don Brown: Unplugged Adapted based on an Article Published in the DeFuniak Springs Herald Breeze June 19, 2008 464

Introduction

Dear Reader,

As I sit down to write this introduction, I find myself reflecting on a childhood memory that has stayed with me throughout my life. Growing up in a small, close-knit community, I learned the value of hard work, honesty, and the power of coming together to overcome challenges. It was a time when a person's word was their bond, and the wisdom of our elders was cherished and passed down from generation to generation. This memory lays the foundation for the lessons and insights I aim to share with you throughout this book.

Now, I'm not just here to preach about hard work and honesty. I'm also here to entertain you. After all, life is full of funny moments, even when you're wrangling stubborn farm animals or running for elected office. So, expect a few good laughs along the way.

Through a combination of memoir and essays, I will take you on a journey that traces the thread from my upbringing to my professional life as a former Florida legislator. By sharing my experiences and the lessons I've learned along the way, I aim to provide you with a unique perspective on risk management, decision-making, public policy, and the value of standing firm when the things you hold dear are challenged.

The following three principals have guided much of my work as a legislator:

1. "It is a little recognized fact that in Western Cultures we tend to focus on symptoms rather than the root cause(s) of our problems. This tendency to focus on symptoms rather than the cause can also be seen in many other aspects of western culture, not the least of which is 'Public Policy.'"

2. "The golden rule of problem solving: Rule #1: Properly identify the problem, Rule #2: Properly identify the problem, and Rule #3: Refer to Rule #1 and Rule #2 before proceeding."
3. "Self-preservation and self-development are common aspirations among all people…However, there is also another tendency that is common among people. When they can, they wish to live and prosper at the expense of others…This fatal desire has its origin in the very nature of man—in that primitive, universal, and insuppressible instinct that impels him to satisfy his desires with the least possible pain." - Frédéric Bastiat

If you find nothing more of value in this collection of essays, it is my sincere hope that these will be as meaningful to you as they have been to me. For a deeper exploration of these themes, please refer to the essay contrasting the views of Sun-Tzu and Frédéric Bastiat in Chapter 5.

In the first part of the book, I will share personal stories that shaped my worldview and guided my approach to business, politics, and faith. These stories will offer a glimpse into a way of life that values hard work, honesty, family, and community—values that I believe are just as important today as they were during my childhood. Plus, I'll sprinkle in some humorous anecdotes about my adventures, like the time I thought it was a good idea to race a pig at the county fair. Spoiler: the pig won.

By sharing these experiences, I hope to inspire you to reflect on the lessons and wisdom you've gained from your own life and the lives of those around you.

As we move into the essays, I will draw upon my experience as a Florida legislator during the "Florida Grand Experiment" to explore the challenges and pitfalls of public policy decision-making. A key focus of these essays will be the importance of identifying root causes rather than merely addressing symptoms when confronting complex problems. Using the example of high homeowners' insurance premiums in Florida, I will demonstrate how these premiums are a symptom of a larger issue—the state's vulnerability to hurricanes and human behavior—and why addressing this problem requires a more nuanced approach than simply treating the symptoms.

Throughout the book, I will also share my insights into the nature of leadership and how these principles can be applied to decision-making in various contexts. Whether you are an insurance professional, risk management expert, policymaker, academic, student, Florida resident, or simply someone interested in decision-making and risk, I believe the lessons and insights in this book will resonate with you and provide valuable guidance for navigating the complexities of our world. And let's be honest, navigating complex issues is a lot easier when you can chuckle at the absurdity of it all from time to time.

As you read through the memoir and essays, I encourage you to reflect on your own experiences and consider how the lessons I share can be applied to your own life and work. By the end of this book, my hope is that you will have gained a new perspective on problem-solving, risk management, and the importance of strong leadership in the face of adversity.

Thank you for joining me on this journey. I am honored to share my story with you and look forward to the insights and conversations that will emerge from these pages.

Sincerely,
Donald Brown

Part 1

Personal Foundations and Early Insights

CHAPTER 1

Reflective Beginnings: Paths of Resilience and Gratitude

Life is a rich mosaic, weaving unique threads of stories—stories of triumph, tribulation, and those serene moments that seamlessly bind our days into years. Reflecting on my journey, I am grateful for the blessings that have shaped my path.

Growing up in a tight-knit community, I learned early on that leadership isn't about titles or power; it's about integrity, resilience, and the ability to unite people towards a common goal. Watching my parents and neighbors navigate hardships with grit and grace, I understood that true leadership emerges in the face of adversity. These early lessons formed the bedrock of my leadership philosophy, emphasizing the importance of honesty, hard work, and collective problem-solving.

A Season of Joy and Reflection

This weekend, as the fragrance of pine and the melody of carols fill the air, I am reminded of the true essence of Christmas. It is a time to celebrate the Christmas story, cherish family and reflect on the divine grace that has guided me through life's challenges.

A Testament to Resilience

Today marks the culmination of a business trip linked to my consultancy role with the Florida Insurance Council. It was a testament to the resilience and dedication that defined my year. As a pastor, I stand prepared to share a message of hope and redemption.

The Canvas of Insurance

Insurance has been the canvas against which I've nurtured my family and served my community. From my legislative tenure in Florida to the thriving agency my wife and I established, each policy has been a covenant of security and trust.

As a consultant to the Association of Bermuda Insurers and Reinsurers, a member of the Florida Building Commission, and Chairman of the Florida Hurricane Catastrophe Fund Advisory Council, I continue to advocate for a delicate balance between integrity and safeguarding. I recall an era when regulations seemed more like entrapments, stifling progress and fairness. It was a period poised for change, and I am proud to have contributed to ensuring the steadfastness of insurance for every citizen.

My voyage to this point is often characterized by those close to me as a testament to tenacity—a quality my wife affectionately associates with my steadfast morals, unwavering ethics, and deep-seated faith. This tenacity, an unyielding refusal to compromise on righteousness and truth, has steered me through life's storms and successes. Some liken me to a bulldog. I always respond: "That is not true. A bulldog can hurt you. I am more like a Chihuahua. All a Chihuahua does is nip at your ankles, but they never shut up."

The Journey of the Pawn Shop

My venture into pawnbroking might seem incongruent with my moral compass, but it was a journey that unraveled the core of my mission: to serve and uplift. By establishing a business that genuinely aimed to assist those in financial need, I created a haven where my community could find support without compromise.

The pawnshop became more than a business; it was a place where I could listen to patrons, understand their needs, and share the "Good News." It drew individuals unaware that solutions could be found through faith.

Retirement from the insurance industry hasn't diminished my dedication to service; instead, it has augmented it, allowing me to infuse my experiences into sermons that touch souls and ignite hope. My church, modest in scale, is equally a source of immense encouragement. We minister to each other.

Luminaries and Life Lessons

Throughout my journey, I've been enlightened and inspired by luminaries like Peter Marshall, Frédéric Bastiat, Dr. Randal Holcombe, and the comedic relief of Ray Stevens. Stevens' anecdotes often strikingly mirror real-life situations, offering more than mere amusement. Some of my all-time favorites are: "It's Me Again, Margaret," "Shriner's Conventions," "The Streak," "The Mississippi Squirrel Revival," "Sittin' Up with The Dead," "The Booger Man," "I'm Getting Sued by Santa Claus," and "No Lawyers in Heaven."

On a more serious note…:

Peter Marshall's works, "The Light and the Glory" and "From Sea to Shining Sea," delve into America's Christian heritage and the role of divine guidance in its founding and growth.

For example, it describes how the Pilgrims' faith influenced their settlement and survival in the New World and discusses George Washington's leadership during the Revolutionary War, emphasizing the role of divine providence in America's founding.

"From Sea to Shining Sea" continues from 1787 to 1837, focusing on America's expansion and challenges. It includes accounts of how the new Constitution was divinely inspired and details the Second Great Awakening, a religious revival that influenced American society and politics during this period.

Both books intertwine historical events with the notion of America's Christian heritage and divine guidance.

Bastiat, with profound gravity, probes into the core of human nature. His views on empathy and understanding as cornerstones across all facets of life, be it in professional, governance, or family realms, have significantly shaped my interactions.

Drawing from my professional experiences, I've been deeply influenced by Bastiat's insights, which highlight a fundamental human trait: we all strive for self-preservation and development, yet there's a common urge to thrive at others' expense.

Bastiat poignantly articulates a profound human truth: "Self-preservation and self-development are common aspirations among all people…However, there is also another tendency that is common among people. When they can, they wish to live and prosper at the expense of others…This fatal desire has its origin in the very nature of man—in that primitive, universal, and insuppressible instinct that impels him to satisfy his desires with the least possible pain."

From a different perspective, Dr. Holcombe uses a powerful illustration to demonstrate the concept of supply and demand. Dr. Holcombe explains: *"If you give away or sell a product or service at less than market value, then you should never expect to be able to meet the demand for that product or service."*

The more I thought about this, the more convinced I became that this simple sentence contained a profound economic principle.

I also realized that I could not wholly understand this principle without the help of a simple illustration.

Dr. Holcombe illustrates: "I have a machine that can legally print $100 bills. The machine will wear out after about 10,000 copies. I am willing to sell each $100 bill for $50. How many would you like to purchase?

If you are smart, I will never be able to satisfy your demand because, with the purchase of every $100 bill, you are getting $50 for nothing."

That is similar to what the government does. It extracts (forcefully) from some and gives to others for nothing.

In the case of homeowners insurance, state regulators or laws passed by the legislature can result in suppressed rates in high-risk territories and inflated rates in low-risk territories. When this happens, it is called a cross-subsidy, i.e., the practice of using funds collected from one group to subsidize another, often higher-risk, groups. Cross-subsidies can distort market signals, resulting in inefficiencies like the overconsumption of underpriced services and the underconsumption of overpriced ones. They can create unfair competitive advantages, discourage innovation, and misallocate resources.

In insurance, for example, they might result in inadequate risk pricing, encouraging risky behavior and making it difficult for more accurately priced competitors to survive, potentially reducing overall market competitiveness and efficiency.

Dr. Holcombe's illustration highlights an economic principle: Demand will always exceed supply if one offers a product or service below market value.

Comparing this to Frédéric Bastiat's quote, we observe complementary perspectives. Bastiat discusses human nature's inclination toward self-preservation and the desire to prosper at others' expense, which aligns with Holcombe's illustration of government redistribution.

Both discuss fundamental economic and behavioral principles, albeit from different angles: Bastiat focuses on individual tendencies and moral philosophy, while Holcombe illustrates the practical economic implications of such tendencies when applied to policy. Their ideas together provide a nuanced understanding of human behavior and economic policy, highlighting the balance between individual desires and societal implications.

Chapter 1 Summary: Reflective Beginnings: Paths of Resilience and Gratitude

Reflecting on my journey in Chapter 1 of "Personal Foundations and Early Insights," I weave together the threads of my life, emphasizing gratitude and resilience. From my roles as a pastor, insurance consultant, to community leader, I share anecdotes that illustrate my dedication to service. Whether navigating the complexities of insurance reform or advocating for integrity in legislative matters, each experience underscores the importance of tenacity, faith, and ethical conduct. Drawing inspiration from luminaries like Peter Marshall, Frédéric Bastiat, and Dr. Randal Holcombe, I invite readers to glean wisdom from their teachings and apply them to their own lives.

Transition to Chapter 2:

As I conclude Chapter 1, reflecting on the wisdom gained from luminaries and personal experiences, there's a natural segue into Chapter 2, where the focus shifts to my childhood foundations. As I invite you to journey back in time, I aim to uncover the roots of my resilience, gratitude, and unwavering faith. These values, instilled in my early years were deeply rooted in the rich soil of my rural upbringing, where every chore and adventure mirrored the timeless tales of Tom Sawyer.

Chapter 2

Under the Magnolia: Lessons from a Rural Upbringing

Growing up in the heart of the countryside, my life was an adventure that would rival Tom Sawyer's. It was like it was straight out of a storybook, filled with tasks, mischief, and lessons learned the hard way. Let me take you through my childhood journey, where each chore was an epic quest, and the old Magnolia tree in our front yard was my kingdom and my nemesis.

The Magnolia Kingdom

Our family home, acquired by my Daddy when I was four years old, was an aged plantation-style dwelling dating back to the late 1800s. It featured spacious porches at the front and back, with an airy corridor dividing the interior, separating Momma and Daddy's sleeping quarters from the rest of our living areas.

This venerable structure stood amidst 14 lush acres, bordered by a meandering creek to the north. Daddy secured this haven for $875, with a modest down payment of $50 and a commitment to a monthly mortgage of $25—a small price for a realm filled with endless possibilities.

A majestic Magnolia tree, distinguished and stoic, stood sentinel over our home, embodying both a bastion of solitude and a vessel for boundless adventure. It was more than a tree; it was a fortress, a pirate vessel, a dragon awaiting conquest. Climbing its towering limbs, I claimed sovereignty over all I surveyed, embracing the world with the audacity of youth.

Yet, the fantasy realm was grounded by the duty of care—for the Magnolia demanded its tribute each autumn. Tasked by Momma, the battle against the falling leaves commenced yearly, turning my enchanted kingdom into an arena of perseverance. Despite its grandeur, the tree tested my mettle with the challenge of its annual shedding, each leaf a call to arms.

The Garden of Life

Beyond the Magnolia's shade, the garden stretched out, a bountiful expanse first tilled by Daddy's hands and later entrusted to Momma and me for harvesting. This patch of land was not just a source of sustenance but a joint venture into agriculture that extended beyond our family table. Each day spent there was a lesson in perseverance.

Toiling in the family garden under the watchful eye of my mother, I learned that leadership is not about instant results, but rather the patience and persistence to nurture growth over time. Just as the seeds we planted required constant care and attention before yielding fruit, I understood that effective leadership involves consistent effort, even when the outcomes are not immediately visible. This early lesson in delayed gratification and the value of sustained commitment has been a guiding principle throughout my leadership journey. This hands-on experience in the garden reinforced a fundamental truth about success and effort: 'Doers get to the top of the oak tree by climbing it. Dreamers sit on an acorn.' Just as the fruit trees in the garden began as mere seeds, my ambitions required not just dreams but active pursuit.

This understanding became the cornerstone of my approach to life and later, my political career. Just as the garden required constant tending and the courage to see beyond the soil, my path to the legislature demanded resilience and a proactive stance—traits that I cultivated from those early days in the garden.

As we unearthed the bounty of vegetables and fruits, our efforts fed us and brought the community to our door, willing to exchange their coins for a share of our harvest.

While laborious, this endeavor swelled our hearts with pride and a sense of contribution to our family's livelihood. Our garden, thus, was more than just soil and produce; it was a testament to the fruits of collective labor and the sweet taste of shared success.

The Leaf-Burning Misadventure

Now, let me recount the tale of one particularly memorable autumn. Tasked with the arduous endeavor of gathering the Magnolia's fallen leaves, I hatched a plan to make even the bravest knights think twice.

Inspired by the epic tales of cowboys and dynamite, I decided to incinerate the leafy dragon's remnants in a blaze of glory.

Foregoing the wisdom of seeking Momma's approval, I was wholly ensnared by the thrill of the challenge. I meticulously arranged the leaves into a colossal pile, envisioning the magnificent bonfire that would ensue.

Remembering the cowboy's wisdom of keeping a safe distance from the explosion, I doused the pile in gasoline, creating a long fuse that allowed me to retreat hastily.

With the stage set, my heart pounded with anticipation as I struck the match, igniting the trail of gasoline. The flame slithered towards the pile with the grace of a dancer, and then—BOOM!

The sky was ablaze with the aerial dance of leaves, soaring higher than I thought possible, creating a spectacle that shook the foundations of our home and the neighbor's peace.

Retribution was swift and fierce. With the speed of a gazelle and the fury of a storm, my Momma made her displeasure known. The lecture was epic, the spanking legendary, and the lesson unforgettable.

Faced with the Herculean task of gathering the leaves once more, nursing a sore bottom and a bruised ego, I understood the gravity of my actions and vowed to never do that again.

This misadventure taught me profound and memorable lessons. More than simply heeding maternal counsel, it forged humility, responsibility, and a keen awareness of the consequences of playing with fire—both literally and figuratively.

As I reflect on those days, with all their trials and triumphs, I can't help but smile. As foolish as some may have been, those adventures shaped me into who I am. They taught me about the importance of wisdom, hard work, and family's enduring love. And just like the Magnolia tree, with its deep roots and towering presence, these lessons have stayed with me, grounding and guiding me through life's many seasons.

The Entrepreneurial Spirit

As my reputation as a young landscaper flourished in our little community, word spread, and soon, my services were in high demand. Among the first to enlist my grass-cutting expertise was my dear, sweet aunt, Aunt Lillian. She wasn't just any client; Aunt Lillian's house became my favorite summer destination, where the afternoons transformed her lawn into a lush masterpiece.

After each session, Aunt Lillian handed me the crisp one-dollar bill and invited me to join her on the front porch. There, we'd spend hours swinging gently, lost in conversation. It was more than just a job; it was a cherished ritual between the wisest of women and a boy eager to learn about the world through her eyes.

The buzz about my lawn-mowing prowess spread, and before long, other neighbors were knocking on our door. This burgeoning enterprise of mine caught Daddy's attention, who one day announced that we were heading to the hardware store. The purpose of the trip was shrouded in mystery, sparking a whirlwind of anticipation as we drove from Portland to Freeport.

Upon arriving, we were met with the familiar warmth of Frank Schissler, the store owner. Daddy's mission was clear: "I'm here to buy a lawn mower and a gas can," he declared. We selected a bright red lawn mower, its hue as vibrant as my enthusiasm. After paying, we loaded our new acquisition and a gas can into the truck, making a pit stop at the local gas station to fill the can and purchase oil for the mower.

The ride home was a profound one. Daddy explained that this lawn mower was a one-time gift. He set the expectations: this mower, the gas, and the oil were mine to manage. It was a rite of passage, an introduction to responsibility and self-reliance. The message was clear: maintain the mower, budget for gas and repairs, and this venture could be the seed for a blossoming future.

True to Daddy's word, that lawn mower and I shared many adventures, cutting through countless yards and summers. Eventually, the day came when the mower could no longer mow, and it was with pride and nostalgia that I used my earnings to purchase its successor. This cycle was not just about lawn care; it was a lesson in diligence, financial management, and the pride of ownership.

That journey from the first swath of grass under the old Magnolia tree to becoming the neighborhood's go-to landscaper was more than a series of chores. It was a chapter in my life where I learned the value of hard work, the importance of community, and the satisfaction of earning my way.

Through the hum of the mower and the scent of freshly cut grass, I found my first taste of independence and the realization that with dedication and care, I could cultivate lawns and my path in life.

Lessons from the Garden

Continuing our journey through the rich imagery of childhood memories, let's delve deeper into the annual ritual of preparing our garden, which intertwined the destinies of my family and the soil we nurtured.

Each spring, as Little League baseball season beckoned with the promise of glory and camaraderie, my father would enlist my help for planting, mainly the sweet potato draws. This task, critical as it was, often found itself at odds with my longing to chase fly balls and home runs.

Daddy, a man of precision and care, had shown me the art of planting and watering with diligence bordering on sacredness. He insisted that water be delivered gently at the base of the plants, a method designed to nurture them without overwhelming them.

However, the lure of baseball games led to hurried and admittedly sloppy watering sessions on my part. Upon witnessing my haphazard approach, Daddy reprimanded me, emphasizing the importance of the task at hand.

Yet, it wasn't until he poured a bucket of water over my head, mirroring the plight of the sweet potatoes under my care, that the lesson sank in. Drenched and humbled, I understood the weight of my actions, vowing to tend our crops with the respect they deserved.

As the garden flourished under the watchful eyes of my Momma and me, it became clear that this patch of earth was more than just a source of sustenance; it was a classroom of life's most enduring lessons. We tended to several acres, including a lush spot lent to us by an aunt. This fertile haven, nestled between two branches, was inaccessible by vehicle, presenting unique challenges and rewards.

Despite the logistical hurdles and the sweltering heat that made the air feel like a heavy blanket, the rich soil yielded bounty when the hills around us bore the marks of the sun's wrath.

Harvesting in the cool of dawn to avoid the midday furnace, we'd carry baskets heavy with the fruits of our labor up a steep incline to our waiting vehicle. During one such journey, burdened by my load and muttering grievances only half-meant, Momma shared a pearl of wisdom that would forever echo in the chambers of my mind: "It's a lazy man who carries a heavy load to avoid a second trip."

Her words, delivered with the calm certainty that only a life of hard-won insights can afford, halted me in my tracks. "What did you say?" I asked, disbelief mingling with intrigue. She repeated, her voice steady and clear, "It's a lazy man who carries a heavy load to avoid a second trip."

The profundity of her statement, simple on the surface yet rich with meaning, unveiled the virtues of balance and foresight to me. Through her guidance, I learned that true efficiency lies not in the burden one can bear in a single effort but in the wisdom to gauge one's capacities, ensuring that the weight of ambition breaks neither spirit nor spine.

This lesson, imparted under the rising sun, taught me to approach life's tasks with measured steps and a patient heart.

My bond with my mother, forged in the sweat and toil of those gardens, was special beyond words. The hours we spent together, whether in prayer or amidst the greenery of our little Eden, were sacred.

Though she has passed, the values and love she instilled in me remain guiding lights in life's journey. Standing by her bedside, alongside my sisters, as her pulse faded was a moment of heartbreaking beauty. It was a testament to the cycle of life, love, and the unbreakable bonds that define us.

Reflecting on these memories, I realize that the garden was more than just a plot of land; it was a legacy of love, lessons, and a connection to something greater than myself. Through the soil, the sweat, and the shared moments of joy and frustration, my parents imparted wisdom that transcends time, nurturing my growth much like the crops we tended together.

In the garden of life, they taught me how to sow, care, and ultimately harvest the fruits of love and labor.

Family Gatherings and Faith

In the vibrant memory of my childhood, woven with chores and lessons, threads of pure joy sparkled amidst the routine. My parents, understanding the balance between duty and delight, often whisked us away on excursions that filled our hearts with laughter and our minds with memories.

Among our cherished adventures was the Bay Fill, a swimming hole cradled by a causeway where the community's families would converge during the sweltering summers. There, amidst splashes and the sweetness of watermelon, we celebrated life's simple pleasures.

Each summer, as if by an unspoken decree, our families would also be enriched and deepened during a grand festival of kinship. This beloved assembly summoned relatives from distant corners of the land under the majestic oak trees in our yard, where the summer breeze danced and whispered secrets of old. There, beneath those ancient boughs, the ties that bound us were fortified, weaving us closer with each shared story and laughter.

Cousins, aunts, and uncles, whom the hustle of life allowed us to meet but once a year, transcended their roles as mere entries in a family tree. They emerged as vibrant threads in the rich mosaic of our collective existence, integral to the narrative of who we were and pivotal in the story of love and kinship that defined us.

This gathering, far more than tradition, was the bedrock of our shared heritage, a testament to the enduring connections that form the essence of family. Beneath the broad oaks, guarded by the ever-watchful summer breeze, we came together to celebrate the ties that, though unseen, were as real and enduring as the earth beneath our feet.

In these moments, under the dappled sunlight, we found the heart of our collective journey, a treasure to be held dear as the very soul of our lineage.

Yet, the fabric of my upbringing in Portland was not solely stitched with leisure moments. It was also filled with the spirit of worship, a practice instilled in me from the tender age of five.

Portland United Methodist Church

Sundays transformed into a pilgrimage, our bare feet carrying us down dusty roads to the Portland United Methodist Church, a distance that seemed to shrink under the weight of anticipation.

The old creek between our home and the sanctuary offered a momentary respite, a place to cool our feet and stir the waters, hoping to glimpse the fish that lurked beneath.

My journey with the church was marked by an unwavering commitment to Sunday school, a record of perfect attendance that became a testament to my devotion. This dedication was not just about being present; it was a journey of spiritual growth nurtured by the wisdom of elders and the vibrant stories of the Bible that took root in my heart.

The revival meetings of summer, intense and stirring, became milestones of my faith, where the conviction of the Holy Spirit was as palpable as the summer heat.

The communal aspect of our church life was vividly showcased through the plays and productions during Easter and Christmas. Mrs. Maude Jones was the director. She would try to get us to behave and learn our lines. Somehow, she would be able to "pull it off". Many of the cast were cousins like David and Larry Godwin, Johnny and Shirley Godwin, and my dearest childhood friend, Judy Martin. This collective effort taught us the value of unity and the joy of shared storytelling.

At fifteen, propelled by my perfect attendance record and perhaps a nudge from destiny, I found myself delivering a sermon in a neighboring church. This experience was as daunting as it was enlightening, marking my first foray into public speaking about faith.

Yet, this unbroken chain of attendance soon met its match against the trials of youth – mumps beset me. Unwilling to see my record tarnished by this setback, I reached out to the pastor with a resolve to attend regardless. His response was a blend of caution and care; he proposed an alternative to safeguard my streak – a private Sunday school session at home.

His reluctance, I later discovered, was not just for my well-being but also his own, as he had never faced the trial of mumps himself. This episode was a lesson in the nuances of community care, teaching me the importance of mutual consideration and the lengths we go to protect and preserve the well-being of our collective flock.

Reflections and Hope

Reflecting on these experiences, it's clear that my upbringing in a faith-filled environment has profoundly shaped the man I've become. The lessons learned behind those old wooden pews, the stories of Jesus' love, sacrifice, and promise of eternal life, have filled me with hope and a longing for reunion with loved ones who have passed on.

My faith, rooted in the love and teachings of my early years, is a beacon that guides me toward a future reunion, not just with my beloved Momma and Daddy but with all my family, in the presence of the divine. This enduring hope, seeded in the fertile ground of childhood memories and spiritual awakening, continues to flourish, a testament to the lasting impact of those sunlit days and starlit nights of worship and wonder.

Having journeyed through the lush paths of my childhood, where each family member and every tree seemed to bestow a lesson, I moved forward to see how these roots foster growth and realization in my life. Let's explore how the seeds planted in youth blossom into a tale of family, discipline, and discovery.

Chapter 2 Summary: Under the Magnolia: Lessons from a Rural Upbringing

In Chapter 2, I explored my rural upbringing, painting a vivid picture of childhood adventures and familial bonds. From the iconic Magnolia tree symbolizing resilience to misadventures like burning leaves, each anecdote reflects key values instilled during my formative years. The narrative seamlessly shifts between recollections of family gatherings, entrepreneurial endeavors, and spiritual experiences, highlighting the profound influence of community, hard work, and faith on my development. Through poignant vignettes, I explore themes of responsibility, humility, and the enduring lessons found in everyday experiences. Ultimately, I emphasize the transformative power of familial love, the wisdom passed down through generations, and the timeless truths discovered amidst the simplicity of rural life.

Transition to Chapter 3:

As I journeyed through the chapters of my life, from the halls of childhood innocence to the corridors of youthful discovery, each step was marked by the guiding lights of family, faith, and community. Chapter 2 illuminated the path of my early years, laying the groundwork for the tales yet to unfold. Now, in Chapter 3, we embark on a deeper exploration—a journey from roots to realization, where the intertwined threads of family bonds, spiritual awakenings, and life experiences weave a tapestry of resilience and revelation. Just as the garden nurtured our crops, my family and faith nurtured my spirit, laying the foundation for a life of discovery and realization.

Chapter 3

From Roots to Realization: A Tale of Family, Faith, and Discovery

Introduction:

Their upbringing shapes every individual's journey, and mine is no exception. My formative years were influenced by three unique pillars: my family, a profound puzzlement, and a beloved dog named Peanut. These elements have intertwined to form the bedrock of my character and guiding principles, shaping me into the person I am today.

My parents' unwavering commitment to discipline and moral integrity left an indelible mark on my leadership style. Through their example, I learned that true leaders must be willing to stand firm in their convictions, even in the face of opposition or adversity. This early lesson in moral courage and the importance of staying true to one's principles has been a cornerstone of my approach to leadership, guiding me through the challenges and temptations of public service.

Family: The Foundation of Values

As a young boy growing up in a small town, I learned the importance of discipline, openness to change, and the unbreakable bonds of familial love. Being the only boy among five sisters, I quickly learned the value of resilience and adaptability.

When I was born, my oldest sister was 16 years old and, in many ways, became a second mother to me. With four older sisters, O'Delia, Vonnie, Bonnie, and Doris, you can imagine I got bossed around a lot. To make matters even more challenging, my baby sister, Karen Diane (Kay), was born just over a year after me and received most of the attention. I will concede that my sisters have a different perspective, and they are probably right. However, these challenges also provided valuable lessons and advantages that I am excited to share.

I vividly remember the chaos of our family's move to a new house and the debates that followed, particularly the one surrounding the installation of an indoor bathroom.

Momma would have supper ready every evening after Daddy came home from work. Our meal would always begin with Daddy offering thanks for the food. With my entire family sitting around a table full of home-cooked food, we would share stories about what was happening in each other's lives. We learned from and cared about one another.

One evening, as we were having this family conversation, my Daddy announced to Momma that the following Saturday, my uncle was coming to help him enclose a portion of the porch to install an indoor bathroom. Before this, we had a two-seat outhouse. It was not fancy, but it got the "job" done.

Upon hearing this announcement, my invalid grandmother, who shared our home and table, proclaimed, "Dewey Brown, have you gone crazy? Why would you want to put that nasty thing in the house?"

At that moment, Grandma could not escape the only paradigm she knew. With time, she learned to appreciate the indoor bathroom, especially during winter. She demonstrated the importance of being open-minded when confronted with new information or technology. Ultimately, we were all happy about this new experience called an indoor bathroom.

This seemingly trivial event taught me the importance of embracing progress while respecting the perspectives of others, a lesson that has stayed with me throughout my life.

Peanut

Another defining moment in my family life was when Daddy brought home a puppy named Peanut, an event my mother deemed almost apocalyptic. Her rule against indoor pets quickly faced a challenge when Peanut fell ill. After much pleading, she reluctantly allowed him inside, albeit restricted to a spread of old newspapers.

Training Peanut was an ordeal, but my mother triumphed, and he soon became an integral part of our family. Watching her discipline and care for Peanut imparted significant lessons in obedience and consequences.

Despite successfully teaching Peanut to obey, he still had one habit that drove Momma crazy: following her everywhere. Whenever we went to the market, Peanut wanted to come along, much to Momma's frustration.

No matter what she did, Peanut would only pretend to turn back to the house but then would find ways to continue the chase after us as we trekked to the market. This did not go over very well with my Momma's discipline-minded demeanor.

After many attempts to dissuade Peanut, Momma had enough. So, out came the switch stick!

She told me, "This is going to cure or kill him." With a stern voice, Momma called Peanut to come to her. Peanut knew what was coming and refused. Momma then told me to catch him, but I objected, explaining that he would associate what she was about to do with me if I caught him. She then told me to grab Peanut, or she would use the switch on me. With that ultimatum in mind, I figured Peanut could stand it better than I could.

It is incredible how quickly we can betray a friend if we think it will cost us something.

So, I caught Peanut. Momma said, "You hold him by the collar, and don't you dare let him go, and I am going to spank him all the way home. Well, at this point, Peanut saw what was coming. Peanut dodged the switch with every lick, and I got spanked all the way home.

In the end Momma accomplishes her goal. Peanut never followed us to the store again. From that day on, whenever we left home, I would tie Peanut to the corner of the house so he couldn't follow us.

It didn't take long for him to realize that he had to learn to obey or that his desire to follow us could lead to his untimely demise.

The lesson was clear: if you hang around with those who misbehave, you are likely to get what they deserve.

Watching my mother's unwavering discipline and care for Peanut instilled in me the significance of consistent, fair rules and the power of unconditional love. The incident where Peanut followed us to the store, despite my mother's efforts to dissuade him, taught me that discipline, when balanced and consistently enforced, is not a bad thing. These early experiences with my family and Peanut laid the foundation for the values that would guide me through life.

Faith and Puzzlement: A Spiritual Journey

My spiritual journey began with a disappearing wart and a mother's faithful prayers. Let me explain.

As I was about to start the 1st grade, Momma noticed something growing on my nose. After careful examination, she concluded that it was a wart. As this wart grew bigger, Momma began to worry that it might cause other kids to make fun of me when I started school.

After a week or two, Momma said we were going to see the doctor about the wart. This scared the dickens out of me because the first thing I thought of was a knife.

So, we made the long drive to town to see the doctor. Momma explained her concern, and the doctor took me into his lap to examine the problem. I was incredibly relieved when he said, "Mrs. Brown, we'll leave that wart alone. It should take care of itself with some time." Momma, however, was not happy and wanted that wart gone.

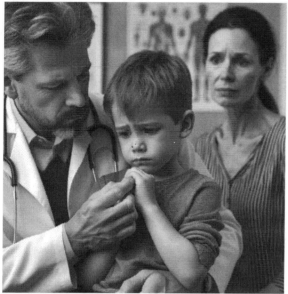

On the drive home, Momma was quiet, and I knew she was thinking about something. After a while, she said, "Don, I got a plan for that wart. Tonight, I will tell you what we are going to do." This scared me even more. Was Momma going to cut that wart off?

I worried all afternoon, not knowing Momma's plan. I was hoping she would forget about it. As I was getting ready to go to bed, Momma came to my room and said, "Don, we need to talk about that wart. This is what we are going to do. We will pray about that wart every night when you go to bed." What a relief, I thought. Prayer is better than a knife any day.

Every night, Momma was faithful. She would come to my room, and we prayed and asked God to take that wart. One morning, after several weeks, I went to the breakfast table, and one of my sisters looked at me and asked, "Don, where is your wart?" I immediately put my finger to my nose, and much to my surprise, the wart was gone.

In doubt, I went to my room and searched my bed, but I couldn't find the wart. At this point, it began to dawn on me that Momma's prayers had been answered. After further reflection, I realized that my prayers had also been answered.

This experience marked the beginning of what I call my 'puzzlement,' a word I heard on a Winnie the Pooh cartoon as a young child. It's funny how some things from our youth can stick with us for the rest of our lives. The question of why we pray, and the nature of its outcomes has always intrigued me.

This experience sparked a profound "puzzlement" within me, a curiosity about the nature of faith and its role in our lives.

Faith and Prayer: A Deeper Exploration

Is faith merely a psychological crutch for the uncertain, or is it the bedrock of human existence, providing substance to our deepest hopes and aspirations? The profound verse from Hebrews 11:1, "Now faith is the substance of things hoped for, the evidence of things not seen," invites us to delve deeper into this intricate tapestry of belief and expectation.

Prayer is often misconceived as a one-way street, merely listing desires and grievances to a celestial being. Yet, the true essence of prayer is far more relational; it's about forging a connection with the divine, the ultimate provider. It's not the act of asking that defines prayer but the profound act of listening, aligning, and harmonizing with the divine will.

In this context, trust is not blind faith but informed assurance. It emerges from the intimate knowledge of the divine nature, gleaned through the persistent pursuit of getting to "know" God. This knowledge transcends mere intellectual understanding; it is experiential, transformative, and deeply personal.

The true mission of prayer is not merely to seek divine intervention in our worldly affairs but to cultivate a relationship with God, to understand His essence, and to align ourselves with His greater purpose. In this alignment, we find the true essence of faith: a dynamic, living connection with the divine that shapes our being, guides our actions, and infuses our lives with meaning beyond the temporal.

As we navigate the complexities of life, these spiritual practices offer a compass, guiding us toward a deeper understanding and a more purposeful existence.

Life Experiences: Lessons in Resilience and Community

Beyond the realm of family and faith, my childhood was marked by experiences that taught me valuable lessons about resilience, consequences, and the importance of community. One such incident occurred in Mrs. Yates' 2nd-grade class, where my buddy and I had a mischievous plan.

You see, our school bus came twice in the afternoon - once for the nearby kids then again about 20 minutes later for the rest of us. Well, we figured out that if we hid in the classroom bathroom until the first bus left, we could jump out the window and have the playground all to ourselves for a bit.

One day, our scheme went haywire. We got stuck in that bathroom longer than a possum playing dead, waiting for the right moment to make our move. By the time we finally jumped out, our bus had vanished.

I found myself in quite a conundrum. It was a good four miles from Freeport Elementary to my house, but I was bound and determined to make it home for supper. So, I set off down the road, full of youthful optimism. I would later regret that decision.

I made it about halfway to Portland when a bus pulled up beside me. Turns out he was Jimmy Brown's grandfather, Mr. Pitts. Jimmy and I were and remain best friends today. It would take another book to tell all our misadventures. To make a long story short, Mr. Pitts hollered at me to get in, but I tried to tell him I was making my way home. He wasn't having any of my sass and threatened to take off his belt. I knew when I was licked. Mr. Pitts knew where I lived, and even though it was off his route, he took me home in time for supper.

But when I got home, Momma had something else in store for me besides a warm meal. Let's just say I had to stand up to eat supper. That night, I reaffirmed my previous decision not ever to do that again.

Looking back, it's hard to fathom how different things were then. The idea of a 2nd grader traipsing down the side of the road nowadays is enough to make your hair stand on end. But back then, the whole community watched out for each other's young'uns.

It was a simpler time, and even though I found myself in a few scrapes here and there, I'm mighty thankful for people like Mr. Pitts, who made sure I didn't stray too far off the path. I miss those days.

This adventure taught me the power of perseverance, the consequences of my actions, and the importance of the caring eyes that watched over us in simpler times.

Mr. Totts' Pig Farm

Another defining moment in my youth was the time I spent working on Mr. Totts' pig farm. The long days of hard work, the camaraderie with Mr. Totts and Mrs. Myrtlowe, and the annual pig vaccination day taught me the value of a strong work ethic, the importance of being part of a tight-knit community, and the resilience needed to overcome life's challenges.

It began on one hot summer day as I was putting the finishing touches on Mr. Conley Martin's lawn. Mr. Totts Brown rolled up in his trusty pickup truck. After a brief exchange with Mr. Martin, Mr. Totts came over and told me that my Daddy had agreed I could lend him a hand. "We've got a storm on the horizon, and there's a mountain of corn that needs picking," he declared. Though I was unfamiliar with Mr. Totts and oblivious to any looming storm, the adventure was too intriguing to pass up.

Upon reaching the farm, I found my cousin David there, which was a relief—like finding a familiar face in a Wild West saloon. We, youngsters, were trained to respect our elders back then, to the point where any grown-up could wave a switch at you if you stepped out of line, and it wasn't considered strange.

After several days of determined labor, we secured the corn, and, as fate would have it, the hurricane veered away.

Mr. Totts, now more a friend than a boss, offered me a job on the farm. My days started before the sun and ended after it had called it a day, filled with a medley of farm tasks.

Our midday break was an event in itself. In my youth, "dinner" referred to this hearty midday meal, not to be confused with "supper," the lighter evening meal. Mrs. Myrtlowe's dinner spread was legendary, a feast of fried chicken, pork chops, fresh vegetables, biscuits, and gravy that would fortify us for the afternoon's work. Following this midday banquet, Mr. Totts would eat till he was full as a tick, then snooze while I helped Mrs. Myrtlowe clean up.

One of the farm's annual highlights was the pig vaccination day. That's when Doc Williams would come out to give all the new pigs their shots. It was like a barnyard ballet with me as the lead dancer, tasked with catching and holding each piglet for their shot.

Let me paint you a picture: There I am, covered head to toe in pig muck, with an ornery 25-pound pig squealin' and wigglin' between my legs. I'm tryin' my darnedest to keep its head clamped between my knees while Doc Williams pokes it in the belly with a needle.

Well, that pig would kick up a ruckus fit to wake the dead! And I'll tell you what, when you've got an angry pig's rear end that close to your face, you learn really quick how to dodge flyin' stuff! By the time we finished with all 50 of them pigs, I was shakin' like a dog passin' peach pits.

But it wasn't all bad—after a hard day's work, I'd wash off in the creek and go for a dip in the swimming hole. There's nothin' better than cool water on a hot day!

Daddy's Ithaca Featherweight

When I was just a ten-year-old, full of curiosity and adventure, my father decided it was time for me to have my own shotgun. Until that moment, I was merely an observer, tagging along with the men from our community on their deer hunting escapades, soaking in the thrill and camaraderie.

One crisp early fall day, during the dawn of the hunting season, I had my first taste of shooting with a .410 shotgun. This moment would unknowingly pave the way for my Christmas gift that year—a single-barrel 20-gauge shotgun. Although it packed a greater kick than the .410, my pride in owning it was immeasurable.

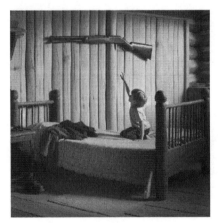

My father owned a majestic 12-gauge Ithaca featherweight pump shotgun, which I admired endlessly. I would watch him clean it, memorizing his every move, yearning to hold and operate it myself. But for the time being, I was relegated to my 20-gauge.

A twist of fate occurred when my dad was hospitalized for some procedures. With my mother preoccupied with preparations to visit him, I saw my chance. I sneaked into their bedroom, where the coveted Ithaca hung on the wall. Climbing onto the bed, I reached for the shotgun, my heart racing with excitement and a tinge of forbidden thrill.

In my naivety and eagerness, I forgot that my father had recently used the shotgun to shoot crows in the corn patch. Determined to pump it, I fumbled with the release mechanism but didn't quite have the strength in my fingers to get it to work.

Having watched my Daddy do it many times, I knew all you had to do was push the safety off and pull the trigger. That's what I did.

The world seemed to explode around me—the deafening blast, the smell of gunpowder, the cloud of dust, and the gaping hole in my dad's bed with cotton and springs hanging out. There was also a large hole in the wall. All of this created a scene of chaos.

My mother's horrified entrance and her relief-filled embrace were followed by the daunting task of confessing to my father in the hospital. His reaction, mirroring my mother's, was of relief that I was unharmed, a testament to the depth of their love and concern, not to mention my vow to not ever do that again. This incident became a profound lesson in respect and responsibility.

Not long after, my solitary hunting expeditions became a regular affair, a testament to the trust and independence granted to me. Momma would pack lunch for me, and I would leave home just before daylight. During a typical day in the woods, I would wade across streams, climb fences, and make it home just before dark.

I recall vividly one such adventure when I stumbled upon a covey of wild quail, their sudden fluttering nearly sending me into a state of shock. At that moment, I thought my world was coming to an end. They were under my feet, in front and back of me, coming from everywhere. If you have ever scared up a covey of wild quail, you know what I mean. Thinking back on that moment now brings a smile to my face.

These experiences, etched in my memory, represent a bygone era of freedom and adventure, where a boy could immerse himself in the wilderness, learning life's lessons through the lens of nature and the responsibility bestowed by a cherished tool of the hunt.

These experiences, filled with laughter, learning, and a bit of mischief, have forever shaped my character and worldview.

Guiding Principles: The Cornerstone of Public Service

The lessons I learned from my family, my spiritual puzzlement, and my life experiences have culminated in the development of five guiding principles that have shaped my approach to public service and decision-making:

1. Less Government: Promoting efficiency and reducing bureaucratic overreach.
2. Lower Taxes: Ensuring citizens retain more of their hard-earned money.
3. Personal Responsibility: Encouraging individuals to own their actions and decisions.
4. Individual Freedom: Protecting the liberties and rights of every person.
5. Stronger Families: Recognizing the family as the foundational unit of society.

These principles, rooted in the lessons of my youth, have served as a compass throughout my career, ensuring that I remain dedicated to serving the public interest and promoting the values that have shaped my life.

As a freshman legislator in Florida, I carried a card bearing these principles in my wallet, determined to avoid the pitfalls common to many in public service. Looking back, I take pride in how these principles are reflected in my legacy, both in my legal achievements and in influencing others through ethical leadership.

Chapter 3 Summary:

In Chapter 3, "From Roots to Realization: A Tale of Family, Faith, and Discovery," I examine the foundational pillars that have shaped my character and worldview. The chapter begins with an exploration of the profound influence of family on my upbringing, highlighting the lessons of resilience, adaptability, and the importance of embracing progress while respecting differing perspectives. Through anecdotes of family debates over the installation of an indoor bathroom and the misadventures with our beloved dog, Peanut, I illustrate how these early experiences laid the groundwork for my guiding principles.

Moving deeper into the realms of faith and spiritual puzzlement, I recount the transformative power of prayer in the disappearance of a childhood wart, sparking a curiosity about the nature of faith and its role in our lives. This section looks into the essence of prayer as a relational journey, cultivating a dynamic connection with the divine and shaping our understanding of faith beyond mere belief.

Life experiences, ranging from mischievous escapades to hard work on Mr. Totts' pig farm, further enriched my character, teaching invaluable lessons in resilience, responsibility, and the importance of community. Through humorous anecdotes of youthful exploits and heartfelt reflections on the bonds of trust forged in simpler times, I illuminate the enduring values instilled by these formative experiences.

The chapter culminates in an exploration of my guiding principles, honed through the crucible of family, faith, and life's trials. Rooted in the values of less government, lower taxes, personal responsibility, individual freedom, and stronger families, these principles serve as a compass guiding my approach to public service and decision-making.

In essence, Chapter 3 is a testament to the profound impact of family, faith, and community on shaping the trajectory of my life. Through the lens of personal anecdotes and reflective insights, I invite readers to embark on a journey of self-discovery, drawing strength from the roots that have nurtured us and the experiences that have shaped us, as we strive to build a brighter future for ourselves and future generations.

Transition to Chapter 4:

As I reflect on the lessons learned from my early years, one pivotal event stands out—the storm that shaped not only my family's history but also my understanding of resilience and courage. Join me now as I move into the harrowing tale of "Til The Storm Passed By," a chapter that illustrates the unwavering spirit of my parents, Dewey and Velma Brown, and the profound impact it had on my life.

Chapter 4

'Til The Storm Passed By

Among the many storms of life, one particularly stands out, not just as a physical event but as a metaphorical one that tested and solidified our family's resilience. This storm, both literal and figurative, was vividly captured in a theatrical production many years later.

In November 2001, Grit & Grace, The Official Folk Life Production of Walton County, Florida, presented a theatrical production titled "Water Under the Bridge".

This production was described in the September 2002 edition of the Southern Living magazine as "…a coming together of stories about the waterways of Walton County."

On a November evening in Freeport, FL, Scene 3 of the production, subtitled" Til the Storm Passed By," told the story of a young couple and their young child and how they encountered the monster hurricane of 1936.

The couple, Dewey and Velma Brown, would become my parents fifteen years later, making me their first and only son.

The Hurricane of 1936

The scene is set in their home in Niceville, FL, in the summer of 1936, where Dewey and Velma say their goodbyes as Dewey sets off on a commercial fishing boat for several days in the Gulf of Mexico. Neither of them knew the drama that would unfold in the intervening days.

Let's listen as the script unfolds as my sisters O'Delia and Kay reflect on that terrible storm…

On a sun-kissed coastline, O'Delia and her little sister Kay were poised with anticipation, watching for the silhouette of their father's boat. Just then, an old family friend, Mr. Mack, approached with a gentle query.

"Hey, girls, what are you doing out here?" he asked, his voice laced with friendly concern.

O'Delia, with a practiced cheer, replied swiftly, "Hi, Mr. Mack. We're here to see if we can spot Daddy's boat come in."

From the vastness of Choctawhatchee Bay, Mr. Mack's gaze settled on a familiar vessel. "See that boat out there? I understand your Daddy used to work on a boat a lot like that," he postulated, sparking memories of yesteryear.

"Yes, Daddy worked for the Saunder Fish Company on a boat in 1936…" began O'Delia. "…One hundred and forty-five feet long!" Kay interjected with wide-eyed awe. O'Delia smiled at Kay's tendency to embellish, "Kay exaggerates. It was more like 45 feet long. But yes, it was "The Billy", caught in the hurricane of '36."

The Narrator chimed in, painting a picture of the past where Captain Billy and his crew, with Dewey among them, set off on a day as promising as any other on the boat named "The Billy" in honor of Captain Billy himself. The men were full of hope and determination despite the uncertain nature of their journey.

(Now going back to that day in 1936)

"What a beautiful day. I feel it in my bones we're bringing home a prize catch," said Alec with a hopeful grin.

Billy, the cap-donned leader, and the soul of "The Billy," instructed Dewey to steer them towards fortune, "Bring us over that reef. I remember some good snapper holes right beyond them," he commanded. Dewey, youngest but strongest on board, responded with a fervent "Yessirree." His spirit soared beyond the present as he envisioned a future where he, too, would command a vessel as grand as the dreams that danced in his head.

The crew ribbed Dewey for his ambitious dreams; even through their jests, there was a sense of camaraderie and an unspoken pact—the kind shared by men who knew the sea's whims all too intimately.

Velma, Dewey's young wife, awaited his return on the sturdy ground with their new child. "How long's it going to be, Dewey? Should I keep supper?" she asked, a tinge of worry beneath her practicality.

"A couple of days," Dewey reassured. "Captain Billy's planning on staying out for a promising haul, given how costly diesel has become." His words, while hopeful, couldn't shield Velma from the specter of concern that loomed as the gulf's mood shifted.

The storm's onslaught began as the waves grew surly. On the deck of The Billy, the crew responded to Captain Billy's orders. The raging elements now dictated their plight. The previously stable vessel was now at the mercy of howling winds and burgeoning waves.

The hurricane bore down with intensity, turning the Gulf of Mexico into a frothy cauldron. The Billy, after exhausting her fight, needed to succumb, letting the storm carry her as it willed.

Below deck, the men settled into a solemn trance, each facing the daunting possibility that their handwritten names might be all that remained after the storm's rage.

(Back on Shore)

Velma, ever the resolute beacon, held onto her faith onshore. She deflected the neighbor's concerns with a grace forged of resolve and love, opting to keep vigil, her gaze tirelessly fixed upon the churning waters, a silent prayer etched upon her lips.

Amidst the post-storm silence, Velma's neighbor brought a somber offering—the obituary printed upon the folds of the local newspaper. The ink seemed to bleed despair as she read the black-and-white pronouncement of Dewey's demise.

The neighbor's hand rested upon hers, his touch suggesting a shared mourning, a unity brought by loss. It read, "Dewey Brown, along with the entire crew of the fishing boat The Billy, perished at sea."

Yet life, as it wants to do, swerved unexpectedly toward hope. Dewey, after days that seemed like an eternity, eventually appeared, walking a path toward home that was lined with hardship but also with determination. Velma, emerging from the shadow of grief to the light of his return, welcomed him with a joyous kiss and embrace that eclipsed all words of reproach.

 Dewey's recount of his return teased a smile from Velma. Despite her instinctive doubt, their reunion was sweetened by the absurdity of fishermen traveling by bus. The trip from Apalachicola, FL, where they were washed ashore, to home took several days as the bus maneuvered on roads blocked by downed trees and bridges damaged by the storm.

Their tale was a tapestry woven from despair and elation; a narrative sealed not only by the bond of the men who braved The Billy's last journey but also by Velma's unwavering faith through the storm.

(Back to the reflections of O'Delia and Kay)

With a nod to the present, O'Delia, matured by the years, still held the youthful radiance that once brightened the old family tales. She gestured toward the Polly Ann and, with Kay, waved to their father. It was an act that sealed the legacy of The Billy and the Brown family alike—one of enduring hope, faith, and the resolute courage of fishermen and their kin.

The Rest of the Story

Adventures on the Polly Ann

In the summer of 1965, a dream that had long lingered within my Daddy finally came to fruition. He became the proud owner and captain of the Polly Ann, a name she bore from her creation, which Daddy chose to honor. She was a 40-foot front rig shrimp boat, her heart powered by a sturdy Waukesha diesel engine. I was fourteen at the time, and the pride that swelled in my chest matched his. Captain Dewey Brown, my Daddy, had achieved his lifelong ambition, and I couldn't have been prouder.

He poured himself into the Polly Ann, dedicating months to refurbishing her. He overhauled the rigging, applied a fresh coat of paint, and tuned up the engine. Daddy treated the Polly Ann with a tenderness usually reserved for family members, sensing her moods and needs with just the sound of her engine.

Our adventures on Choctawhatchee Bay were relentless in pursuit of the elusive "big haul." Seasonally dictated, our shrimping efforts sometimes stretched into the night. With the boat stocked with a hundred gallons of diesel and six hundred pounds of ice, we would set out for a week at a time, Daddy's intimate knowledge of the bay guiding us.

We faced an unexpected challenge while shrimping near Fort Walton Beach one summer night. We prepared for our night of work after seeking refuge from the day's heat in a secluded cove. However, shortly after beginning, Daddy sensed something amiss with the Polly Ann. The engine's temperature was rising dangerously, demanding immediate attention.

Despite his arthritis, which had cruelly stripped him of much of his physical prowess, Daddy sprang into action. The engine's roar nearly drowned out his voice as he enlisted my help. The task fell on me because I could maneuver into the cramped quarters of the engine room where he could not.

Our predicament stemmed from a clogged intake pipe choked by seagrass we had unwittingly collected. This obstruction threatened to overheat the engine, potentially stranding or damaging the Polly Ann. Despite my fears of the spinning belts and pulleys and the engine's scalding heat, Daddy handed me a screwdriver and pliers and urged me to clear the blockage.

The task was daunting. Loosening a clamp and removing a hose to access the intake pipe, I was startled by the eruption of water that ensued, creating a chaotic

mist of steam. It was a frantic, fear-inducing moment, further amplified by the sudden blare of a tugboat's horn.

Realizing the imminent danger of collision, my urgency surged. With Daddy shouting instructions from above, I struggled to reattach the hose and secure the clamp amidst the engine's deafening noise. My hands fumbled, but I completed the task just in time for Daddy to steer us out of the tugboat's path, avoiding disaster.

That was my first brush with real danger on the water, a rite of passage in a way. It seemed almost routine for Daddy, but it was a profound lesson in responsibility and courage for me.

Amidst the countless days spent on the Polly Ann, I found solace and freedom by climbing to the top of her mast. With the wind in my face and a panoramic view of the bay, I felt at peace there. He knew exactly where to look whenever Daddy couldn't find me on deck.

Those summers on the Polly Ann with Daddy are etched deep in my memory, a testament to the lessons learned and our unspoken bond. The challenges we faced, the close calls, and the tranquil moments of beauty on the bay shaped me in ways I'm still understanding. Through it all, the Polly Ann was more than just a boat; she was a classroom, a sanctuary, and a cherished family member.

The Final Lesson

The final journey I shared with Daddy on the water came years after I had moved to Pensacola for my studies at the University of West Florida. Home for the weekend, I welcomed his invitation on Saturday morning to go oystering together. His arthritis had significantly worsened, and the thought of him being alone on the water was something that concerned me.

We set off aboard the Polly Ann, navigating out of Alaqua Creek and across Choctawhatchee Bay towards a spot where Daddy knew of an abundance of oysters. Once anchored, he proposed I start tonging the oysters. Having kept in shape from years of high school weightlifting, I eagerly accepted, perhaps a bit keen to impress him.

Oyster tongs, resembling two large yard rakes joined on long handles, are a traditional tool in this craft. They are cumbersome and demand considerable upper body strength, scooping oysters into their rake-like basket from the bay's bottom. I was confident in my youth and vigor to manage the task.

After about 45 minutes, visibly tired, Daddy suggested taking over. As he contributed to our haul, our conversation flowed effortlessly, punctuated by my tasks of washing and managing the oysters.

He persistently declined despite my repeated offers to resume the work over the next four hours. It dawned on me then, not only his enduring strength but perhaps a more profound lesson he intended to impart, though its essence eluded me.

Our dialogue dwindled to silence. When Daddy finally conceded we had enough oysters, a reflective quiet enveloped our return journey. My mind churned over the day's events, culminating in a question about the lesson he aimed to teach through his prolonged labor.

His initial evasion gave way to a revelation marked by a knowing smile. To my question, "What is the point you were trying to make?" he replied, "There is a difference between a boy and a man. Don't ever forget it." A simple yet profound distinction that, at the moment escaped my complete comprehension. Was this a commentary on my strength or his? The message was cryptic to my younger self.

Years later, the depth of Daddy's wisdom has become more evident. Youth often blinds us with a sense of invincibility, akin to the hare in Aesop's fable, brimming with confidence yet lacking the perseverance emblematic of the tortoise. Despite the pain, Daddy's enduring toil that day was a testament to the virtues of tenacity and resilience over sheer might and speed.

He aimed to teach me that life's challenges, unexpected hardships, and obstacles don't spell defeat unless we permit them. As he sought to convey, the essence of manhood lies in the unwavering resolve to persevere in fulfilling our duties despite our adversities.

That conversation remains a cherished memory, a pivotal lesson from Daddy that has guided me through life's tumultuous seas. It was among the last of its kind we shared, a parting gift of wisdom from a father to his son.

A Son's Reflection

An unexpected call upended my world a few months after that final lesson on the water. Daddy, the indomitable force of my childhood, was facing a battle unlike before. The diagnosis was grim: cancer, necessitating the removal of a third of one of his lungs.

Seeing him in the ICU for the first time after his surgery, I was confronted with a sight I had never imagined—my father, the epitome of strength and resilience, rendered vulnerable, his hands bound and a tube stealing his voice. Yet, the look in his eyes narrated a tale of sorrow and dependence, a stark contrast to the man I had always known.

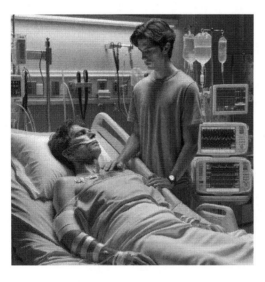

Despite the odds, he didn't succumb to despair. Gradually, he progressed from the ICU to a regular hospital room, embarking on a painstaking journey toward recovery.

His return home, however, marked the beginning of a different reality. Daily tasks became Herculean challenges, and cancer treatments only exacerbated his frailty.

The situation took a darker turn when seizures began to wrack his body, leading to further tests that unveiled a devastating development—a tumor had taken residence in his brain.

The trajectory from that point seemed to steepen, a steep decline that led to his passing at 63 on May 11, 1974. In the wake of his departure, I yearned for just one more day with him aboard the Polly Ann, to navigate the waters together, to share in the silence and the spoken words that filled our days. I'm left wondering if he would view my life's endeavors with approval and if pride would light his eyes at the mention of my achievements.

Despite the absence of definitive answers, a part of me believes that someday, those questions will be resolved. It's a hope that bridges the divide between the past and the present, a silent conversation that continues beyond the bounds of this earthly existence.

Chapter 4 Summary: Til the Storm Passed By

This chapter recounts the narrative of a young couple, Dewey and Velma Brown, facing the monstrous Hurricane of 1936. Vivid storytelling sets the scene in Niceville, FL, where Dewey embarks on a fishing expedition, unaware of the impending calamity. As the storm ravages the Gulf of Mexico, Dewey's wife, Velma, stands vigil onshore, grappling with uncertainty and fear.

The narrative intertwines reflections from Dewey and Velma's daughters, O'Delia and Kay, as they recount the family's ordeal. Despite the initial despair of Dewey's presumed demise, his miraculous return after days adrift at sea becomes a beacon of hope amidst the devastation.

Transitioning to the Brown family's later endeavors, the chapter shifts focus to Dewey's fulfillment of a lifelong dream—the ownership of the Polly Ann, a shrimp boat symbolic of resilience and determination. Through shared adventures on Choctawhatchee Bay, Dewey imparts invaluable lessons to his son, shaping his character and understanding of life's challenges.

The narrative culminates in a poignant moment between father and son, as Dewey imparts a profound lesson on manhood and perseverance during a final oystering expedition. However, the chapter takes a somber turn as Dewey's health deteriorates, ultimately leading to his passing. Yet, amidst the grief, the legacy of resilience and courage endures, guiding the protagonist toward a future marked by education and public service.

Chapter 4 serves as a testament to the indomitable human spirit in the face of adversity, weaving together themes of family, resilience, and the enduring impact of life's storms.

Transition to Chapter 5:

As the stormy waters of my family's past settled, a newfound sense of purpose and direction emerged. Guided by my father's lessons of resilience and determination, I embarked on a journey that would shape my character and define my legacy. The echoes of leadership and brotherhood reverberated from the tumultuous seas of our fishing expeditions to the tranquil bay of academic pursuits. During these formative years, I encountered an organization that would become the cornerstone of my personal growth and leadership development - the Order of DeMolay. Join me as I delve into the transformative echoes of my journey through leadership and legacy in DeMolay.

Part 2

Professional Beginnings and Political Ascent

Chapter 5

Transformative Echoes: A Journey Through Leadership and Legacy in DeMolay

Introduction

As a teenager, I struggled to find my place in the world. Academic and athletic achievements failed to provide the purpose and self-worth I desperately sought. That all changed when I was introduced to the Order of DeMolay. My journey through DeMolay was a crucible that forged my leadership skills and philosophy. Through the guidance of dedicated mentors and the challenges of taking on increasing responsibilities, I learned that leadership is about service, empowerment, and the ability to inspire others towards a shared vision. The lessons of humility, accountability, and the transformative power of mentorship that I gained in DeMolay have been essential guideposts in my own leadership journey, shaping my commitment to fostering growth and development in those I lead.

The Bob Arrington Chapter

My journey began in the Bob Arrington Chapter, a name that would represent a pivotal chapter in my life story. As I stepped into this new world, I was immediately struck by the atmosphere of acceptance, friendship, and camaraderie that permeated every interaction. Among a group of like-minded young men, I found a sense of belonging that had previously eluded me.

Mentorship and Character Development

Under the guidance of dedicated advisors like Harold Gillis, Alvin Spencer, Don Harrison, J.B. Coon, Clerk of Court, and Coach Philip Anderson, I began to discover my potential. These men, who generously gave their time and wisdom, became more than just mentors; they were the architects of my character. Their unwavering support and exemplary conduct taught me the importance of leadership, responsibility, and the impact of a positive role model.

Becoming a Chapter Leader

As I progressed through the ranks of DeMolay, I set my sights on becoming a chapter leader. The path was challenging, demanding hard work, dedication, and perseverance. Yet, with each challenge overcome, I felt myself growing stronger, more confident, and more capable of making a difference in the lives of others.

The DeMolay Parade

One of the most memorable experiences during my time as Master Councilor was organizing a local DeMolay parade in our hometown. What started as a simple idea quickly grew into an ambitious undertaking that tested our resolve and showcased the power of our collective determination.

We envisioned a grand event celebrating our chapter and engaging the entire community. Our plans included inviting multiple units from the Shriners, a military color guard, local law enforcement, and first responders. We even dared to dream of having a military flyover during the parade, a feat that seemed nearly impossible for a group of young men to arrange.

The Phone Call to Eglin Air Force Base

One of the most pivotal moments in our planning process came when I decided to call Eglin Air Force Base to inquire about the possibility of having a military flyover. It was a daring idea born from the enthusiasm and ambition of a young mind.

With a mixture of nervousness and determination, I dialed the number. I still feel the phone's weight in my hand as my heart raced with each ring. When I asked to speak with the base commander, never in a million years did I expect to be transferred directly to their office. The conversation that followed was surreal.

Explaining our vision for the parade and expressing our desire for a military flyover, I waited for a response. The pause on the other end of the line felt like an eternity. I feared our request would be dismissed outright. However, to my surprise and delight, the officer commended our ambition but politely informed me that I'd have to wait for a response. In my head, I pictured Radar from M*A*S*H being called in to shuffle through paperwork, and my hopes weren't high.

Fast-forward a few days, and there I was, walking the halls of my school, when I was called to the principal's office. Surprised by the summons, I figured I was in big trouble about something.

When I got to the office, the principal was waiting for me. He said, "I don't know what you have done now, but Eglin Air Force Base is on the phone, and they want to speak with you. My mind raced as I took the receiver. An officer on the line inquired about my identity and the reason behind my call from days ago. With a deep breath, I shared our vision for the parade and reiterated our wish for a flyover.

The officer's pause was palpable and then came a chuckle, not of mockery but of admiration. He explained that a flyover wasn't within his purview but offered something unexpected – a color guard for our event. My heart soared. I eagerly relayed the details needed for the color guard, thanked the officer with more gratitude than I could express, and hung up, a mix of elation and disbelief coursing through me.

The news of this development spread like wildfire among our DeMolay chapter members. It was more than just a boost for our parade; it was a stamp of recognition, a nod from those in high places that what we were doing was significant.

Looking back, I realize the phone call represented more than securing a color guard for our event. It was a turning point in our planning process, a moment that taught us the value of reaching for the stars and believing in ourselves and our vision. It demonstrated that we could achieve extraordinary things with passion, perseverance, and willingness to take bold steps.

The Parade's Success

On the day of the event, everything came together seamlessly. The Shriners arrived with colorful parade units, including go-carts, motorcycles, clowns, and live camels. Local law enforcement and fire departments joined, adding to the festive atmosphere. True to their word, the military color guard marched proudly at the head of the procession, lending an air of solemnity and respect to the occasion.

Watching the parade unfold, I felt an overwhelming sense of pride and accomplishment. The sight of our chapter members marching alongside the various participants, with the community lining the streets to cheer us on, was a moment I will never forget. It was a testament to the power of perseverance, the strength of our brotherhood, and the impact a group of dedicated young men could have on their community.

The Flower Talk

Another of the most significant milestones in my DeMolay journey was memorizing and delivering the "Flower Talk." This poignant oration, which speaks to mothers' enduring love and sacrifice, struck a deep chord within me. As I committed each word to memory, I reflected on my mother's profound impact on my life. The Flower Talk became more than just a speech; it was a tribute to the unsung heroes who shape our lives and a reminder of the gratitude we owe them.

Delivering the Flower Talk to audiences was a transformative experience. As I stood before the altar, surrounded by the symbolic white and red flowers representing the love of mothers' past and present, I felt a profound connection to something greater than myself. Through my words, I hope to have touched the lives of those who listened, inspiring them to cherish and honor the love and sacrifices of their own mothers.

Awards and Recognition

As I continued to grow within DeMolay, my efforts were recognized through awards and honors that held deep personal significance. The Merit Bars I earned, each representing a specific area of achievement, were tangible reminders of my commitment to personal growth and service. From the Ritual and Visitation bars to the Athletics and Scholastics bars, these achievements showcased the well-rounded development that DeMolay fostered within me.

Three awards stand out as the pinnacles of my DeMolay journey:

1. The Representative DeMolay Award was bestowed upon me for exceptional service, leadership, and participation.
2. The Past Master Councilor Meritorious Service Award, presented to me upon completing my term as Master Councilor.
3. The Degree of Chevalier, the highest honor in DeMolay, which recognized exceptional leadership, service, and character.

Reflecting on my DeMolay experience, I realized I was part of something larger than myself. DeMolay's legacy spans generations and includes some of history's most respected and influential figures. From Walt Disney, whose creative genius has touched the lives of millions, to John Wayne, the embodiment of American valor and integrity, DeMolay has shaped the character of countless leaders in every field.

Other notable DeMolays include Carl B. Albert, former Speaker of the U.S. House of Representatives; Walter Cronkite, the most trusted voice in American journalism; and Fran Tarkenton, NFL quarterback and Hall of Fame inductee. In their own words, these men have attributed their success and moral compass to the lessons learned and values instilled during their time in DeMolay.

Former Florida Governor and 1983 Presidential candidate Reubin Askew said: *"DeMolay played an important role during the formative years of my life. It gave me one of my earliest opportunities to learn about leadership and brotherhood. The values taught in DeMolay continue to be highly relevant and necessary to character development in young people in today's difficult world."*

Senator Jack Latvala is another notable former DeMolay from Florida.

In Walt Disney's words, "*I feel a great sense of obligation and gratitude toward the Order of DeMolay for its important role in my life. Its precepts have been invaluable in making decisions and facing dilemmas and crises. DeMolay stands for all that is good for the family and our country. I feel privileged to have enjoyed membership in DeMolay.*"

Other notable former DeMolays were:

- **Neil Armstrong**, the test Pilot, Astronaut, and the First Human Being to walk on the moon, and
- **Mel Blanc**, the Comic and famous cartoon voice best known as the voice of Bugs Bunny.
- **Earnest Borgnine** was a famous actor and Academy Award Winner.
- **Terry Bradshaw** was an NFL quarterback who led the Pittsburg Steelers to four Super Bowl Championships and was a Pro Football Hall of Fame Inductee.
- **Roy Clark** was a musician, Guitar Player, and TV Personality.
- **Buddy Ebsen** was an Actor, Dancer, and Vaudeville performer best known as Jed Clampet on the TV series The Beverly Hillbillies.
- **Paul Harvey** was a famous radio journalist.
- **Chet Huntley** was a famous TV Newscaster.
- **Burl Ives** was a musician, balladeer, and actor.
- **Dick and Tommy Smothers** were the World-Famous banjo/guitar-playing comedy team "The Smothers Brothers."

These testimonies serve as a powerful reminder of the enduring impact of DeMolay and the universal truths it embodies. The values of leadership, integrity, and service, which lie at the heart of the organization, transcend time and individual circumstances.

Looking back on my DeMolay journey, I am filled with a profound sense of gratitude. The experiences, lessons, and friendships forged within the Bob Arrington Chapter have left an indelible mark on my life. Friends like Jimmy

Brown, Eddie Weidenhaft, Bill and David Green, Edward and LeRoy Holden, John Keegan, John and Charlie Day, David Thomas, and Bubba Schultz contributed to one another's growth.

The Impact of DeMolay

The impact of DeMolay extends far beyond the boundaries of the chapter room. The principles and values instilled during those formative years have guided me through every aspect of my adult life, from personal relationships to professional endeavors.

As I reflect on the profound impact DeMolay has had on my life, I am reminded of the words of the Flower Talk, which so eloquently captures the essence of the organization's teachings:

> "Far in the dim recesses of her heart,
> where all is hushed and still, She keeps a shrine.
> 'Tis here she kneels in prayer
> While from above, long shafts of light upon her shine.
> Her heart is flower-fragrant as she prays.
> Aquiver like a candle flame,
> each prayer takes wing to bless the world she works among,
> to leave the radiance of the candles there."

These words, etched in my memory and engraved upon my heart, are a constant reminder of the love, sacrifice, and guidance that have shaped my life. They are a tribute to the mothers, fathers, and mentors who have illuminated my path and a call to honor their legacy through a life of purpose and service.

I am filled with hope and determination as I look to the future. The foundation laid by DeMolay will continue to guide my steps and inform my choices. While the specific challenges and opportunities that lie ahead may be unknown, I am confident that the principles and values instilled by this remarkable organization will provide the strength, wisdom, and resilience needed to navigate whatever path life may present.

In sharing my DeMolay story, I hope it will inspire others to seek out this organization's transformative power. To young men searching for purpose, belonging, and the chance to make a difference, I offer this invitation: step into the world of DeMolay, embrace its teachings and be molded by its timeless values.

I extend my heartfelt thanks to the parents, mentors, and advisors who tirelessly dedicate themselves to the DeMolay mission. Your guidance, support, and unwavering belief in the potential of young men are the bedrock of this organization's success. You are shaping the future leaders of our communities, nation, and world through your efforts.

Ultimately, the true measure of our lives is not found in the accolades we receive or the titles we hold but in our impact on others and the legacy we leave behind. Through organizations like DeMolay, which foster character, leadership, and service, we can ensure that our legacy will be one of purpose, integrity, and enduring significance.

As we delve deeper into the essence of leadership and personal development, it is important to consider the philosophies that can guide us in overcoming internal and external challenges. Two profound quotes from Sun-Tzu and Frédéric Bastiat offer valuable insights into understanding ourselves and our interactions with others. These insights are particularly relevant as we reflect on our personal growth and the lessons learned through our experiences.

In the following essay, we will explore the contrasting yet complementary perspectives of Sun-Tzu, the ancient Chinese military strategist, and Frédéric Bastiat, the 19th-century French economist and philosopher. Sun-Tzu emphasizes the importance of knowing oneself and one's adversaries, while Bastiat highlights the inherent human desire for self-preservation and the temptation to prosper at the expense of others. By examining these perspectives, we can gain a deeper understanding of how self-awareness and ethical decision-making play crucial roles in effective leadership.

This essay serves as a bridge between the personal reflections shared in this chapter and the broader themes of leadership and public policy that follow. It underscores the importance of introspection and ethical considerations in shaping our actions and decisions.

Sun-Tzu – Frederic Bastiat

In the realm of personal growth and success, two seemingly contrasting philosophies emerge from the words of Sun-Tzu and Frédéric Bastiat. Sun-Tzu emphasizes the importance of knowing oneself and one's enemy to secure victory, while Bastiat highlights the inherent human desire for self-preservation and the temptation to prosper at the expense of others. However, upon closer examination, these two perspectives converge to reveal a powerful truth: the key to overcoming our own weaknesses lies in understanding ourselves deeply.

Sun-Tzu's words, "If you know neither the enemy nor yourself, you will succumb in every battle," ring true not only in the context of military strategy but also in the battles we face within ourselves. Our greatest enemy often lies within – our own doubts, fears, and self-destructive tendencies. By failing to recognize and confront these internal adversaries, we leave ourselves vulnerable to repeated defeats in our personal and professional lives.

This is where Bastiat's insight into human nature becomes particularly relevant. He observes that while people aspire to self-preservation and self-development, they also possess an innate desire to satisfy their wants with the least effort possible, even if it means prospering at the expense of others. This "fatal desire" can manifest in various forms, such as procrastination, cutting corners, or exploiting others for personal gain.

To overcome these self-defeating impulses, we must first acknowledge their existence within ourselves. By developing a keen self-awareness and understanding our own strengths and weaknesses, we can begin to recognize when our actions are driven by this "primitive, universal, and insuppressible instinct." Only then can we consciously choose to resist these temptations and redirect our efforts towards more constructive and ethical pursuits.

Moreover, by knowing ourselves deeply, we can identify the unique talents and abilities that set us apart. By focusing on these strengths and leveraging them to create value for others, we can achieve success and fulfillment without resorting to the self-serving tactics that Bastiat warns against. In this way, self-knowledge becomes not only a defense against our own weaknesses but also a powerful tool for personal growth and achievement.

In conclusion, the words of Sun-Tzu and Bastiat serve as a reminder that the path to success is paved with self-awareness. By understanding our own nature, confronting our weaknesses, and leveraging our strengths, we can overcome the internal battles that hinder our progress. In the end, knowing ourselves is not just a matter of self-preservation; it is the key to unlocking our full potential and achieving victory in all aspects of life.

As we conclude this exploration of leadership and personal growth through the lens of Sun-Tzu and Frédéric Bastiat, let us summarize the key takeaways from this chapter. Understanding our strengths and weaknesses, recognizing the ethical implications of our actions, and striving for continuous self-improvement are fundamental to effective leadership.

In the summary that follows, we will revisit the main points discussed in this chapter, highlighting the lessons learned from my experiences in DeMolay and their lasting impact on my approach to leadership and public service. These reflections will set the stage for the subsequent discussions on public policy and risk management, illustrating how personal development and ethical leadership can guide our professional endeavors.

Summary of Chapter 5:

Chapter 5 of my book chronicles my transformative journey through leadership and legacy in the Order of DeMolay. Introduced to the organization as a teenager, I found a sense of purpose and belonging that had previously eluded me. Under the guidance of dedicated mentors and advisors, I began to discover my potential and embrace the values of leadership, responsibility, and service. As I progressed through the ranks of DeMolay, I took on leadership roles within my chapter, culminating in organizing a local parade that showcased the power of perseverance and collective determination.

The chapter also highlights significant milestones in my DeMolay journey, including memorizing and delivering the poignant "Flower Talk" and receiving awards and recognition for my contributions. Through reflections on the impact of DeMolay and the enduring legacy of its principles, I offer an invitation to others to embrace the transformative power of the organization and continue its mission of shaping future leaders.

Transition to Chapter 6:

As the echoes of my transformative journey through leadership and legacy in DeMolay faded into the background, new horizons beckoned, promising fresh challenges and opportunities. Guided by the principles instilled during my formative years, I navigated the corridors of Freeport High School, where the seeds of leadership and public service were first sown. Join me as I embark on a retrospective journey through the early education and influences that shaped my political career and laid the groundwork for the professional endeavors that would follow.

Chapter 6

My Political Career - Early Education and Influences

Freeport High School

My voyage into leadership and public service took root in the vibrant corridors of Freeport High School, nestled in the heart of Northwest Florida, during the transformative year of 1966. Surrounded by the palpable energy of youthful ambition and camaraderie, I boldly decided to run for student council president.

Following a campaign that was as spirited as it was brief, I found myself at the helm of the student council, steering it through a year of memorable leadership. This initial brush with leadership was merely the beginning; I also took on the mantle of senior class vice president, further solidifying my dedication to serving my peers and refining my emerging leadership skills.

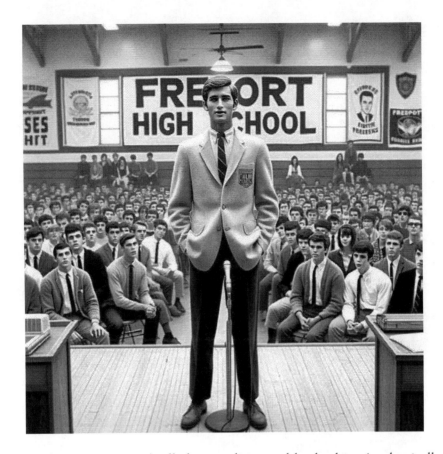

However, the journey wasn't all about politics and leadership. Academically, life at Freeport High, a quaint rural school, presented its own set of challenges. As a member of the smallest graduating class in 1969, with only 28 students, I often humorously remind myself that I was not the valedictorian.

Okaloosa-Walton Junior College

That summer, I embarked on a new chapter at Okaloosa-Walton Junior College, starting with a course in remedial reading. Back then, my aspirations were modest at best. I aimed no further than a technical program in drafting, just enough education to secure a job and embark on the so-called 'real life.' Little did I know Mr. Jenson was about to change the course of my life.

The Influence of Mr. Jenson

Mr. Jenson, the lead instructor of the drafting program, was the epitome of distinction—well-dressed, with a thin mustache, exuding a gentle yet authoritative presence that hinted at a military background. His attention to each student, especially in a program as intimate as ours, allowed for a rare and invaluable mentorship.

His daily check-ins at my desk and gentle encouragement to consider further education planted the seeds of potential within me. His question, "Mr. Brown, have you considered going on to get your 4-year degree?" became a familiar refrain, challenging my self-imposed limitations.

The turning point came with his unexpected offer to hire me as his student assistant in the drafting lab—an offer that transformed our relationship from instructor-student to friend. Mr. Jenson's belief in my potential led me down a path I had never imagined.

Although Mr. Jenson and I eventually lost touch, and I presume he has since passed, his impact remains indelible. To Mr. Jenson, wherever you are, I offer my deepest gratitude for igniting the spark of ambition and confidence within me.

This journey, from the hallways of Freeport High through the encouragement found at Okaloosa-Walton Junior College, was not a direct path to the political and professional arenas I would later navigate.

After my youth and junior college achievements dimmed in the rearview mirror, I earned a B.S. in Industrial Technology from the University of West Florida at Pensacola, FL. Ultimately, I returned to DeFuniak Springs, where I started my first job at the First National Bank of DeFuniak Springs.

It was unusual but the bank was also home to the First National Insurance Agency of DeFuniak Springs, Inc. of which I later became the president.

In the next chapter, we'll explore how the seeds of education and early influences blossomed into my future career and became the foundational blocks of my professional and political career.

Summary of Chapter 6:

Chapter 6 describes the formative years of my political career, beginning with my time at Freeport High School and Okaloosa-Walton Junior College. At Freeport High, amidst the vibrant atmosphere of youthful ambition, I made my first foray into leadership by running for student council president. This experience, coupled with my role as senior class vice president, solidified my dedication to serving my peers and honing my leadership skills. Transitioning to Okaloosa-Walton Junior College, I initially harbored modest aspirations, aiming for a technical program in drafting.

However, the influence of Mr. Jenson, the lead instructor of the drafting program, proved pivotal. His encouragement and mentorship planted the seeds of possibility within me, ultimately leading me to pursue a 4-year degree and embark on a path that would shape my future career. Despite losing touch with Mr. Jenson, his impact remains profound, serving as a testament to the transformative power of mentorship. This chapter sets the stage for the subsequent exploration of how these early influences and educational experiences laid the foundation for my professional and political career, culminating in my role as president of the First National Insurance Agency of DeFuniak Springs, Inc.

Transition to Chapter 7:

Leaving behind the corridors of education and early influences, I returned to DeFuniak Springs, where my professional journey truly began. Join me as I recount the pivotal moments that shaped my career and propelled me into the dynamic intersection of finance, insurance, and public service.

Chapter 7

My Political Career - Professional and Political Beginnings

I returned to DeFuniak Springs, where I started my first job at the First National Bank of DeFuniak Springs. This career would navigate the complexities of the banking and insurance industries.

This period was not merely a job but a foundational experience, setting the stage for a lifetime dedicated to financial services. The lessons learned, the confidence gained, and the paths taken all trace back to the encouragement of those like Mr. Jenson, who saw potential where I saw limits.

Taking the Helm at First National Insurance Agency

My story took a decisive turn when an opportunity landed in my lap that would indelibly mark the contours of my professional life. It was the moment when the president of the insurance agency I had served with decided to retire, leaving behind a legacy and a vacancy I was chosen to fill.

Stepping into the role of president at the First National Insurance Agency of DeFuniak Springs, Inc., was more than a promotion; it was a spotlight on my capacity for leadership, my commitment to excellence, and my profound dedication to the well-being of our community.

The Challenge of Acquisition

The year 1983 unfurled a tapestry of significant changes. The bank, our parent institution, was sold, thrusting the insurance agency—and, by extension, me—into a mixture of uncertainty.

The agency was nudged out of its familiar nest, and I stood at a crossroads, facing a choice that would dictate the future course of my career. On one hand, I had the opportunity to stay within the newly restructured bank; on the other, I could relocate the insurance agency and continue my role as its president.

My choice? I opted for the latter, propelled by an unshakeable belief in the agency's mission and my integral role within it. This decision to shepherd the agency through its transition and to maintain my leadership was a declaration of my allegiance to my core principles and to the community that had entrusted me with its faith.

In the pivotal year of 1984, my wife Diane and I found ourselves on the cusp of a decision that promised to redefine our professional and personal trajectories. We boldly approached the board of directors of the insurance agency with a proposition that was as daring as it was decisive: to purchase the agency outright.

Fortuitously, with the support of one of the insurance companies we represented, we secured 100% financing for this venture. However, this financial windfall was not without its stipulations—two stringent conditions were attached to this lifeline.

Firstly, we were tasked with achieving a 25% premium growth with the financing insurance company. Secondly, a specific target in life insurance production was set before us.

The stakes were unambiguous: fall short of these targets, and we would see our loan interest rate surge from a manageable 7% to a staggering two points above the New York Prime rate, which, at the time, towered significantly higher.

Faced with this trial, Diane and I assessed our ambition against the backdrop of risk. After considerable reflection, we chose to rise to the challenge, keenly aware of the arduous journey ahead to meet those stringent loan conditions.

However, unforeseen challenges soon came our way. In 1985, the Florida legislature-initiated discussions on insurance reforms, including a particularly contentious proposal for a 25% rate rollback on all general liability insurance.

This legislative move, which seemed to be a concession to trial lawyers, cast our venture into turmoil. Spooked by the legislative changes, the insurance company that had backed our financing decided to retreat from the Florida market. This departure struck a dire blow to Diane and me, imperiling our capacity to meet the loan's critical conditions.

Confronted with this daunting uncertainty, I contacted the financing company, seeking clarity on their stance regarding the loan's severe interest rate penalties. After a series of nerve-wracking attempts and an atmosphere thick with tension, the grim confirmation came: the interest rates would indeed skyrocket, the fulfillment of the original conditions rendered moot by their market exit.

This turn of events weighed heavily upon us. Throughout the seven-year term of the loan, Diane and I grappled with the burden of tens of thousands of dollars in retroactive interest adjustments. By the time we had fully repaid the loan, our financial standing had deteriorated, plunging us deeper into debt than we were at the inception of our agency's acquisition.

The financial strain reached a point where we were compelled to borrow from friends and family, catapulting our debt to staggering new heights.

Yet, this ordeal was far more than a fiscal quagmire; it was a transformative chapter in my life, pushing me toward public service. Fueled by a resolve to shield others from the precariousness wrought by legislative caprices and the volatility of financial markets, I was propelled to run for office.

This episode, fraught with adversity and invaluable lessons, catalyzed my commitment to champion policies designed to safeguard individuals and small businesses against the capricious currents of legislation and market dynamics.

Beginning about 1985, Barrett Glover, the local jail chaplain, invited me to join him each Thursday night for Church services for the inmates. His passion for serving others was extraordinary.

He also had a keen eye on politics and encouraged me to get involved in local party politics. At first, I made the excuse that I was too busy with my business, but he was unrelenting. With his encouragement in 1988, I ran for the local Republican State Committeeman position, not knowing what would unfold.

Within weeks of winning that election, I received a visit from the County Clerk of Court. She informed me of a vacant position on the Board of County Commissioners. The Governor had removed a previous Commissioner from office for official misconduct.

She wanted me to apply to be appointed to fill that vacancy. I explained that I was too busy with my business to take on a new responsibility of such a magnitude. Unbelievably, two hours later, I found myself writing my resume. To make a long story short, a few days later Governor Bob Martenez appointed me to the Walton County Commission to fill the unexpired term of the commissioner he had removed.

This turned out to be an initiation by fire. I was 37 years old, and most of the other Commissioners were old enough to be my father. I was immersed in public service (and county politics) within days.

After two years, I decided to run for office. During that election, commissioners did not run county-wide; they ran in single-member districts. I was a registered Republican in a county that remained majority Democrat. My district was registered heavily Democrat. When the election was over, I had lost by 42 votes. Needless to say, I was disappointed. I enjoyed serving my County. The truth is, I was "hooked."

Personal Tragedies

In 1993, my life's path veered into an abyss of sorrow I could never have foreseen. It was the year my teenage son, full of dreams and the promise of youth, was cruelly snatched away from us in a car accident.

The tidal wave of shock and grief that followed left me adrift in a sea of despair, rendering me virtually paralyzed, unable to muster the strength to engage with our family business. This venture had been a source of immense pride and sustenance for us.

As if the heavens hadn't already exacted a heavy toll, the year 1995 brought with it another profound loss. My mother, who had been a beacon of strength and love throughout my life, passed away, adding layers of grief to an already burdened heart. Her absence left a void, deepening my incapacity to shoulder my responsibilities at work as I grappled with an overwhelming sense of loss.

During these dark times, my wife Diane emerged as the pillar of strength that held our world together. Her resilience and unwavering dedication became the lifeline that kept our business—and, by extension, our family—afloat. She navigated the storm gracefully, even as she bore her grief, and stood by me as I stumbled through the shadows of sorrow.

Diane's unwavering support was the lone hope in an otherwise engulfing darkness.

Stepping into Politics

As the relentless march of time gradually moved us forward, I began to discern faint glimmers of light piercing through the gloom. In this period of profound searching, I found an unexpected source of solace in politics. Encouraged by a friend, Norm Davis, I ran for State Representative for House District 5 in 1996.

This step into the political arena was not driven by a strategic career ambition. Still, rather, it was born out of a desperate need to find a diversion, a respite from the consuming grief that had come to define my existence.

This foray into public service initially sought to distract and detach me from the pain, eventually opening new avenues of purpose and engagement for me. It began in the depths of personal tragedy but led to a path of recovery and renewed commitment, marking the start of a new chapter in my life.

Diving headfirst into the campaign trail, I found myself weaving through a sea of faces and stories, each meeting an opportunity to share my earnest vision for what good governance could look like. Despite pouring every ounce of vigor into the campaign, the final tally left me short of victory by a heartbreakingly narrow margin of just a few hundred votes.

Yet, instead of serving as a deterrent, this defeat only stoked the fires of my determination. It became a crucible from which I emerged not discouraged but fortified with invaluable lessons and a more vigorous resolve to mount another run.

Resilience and Purpose

Reflecting on this chapter of my life, I see a narrative woven from threads of resilience, purpose, and the intersection of my professional and personal journeys. The challenges and tragedies I faced, from the financial strain of acquiring the insurance agency to the devastating losses of my son and mother, tested my mettle and shaped my character in profound ways.

Yet, through it all, my wife Diane's unwavering support and my drive to find purpose in the face of adversity propelled me forward. My entry into politics, initially a means of escape from grief, became a path to renewed commitment and public service.

These experiences, as painful and transformative as they were, prepared me for the trials and triumphs in my political career. They instilled in me a deep sense of empathy, a fierce determination to overcome obstacles, and a resolute commitment to making a difference in the lives of others.

Summary of Chapter 7:

Chapter 7 of my book delves into the pivotal moments that marked the beginning of my professional and political journey. Returning to DeFuniak Springs, I embarked on my first job at the First National Bank, laying the groundwork for a lifetime dedicated to financial services. However, it was my transition to the role of president at the First National Insurance Agency that served as a turning point, highlighting my capacity for leadership and dedication to community service. The challenges of acquisition in 1983 tested my resolve, leading to a daring decision to purchase the agency outright in 1984. Yet, unforeseen legislative changes in 1985, coupled with the exit of our financing insurance company, plunged us into uncertainty and financial strain.

This tumultuous period catalyzed my entry into public service, fueled by a determination to shield others from legislative caprices. Encouraged by local jail chaplain Barrett Glover, I ventured into local party politics, eventually leading to my appointment to the Walton County Commission. Tragedy struck in 1993 with the loss of my teenage son in a car accident, followed by the passing of my mother in 1995, leaving me adrift in grief.

Amidst this darkness, politics emerged as a source of solace, leading me to run for State Representative in 1996. Though initially driven by a need for diversion, this foray into public service ignited a renewed sense of purpose and commitment. Despite the initial defeat, the campaign fortified my resolve, setting the stage for future endeavors. This chapter explores the resilience and purpose that emerged from personal tragedy, shaping my character, and guiding my path toward public service. As I close this chapter, the stage is set for an exploration of my journey into the State Legislature, where personal challenges and political aspirations intersect in profound ways.

Transition to Chapter 8:

Leaving behind the tumultuous landscape of personal challenges and legislative confrontations, I stepped into the realm of state politics with a newfound determination and resilience. Join me as I navigate the intricate corridors of the Florida legislature, facing monumental events and forging enduring friendships that would shape my legislative career.

As I transitioned into state-level governance, the balance between personal dedication and professional responsibilities became ever more crucial.

Part 3

LEGISLATIVE CAREER AND MAJOR THEMES

Chapter 8

My Political Career - State Representative Career – Personal Challenges and Reflections

Election Victory

As the calendar flipped to 2000, it ushered in a fresh opportunity that I seized with a newfound determination, tempered by previous setbacks. The road to the election was fraught with challenges, both in the primary and the general election.

However, my perseverance, fueled by relentless effort, strategic adjustments based on past lessons, and an unwavering belief in the possibility of success, bore fruit. I emerged victorious, earning the honor of representing House District 5 as its State Representative.

The backdrop to my triumph was the tumultuous and now-legendary presidential contest between George W. Bush and Al Gore. The drama of that election night, with its hanging chads and recounts that captured the nation's attention, added an unforgettable layer of historical significance to my victory.

Amidst the whirlwind of national scrutiny and political fervor, my election victory was a profoundly personal milestone intertwined with a momentous event in American political history.

As a State Representative, I faced numerous challenges that tested my leadership mettle and commitment to my core values. In moments where political expediency and personal convictions clashed, I drew upon the early lessons of integrity and moral courage instilled by my upbringing. Standing firm in my principles, even when it meant going against the tide of popular opinion or political pressure, I learned that true leadership requires the strength to make difficult choices and the humility to bear the consequences. These experiences refined my leadership philosophy, emphasizing the importance of integrity, courage, and the willingness to put principles before politics.

Early Legislative Experiences

Upon my arrival in Tallahassee to take the oath of office, I found myself thrust into the heart of a maelstrom. The presidential election, hanging in the balance and shrouded in uncertainty, transformed the city into a buzzing hub teeming with journalists from every corner. This charged atmosphere set the stage for the commencement of my legislative journey.

In the whirlwind of those initial weeks, amidst the fervor and chaos of a nation fixated on hanging chads and court decisions, I began laying down the foundations of enduring friendships. These early connections, forged in the distinctive crucible of political tension and shared aspirations, would strengthen and deepen throughout my eight years of service.

Among these relationships, one stood out significantly—Dennis Ross, who would become my best friend and most trusted colleague in the journey ahead.

Our friendship was more than just a product of shared goals or mutual interests; it was a bond that would be rigorously tested through personal and professional trials and challenges.

The State Administration Committee

My journey into the heart of legislative work began with my assignment to the State Administration Committee, a role that ushered me into the intricate dance of governance and the dynamic personalities that guide its rhythm.

At the helm of this committee was Fred Brummer, a figure whose reputation as a professional CPA and formidable character had reached me long before our paths crossed. Known for his rigorous standards and a demeanor that could oscillate between stern and downright intimidating, Fred stood as a formidable presence in the committee room.

During my inaugural year on the committee, we became involved in a particularly thorny issue that tested my principles' resolve against the pressures of legislative dynamics.

I had made a vow to my constituents, a pledge to rigorously examine the details of any bill before lending it my vote. This dedication to scrutiny and due diligence soon placed me in a precarious position with Chairman Brummer, who was keen on securing my support for the bill in question.

My unwavering stance sparked a palpable tension between the Chairman and myself, casting a shadow over several days of committee work. Bearing the weight of this discord, I resolved to confront the issue head-on. I sought out Chairman Brummer in his office to clarify my position and, if necessary, resign from the committee should my principles be deemed a misfit for his expectations.

The meeting that ensued was a remarkable departure from the tension that had preceded it. Chairman Brummer received me with an openness that paved the way for a frank and insightful exchange. I presented my case with unvarnished honesty, ready to step down if that was the price of maintaining my integrity.

To my astonishment and relief, Chairman Brummer responded not with the anticipated rebuke but with grace and understanding. He acknowledged the depth of my commitment to my constituents and, far from wanting me to resign, he expressed a keen desire for me to remain on the committee. He recognized the potential in our collaboration, envisioning a path forward where our relationship could evolve into something both productive and meaningful.

This encounter, which began as a collision of principles and duty, blossomed into a profound friendship with Chairman Brummer. Our bond, forged in the fire of that initial confrontation, became a testament to the power of mutual respect and understanding. It underscored the truth that even amidst the most heated disagreements and the pressures of high-stakes decision-making, there lies the potential for building bridges, fostering connections, and achieving collaborative success.

Reflecting on my intense discussions with Chairman Brummer, I realized the importance of being adaptable and open to changing one's stance when presented with compelling evidence. It was a moment that tested my convictions but also underscored a vital principle: 'The world belongs to the man who is wise enough to change his mind in the presence of facts.' This mindset was crucial as we navigated the complexities of legislation, and it became even more relevant as we faced the global upheavals that followed 9/11.

9/11 and Its Impact

In 2001, the tides of change swept through the halls of the Florida legislature, heralded by Speaker Tom Feeney's gracious invitation to attend a legislative conference in New York City. Seizing this opportunity with both hands, Diane and I set off, hearts brimming with anticipation for the knowledge to be gained and the new connections to be made.

A standout moment of our trip was an evening designed to bring the Florida legislative delegation closer together, dining at the Windows of the World Restaurant on the 110th floor of the North Tower of the World Trade Center. It was mid-August 2001, and the night unfolded in a display of camaraderie and breathtaking views, etching itself as an indelible memory for everyone present.

Soon after, I found myself in Columbus, OH, for a training conference with the National Organization of Insurance Legislators. The calendar pages turned to September 11, 2001; a date marked for my return flight to Tallahassee. However, destiny had penned a different narrative for that day—one of tragedy and heartbreak.

The morning's events, a terror attack of unimaginable scale, abruptly halted not just my travel plans but also the very pulse of our nation. As the harrowing news broke, it became apparent that my flight was one of countless grounded, a trivial detail against the backdrop of a national catastrophe that would indelibly change the course of our collective history.

The days following that fateful morning, I was boarding a city bus bound for the airport. The atmosphere was thick with a real sense of unease, a silent testament to the events that had abruptly stopped the heartbeat of our entire nation. Upon my arrival, I was greeted by the stark reality that only two rental cars remained—an omen, perhaps, of the journey that lay ahead. With a deep sense of urgency, I secured one for myself, embarking on the long drive home.

As the miles stretched out before me, my sole companion was the radio, its broadcasts unfolding the full scope of the tragedy of September 11th. Each update and bulletin painted an increasingly vivid picture of the horror that had developed.

It was a journey of physical distance and a profound and solemn transformation in my understanding of the world. The events of that day, relayed through the speakers, were a constant companion, marking every mile with a shift in my perception of our shared reality.

It was a solemn journey home that underscored the profound impact of those events, not just on my own life but on the fabric of our nation and the world. As I navigated the road back to the familiar, I was acutely aware that nothing would ever be quite the same again. The tragedy of 9/11 had redrawn the contours of our reality, leaving an indelible mark on our collective consciousness.

Solidarity in Service: A Weekend with the National Guard

As we navigated the post-9/11 world, the themes of service, sacrifice, and community became even more poignant. This era of heightened patriotism and unity brought a unique experience that deepened my appreciation for those who serve in our armed forces. During this time, I had the distinct honor of spending a weekend with the National Guard. This experience broadened my perspective on military service and reinforced my commitment to public service.

In the bracing winter of 2002, I was embroiled in a remarkable adventure that would leave an indelible mark on my memory. The journey commenced with a call from John Keegan, a seasoned veteran poised on the cusp of retirement, serving as a National Guard recruiter. His invitation was anything but ordinary: a weekend exercise with the Chipley National Guard unit at Fort Rucker, Alabama.

Our arrival on a frigid Saturday morning heralded the beginning of an intense day. Amidst the chill, camaraderie blossomed as I mingled with the troops, each a guardian of our nation's peace. The morning's highlight was an extraordinary chance to handle the formidable M240 and M249 machine guns, instruments of defense wielded by these dedicated soldiers.

Lunch was a stark reminder of military pragmatism, with MREs serving as our sustenance, followed by a live fire exercise. Here, I was a spectator of the troops' precision and teamwork, their strategic maneuvers a ballet of disciplined force. As dusk fell and the cold deepened, another exercise illuminated the night, tracer rounds painting arcs of fire against the dark sky, inadvertently igniting the woods in several places.

The true test of endurance came with nightfall. Considering my unfamiliarity with the biting cold, John offered a retreat to a motel. Yet, I resolved to stand in solidarity with the troops, embracing the raw elements they faced without flinching. Nestled under a tree, cocooned in a multi-layered sleeping bag, I found a semblance of warmth, drifting into sleep under the watchful eyes of the stars.

As I awoke to a frost-covered dawn, the troops' lively chatter greeted me, their resilience as radiant as the rising sun. The morning camaraderie was palpable, a testament to the unspoken bonds forged in the crucible of shared hardship.

Our return to the Armory in Chipley was a procession of pride, the cleaning of equipment, and a ritual of respect for the tools that serve our nation's defense. Amidst this routine, a lighthearted wager among the troops came to light, betting on my overnight stay — a moment of levity in the solemnity of their duty.

This weekend was not merely an exercise in military prowess but a profound lesson in the valor and solidarity of those who wear uniforms. My admiration for these men and women is boundless, and their commitment to duty and to one another is a beacon of the spirit that guards our nation. In my prayers, I seek strength for their hands, swiftness for their feet, and unerring precision for their aim. May God bless these steadfast guardians of our liberty and the land they protect.

As I left Fort Rucker, my reflections on teamwork, discipline, and commitment followed me back into the realm of public service, offering fresh insights as I considered my path toward reelection and the continuing journey of serving people with unwavering dedication.

Reelection and Reflection

In the vibrant tapestry of 2002, I once again hit the campaign trail, my heart set on reelection. My campaign was like a marathon, where the cheering of my constituents propelled me to a comfortable victory that whisked me back to the familiar corridors of Tallahassee.

Summary of Chapter 8:

Chapter 8 of my book chronicles the early years of my tenure as a State Representative, marked by triumphs, challenges, and profound personal reflections. It begins with the exhilarating victory in the 2000 election, amidst the backdrop of a historic presidential contest. Upon taking office, I found myself embroiled in the whirlwind of legislative duties and the camaraderie of newfound friendships, notably with Chairman Fred Brummer. Our early encounters tested my principles but ultimately laid the foundation for a deep and productive relationship.

The chapter also delves into the seismic impact of the 9/11 terrorist attacks, detailing my harrowing journey home during the aftermath. Amidst heightened patriotism and unity, I had the honor of spending a weekend with the National Guard, a transformative experience that deepened my appreciation for military service.

As the chapter draws to a close, it reflects on my successful reelection campaign in 2002, highlighting the resilience and commitment that would define my legislative career. Through triumphs and trials, this chapter is a testament to the enduring pursuit of making a positive difference in the lives of those I served.

Transition to Chapter 9:

Chapter 9 plunges into the heart of my political career, exploring the highs, lows, and unexpected twists that defined my time in the Florida House of

Representatives. From legislative achievements to hard-fought battles, this chapter paints a vivid picture of the challenges and triumphs that shaped my path. So, buckle up as we explore the intricacies of governance and the art of legislative warfare in "My Political Career - Legislative Achievements and Battles."

Chapter 9

My Political Career - Legislative Achievements and Battles

Upon my return, the new Speaker of the House, Johnny Byrd, like a maestro ready to conduct an orchestra, handed me my new score: a fresh set of committee assignments. Among these, the insurance committee resonated with my background as an insurance agent, fitting me perfectly.

The Workers' Compensation Reform Battle

That year, the legislative orchestra faced a particularly dissonant piece of music: the thorny issue of workers' compensation reform. With the controversy swirling around it like a tempest, Speaker Byrd created a Select Committee dedicated to this discord in a move akin to forming a special task force.

My friend Dennis Ross was appointed as the chairman, and I was entrusted with the task of transforming this discord into harmony as his vice chair.

Embarking on this quest was akin to diving into a complex symphony, with each session demanding a meticulous composition of solutions. Despite navigating the legislative labyrinth, we emerged with a bill that held the promise of being the masterpiece we needed.

However, as this bill took center stage in the full insurance committee, it hit a sour note. A staggering 38 amendments loomed before us, each threatening to turn our carefully composed symphony into a chaotic medley, potentially inflating the cost of workers' compensation insurance in Florida instead of mitigating it.

In the heat of the debate, I couldn't help but notice an uninvited percussionist joining our ensemble—rate creep. Each amendment was like an errant drumbeat, threatening to throw our carefully crafted harmony off balance, driving costs higher with every strike.

Despite our concerted efforts to keep the rhythm steady and costs down, the committee chairwoman, wielding her baton with a decisive stroke, adopted all 38 amendments. This move, much to our chagrin and Speaker Byrd's dismay, was akin to ending our symphony on a series of unresolved chords, leaving us to ponder the composition that could have been.

In the wake of that fateful committee melee, I received an unexpected summons from Speaker Byrd, akin to being called into the headmaster's office after a particularly inventive but ill-advised practical joke at school. He was on a quest to perform a legislative Houdini act over the weekend, aiming to transform our beleaguered bill into a phoenix ready to rise anew.

But here's the catch—I had conditions. My first demand was akin to asking for a magician's assistant to vanish momentarily: I suggested that his right-hand man, Representative Dudley Goodlett, might enjoy a leisurely weekend away from the fray, not wanting him soiled by the fling stuff.

The second call, a plot twist worthy of a detective novel, was to the committee chairwoman, the mastermind behind the avalanche of amendments. Despite Byrd's initial bafflement, reminiscent of a puzzled Sherlock Holmes, I laid out the plan: we needed her to pull a legislative rabbit out of the hat with a strike-all amendment first thing Monday, effectively hitting the undo button on the previous act. All she had to do was read the script.

To his credit, Speaker Byrd played along with our caper.

Cue the emergency conclave—a secretive gathering that might as well have been a meeting of the Illuminati. With Chairman Ross off being a dutiful dad at a Little League game, alternating between cheering and consulting his phone like a Wall Street trader during a stock market crash, the rest of us—Gerald Wester, Mary Ann Stiles, and Tammy Perdue—huddled in our clandestine chamber, drafting what would be the bill's salvation, all while adhering to the Speaker's edict: "Fix the problem!"

Convening a committee at the ungodly hour of 8:00 AM on a Monday was as unconventional as serving breakfast for dinner, yet there we were. Now seemingly following a script worthy of Broadway, the chairwoman introduced the magic wand of legislative amendments—the strike-all. With the flash of a matador, the amendment was adopted, and our bill was not just back on track; it was set to be the show's star.

Returning to navigate the complex legislative landscape, we had a mountain of work before us. With our precious bill in tow, we navigated the jungle of remaining committees. Each step was like tiptoeing through a minefield, full of suspense. You could almost hear the dramatic music crescendo as we pondered, "Will our baby bill get diluted in the wash again?"

The spectacle unfolded like a prime-time drama, with stakeholders glued to their seats, eyes darting across the rotunda from the House to the Senate, searching for any whisper of rebellion. Amid this high-stakes poker game, one figure stood out, a certain Mr. T.K., with an interest as sharp as his initials. Each time the bill edged forward, he'd pop up with the urgency of a meerkat on the lookout, "Is everything all right—are we still on track?"

Oh, the mischief in my heart couldn't resist. "Haven't you heard what happened?" I'd drop, dangling the bait with the finesse of a cat playing with a mouse, then swivel on my heel and leave, my laughter echoing down the hallways. We were, in fact, cruising along, but who could resist such a ripe opportunity for a bit of fun?

This little dance became our ritual, a brief interlude of fun amidst the tempest of legislative warfare. "Hey, is everything OK?" T.K.. would ask, eyes wide, the picture of concern. And there I'd be, ready with my now-infamous line, "Haven't you heard...?" leaving the question hanging like a cliffhanger at the end of a soap opera episode.

Reflecting on that era, it was filled with relentless effort, high stakes, and a sprinkle of legislative wizardry, all in the service of navigating the intricate maze of governance. And, if nothing else, it underscored the notion that even within the solemn halls of lawmaking, there's room for a touch of mischief and enchantment.

In the cauldron of high drama and nail-biting moments, these slices of humor were our shared secret, a way to lighten the load, if only for a moment. It turned the intrigue into something memorable but tinged with the mischief that keeps the spirit alive, even when the stakes couldn't be higher.

My time in the limelight of Speaker Johnny Byrd's legislative circus was anything but dull, securing me a place in the legislative annals with an unprecedented 16 committee assignments over two years—a record that left the clerk of the Florida House wondering if I had mastered the art of cloning.

What followed was nothing short of a legislative symphony, leading to a bill that would slash workers' compensation costs by as much as 70% in the ensuing years—a feat of financial acrobatics that would make even the most seasoned trapeze artist dizzy.

The maestro of this circus? None other than Dennis Ross, whose leadership and tenacity were the twin engines propelling us toward victory.

Looking back, it was a period steeped in hard work, high stakes, and a dash of legislative dexterity, all dedicated to steering through the complexities of governance. And, if nothing else, it proved that even in law-making, there's room for mischief and magic.

The Saga of HB145

In 2004, the voters granted me the honor of returning to the Florida House, a privilege that filled me with anticipation for the term ahead, especially with Allen Bense poised to take the reins as Speaker. His leadership promised a new direction, and I was ready to play my part.

With a sense of responsibility and excitement, I accepted the position of Chair of the State Administration Council. I also served on the Fiscal Council, Rules & Calendar Council, and, fittingly, the Insurance Committee.

The 2005 regular session was a whirlwind of legislative activity for me. I took the initiative to file 18 bills, a mix that included both local and broader-reaching proposals. Of these efforts, 13 managed to clear the hurdles of the legislative process, receiving the Governor's approval or being Adopted by Publication—a testament to the hard work and negotiation behind the scenes.

Notably, three of those successful bills were local initiatives concerning Bay County. Although this area lay outside my district, I filed them as a gesture of support for Speaker Bense, a move that underscored the collaborative spirit of our work.

However, not every battle was won. One piece of legislation, HB1513, aimed at civil justice reform, fell short of passage. This bill held significant importance for me, representing a challenge we faced in striving for a more equitable legal landscape.

The journey of HB1513, from its inception to its eventual stall in the legislative process, is a story of the complexities and nuances of lawmaking—a narrative of aspiration, effort, and, sometimes, unfulfilled goals.

The 2006 regular session was akin to juggling flaming torches while riding a unicycle—busy doesn't even start to cover it. I tossed six bills into the legislative circus, but the real showstopper was HB145, Apportionment of Damages in Civil Actions.

Working on this bill was like assembling a 1000-piece puzzle, blindfolded, with the pieces constantly moving. It wasn't just a solo act; it was a full-on ensemble performance, and it turned out to be one of the star acts of my legislative career.

For years, repealing the Joint and Several Liability doctrine had been like the Holy Grail for Republican conservatives. Explaining this doctrine here would be like trying to recite the entire dictionary backward—tedious for you and a Herculean effort for me. But the behind-the-scenes political saga? Now, that's a tale worth telling, with enough twists and turns to keep even the most seasoned Capitol Hill veteran on their toes.

The adventure started with a message from Governor Jeb Bush's office, hand-delivered by a delegation that could have quickly passed for a band of messengers from a medieval court. Given my infamous dive into legal reform the year before—a spectacular belly flop by legislative standards—it seemed the Governor had pegged me as the court's jester willing to charge into battle with his tort reform banner.

My initial reaction was like being asked to perform a high-wire act without a net: intriguing but perilous. I needed to see this proposed act of legislative acrobatics for myself. I wasn't about to put on a show with a watered-down bill that would barely get a round of polite applause. No, if I was going to face the lions in the arena, particularly those of the legal profession, I wanted to ensure it was worth the spectacle

Upon reviewing the "Governor's" bill, I found it surprisingly to my liking, but here came the plot twist. I relayed back to the Governor's heralds, with a twinkle of mischief, that I'd be delighted to sponsor the bill under one minor condition: they remind the Governor that, unless my memory of the Florida Constitution was as faulty as a carnival fortune-teller's predictions, he didn't exactly have a bill filing slot in the legislature.

The bill, if filed, would be under my banner, making it "my" bill, not "his." My attempt at jesting fell flat, lost in translation like a clown at a mime convention. Nonetheless, my message was conveyed with the solemnity of a royal decree, albeit by jesters who didn't quite catch the joke.

A few sunsets after I had agreed to juggle the Governor's legislative hot potato, I found myself navigating the maze of the House office building. Like a scene out of a spy movie, Governor Jeb Bush spotted me from across the room in a move as smooth as a seasoned diplomat. With a gesture that could rival a knight summoning his squire, he beckoned me over.

Flashing a grin that could light up the gloomiest of legislative sessions, he asked if I had indeed filed "my" bill. I confirmed with a nod, adding a sprinkle of gratitude for his boldness in championing such a hot-button issue. But I couldn't resist adding a dash of spice to our exchange.

With a smile still playing on my lips, I issued a playful warning to the Governor. If he dared to fold under the fiery gaze of the trial bar, I'd regale my constituents with tales of the Governor's newfound career as a "sissy."

The joke landed with the finesse of a pie to the face—messy but undeniably amusing. While the Governor caught the jest, he couldn't help but stiffen at the mere thought of being dubbed a daisy in the face of adversity.

His comeback was swift and sure, a knight's vow to stand firm. And me? I played the role of the skeptical rhymester, promising to sing songs of his bravery or cowardice, depending on how the saga of HB145 unfolded.

As we rolled up our sleeves to dive into the nitty-gritty of advancing the bill, our interactions were peppered with humor-filled challenges. We tossed back and forth the gauntlet of commitment to sound public policy, all the while knowing that the circus of distractions wouldn't be far behind. Our banter, a blend of jest and earnestness, became the soundtrack to the serious work at hand, proving that a bit of laughter goes a long way, even in the thick of legislative battles.

Walking into Speaker Bense's office felt like being called to the principal's office after an audacious but ill-advised caper. The word was out: I had filed the bill and was under the microscope.

Speaker Bense laid it out for me with a mix of concern and incredulity. He worried that, as someone who wasn't exactly a legal eagle, I might not be able to stand up to the barrage of questions and scrutiny coming my way. It was like being told I was about to enter a duel with a water pistol.

With a blend of naivety and determination, I assured him of my commitment to cramming like a college student before finals. Speaker Bense, with the wisdom of someone who's seen too many freshmen flunk out, knew the Herculean task I had unwittingly signed up for.

His next move was something of a legislative lifeline. Concerned that this critical piece of legislation was in the hands of, let's say, a less-than-ideal champion, he assigned me a pair of legal Yodas.

George Meros and William Large were tasked with transforming me from a legislative novice into something resembling a Jedi. Starting with the equivalent of a legal empty cup, they poured in as much knowledge as possible.

Reflecting on that time, I'm still amazed at how much information they packed into my brain's limited real estate. It was akin to stuffing a Thanksgiving turkey with all the fixings into a pigeon.

And then, as if by magic—or perhaps a nod from "Leadership"—HB 145 was streamlined to face only two committee assignments. It was a subtle but clear sign that, despite the odds, there might be a fighting chance for both the bill and its rookie sponsor. Standing before the Judiciary Committee felt like stepping into the gladiator arena, armed with nothing but a slingshot while facing a legion of trial lawyer lions. They were the elite, ready to pounce with their superior legal acumen on a non-lawyer like me. Little did they know, George Meros and William Large had turned me into a legal David, ready to sling my well-prepared stones.

The initial phase of presenting the bill was like the calm before the storm—scripted and straightforward, with me reciting my lines. But as soon as we moved to the question-and-answer round, it was as if someone yelled, "Release the hounds!" Questions were thrown at me like ninja stars; each aimed to trip me up and send my bill crashing down before it even ran.

My legion of legal experts sat at the ready, like warriors waiting for their moment to charge. Yet, as the barrage of questions flew, something incredible happened—I found my groove. Representatives Ambler, Gelber, and Seiler, all courtroom gladiators in their own right, launched their verbal javelins, but I repelled each one, fueled by hours of rigorous preparation.

Just as the committee seemed ready to move on, a well-dressed lawyer stepped up to the plate, prepared to swing at my bill with all his might. Tradition dictates sponsors retreat at this point, but I stood my ground, unwilling to cede an inch in this battle of wits.

Then, in the heat of the moment, a sneeze ambushed me. I politely turned away from the lawyer, covered my mouth, and let it rip loud enough to echo through the chamber. The lawyer, oblivious to the sneeze but fully aware of the sound, froze mid-critique. Seizing a devilish opportunity, I leaned in and whispered, "Sorry about that, I think I just sneezed on you," while pretending to brush off his shoulder, even though I had not actually sneezed on him at all.

His look of utter dismay was a masterpiece I wish I could have framed. The poor man, convinced he was now wearing my sneeze, lost all composure and beat a hasty retreat, leaving his arguments in tatters. Little did he know, it was all an innocent trick, and his suit remained pristine, untouched by my sneeze.

Shanta Combs, a front-row witness to my impish improvisation, fled the scene, laughter betraying her exit. The spectacle derailed the opposition's momentum, and when the vote was called, it was a victory by a hair—seven Yeas to five Nays, with two abstentions.

As the dust settled, it was clear: we had won this skirmish, but the war for HB145 was far from over. Yet, in that moment, we knew we had not just survived; we had thrived, sneeze and all.

The journey of HB145 next led me to the Justice Council, a meeting presided over by Representative Kyle. This saga chapter was the eye of the hurricane—an eerily quiet session that culminated in an eight-to-two vote in our favor.

But the test was yet to come: the bill was to face its final hearing on the House floor.

Here, the rules of engagement shift dramatically. No longer could I lean on the crutch of my legal brain trust should the opposition corner me. It was just me, my wits, and the bill against the world.

The presentation of the bill unfolded without hitches. The questions thrown at me felt like reruns of a show I had watched too many times. Confidence began to seep in, but then, as expected in any good drama, the twist arrived.

Representative Jack Seiler, one of the House's legal luminaries, proposed an amendment so cunning it threatened to erase all our hard work with a single stroke.

As he stood to detail his amendment with the finesse of a seasoned scholar, a wave of panic washed over me. Speaker Bense's earlier warnings transformed from abstract advice to a palpable challenge staring me down.

I was in the spotlight, and playing to Seiler's legal prowess was not an option.

As the moment for my rebuttal arrived, gears turned rapidly in my head, piecing together a counterstrategy. It was time to navigate this chess game with a move they didn't see coming.

As I rose to address the chamber, my brain sprinted like a caffeinated squirrel.

I kicked off by tipping my hat to Representative Seiler for his masterclass on his amendment. I even acknowledged his prowess in the legal arena, suggesting everyone hang on to his every word.

But then, I pivoted. "However," I began, "his explanation is just one side of the story, and, folks, I'm here to paint you a different picture." With that, I launched into my spiel, hand raised with three fingers proudly displayed as if I were about to swear in for jury duty.

Imagine, if you will, each finger symbolizing a defendant in a courtroom drama worthy of daytime TV. The plot thickens with the court decreeing the first defendant as the villain of the piece, responsible for 80% of the mischief, while the other two were mere bit players, each with a 10% cameo in our plaintiff's misfortune.

Now, for the twist in our tale. If Seiler's amendment were to pass, it would be akin to a surprise development that leaves the audience gasping.

Picture this: our main antagonist, despite his starring role in the debacle, is as broke as a joke, not a penny to his name nor an insurance policy to call upon.

Enter the trial lawyers, stage left, offering him a deal to bow out gracefully for a token amount.

The next act sees our lead villain's name magically erased from the drama, leaving our supporting characters to foot the bill for the entire production.

And, just when you thought the plot couldn't thicken any further, another defendant takes his final bow, leaving our last man standing—a mere understudy with only a 10% role—suddenly spotlighted as the sole bearer of the financial burden.

Here I stood, my narrative culminating with only the middle finger left aloft—a lone survivor in this legal thriller.

"Now, I realize the optics of just this one finger standing might be a bit... pointed," I quipped, "but let's focus on the story, not the storyteller's props."

The chamber erupted in laughter, a welcome interlude in the high-stakes drama of legislative debate. Even the Speaker, caught between decorum and amusement, couldn't help but shake his head at the audacity of the performance.

When the dust settled and the laughter subsided, the verdict on Seiler's amendment came down—it was defeated. Perhaps this is a testament to the persuasive power of a well-spun yarn or to the universal appeal of a good joke at the right moment.

And so, the saga of HB145 reached its grand finale, not with a whimper but a ceremonial bang in the Cabinet meeting room, crammed to the rafters with an eager public and the ever-watchful press to witness the Governor sign this newborn bill. The atmosphere was electric, 'with the anticipation of victory lap speeches from the political gladiators who had championed this legislative beast through the gauntlet.

Governor Bush took the stage first, his words painting the arduous journey and triumph of HB145. Following him, Senate President Tom Lee and Senator Daniel Webster, the valiant Senate sponsor of the bill, shared their pieces of the story, each adding layers to the epic. Speaker Allen Bense, ever the succinct statesman, offered brief remarks before the spotlight swiveled my way.

Standing there, basking in the glow of legislative success and the assembled crowd's attention, I launched into my thank-you's, tipping my hat to the legion of lawmakers, lobbyists, and legal scholars who had toiled tirelessly to lay the golden bricks on the road to this moment.

But then, a mischievous impulse took hold, a last bit of unfinished business that begged for closure. With the room hanging on my every word, I pivoted, eyes on Governor Jeb Bush, and declared, "Governor Bush, in an arena filled with far too many men that are sissies, I want to thank you for being a real man."

The Governor, quick on the uptake and possibly foreseeing the potential for this quip to spiral into a diplomatic incident, clapped a hand on my shoulder with a mix of camaraderie and mild alarm. "Brown, if you don't get away from that microphone, you're going to get us all in trouble," he half-joked, half-pleaded, his words a lifeline thrown to a man blissfully diving headfirst into hot water.

His reaction, a perfect blend of humor and urgency, only added to the moment's levity. It was a fitting end to a legislative journey that had seen its fair share of battles, laughter, and, above all, camaraderie.

As I stepped away from the microphone, I couldn't help but think that this adventure in lawmaking, with all its ups and downs, had been one for the books.

The Speakers Race

As the curtains began to close on the 2006 Legislative session, another act was taking center stage, brewing its blend of drama. The race for the next Speaker of the Florida House was heating up, a contest of wills between my good friend Dennis Ross and Marco Rubio. The air was thick with anticipation and political maneuvering.

Amidst the mounting pressure of the campaign, Dennis made the difficult decision to withdraw, leaving Marco as the sole remaining candidate.

My involvement in Dennis's campaign had been deep and passionate, so the outcome was a bitter pill. I braced myself for a future under the Rubio administration where my role, I assumed, would be significantly less influential than it might have been under Dennis. After all, "To the victor goes the spoils," or so the adage goes.

Imagine my surprise when, a week or two after the dust had settled, my phone rang with an unexpected caller: Speaker Designate Rubio himself. He expressed a wish to meet in my office. Curiosity piqued, and perhaps a bit wary, I agreed to the rendezvous.

Marco arrived with a demeanor that was all smiles and enthusiasm, brimming with talk of his plans and dreams now within reach as the future Speaker. His enthusiasm was evident, but I couldn't help questioning why he chose to share this vision with me, considering my recent affiliations.

After hearing him out, I felt the need to express my stance. I confessed that the Ross campaign had been a deeply emotional journey for me, and I wasn't quite ready to jump ship and pledge my undying loyalty to his administration just yet.

Marco cut me off before I could go any further, his message clear and unexpectedly humble. "You misunderstood my visit," he clarified. "I'm not here to demand your allegiance. I'm here to earn your respect. I want you on my leadership team."

His words caught me off guard, leaving me momentarily speechless. I managed to cobble together a response, saying, "Well, if it's my respect you're after, you've got your work cut out for you. So, better get started." Looking back, I cringe at how awkwardly I phrased it.

But in that moment, Marco's unexpected outreach reshaped the narrative I had anticipated for our future interactions. It was a clumsy exchange, perhaps, but it marked the beginning of a new chapter where respect and leadership were not assumed but earnestly sought.

The Property Insurance Bill Debate

As the 2006 Session drew to a close, we were confronted with a final, unresolved issue that cast a long shadow over the proceedings. The matter at hand was a bill concerning Florida's property insurance market, a topic that had seen its share of contention.

Throughout the session, this bill had been repeatedly amended, and it had just returned from the Senate adorned with new amendments. These changes sat uneasily with me, and I struggled to support the bill's final version.

Despite my reservations, I had resigned myself to support the bill in silence, harboring a hope that we could address its shortcomings in the next legislative session. However, as the clock ticked towards the end of our final night, around 11:15 pm, the bill was brought forth for its final passage. I had no intention of speaking out—until Marco approached me. He urged me to voice my concerns during the debate, a request that took me by surprise but one I ultimately chose to honor.

Standing before my colleagues as the session neared its conclusion, I decided to share not just my apprehensions about the bill but to frame them within a broader historical context.

"Members," I began, "I hadn't planned to speak. Yet, I wish to recount the story of a man who lived long ago in a faraway place, Leonidas, a Spartan warrior whose mother's words to him were, 'Come home with your shield or on your shield.'

Leonidas was warned that the Persians were coming and that their archers were so many that their arrows would block the sun, to which Leonidas said, "All the better, for we will fight in the shade."

"For three days, the Spartans repelled the best of the Persian warriors. They were called the 'Immortals.'"

"On the third day, the Spartans were betrayed by one of their own. With the inevitable in view, Leonidas and his warriors took their position on a small spit of sand, and back-to-back, they fought with their swords until they had no swords. They then fought with their hands until they had no hands. They then fought with their teeth until the last man was dead."

I continued, drawing parallels between Leonidas's legendary stand and our present circumstances. "Leonidas's story is not just one of courage but of the indomitable spirit in the face of impossible odds. It speaks to the essence of sacrifice for a greater cause and the profound impact such actions can have on history.

Though steeped in the annals of ancient warfare, his legacy resonates with our civilization's values today—courage, sacrifice, and the unyielding pursuit of what is right."

With the chamber hanging on my words, I concluded, "Tonight, I stand before you, inspired by Leonidas's example. Should we face such inadequacies in our legislative efforts in the future, know that I will choose to stand firm in my principles, even at the cost of my political career. Let this be my Thermopylae."

The following summer, I was recognized as the Florida Chamber of Commerce Legislator of the Year, an honor for which I was deeply grateful, particularly for the passage of HB145. My gratitude extends to George and William, whose guidance and support were invaluable throughout this journey. Their wisdom prepared me for our legislative battles and reminded me of the enduring power of standing firm in one's convictions, regardless of odds.

Reflecting on these legislative achievements and battles, I see a tapestry woven from threads of perseverance, principle, and the power of collaboration. The challenges we faced, from the workers' compensation reform to the saga of HB145 and the property insurance bill debate, tested our mettle and shaped our understanding of what it means to be a legislator and a leader.

These experiences taught me the importance of standing firm in one's beliefs, even when the odds seem insurmountable. They highlighted the value of humor and wit in navigating tense situations and the transformative potential of building bridges and fostering respect, even among political adversaries.

As I look back on this chapter of my life, I am filled with gratitude for the lessons learned, the friendships forged, and the opportunity to serve the people of Florida. These legislative battles, with all their triumphs and tribulations, have left an indelible mark on my journey and have prepared me for the challenges and opportunities that lie ahead.

Anticipation and Resolve

Election season within the Florida Legislature had rolled around again, and the privilege of being re-elected humbled me. The prospect of collaborating with Speaker Marco Rubio's new leadership team filled me with anticipation and resolve.

Summary of Chapter 9:

Chapter 9 of my book explores the intricate world of legislative battles and victories, showcasing my determination, resourcefulness, and strategic approach as a lawmaker. It opens with Speaker Johnny Byrd entrusting me with a pivotal role in the insurance committee, a fitting assignment given my background as an insurance agent. This sets the stage for the challenging Workers' Compensation Reform Battle, where my colleagues and I navigate a complex landscape of legislative maneuvers to craft a bill that seeks to provide solutions amidst a storm of controversy.

The narrative unfolds like a gripping drama, with each amendment and committee session adding layers of tension and intrigue. My resourcefulness comes into play as I orchestrate a plan to salvage the beleaguered bill, employing negotiation and quick thinking to overcome opposition and bureaucratic obstacles. The recounting of my legislative efforts, from private meetings to unexpected moments of levity, offers a glimpse into the human side of lawmaking, where humor and camaraderie coexist amidst the high-stakes battles.

The saga of HB145 emerges as a significant part of my legislative career, a determined effort to repeal the Joint and Several Liability doctrine. My narrative navigates the intricate political landscape, weaving a tale of strategic alliances, unexpected challenges, and moments of humor amidst the gravity of legal debate. From light-hearted exchanges with Governor Jeb Bush to outmaneuvering legal adversaries with a well-timed sneeze, my journey is marked by a blend of determination, courage, and unwavering conviction.

As the narrative unfolds, themes of sacrifice, principle, and collaboration emerge as guiding principles in my legislative journey. The retelling of historical anecdotes, such as the saga of Leonidas, lends depth and gravitas to the message, underscoring the timeless values of courage and sacrifice in the pursuit of justice. My Thermopylae moment, delivered with passion and conviction on the House floor, is a testament to my commitment to principle, even in the face of political adversity.

In the final act, the narrative shifts to the Speaker's Race and the property insurance bill debate, offering a glimpse into the inner workings of political maneuvering and moral conviction. Despite past allegiances, Speaker Designate Marco Rubio's unexpected outreach reflects a theme of respect and leadership, underscoring the importance of collaboration and mutual respect in the legislative process.

As the chapter draws to a close, the narrative culminates in a moment of recognition and gratitude as I am honored as the Florida Chamber of Commerce Legislator of the Year. The passage of HB145 and the guidance of mentors George Meros and William Large are poignant reminders of the enduring power of principle and collaboration in pursuing legislative success.

In summary, Chapter 9 offers a rich tapestry of legislative battles and victories, showcasing the complexity and humanity of the lawmaking process. Through vivid storytelling and thoughtful reflection, it captures the essence of my legislative career, highlighting the enduring values of courage, sacrifice, and collaboration in pursuing justice and principle.

Transition to Chapter 10:

In reflecting on the tumultuous events surrounding House Bill 1A and the broader implications for leadership and principles, it's clear that my legislative journey has been marked by both triumphs and challenges. As I bid farewell to the halls of the Florida House of Representatives, I'm filled with a mix of emotions—gratitude for the opportunity to serve, pride in the stands I've taken, and a sober recognition of the compromises that sometimes accompany leadership.

In the wake of the passage of HB1A and my subsequent resignation, I find myself contemplating the essence of leadership and the delicate balance between principles and pragmatism. It's a question that has haunted me for years and one that continues to shape my perspective on governance and public service.

As I turn the page on my political career, I'm reminded of the words of wisdom passed down by my parents and the unwavering support of my beloved wife, Diane. Their guidance and love have sustained me through the highs and lows of public life, and for that, I am profoundly grateful.

Now, as we consider the intricacies of Florida's insurance landscape, I invite you to join me in a journey of exploration and reflection. From the challenges of the homeowners' insurance crisis to the broader themes of leadership and integrity, our path forward is paved with lessons learned and insights gained. Together, let us navigate these waters with humility, courage, and a steadfast commitment to the values that define us.

Chapter 10

My Political Career - Conclusion and Reflections on Leadership

However, as we began to navigate the intricacies of governance under this new administration, it became evident that the devastating hurricanes of 2004 and 2005 had sown the seeds for another tempest, a political storm.

The horizon was darkened by the looming presence of Charlie Crist, a figure whose reputation as a political opportunist suggested he would not let the ensuing crisis go unexploited.

The Homeowners' Insurance Crisis

In this charged atmosphere, Speaker Rubio entrusted me with the chairmanship of the Jobs & Entrepreneurship Council. This role placed me at the helm of oversight for the Committees on Business Regulation, Financial Institutions, Insurance, Utilities, & Telecommunications, underscoring the weight of the responsibilities now resting on my shoulders.

As the legislature convened, the air in Tallahassee was thick with tension. The back-to-back storm seasons had left the homeowners' insurance market in disarray, fueling widespread discontent among the members.

The rhetoric of those who perceived this crisis as an opportunity for political gain further aggravated the situation.

It was against this backdrop that Speaker Rubio summoned me to his office, his concern palpable. The crisis surrounding homeowners' insurance rates was spiraling, and he asked that I spearhead our collective search for a resolution.

Acutely aware of the charged atmosphere and the importance of considering every member's perspective, he ensured that their proposals were diligently evaluated to uncover the most viable solution.

Establishing Guiding Principles

Understanding the Herculean nature of the task at hand, I proposed an alternative strategy. Instead of wading through the morass of competing ideas—an approach that threatened to yield a quagmire of extreme and potentially perilous policies—I suggested we first establish a set of guiding principles.

These principles would serve as our compass, ensuring that our debate remained anchored and that each proposal was measured against a consistent and rational yardstick, thereby mitigating the risks posed by reactionary and populist proposals.

After a week of intense deliberation and collaboration, we emerged with a framework of ten guiding principles. This achievement was not merely procedural; it represented a beacon of reason amid a storm, a testament to our collective commitment to navigate the tumultuous waters of policymaking with foresight and steadiness.

The "Ten Guiding Principles" document encapsulated our approach to addressing the hurricane crisis. It emphasized the importance of using private sector capital over public debt, allowing the free market to operate, and cautiously implementing government interventions when necessary. The principles also highlighted the need for personal responsibility in living choices, limiting subsidies to primary residences, and promoting home fortification and appropriate building codes.

Furthermore, the principles provided a framework for expanding the Florida Hurricane Catastrophe Fund (FHCF) judiciously and temporarily, ensuring fairness and market pricing. They also stressed the importance of a comprehensive and understandable implementation plan and the consideration of non-insurance remedies, such as property tax relief.

The "Hurricane Crisis Concepts" document delves deeper into the specific strategies and considerations for addressing the crisis. It identifies three interrelated problems: the political crisis, the insurance crisis, and the hurricane crisis. The document proposes a mix of short-term, intermediate, and long-term solutions, ranging from consumer protections and mitigation efforts to reforms in the Florida marketplace and Citizens Property Insurance Corporation. It also highlights the negative outcomes of flawed government-run insurers and emphasizes the need for a multi-faceted approach that includes growth management, improved building codes, mitigation, and raised public awareness of risk.

In the appendix of this book, you'll find the documents summarized above. These documents are not just pieces of paper but a testament to our collective effort to steer our state through one of its most challenging periods, guided by a unfaltering commitment to principle-driven policymaking.

For those interested in understanding the depth of our strategy, I encourage you to consult these sections. They encapsulate our approach's essence and vision for overcoming the crisis.

As we laid down these guiding principles, it became apparent that standing by them would sometimes mean standing alone. The principles we championed required not just understanding and collaboration, when possible, but more importantly, the fortitude to uphold them even in the face of overwhelming opposition.

In such times, when it felt like we were surrounded yet alone in our convictions, Shakespeare's whimsical words often came to mind: "It's nice to be among friends…even if they are somebody else's." These words took on a sardonic twist, reflecting our solitude in the legislative arena where, despite the lack of support, we remained steadfast in our commitment to what was right.

The Capitulation on House Bill 1A

I wish I could report a happy ending to this story, but fate would not cooperate. In an extraordinary legislative maneuver, a special joint select committee on insurance was called. The House and Senate delegations met in the Knot building. The mood was tense.

The Senate delegation advanced a plan totally inconsistent with the Guiding Principles established by the House, and persuasive arguments were advanced. The plan hinged on leveraging debt-based financing for future hurricane damage. In other words, self-insuring the risk.

To accomplish this magic, the Florida Hurricane Catastrophe Fund would grow exponentially. The argument was, "Don't worry. If a storm strikes, we'll borrow the money." My retort was, "How do you plan to repay the debt?" "We'll pass a special assessment on all policyholders in the state to repay the debt." I could hear my former boss at the bank who loved to remind foolish borrowers, "You can't drink yourself sober, and you can't spend yourself out of debt."

The Senate proposal went further. Citizens Property Insurance Company (Citizens), the State's insurer of last resort, would be authorized to assess all policyholders for post-storm shortfalls. Citizens rates would also be rolled back, rates that had already been declared inadequate.

To my dismay, abandoning our principled stance, the House delegation capitulated and celebrated a hollow victory, convinced the issue was resolved. I, however, could not contain my frustration. My words, particularly to a fellow House member and insurance agent, were harsh and, in hindsight, regrettable. "You are less than worthless—you should know better," I admonished, a statement born of disillusionment rather than malice.

The bill was discussed in the House and Senate chambers the following week. Before the scheduled House vote, I received a call to the Speaker's office. As I entered the room, Speaker Rubio appeared anxious.

He asked, what I believed at the time to be, a rhetorical question, "Don, what are we fixing to do?" I responded, "Mr. Speaker, this bill will result in something like a death spiral. It will be complicated to undo."

His retort was, "I have members of this House ready to commit mutiny and a Governor with an 80% approval rating. Don, what you don't understand is that when you are in leadership, there are occasions when you must do things you don't want to do."

My response, though earnest, was met with a stark reminder of the sacrifices leadership sometimes demands, sacrifices that, in this instance, I could not conscionably make. "Marco, you may have a point," I conceded, albeit with a bitterness that betrayed my frustration. "I forgot about that 'leadership' quagmire."

Resignation and Reflection

Retreating to my office's solitude, I pondered the weight of our decisions and the path they had set us on—a path I could no longer follow. There, amidst the quiet acceptance of the inevitable, I penned my resignation letter, a tangible symbol of my protest.

The subsequent votes in both the Senate and House only underscore the magnitude of our collective folly. With the Senate's unanimous approval and the House's overwhelming majority, only Dennis Ross and I stood in dissent. It was a somber affirmation of a journey fraught with compromise that, despite our best efforts, ended not with a resolution but with a profound sense of what might have been. In the face of this kind of adversity, it's easy to complain or hope for change, but real leadership demands action. "The pessimist complains about the wind; the optimist expects it will change; the realist adjusts the sails." This pragmatic approach has always been my guide.

In the intervening years, this question has plagued me, "Can the abandonment of one's principles be rightly blamed on the demands of "leadership"? I thought leadership was about leading, not surrendering to the majority.

Having asked this question of myself hundreds of times and others nearly as many, the consensus sounds like this:

The tension between adhering to one's principles and navigating leadership demands is complex and nuanced. Indeed, leadership is fundamentally about guiding, influencing, and making decisions aligning with a vision or values.

However, the practical reality of leadership, especially in political and organizational contexts, often involves balancing competing interests, negotiating compromises, and sometimes making concessions to achieve broader goals or to maintain unity and function within a group or institution.

Abandoning one's principles due to the pressures of leadership can be viewed critically for several reasons:

1. **Core Values and Integrity**: Leadership is deeply intertwined with the notion of integrity and the unyielding adherence to a set of core values or principles. When leaders forsake their principles, it can raise questions about their integrity, reliability, and leadership authenticity.

2. **Vision and Direction**: Effective leadership requires a clear vision and the ability to inspire others towards that vision. Surrendering to the majority without consideration for core principles can lead to a loss of direction and purpose, undermining the leader's ability to inspire and lead effectively.

3. **Trust and Respect**: Leaders are often respected for their commitment to their values and ability to stand firm in challenging situations. Compromising on principles, especially under pressure, can erode trust and respect among followers, colleagues, and the broader community.

However, leadership also involves pragmatism and the capacity to navigate complex, dynamic environments. This sometimes requires compromise and flexibility, including:

1. **Strategic Compromises**: In some cases, leaders may choose to compromise on specific issues as a strategic decision to achieve more significant, overarching goals or to prevent worse outcomes.

2. **Consensus Building**: Effective leadership often requires consensus among diverse groups with competing interests. This can necessitate concessions to ensure collaboration and progress.

3. **Responsibility to Stakeholders**: Leaders must consider the needs and well-being of all stakeholders, which can sometimes mean prioritizing collective or long-term benefits over personal principles.

In conclusion, while leadership is fundamentally about leading rather than surrendering, the complexities of real-world leadership can sometimes require difficult choices and compromises. The key is finding a balance that allows for effective governance and progress while maintaining integrity and staying true to core principles as much as possible.

Leaders are often judged by their adherence to principles and their ability to navigate these complexities and make decisions that serve the greater good.

The bottom line, in my opinion, in the case of House Bill 1A, is that all the preparation and argumentation for reasoned and sound public policy was cast aside in favor of the whining of a demagogue. How soon we forget the lessons of the past. House Bill 1A became a sad reminder of how weak the commitment of many to what we call "our principles."

We can frame and mount them on the wall, laminate them, and carry them in our wallets, but if we cannot defend them at our "Thermopylae," we are not worth the salt in our bread.

As the discussion of House Bill 1A ends and after years of deep reflection, I remain proud of the stand that Dennis Ross and I took. I also concede that, based on the definition of leadership that some hold, I may have failed, and I'm OK with that.

Final Farewells

The regular sessions of 2007 and 2008 were personally painful. After the passage of HB1A in the Special Session of 2007A and my subsequent resignation as Chairman of the Jobs & Entrepreneurship Council, I remained Vice Chairman of the Jobs and Entrepreneurship Council and Chairman of the Insurance Committee.

In 2007, I filed nine bills. All died in committee except for two local bills.

In 2008, I filed six bills, all of which died. The only productive work I was allowed to do was in the Insurance Committee, where public hearings were conducted on the state of the property insurance market after HB1A.

After the Insurance Committee received several hours of testimony under oath, a 10-page report was issued and provided to Speaker Marco Rubio. A copy of that report titled "Letter to Speaker Marco Rubio" is in this book's Appendix.

As the 2008 legislative session ended, so did my legislative career. It was a bittersweet reflection on all the successes and failures and an opportunity to say goodbye to friends and colleagues.

There were several memorable farewells on the last day. First was the staff that had worked so hard on the issues that were so important to me. They were the best, and I consider many of them friends.

Second, I had a particularly emotional final visit to my office with Mark Delegal and Allen McGlynn. They had been intimately involved in much of the legislation I had worked on over the eight years I had served. Jim Massie also offered a heartfelt goodbye.

I noted that Mark, Allen, and Jim were the only lobbyists who said goodbye. I consider all three of them dear friends to this day.

Finally, I met my dear friend Dennis Ross in the Rotunda to exchange our goodbyes. So many memories flooded my mind as we embraced (briefly), shook hands, and assured one another that we would stay in touch. Driving home for the last time as a State Representative was difficult, filled with so many memories.

As I write this chapter describing my years of public service, eight of which were in the Florida House of Representatives, it has allowed me to reflect deeply on those years. That reflection is now seasoned by the intervening years, which provides a much broader perspective. I continue to carry with me a belief that has long informed my view of governance: 'My reading of history convinces me that most bad government has grown out of too much government.'[1]

I am profoundly grateful and honored for the opportunity that my constituents give me to serve. I am also profoundly thankful for the life lessons my Momma and Daddy taught me. Finally, to my loving wife Diane, I could not have served without your help. So much work was piled on you, but you gladly bore it out of love, and I am eternally grateful. I Love You, Sweetheart.

---

[1] https://www.brainyquote.com/quotes/john_sharp_williams_193114

Summary of Chapter 10:

Chapter 10 of my book describes a pivotal period in my political career, marked by the challenges and crises that emerged after devastating hurricanes in 2004 and 2005. As I navigated the intricacies of governance under a new administration, it became evident that these natural disasters had sown the seeds for a political storm, with the looming presence of figures like Charlie Crist adding to the tension.

Amidst this charged atmosphere, Speaker Rubio entrusted me with the chairmanship of the Jobs & Entrepreneurship Council, placing me at the forefront of oversight for critical committees. The legislature convened amidst widespread discontent over the state of the homeowners' insurance market, fueled by the aftermath of back-to-back storm seasons and escalating political rhetoric.

In response to the crisis surrounding homeowners' insurance rates, Speaker Rubio summoned me to his office, tasking me with spearheading our search for a resolution. Recognizing the need for a measured approach amidst the charged atmosphere, I proposed establishing a set of guiding principles to anchor our debate and evaluation of proposals. After intense deliberation, we emerged with a framework of ten guiding principles, representing a beacon of reason amid the storm of political maneuvering.

These principles emphasized the importance of utilizing private sector capital, allowing the free market to operate, and implementing government interventions cautiously. They also underscored the need for personal responsibility, limiting subsidies, and promoting home fortification. Additionally, the principles outlined a comprehensive approach to expanding the Florida Hurricane Catastrophe Fund and considering non-insurance remedies.

Despite our efforts to uphold these principles, the legislative process took an unexpected turn with the introduction of House Bill 1A. This bill, which expanded government intervention and adopted unsustainable financing mechanisms, was a departure from our established guiding principles. Despite my objections and warnings about the potential consequences, the House delegation ultimately capitulated. They celebrated what they viewed as a victory while disregarding the principles we had fought to uphold.

The passage of House Bill 1A marked a sobering realization of the challenges inherent in principled policymaking within the political arena. Despite our best efforts, the allure of short-term political gains and the pressures of leadership led to compromises that undermined the integrity of our principles. Reflecting on this chapter of my political career, I am reminded of the importance of steadfast commitment to principles, even in the face of adversity and political expediency.

Transition to Chapter 11:

Now, as we turn the page and begin Chapter 11, I invite you to join me on a journey of exploration and reflection. From the lessons learned in my small-town upbringing to realizing those values in my professional life, this chapter delves into the intricate interplay between personal roots and professional wisdom. So, let's embark on this journey together, bridging youthful lessons with the insights gained over a lifetime of public service.

Chapter 11

From Roots to Realization - Bridging Youthful Lessons and Professional Wisdom

Growing up in a small town, you quickly learn that every handshake matters and that your reputation is built on a mix of goodwill and hard work. My early days weren't characterized by the incessant buzzing of smartphones or the constant chatter of cable news. Instead, life revolved around the rhythms of community gatherings, school events, and seasonal celebrations that marked the passage of time in our close-knit community.

As a kid, I spent countless hours helping on my family's farm after school. There, I learned the value of a hard day's work, the patience required to see a crop through to harvest, and the resilience needed when things didn't go according to plan. More than mere chores, these tasks served as my first lessons in responsibility and problem-solving—skills that would later form the foundation of my professional life.

In politics and insurance, like in farming, you quickly learn that not every seed you plant flourishes. I took the lessons from the farm—about nurturing, timing, and adapting—and applied them to my roles in public service and business. Sometimes, that meant crafting legislation that would take months, even years, to come to fruition. Other times, it meant navigating the complex needs of constituents or clients with just the right balance of tact and firmness.

My journey from the fields of my family farm to the halls of the Florida House wasn't a straight line. Each step, setback, and success along the way constituted a chapter in the larger narrative of personal growth and public service. The values instilled in me by my family—honesty, diligence, and a deep-rooted sense of community—guided my every decision, whether at a town hall meeting, in a committee meeting, or negotiating a crucial insurance reform.

Reflecting on these transitions, I see a tapestry of experiences, each thread colored by the lessons of my youth. This blending of personal upbringing with professional endeavors just didn't happen. It was a deliberate process of applying the old lessons to new challenges, a problem-solving method informed by a lifetime of learning and living in a world where your word is your bond, and your reputation is your most valuable asset.

Ultimately, this journey from roots to realization isn't just about the roles I've played or the positions I've held. It's about how the core principles learned early can lead to meaningful, impactful work. It's about making a difference, one day, one decision at a time. And as I look back, I'm grateful for every lesson, every challenge, and every opportunity to serve. They've all shaped the person I am today in ways I could never have imagined standing in those fields all those years ago.

Summary of Chapter 11:

In Chapter 11, I discuss my formative experiences growing up in a small town and the profound impact they've had on my approach to public service and leadership. Growing up amidst the rhythms of community life and the responsibilities of family farming instilled in me the core values of hard work, integrity, and resilience.

I draw parallels between the lessons learned on the family farm—about nurturing, adapting, and problem-solving—and their application in the realms of politics and insurance. Whether crafting legislation, navigating constituent needs, or negotiating insurance reforms, these early lessons guided my professional endeavors.

My journey from the fields of my family farm to the halls of the Florida House of Representatives was characterized by a deliberate process of blending personal upbringing with professional challenges. Each setback and success along the way became a chapter in a larger story of personal growth and public service.

Reflecting on this journey, I emphasize the importance of applying old lessons to new challenges—a problem-solving method informed by a lifetime of learning and living by honesty, diligence, and community values. Ultimately, this journey from roots to realization underscores the transformative power of personal values in driving meaningful, impactful work in the realm of public service.

As we conclude this chapter, we transition to a deeper exploration of specific strategies and policies that address pressing issues in state policy, beginning with the challenges of reducing Florida homeowners' insurance premiums.

Transition to Chapter 12:

In Chapter 11, I reflected on the lessons learned from my upbringing and professional endeavors. In Chapter 12, I turn my focus towards the intricate world of insurance. This transition mirrors the journey from personal growth to a deeper exploration of the complexities within the realm of insurance and public policy. So, let's now explore specific strategies and policies to reduce Florida homeowners' insurance premiums, addressing one of the most pressing issues in state policy.

Part 4

ESSAYS ON INSURANCE AND PUBLIC POLICY

CHAPTER 12

Introduction to the Chapters on Insurance

In my journey through the snarl of homeowners' insurance, I've stumbled upon truths and myths, learning lessons that are as valuable as they are hard-earned. Allow me to share a story with you, drawn from experience and insight, a narrative from the core of the "Florida Grand Experiment."

Imagine a state battered by hurricanes, where wealth and population patterns play out in a theater of risk and responsibility. Florida, my beloved state, served as the stage for this grand experiment, where the quest to tame high homeowners' premiums unfolded like a modern tragedy, revealing the foolishness of mistaking symptoms for the disease. (A Hint: Florida's problem is not high homeowners' insurance premiums. Florida's problem is hurricanes and stubborn human behavior. More on that later…)

As we journey through the following chapters, we will unravel the complex tapestry of insurance, where the threads of political decisions, natural disasters, and human behavior intertwine. Envision a world where building codes and human choices emerge as the unsung heroes, where the battle is waged not only against nature's fury but also against our inclination to build castles on sand.

Before we get too deep into the weeds on such a technical subject, I want to pause and welcome you to the book section, where we delve into the world of insurance and public policy. Now, I realize the topic of insurance and public policy may not be the most riveting subject for everyone. But trust me, it's much more interesting than you might think! Let me tell you a little story that might just change your mind.

Years ago, I felt the same way you do - like this stuff was about as exciting as watching paint dry. That is until I met my study partner. You see when I was preparing for my insurance agent's license exam, I recruited a pretty young lady from my church to help me out. Not only did she make the studying process much more enjoyable, but we ended up getting married! And that was over 45 years ago.

Now, I don't know what that has to do with making insurance and public policy more interesting, but I'll tell you what I do know—I'm going to make sure this discussion is anything but dull. As we dive into this topic, I will sprinkle in some "entertainment breaks" to keep you on your toes. At times, the humor will serve to illustrate a point, while at others, it will be purely for unadulterated entertainment. Think of it as a little reward for making it through the more technical stuff.

So, keep your eyes peeled because you never know when one of these little interludes might pop up. Who knows, maybe you'll even learn something along the way! Let's get started, shall we?

Insurance and public policy play a fundamental role in our lives, often in ways we don't even realize. From the obvious, such as health and property insurance, to the more obscure, like liability and reinsurance (insurance for insurance companies), these mechanisms create a safety net that allows us to take risks and step boldly into the future. In the following chapters, we will explore how these policies are crafted, the impact they have on our daily lives, and the ongoing debates surrounding them.

Now, you may say, "I'm just not interested in politics and public policy" but you should realize that "Just because you do not take an interest in politics doesn't mean politics won't take an interest in you!" Navigating the stormy waters of

Florida's insurance landscape has taught me that policy changes can affect us all, whether we want them to or not.

I learned this firsthand when a constituent approached me after a town hall meeting, looking rather puzzled. "You know," he said, "I didn't care much about insurance and politics before, but now my premiums have doubled, and I can't keep up. What changed?"

"Well," I replied, "the weather might have remained the same, but the political climate has certainly shifted." His eyebrows furrowed, and he nodded thoughtfully, clearly realizing that changes in the law governing insurance weren't just theoretical exercises for lawmakers—they had real-world implications that touched his wallet.

Insurance and public policy are deeply intertwined and shifts in one inevitably affect the other. While synthesizing this landscape isn't always easy, it's crucial to stay informed and actively participate in shaping the policies that affect our homes, businesses, and communities.

Understanding these changes can help us weather the storm, even if it means keeping an eye on the political tides and staying ahead of the curve. Because if you don't take an interest in politics, you might find yourself caught in a political tempest you never saw coming.

Now, let's explore the key themes and discussions that will unfold throughout these essays, including how reducing losses can significantly lower Florida homeowners' insurance premiums. We will then move on to more complex discussions, such as the intricacies of managing risks in the face of Florida's hurricane exposure. Each section aims to demystify insurance and public policy elements, providing a solid understanding enriched by anecdotes from my own experiences in the field.

Together, we'll navigate these often-choppy waters, making stops along the way for those promised breaks—little oases of humor and insight to refresh and engage. By the end of this journey, I hope to have informed you and entertained and shown you the unexpected excitement hidden within the world of insurance and public policy.

We'll get our toes wet by dissecting the foundational elements of insurance, from the basic principles of risk versus uncertainty, as illuminated by the esteemed Dr. Frank H. Knight, to the nuanced dynamics of residential property insurance in a state perennially dancing with the forces of nature. Each chapter builds upon the last, creating a rich tapestry of insights that lay bare the challenges and opportunities inherent in the quest to safeguard homes, livelihoods, and legacies against the capriciousness of the elements.

After we unravel the layers of reinsurance (*insurance that an insurance company purchases to limit its risk by sharing some of its potential losses with other insurers*) and its pivotal role in Florida's insurance landscape in Chapter 29, "Beyond the Storm – How Reinsurance Protects Florida's Homeowners," we transition to Chapter 30, "Navigating the Complexities of Florida's Property Insurance Market." This chapter serves as a lighthouse, illuminating the nuanced shores of Florida's property insurance market. Here, we dissect the interplay of human decision-making, market forces, and regulatory frameworks, guided by the intellectual beacons of the Ellsberg Paradox, Knight's distinction between risk and uncertainty, and Bastiat's poignant observations on the unintended consequences of well-meaning interventions.

Some will purposefully choose not to join us on this journey, whether out of spite or despise.

To those wayward travelers, we say:

"May Those That Love Us - Love Us.

And, For Those That Don't,

May God Turn Their Heart.

And, For Those Whose Hearts He Cannot Turn,

May He Turn Their Ankle

So That We Will Know Them by Their Limping."

In our story, this adage finds its place not just as a witty remark but as a profound reflection on the journey of understanding and influence, a reminder that not all will walk with us in the quest for change.

Let's switch gears and get a bit more casual as we dive into the quirky insurance world in sunny Florida. Imagine we're strolling down the 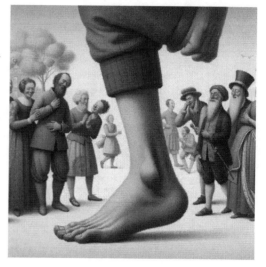 hallways of lawmaking and tiptoeing through the minefields of risk assessment while trying to figure out the wild world of human behavior. It's like trying to predict Florida weather – a bit unpredictable, often surprising, but always interesting.

So, grab your metaphorical backpack, and let's embark on this adventure together. We will sift through the sands of time to learn from the past, look around at our current state, and peek over the horizon at what the future might hold. And what's our map through this journey? The Florida Grand Experiment – sounds like a theme park ride. We'll dodge the pitfalls, navigate through the perils, and maybe find some hidden treasure of wisdom, change, and growth in the crazy world of homeowner's insurance.

Summary of Chapter 12:

Chapter 12 introduces a series of chapters dedicated to unraveling the intricacies of insurance, particularly within the context of Florida's unique challenges and opportunities. Drawing from personal experiences and insights gained throughout my career, I embark on a journey to dissect the foundational elements of insurance and shed light on the complex dynamics shaping the homeowners' insurance landscape.

The chapter vividly depicts Florida as the stage for a grand experiment in taming high homeowners' premiums, highlighting the intersection of political decisions, natural disasters, and human behavior. It sets the stage for a deeper exploration of insurance principles, risk assessment, and regulatory frameworks, inviting readers to delve into the nuances of an industry shaped by both external forces and internal dynamics.

As the narrative unfolds, key concepts such as risk versus uncertainty, the role of reinsurance (insurance for insurance companies), and the unintended consequences of regulatory interventions are explored. Through a blend of intellectual discourse and real-world anecdotes, the chapter navigates the complexities of Florida's property insurance market, offering valuable insights into the challenges homeowners, policymakers, and industry stakeholders face.

Moreover, the chapter adopts a playful tone, acknowledging the insurance world's quirky nature while emphasizing its implications' seriousness. It invites readers to embark on an adventure of discovery, promising to uncover hidden treasures of wisdom, change, and growth amidst the unpredictable landscape of homeowner's insurance.

Ultimately, Chapter 12 sets the stage for a deeper dive into the strategies and policies to reduce Florida homeowners' insurance premiums, offering readers a glimpse into the transformative potential of informed decision-making and strategic planning. Through a blend of humor, intellect, and personal reflection, the chapter lays the groundwork for an enlightening exploration of one of the most pressing issues in state policy.

Chapter 13

Introduction to the Chapters on Insurance
The Evolution of Insurance: From Ancient Practices to Modern Risk Management

Insurance has ancient roots intertwined with the development of civilization itself. From its origins as a simple system for mitigating risks through communal efforts, insurance has transformed into a complex network of specialized companies and products offering diverse coverage options. Comparing early forms of insurance with modern practices reveals how far risk management has come and highlights the transformation of perceptions around risk.

Early Forms of Insurance

The earliest forms of insurance were primitive and based largely on mutual aid. In ancient civilizations, such as Babylon and China, merchants used methods to distribute risk among multiple parties.

1. Babylonian Code of Hammurabi (c. 1750 BC): One of the oldest known insurance methods was recorded in the Code of Hammurabi. This code included a system where a merchant receiving a loan paid the lender an additional sum to waive the loan should the shipment be stolen.[2]
2. Ancient Greece and Rome: The Greeks and Romans had forms of guilds or benevolent societies that provided financial support to families of deceased members, essentially providing an early form of life insurance. Maritime traders also utilized bottomry contracts, enabling ship owners to secure loans for funding their voyages. If the ship was lost at sea, the loan would be forgiven, but if it returned safely, the lender received both the principal and interest.[3]
3. Ancient China (Zhou Dynasty, 1046-256 BC): Merchants and traders would distribute their goods across multiple vessels when traveling on treacherous rivers. By spreading the risk of loss, they reduced the potential impact of a single vessel sinking or being robbed.[4]

These early forms of insurance were fundamentally communal and based on the principle of mutual assistance. They were not driven by profit but by the necessity to stabilize communities and protect individuals from the capriciousness of fate, whether it be piracy, fire, or death.

---

[2] https://en.wikipedia.org/wiki/History_of_insurance
[3] https://greekreporter.com/2024/04/01/insurance-ancient-greece-pioneer-mitigating-risks/
[4] https://www.swissre.com/dam/jcr:eb1aba5f-05ca-4bd4-bfe6-d42a6ed6b8c5/150Y_Markt_Broschuere_China_Inhalt.pdf

Medieval Innovations

Insurance practices evolved significantly during the medieval period, particularly with the advent of maritime insurance. The expansion of trade during this era, especially in maritime cities like Genoa, necessitated the development of more sophisticated methods to manage the risks associated with sea voyages.

1. Medieval Guilds: In medieval Europe, guilds served a dual purpose as trade unions and early insurers. Guild members contributed to a communal fund, which could then be used to support individuals facing personal or professional crises.
2. Standalone Insurance Policies (14th century): The medieval period saw the emergence of standalone insurance policies, marking a shift from insurance being tied exclusively to lending agreements.

The Rise of Modern Insurance

1. **Great Fire of London (1666):** The Great Fire of London led to significant developments in property insurance. Following the disaster, Nicholas Barbon introduced the first fire insurance company, which not only marked the beginning of modern property insurance but also introduced the practice of risk assessment. The devastation also led to the establishment of fire brigades to reduce risks by quickly extinguishing flames.[5]
2. **Lloyd's of London (1686):** The first modern insurance company, Lloyd's of London, was established to provide marine insurance for ships and their cargo. The company's innovative approach to risk assessment and underwriting set the standard for the insurance industry.[6]

---

[5] https://www.history.com/this-day-in-history/great-fire-of-london-begins
[6] https://www.argolimited.com/wp-content/uploads/2020/07/Learn-About-LLoyds.pdf

3. **Life Insurance:** The first known life insurance policy was issued in England in 1583. However, it was not until actuaries like Edmund Halley developed mortality tables in the 17th century that life insurance became a viable commercial enterprise.[7]

Evolution of Risk Perception and Management

The perception of risk and the management strategies employed by insurers have undergone significant changes from ancient times to the modern era. Initially, risk was perceived as an act of fate or gods, with insurance practices embedded in communal and mutual aid systems. As trade expanded and economic activities became more complex, the perception of risk shifted towards a more calculable and manageable component of commerce.

In the 20th century, the insurance industry underwent significant changes driven by technological advances, data analysis, and a growing understanding of risk. The introduction of actuarial science allowed insurers to assess and price risk more accurately, leading to the development of a wide range of insurance products tailored to specific needs and circumstances.

Modern risk management in insurance uses sophisticated actuarial science to quantify risks and set premiums accordingly. The introduction of probability theory and later developments in statistics allowed insurers to model risks more accurately and spread them effectively across a larger pool of insured entities. Key aspects of modern insurance practices include:

1. **Diverse Risk Management:** Today's insurance industry offers coverage for a wide variety of risks beyond just maritime or fire-related losses. From health insurance to auto insurance and even cybersecurity coverage, companies have specialized in providing comprehensive policies tailored to individuals' and businesses' specific needs.

---

[7] https://www.swissre.com/dam/jcr:e8613a56-8c89-4500-9b1a-34031b904817/150Y_Markt_Broschuere_UK_EN.pdf

2. **Risk Pooling and Underwriting:** Modern insurance practices involve pooling risks from a large group of policyholders to spread the financial impact of individual claims. Underwriting, a critical aspect of risk assessment, helps insurers identify potential risks and set premiums accordingly.
3. **Reinsurance:** Insurers transfer portions of their risks to other companies through reinsurance, reducing their potential financial losses from major claims events like hurricanes. This practice improves the stability of insurance companies by limiting their exposure to catastrophic risks.[8]
4. **Regulatory Frameworks and Consumer Protections:** Insurance regulation has become an integral part of modern insurance practices, ensuring solvency and fairness. Governments now mandate consumer protections, including clear policy documentation, claims handling procedures, and financial safeguards, to prevent fraud and misuse.
5. **Advanced Technologies:** Today, risk management also incorporates advanced technologies such as big data analytics, artificial intelligence, and blockchain to improve accuracy, efficiency, and transparency in insurance practices.

Changing Perceptions of Risk Management

Early forms of insurance were often intertwined with gambling, as bets were placed on the success of voyages or other uncertain outcomes. Today, insurance is less about gambling and more about carefully assessing and managing risks through data analysis and actuarial science. Modern insurers employ sophisticated modeling techniques to estimate probabilities and minimize uncertainty.

Moreover, the public perception of insurance has evolved from viewing it as a luxury for the wealthy to a necessary tool for personal and financial security. While debates about regulation, premiums, and claim procedures persist, insurance

---

[8] https://www.casact.org/sites/default/files/database/proceed_proceed29_29022.pdf

remains a crucial part of modern life, protecting individuals and businesses from financial catastrophe.

Conclusion

The journey from ancient mutual aid systems to modern insurance corporations illustrates a profound shift in risk management. What began as a community-based practice to mitigate the harsh consequences of unpredictable events has evolved into a complex industry that uses sophisticated technology to manage risk on a global scale.

This evolution reflects broader economic and societal changes, highlighting how fundamental the concept of risk management has been throughout human history. As we continue to face new challenges and risks, the insurance industry's ability to adapt and innovate will remain crucial in providing security and stability.

Transition to Chapter 14:

Reducing insurance premiums by focusing on risk mitigation is only one part of the solution. We must examine the underlying market dynamics to understand better how to tackle Florida's insurance challenges comprehensively. By recognizing how market price signals influence consumer behavior, particularly in the face of government intervention and distorted pricing, we can gain valuable insights into the overarching issues affecting Florida's insurance market. This next chapter, 'Outlining the Overarching Challenges Facing Florida's Insurance Market,' will explore these concepts in detail, providing critical guidance for future policies.

Chapter 14
Navigating Florida's Insurance Market: Challenges and Opportunities

Introduction: Thought Experiment

Let me ask you a trick question: "How much do you believe it will cost the people of Florida the next time a $50 billion hurricane strikes our coast?"

It will cost $50 billion. The amount is not the question. The question is, "Who will pay the bill?"

You repeat the question to me, assuming the answer should be obvious: "What do you mean - Who will pay the bill?"

Unfortunately, my response reveals the "not so obvious" and includes more questions. "Hopefully, the insurance industry will cover most of it. But in some cases, insurance companies go bankrupt. Then who pays? The Florida Insurance Guaranty Association will pick up part of the tab, but who will pay the rest? It will be paid by the homeowner."

But you ask, "What if the homeowner doesn't have the money to pay?"

Then, it will be reflected in a reduction in the homeowner's net worth, even when that results in a negative number.

Here is the hard reality: someone must pay the bill once the damage is done.

We cannot change the direction or intensity of tropical storms.

So, the real question is, "What could we have done to reduce the size of the loss?"

The only meaningful way to reduce the size of that loss would have been to reduce the risk, i.e., through building code enforcement, mitigation, and, most importantly, a change in human behavior. If all we do is quibble over the insurance price and fail to address the real problem, our need for Band-Aids and Tylenol will never be diminished.

What is The Problem:

Florida's geography and climate make it uniquely vulnerable to hurricanes and flooding. Yet, our prosperity and rapid population growth have led to the stubborn behavior of building in high-risk areas and expecting someone else to pay for the damage when disasters strike.

High premiums, affordability concerns, and lack of insurance availability are not the problem but merely symptoms. Hurricanes and risky human behavior represent the core problems driving these issues. Addressing symptoms without reducing risk through thoughtful planning and resilient construction will leave homeowners and taxpayers vulnerable.

In fact, I would argue that when policymakers focus on symptoms rather than the root problem, they unwittingly send exactly the wrong message to Florida consumers. Let's spend a few minutes considering the value of "Market Price in Risk Management."

The Function of Market Price in Risk Management

From the introduction, it's clear that hurricanes and risky building behavior are the root problems. High premiums and affordability issues are merely symptoms. This sets the stage to argue that ignoring market signals by suppressing prices leads to unintended consequences, particularly in high-risk areas.

1. The Function of Price in an Open and Competitive Market:

In an open and competitive market, price serves several critical functions:

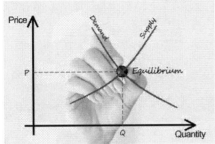

Signaling: Prices convey information about the relative scarcity or abundance of a good or service. High prices indicate scarcity or high demand, while low prices suggest abundance or low demand.

- **Resource Allocation:** Prices help allocate resources efficiently by guiding producers and consumers to make informed decisions about what to produce and what to consume.
- **Incentivizing:** Prices incentivize producers to supply goods or services that are in high demand and consumers to use resources wisely.

In the insurance industry, particularly in areas prone to natural disasters like Florida, pricing should reflect the actual risk associated with insuring properties in high-risk zones. When insurance premiums accurately reflect the risk of loss from hurricanes and floods, they serve several critical functions:

- **Risk Awareness:** High premiums signal high risk, encouraging consumers to reconsider their decisions about where and how they build or buy homes.
- **Behavior Modification:** Accurate pricing incentivizes building in safer areas or investing in risk mitigation measures like improved construction standards or flood defenses.
- **Resource Allocation:** Reflecting true costs ensures that resources are directed toward enhancing resilience, such as funding infrastructure improvements or emergency preparedness.

2. Changes in Human Behavior When Deprived of Actual Costs:

Depriving consumers of the actual price or cost of their decisions, particularly in the context of insurance, can lead to several behavioral changes:

- **Overconsumption:** If prices are artificially low, consumers may use more of a good or service than they would if faced with the true cost. This can lead to inefficient resource allocation and waste. In the case of insurance, this could mean higher claims rates and greater financial strain on the insurance system.

- **Underestimation of Risk:** When insurance premiums are artificially low and do not reflect the true risk of living in high-risk areas, consumers may perceive these areas as safer than they are, leading to increased development in vulnerable zones.
- **Moral Hazard:** When individuals are insulated from the consequences of their actions, they may take more risks or engage in behavior they would otherwise avoid. For example, if flood insurance is heavily subsidized, homeowners may be less likely to invest in flood-proofing their homes.

3. Impact of Government Intervention on Human Behavior:

Government intervention in the insurance market, such as suppressing prices or fostering cross-subsidies, can have profound impacts on human behavior. In fact, there can be an even more sinister effect. To the extent that government intervention focuses on symptoms, such as high insurance premiums, rather than to root cause of those high premium, i.e. hurricanes and human behavior, is the extent to which consumers may be misled to believe their behavior is desirable. After all, the government, by misplacing their emphasis sends a signal of approval, the result of which is to:

- **Encouraging Risky Behavior:** If the government subsidizes insurance premiums or suppresses prices, it can encourage people to build in high-risk areas, knowing that they will not bear the full cost of potential disasters. This can lead to increased development in vulnerable regions, exacerbating the potential for catastrophic losses.
- **Disincentivizing Mitigation:** When individuals do not face the true costs of their decisions, they may be less likely to invest in mitigation measures, such as fortifying their homes against hurricanes or adopting resilient building practices. This can lead to greater damage and higher costs when disasters strike.

- **Distorting Market Signals:** Government intervention can distort market signals, making it more difficult for producers and consumers to make informed decisions. This can lead to inefficiencies and unintended consequences, such as the overdevelopment of high-risk areas or the neglect of risk-reducing technologies.

4. Case Studies of Suppressed Prices Leading to Risky Building Behavior:

- **National Flood Insurance Program (NFIP):**

Established in 1968, the NFIP provides federally backed flood insurance to homeowners in flood-prone areas. The government often subsidizes premiums, making them artificially low and disconnecting them from the true risk and cost of flooding.

- **Impact on Behavior:**

Studies have shown that artificially low premiums encourage people to build and remain in high-risk flood zones. According to the Congressional Research Service, about 1% of properties covered by the NFIP account for over 25% of claims due to their repeated flooding.

- **Consequences:**

The NFIP is now significantly in debt, and premiums do not reflect the true cost of the risk, leading to ongoing financial liabilities. The program also incentivizes rebuilding in the same vulnerable locations, increasing taxpayer exposure.

- **Hurricane Sandy Recovery:**

After Hurricane Sandy devastated the northeastern U.S. in 2012, the government provided substantial financial assistance to homeowners through disaster relief and insurance programs.

- **Impact on Behavior:**

Many homeowners used the aid to rebuild homes in the same flood-prone areas, despite the inherent risks. A study by Stony Brook University found that more than 75% of the New York coastal population continued to live in vulnerable locations post-Sandy.

- **Consequences:**

The continued rebuilding in high-risk zones increases the likelihood of future losses and worsens the long-term impact of climate change on coastal communities.

- **Florida Property Insurance Market:**

Florida's state-run Citizens Property Insurance Company was initially designed as an insurer of last resort. However, artificially low premiums made it attractive, leading to an influx of homeowners seeking coverage.

- **Impact on Behavior:**

Citizens' subsidized rates encouraged building and development in hurricane-prone areas without appropriate risk mitigation. Over time, Citizens became one of the largest property insurers in the state, exposing taxpayers to significant financial risk.

- **Consequences:**

With increased exposure due to market distortions, Florida taxpayers could be liable for billions in damages after a major hurricane.

Conclusion:

By refusing to address the root problem and focusing on symptoms like high premiums, government intervention sends the wrong message about building homes in dangerous places. Consumers need accurate price signals to understand the true risks and make informed decisions. When governments suppress these signals, they create incentives that exacerbate risky behavior and contribute to greater long-term costs.

Jackie Bueno Sousa, in the Miami Herald on July 7, 2009, eloquently captured this issue:

"Magicians will tell you that one of the keys to a successful illusion is the willingness of the audience to believe that what it is seeing is real. The building really is levitating. The elephant really is walking on water. But, of course, it's not real, which is why the show always must end. You can sustain trickery for only so long. And so, it is with Florida's property insurance market. We want to believe that rates can be controlled. That government can permanently suppress free-market forces, that most of us can afford to live in coastal areas. But sooner or later reality takes hold."

This quote perfectly underscores the illusion of sustainability in Florida's property insurance market. The belief that rates can be controlled indefinitely, and that government intervention can suppress market forces is as fleeting as a magician's trick. Sooner or later, reality—and its accompanying costs—must be faced.

To reflect on a positive example of how Florida can better cope with nature's fury, please consider:

Babcock Ranch: A Case Study in Resilience

Babcock Ranch in Florida is an excellent example of a community that proactively addresses these challenges through strategic planning and resilient building practices. Here are the key strategies that set this community apart:

1. Elevated Construction and Strategic Location:

Built 25-30 feet above sea level, Babcock Ranch avoids the storm surges and flooding that devastate many other parts of Florida.

2. Sustainable and Resilient Infrastructure:

- Underground Utilities: All power and communication cables are buried to protect them from wind and falling debris.
- Solar Power Integration: With a solar farm of 700,000 panels, Babcock Ranch generates more electricity than it consumes, and it features battery storage to maintain power.
- Smart Stormwater Management: Integrated smart technology and stormwater management systems anticipate rainfall and lower retention pond levels preemptively to reduce flood risk.

3. Building Codes and Construction Practices:

- Enhanced Building Codes: Buildings are constructed according to updated codes emphasizing load continuity, which helps them withstand stronger winds.
- High-Performance Materials: Using Structural Integrated Panels (SIPs) enhances energy efficiency and provides structural integrity.

4. Community Design and Landscaping:

- Native Landscaping: 75% of landscaping uses native plants that contribute to stormwater management and resilience.
- Community Layout: Streets and layouts facilitate natural water flow, preventing water accumulation in populated areas.

5. Educational and Community Engagement:

- Solar Education Center: The center promotes awareness of sustainable practices and resilience among residents.

Babcock Ranch's approach to resilience should serve as a benchmark for future developments in hurricane-prone areas. The community sets a practical example of how effective planning, and proactive measures can dramatically reduce risks.

So, how should Florida address this problem associated with "Living in Paradise?"

A Tutorial on Problem-Solving:

The first step in solving any real-world problem is to clearly define and understand it:

1. Identify the Problem:

Recognize that an issue needs addressing. In Florida's case, hurricanes and risky building behavior are the core problems, not high premiums alone.

2. Gather Information:

Collect data, facts, and observations to understand the problem's background, including previous attempts at solutions.

3. Analyze the Problem:

Break it down into manageable parts. Identify root causes and contributing factors.

4. Define the Problem Statement:

Clearly state the issue, the desired outcome, and any constraints.

Understanding the problem lays the foundation for more targeted solutions.

Consider These

The 9 Guiding Principles for Insurance Legislation

Guiding Principles for Insurance Legislation:

Future property insurance legislation should align with these guiding principles:

1. Principle #1: Pay for hurricane risk with private capital rather than public debt.

    - Discussion: Paying premiums upfront enables choices, while taxing for losses afterward limits freedom. Maximize private-sector resources to cover potential hurricane losses.

2. Principle #2: Free-market competition best ensures insurance availability and affordability.

    - Discussion: Rates should be adequate to cover risks based on sound actuarial science. Excessive regulation stifles competition, leading to unstable price fluctuations.

3. Principle #3: Government intervention should be limited, cautious, and temporary.

    - Goals:
        - Minimize interference in private insurance markets.
        - Limit the duration of interventions.
        - Implement cautiously and regulate carefully.

4. Principle #4: People have a right to live where they choose but shouldn't expect others to subsidize risky choices.

5. Principle #5: Subsidized insurance should not cover investment or vacation properties.

6. Principle #6: Subsidies for primary residences should be temporary.

    - Discussion: Focus on helping Floridians insure their homes rather than subsidizing leisure or investment properties.

7. Principle #7: Government must act to protect citizens, including:

    - Fortifying homes through building codes and mitigation.
    - Direct subsidies for low-income or fixed-income homeowners at risk from rising costs.

8. Principle #8: Policy solutions must have comprehensive implementation plans that outline:

    - Homeowners' responsibilities.
    - Insurers' obligations.
    - Government's role.

9. Principle #9: Consider tax relief and non-insurance solutions to reduce homeownership costs.

Evaluating Future Legislation:

Proponents of future legislation should answer questions that reveal how closely proposals align with the above principles:

1. Does this legislation address hurricanes and human behavior directly?
2. How will it impact the affordability and availability of insurance?
3. Does it encourage risk reduction through building codes or incentives?
4. How does it affect reliance on Citizens Property Insurance Company?
5. Will it mitigate fraud and litigation?
6. Is it climate-change-ready?

Call to Action:

The future of Florida's insurance market relies on recognizing hurricanes and building behavior as the root problems. By adopting these guiding principles and asking critical questions, policymakers can make informed decisions that improve insurance affordability and availability without exposing taxpayers to unnecessary risks. Now is the time to shift the focus from symptoms to root causes, ensuring Florida's insurance landscape is resilient and secure for all.

Several academic studies were consulted when writing this chapter. Many of the opinions expressed here are supported by conclusions found in those studies. For a list of the studies and a summary of their findings, please refer to "Summary of Academic Research" in the Appendix.

Summary of Chapter 14:

Chapter 14, "Outlining the Overarching Challenges Facing Florida's Insurance Market," thoroughly analyzes how market price signals function in open and competitive markets. It emphasizes the critical role that accurate pricing plays in influencing consumer behavior, guiding them toward risk mitigation measures and responsible building practices.

Key takeaways include:

- **Function of Price:** Price signals help allocate resources, incentivize responsible behavior, and indicate high-risk areas through increased premiums.

- **Behavior Changes:** When consumers don't receive accurate pricing signals, they tend to underestimate risks, overconsume insurance resources, and take on moral hazards.

- **Government Intervention:** Government interference, such as suppressing premiums or fostering cross-subsidies, distorts market signals and encourages risky behavior. Subsidies often result in unintended consequences, leading to overdevelopment in high-risk zones.

- **Case Studies:** The chapter examines real-world cases, such as the National Flood Insurance Program (NFIP) and Florida's state-run Citizens Property Insurance Company, demonstrating how distorted pricing and government intervention encourage risky building behavior and fail to address root causes.

The chapter concludes that addressing these issues requires recognizing and correcting misguided market signals to ensure consumers understand the risks and make informed decisions.

Transition to Chapter 15:

As we move forward, understanding the impact of market signals on consumer behavior provides a clearer picture of how to guide future policy decisions. In the following chapter, 'The Key to Reducing Florida Homeowners' Insurance Premiums: Reduce Losses!' we will focus on actionable strategies to mitigate the root causes of rising premiums. By combining accurate pricing with comprehensive risk reduction measures, policymakers can better protect homeowners while fostering a more resilient insurance market.

CHAPTER 15

The Key to Reducing Florida Homeowners' Insurance Premiums: Reduce Losses!

Is the key to trimming Florida's soaring homeowners' insurance premiums as straightforward as slicing a hot knife through butter, merely by cutting losses? At first glance, this notion seems plausible. After all, insurance is fundamentally a game of numbers, where reducing the outlay (losses) should, in theory, diminish the cost to the insured (premiums). Yet, as we peel back the layers, we uncover a complex tapestry of factors influencing insurance costs, making the argument fundamentally sound yet overly simplistic.

The Core Argument: A Closer Look

At its heart, the statement posits that loss reduction is the only route to lower insurance premiums. This principle is analogous to stating that the best way to keep your feet dry is to avoid the rain entirely—an undeniable truth, but not always feasible or the only solution. In Florida's insurance landscape, loss reduction equates to a decrease in claims stemming from natural disasters, theft, and other insurable events. Historically, areas with lower loss records enjoy lower premiums, a clear correlation supported by risk management principles.

For example, implementing stricter building codes, such as requiring hurricane shutters or impact-resistant windows, can significantly reduce the damage caused by hurricanes, leading to fewer claims and, ultimately, lower premiums. Similarly, encouraging homeowners to invest in loss prevention measures, like installing security systems or reinforcing roofs, can help mitigate the risk of theft or damage from severe weather events. We will discuss more examples in the next chapter titled "Code Plus."

Exploring the Other Side of the Coin

However, likening the insurance premium dilemma to simply reducing losses is akin to suggesting that driving less is the best way to improve a car's fuel efficiency. It disregards the intricacies of engine performance, aerodynamics, and alternative fuels.

Similarly, several other factors play critical roles in insurance premium calculations:

- **Growth Management:** Proper urban planning can mitigate risks. For instance, restricting development in flood-prone areas can lead to fewer claims related to flooding.

- **Building Codes:** Stronger building codes ensure more resilient structures. Florida's stringent hurricane-proofing measures post-Hurricane Andrew exemplify how enhanced building standards can reduce damage and, subsequently, losses.

- **Legal Reform:** The litigious environment in Florida, mainly concerning insurance claims, often leads to higher settlement costs. Legal reforms to reduce frivolous lawsuits could lower the insurance companies' expenses, impacting premiums.

- **Efficiencies in the Insurance Delivery System:** Streamlining operations and utilizing technology can reduce administrative costs for insurers, potentially allowing for lower premiums.

To understand the importance of reducing losses and mitigating risks, we should examine how Hurricane Ian significantly impacted Florida's insurance market and led to legislative reforms.

Hurricane Ian, which struck Florida in September 2022, has become a pivotal event in the state's insurance landscape, much like Hurricane Andrew in 1992. Ian, a Category 4 hurricane, was one of the most powerful storms to make landfall in Florida, causing estimated damages between $41 and $70 billion, including up to $17 billion in uninsured flood damage.[9] This event has significantly tested the resilience of Florida's insurance market, already strained by high premiums and insurer insolvencies.

Rising Insurance Premiums

Even before Ian, Florida's homeowners faced the highest insurance premiums in the United States, with an average annual cost of $4,321, three times higher than the national average.[10] The aftermath of Ian has exacerbated this situation, with projections indicating that insurance premiums could rise by up to 40% or more.[11] This increase is attributed to the high risk of hurricanes, rampant roof

---

[9] https://www.marshmma.com/us/insights/details/understanding-the-florida-insurance-market.html
[10] https://www.climatechangenews.com/2022/10/21/hurricane-ian-could-push-insurers-out-of-florida/
[11] https://winknews.com/2023/05/09/florida-homeowners-insurance-crisis-higher-premiums/

replacement claim fraud schemes, and the state's litigious environment, which has led to a surge in insurance litigation.[12]

Insurer Insolvency and Market Withdrawal

The devastation wrought by Ian has posed a significant threat to the solvency of many insurance companies operating in Florida. Several insurers declared bankruptcy or withdrew from the market, further destabilizing the state's insurance landscape.[13] This trend is not new; even before Ian, six insurance carriers declared insolvency within a year, and others stopped writing new policies due to the unsustainable financial pressure from rampant litigation and soaring reinsurance costs (*insurance that an insurance company purchases to limit its risk by sharing some of its potential losses with other insurers*).[14]

Legislative Response

In response to the challenges posed by Hurricane Ian and the ongoing insurance crisis, the Florida legislature has enacted several measures to stabilize the market and protect homeowners. These include reforms to reduce litigation, strengthen consumer protections, and ensure insurance companies' financial stability.[15] For example, a property insurance reform bill signed by Governor Ron DeSantis in December 2022 aims to increase competition and reduce the cost of claims by prohibiting the use of assignment of benefits (*a practice where a policyholder transfers their insurance claim rights to a third party, typically a contractor or service provider*) for policies issued on or after January 1, 2023.[16] Additionally, the bill

---

[12] https://www.marshmma.com/us/insights/details/understanding-the-florida-insurance-market.html
[13] https://www.climatechangenews.com/2022/10/21/hurricane-ian-could-push-insurers-out-of-florida/
[14] https://www.npr.org/2022/10/06/1127083845/hurricane-ian-florida-property-insurance
[15] https://www.marshmma.com/us/insights/details/understanding-the-florida-insurance-market.html
[16] https://www.marshmma.com/us/insights/details/understanding-the-florida-insurance-market.html

tightens the timeframe for insurance companies to respond to claims and make coverage determinations.

Ian Conclusions

Hurricane Ian has underscored the critical challenges facing Florida's insurance market, from skyrocketing premiums to the risk of insurer insolvency. The state's legislative efforts to address these issues reflect a recognition of the need for comprehensive reforms to ensure the affordability and availability of homeowners insurance. As Florida continues to grapple with the impacts of climate change and the increasing frequency of severe weather events, the resilience of its insurance market remains a key concern for policymakers, insurers, and homeowners alike.

Understanding the historical effects of Hurricane Ian on our insurance market and the following legislative response emphasizes the interconnectedness of catastrophic events and insurance market stability. This demonstrates why reducing losses remains crucial for stabilizing premiums, prompting us to focus on comprehensive strategies to minimize the impact of such disasters on Florida's homeowners' insurance landscape.

The Unavoidable Truth

Despite the multi-faceted approach to managing insurance costs, the argument circles back to loss reduction as a critical lever. It's akin to a multi-pronged strategy in a battle; while diversifying tactics is crucial, striking at the heart of the enemy—here, the losses—is paramount.

This perspective necessitates scrutinizing any proposed property insurance legislation in Florida through the lens of loss reduction. Will the proposal make homes safer, reduce potential damage, or reduce insurers' financial risk?

Reducing losses requires a collaborative effort from homeowners, insurers, policymakers, and the community. Homeowners can take proactive steps to protect their properties, insurers can incentivize loss prevention measures through discounts or premium reductions, policymakers can implement regulations prioritizing safety and resilience, and communities can work together to create a preparedness and risk mitigation culture.

Conclusion: A Balanced Viewpoint

While it's overly simplistic to claim that reducing losses is the *only* way to lower homeowners' insurance premiums, **it is a foundational strategy**. It's a piece of a giant puzzle that includes regulatory, construction, and operational reforms. Yet, without addressing losses, efforts in other areas might only yield marginal benefits.

Looking Ahead

Future discussions must continue to explore innovative ways to mitigate risks, including technological advancements in home safety, community planning, and even climate change adaptation strategies.

In conclusion, while it's simplifying to say reducing losses is the sole path to lower insurance premiums, it's a critical component that cannot be overlooked.

As a seasoned observer and participant in the insurance industry, I've seen firsthand the impact of comprehensive strategies that address loss reduction and other contributing factors. The quest for affordable insurance in Florida is a complex puzzle, but we can move closer to a solution focusing on loss reduction as a cornerstone.

In this chapter, we got a good look at why it's super important to cut down on losses to ease the financial weight of insurance. It's like finding a more thoughtful way to handle money, right? Now, we're moving on to something called "Code Plus." Here, we'll take the idea of preventing losses a step further and check out some practical steps to make our homes and infrastructure tougher.

Summary of Chapter 15:

Chapter 15 argues that reducing losses is key to lowering Florida homeowners' insurance premiums. While seemingly straightforward, this assertion is unpacked to reveal its complexities and multifaceted implications within the insurance landscape.

The chapter emphasizes the direct correlation between loss reduction and premium costs, drawing parallels between risk management principles and insurance premiums. By implementing measures to mitigate risks, such as stricter building codes and investment in loss prevention technologies, homeowners can potentially reduce the frequency and severity of insurance claims, leading to lower premiums.

However, the chapter also acknowledges the broader context surrounding insurance premium calculations, highlighting additional factors such as growth management, legal reform, and efficiencies in the insurance delivery system. While loss reduction remains a critical lever in premium reduction efforts, a comprehensive approach that addresses various contributing factors is essential for meaningful change.

The chapter concludes with a call for collaborative efforts from homeowners, insurers, policymakers, and communities to prioritize loss reduction strategies. It emphasizes the importance of regulatory reforms, technological advancements, and community resilience in creating Florida's sustainable and affordable insurance landscape.

The chapter hints at future discussions exploring innovative solutions to mitigate risks, enhance building resilience, and adapt to evolving climate challenges. It underscores the need for a balanced approach integrating loss reduction efforts with broader policy reforms and community initiatives.

Overall, Chapter 15 provides a nuanced examination of the role of loss reduction in reducing homeowners' insurance premiums in Florida. It underscores the complexity of the insurance landscape while emphasizing the importance of prioritizing strategies that address the root causes of insurance losses.

Transition to Chapter 16:

In Chapter 15, we explored the imperative of reducing losses to alleviate Florida homeowners' insurance premiums. In Chapter 16, we pivot to a comprehensive examination of enhanced building standards. We thoroughly examine how strengthening our buildings with solid codes and clever engineering can pay off, especially when facing the wild side of Florida's weather. It's about ensuring our homes aren't just places to live but strongholds that stand tall against nature's challenges. Let's get into it!

Chapter 16

Code Plus: Elevating Florida's Defense Against Hurricanes Through Enhanced Building Standards

Reducing Florida homeowners' insurance premiums hinges on minimizing future losses or claims, a necessity underscored by the insurance market's struggles post-Hurricane Andrew. This event, striking in 1992, revealed the insurance industry's underestimation of risk and inadequate reserves for catastrophic losses,

spotlighting the vulnerability of Florida's insurance market to major hurricanes and the limitations of existing risk models.

"Code Plus" refers to the concept of enhancing building codes and standards beyond the minimum requirements to create more resilient structures that can better withstand the forces of nature, particularly in hurricane-prone areas like Florida. By implementing these enhanced standards, the goal is to reduce the amount of damage and losses incurred during severe weather events, ultimately leading to lower insurance claims and more affordable premiums for homeowners.

When I first heard about the concept of "Code Plus" for elevating Florida's defense against hurricanes, I couldn't help but be reminded of that classic quip,

"It is hard to understand how a cemetery raised its burial costs and blamed it on the high cost of living." Yes, it sounds contradictory, but sometimes logic isn't exactly straightforward regarding legislation, just as it isn't regarding cemeteries.

Now, you'd think that after years of hurricane devastation, implementing higher building standards would be a no-brainer, right? Well, not exactly. Picture this: I'm sitting in a conference room packed with real estate developers, insurance agents, and local government officials. The day's topic was the new "Code Plus" standard, which would require enhanced building codes for homes and buildings, particularly those in hurricane-prone areas.

A representative stood up and started explaining the new regulations, and you could almost see the room collectively holding its breath, waiting for the other shoe to drop. The guidelines were detailed and comprehensive, aiming to minimize property damage by requiring impact-resistant windows, reinforced roofing systems, and elevated foundation structures.

But as soon as the cost estimates were mentioned, one developer muttered under his breath, "Code Plus? More like 'Cost Plus!'" he said it a little too loudly, and it sent ripples of laughter across the room. But the truth is, many developers were skeptical because higher costs often trickle down to homeowners, who are not eager to see their wallets emptied.

One official voiced his opinion: "It's just like the cemetery—people don't see the value until they're six feet under!" While that analogy hit a little too close to home for some, he had a point. Investing in stronger building standards might seem expensive now, but it's a lot cheaper than rebuilding your house after the next Category 5 hurricane tears through your neighborhood.

Another insurance agent chimed in with a grin, "Well, it's like giving up dessert before the holidays—it's not fun, but you're better off in the long run!" That comparison struck a chord, and the room began to warm up to the idea.

While these discussions highlight the practical challenges of implementing enhanced building standards, the underlying science supports the need for such measures, as evidenced by the University of Florida's Engineering Study that we will discuss later in this chapter.

We walked away that day with a greater understanding that while Code Plus wasn't the cheapest solution, it offered a strong defense against the astronomical costs of rebuilding. Hurricanes aren't going to stop, but at least we can ensure the next storm won't blow us back to the Stone Age.

Sometimes spending a little more upfront can save you a lot of heartache—and a lot more dollars—down the line. At least, that's how we rationalized it. After all, they say, "Nothing is foolproof to a sufficiently talented fool," but Code Plus gets us one step closer to hurricane-proofing Florida homes.

Just as a cemetery can't rationalize its price hikes on the high cost of living, we can't afford to shy away from necessary improvements to Florida's building standards to protect against devastating hurricanes. While these measures may have short-term costs, the long-term benefits outweigh the initial expense. With this in mind, let's explore the specific strategies involved in the 'Code Plus' initiative and how it contributes to elevating Florida's defense against hurricanes. Now, back to our discussion on catastrophe models...

Before Andrew's havoc, it appears the insurance industry relied on models blissfully ignorant of the skyrocketing property values and the rapid densification of populations in areas most vulnerable to hurricanes. The catastrophe spotlighted Florida's insurance market's fragility, revealing the shortcomings of existing risk assessment models.

The challenge confronting Florida's insurance market transcends the mere mechanics of hurricanes—their intensity or frequency. Despite the long-standing history of hurricanes threatening the region, the pivotal issue lies in the dramatic swell in exposure fueled by population growth and coastal property development.

At the heart of Florida's property insurance crisis lies a narrative far more complex than Mother Nature's wrath. The real story, as unveiled by the insightful research documented in "The Deadliest, Costliest, and Most Intense

US Tropical Cyclones From 1851-2010,"[17] shifts the focus from the force of hurricanes to the human factors exacerbating their impact: *swelling population growth and the burgeoning concentration of wealth along the coastline.*

Jarrell et al.'s 1992 study[18] sheds light on a sobering reality: most U.S. coastal dwellers had never braced for a major hurricane, underscoring a widespread unpreparedness and ignorance of the looming threat. This danger has only intensified, with an estimated 50 million individuals migrating to coastal areas over the last quarter-century,[19] markedly amplifying the potential for destruction and loss in the face of a hurricane.

Despite the apparent dangers, the allure of coastal living has led to a marked increase in population density in these areas, thus exacerbating vulnerability to natural disasters. This trend has been further emphasized by a 15.3% increase in coastline county populations since 2000[20], with a projected global rise in coastal inhabitants posing additional risks due to climate change and rising sea levels.

The phenomenon of "blue space" benefits, suggesting a positive impact of water proximity on mental health, often outweighs the perceived risks for many.

---

[17] "The Deadliest, Costliest, and Most Intense U.S. Tropical Cyclones From 1851-2020" provides a detailed look into the historical impact of tropical cyclones, underscoring the significant role of population growth in risk concentration along coastal areas.
[18] https://www.aoml.noaa.gov/hrd/Landsea/deadly/index.html
[19] https://climate.nasa.gov/news/2680/new-study-finds-sea-level-rise-accelerating/
[20] https://www.census.gov/library/stories/2019/07/millions-of-americans-live-coastline-regions.html

This escalation in coastal development and inflation sets the stage for even non-major hurricanes to inflict significant economic damage. The 2008 hurricanes stand as a testament to this, as despite not attaining major hurricane status at landfall, they ranked among the 30 costliest,[21] courtesy of the dense mesh of property and population in their wake.

Historical data on hurricane intensity and frequency indicate fluctuations, with a notable decrease in landfalling hurricanes from 1961-2000 compared to earlier records.[22]

The plight of Florida's property insurance sector post-Hurricane Andrew is a multi-layered saga, with the spike in population and the aggregation of property values in hurricane-prone zones playing central roles. These elements have heightened the exposure and potential losses from hurricanes, presenting insurers with the daunting task of maintaining solvency.

This predicament calls for a radical reevaluation of risk management strategies, encompassing risk transfer mechanisms, enhancement of building codes, and revision of insurance policies, to forge a bulwark against the financial upheavals of future hurricanes.

Unraveling the Data: A Comprehensive Examination

Historical Context of Hurricanes Pre-Andrew:

An analysis of historical data unveils a tapestry of fluctuating hurricane activity over the decades, marked by ebbs and flows in both the intensity and frequency of these formidable storms.

Delving into the archives, we discern a period from 1961 to 2000 characterized by a relative lull in the ferocity and occurrence of hurricanes making landfall in

---

[21] https://en.wikipedia.org/wiki/List_of_costliest_Atlantic_hurricanes
[22] https://www.ipcc.ch/report/ar6/wg1/

the United States, especially when juxtaposed with the earlier epoch spanning from 1901 to 1960.

However, this discernible decline in hurricane landfalls during the latter half of the 20th century did not diminish the historical prevalence of significant storm events before a notable resurgence in the early 21st century.

The Aftermath of Andrew: A Turning Point:

The cataclysm wrought by Hurricane Andrew in 1992 served as a watershed in the annals of Florida's insurance market, starkly exposing the industry's lack of readiness for such cataclysmic events.

The resurgence of hurricane landfalls in the 2000s, evoking memories of the tumultuous 1950s, and the impact of notable storms such as Charley (2004), Andrew (1992), and Hugo (1989), have rigorously tested the resilience of the state's insurance framework against the renewed vigor of nature's fury.

The Human Element: Population Growth and Coastal Expansion:

The dramatic swell in population and development along the state's coastlines are at the heart of the escalating challenges confronting Florida's insurance sector.

Citing 1990 census data, the observation that 85% of U.S. coastal residents had not faced a major hurricane strike underscores a pervasive underestimation of risk. Yet, as mentioned earlier, the subsequent quarter-century has witnessed an influx of approximately 50 million people to these coastal zones, substantially altering the risk landscape. This demographic shift has not only concentrated assets but has also magnified exposure in areas prone to hurricanes, amplifying the state's susceptibility to the economic repercussions of such natural calamities.

Evolving Threats and Financial Vulnerability:

The relentless march of coastal development, alongside inflationary pressures, portends that even hurricanes of lesser magnitude and tropical storms are poised to exact a heavier toll in terms of damage costs.

Synthesis and Path Forward:

The difficulty faced by Florida's property insurance market in the wake of Hurricane Andrew transcends simplistic attributions to shifts in hurricane dynamics alone. Instead, the confluence of the historical variability of hurricane activity, the exponential growth in coastal populations and development, and the increased exposure to hurricane risks collectively forge the crucible of challenges afflicting the insurance landscape.

This intricate mosaic of factors heralds the imperative for adaptive and multifaceted strategies in risk assessment, risk transfer mechanisms, fortifying building codes, the recalibration of insurance policies, and holistic community planning. Such endeavors are essential to ameliorate the future financial strains on Florida's property insurance market, ensuring resilience in the face of the inevitable tempests.

Elevating Hurricane Resilience: Insights from the University of Florida's Engineering Study

The most effective way to reduce Florida homeowners' insurance premiums is to reduce future losses.

While this statement oversimplifies the complex problem Florida faces, it does draw attention to the need for construction techniques that increase the likelihood that homes will be capable of withstanding high wind conditions.

For instance, many claim that Florida has one of the best Building Codes in the United States, but can improvements to the Code reduce future losses?

I believe the answer is an emphatic "Yes" based on a review of recently published research.

In 2019, the University of Florida's Engineering School of Sustainable Infrastructure and Environment, within the Department of Civil and Coastal Engineering, unveiled a pivotal report titled "**Investigation of Optional Enhanced Construction Techniques for the Wind, Flood, and Storm Surge Provisions of the Florida Building Code.**"[23] This comprehensive study underscores the critical nature of hurricane mitigation efforts in Florida, charting the evolution and impact of building construction advancements since the Florida Building Code was implemented in 2002.

The report meticulously documents the tangible benefits these advancements have conferred upon the structural integrity of residential buildings in the face of hurricanes, with a notable decrease in wind damage post-Hurricanes Charley (2004); Irma (2017), Michael (2018).

Despite the robustness of Florida's building codes, the study reveals that vulnerabilities in the building envelope systems continue to be a significant source of economic losses.

Drawing upon insights from FEMA and the Florida Department of Environmental Protection, the report presents an array of enhanced construction recommendations that surpass the standards set by the 6th and 7th Editions of the Florida Building Code.

23

http://www.buildingasaferflorida.org/assets/Final%20Prevatt%20UF%20EnhancedBuildingOptions%20for%20FBC%20-%20FINAL27Dec2019%20(2)1.pdf

These recommendations are geared towards bolstering wind resistance in new constructions and enhancing resilience against hurricanes.

Highlighted below are the key proposed enhancements, along with a brief commentary on their significance:

1. **Wind Resistance Improvement:**

- **Design Wind Load Standard Update:** Incorporating ASCE 7-16 for wind load calculations ensures adherence to the latest research and provides more precise estimations.

- **Roof Sheathing Attachment:** Utilizing roof sheathing ring shank nails (RSRS) for attachment offers a fortified, reliable solution capable of withstanding high wind velocities.

2. **Resistance to Wind-borne Debris:**

- **Sheathing Requirements:** A minimum plywood thickness specification fortifies the building envelope against debris impacts.

- **Glazing and Door Protections:** Requiring impact-resistant coverings for windows, doors, and garage doors critically mitigates the risk of breaches that lead to internal pressurization and subsequent water intrusion.

3. **Roof Coverings Wind Resistance:**

- **Enhanced Performance Standards:** Implementing rigorous requirements for roofing materials, such as ASTM D7158 Class H for asphalt shingles, directly addresses one of the primary avenues for water intrusion.

4. **Wall Coverings Wind and Water Intrusion Resistance:**

   - **Strengthening Wall Coverings:** Improved performance criteria for various siding materials enhance their durability and resistance to wind and water forces.

5. **Roof Water Intrusion Resistance:**

   - **Sealed Roof Deck and Ridge Vents:** Emphasizing the creation of a secondary water barrier and tested ridge vents tackles critical vulnerabilities in roofs during hurricanes.

6. **Windows and Doors Wind and Water Intrusion Resistance:**

   - **Enhanced Performance Requirements:** Establishing rigorous standards for windows and doors ensures they can withstand hurricane-induced pressures.

7. **Soffit Resistance:**

   - **Soffit Performance Improvements:** Ventilated soffits tested for wind and wind-driven rain resistance and mandatory in-progress inspections aim to fortify a common failure point in buildings during storms.

8. **Other Best Practices:**

   - **Gutters and Staple Use:** Evaluating gutters for wind load resilience and advocating for eliminating staples in the Florida Building Code underscores the importance of attention to detail for overall building envelope resilience.

These meticulously designed enhancements target the nuanced vulnerabilities identified through extensive hurricane damage assessments and research. By concentrating on augmenting both wind and water intrusion resistance, these measures promise to elevate the overall durability and resilience of buildings in hurricane-susceptible regions, potentially diminishing damage and loss during such disasters.

This approach embodies a comprehensive strategy for constructing a more hurricane-resistant building envelope, emphasizing the crucial role of fastener types, material standards, and installation techniques.

However, implementing these enhanced building standards comes with potential challenges and obstacles. One significant hurdle is the increased cost of higher-quality materials and more stringent construction practices. Homeowners and developers may be reluctant to invest in these upgrades, particularly if they are not mandatory or if the perceived benefits do not outweigh the additional costs.

Another challenge is ensuring consistent enforcement of these enhanced standards across the state. Building code enforcement can vary from one jurisdiction to another. Ensuring that all new construction adheres to the "Code Plus" standards would require a concerted effort from local building departments and inspectors.

Additionally, some stakeholders in the construction industry who are accustomed to traditional building methods and materials may resist. Educating and training contractors, architects, and engineers on the importance and proper implementation of these enhanced standards will be crucial for their successful adoption.

Despite these challenges, the potential benefits of "Code Plus" in reducing losses and stabilizing the insurance market in Florida are significant. By investing in more resilient construction practices, the state can mitigate the impact of future hurricanes, protect homeowners' investments, and create a more sustainable and affordable insurance environment.

In the swirling storm of Florida's hurricane season, homeowners' insurance premiums stand like a lighthouse, guiding through financial storms but at a cost that can sometimes feel as steep as the waves themselves.

The statement that the only way to effectively reduce these premiums is by minimizing future loss or claims is akin to saying the best way to avoid getting wet in a downpour is not to step outside. While fundamentally true, it oversimplifies the factors that soak Florida's insurance landscape.

Imagine, if you will, Florida as a vast archipelago of homes, each island bracing for the next hurricane. The traditional approach has been to build levees—insurance policies—to keep the floodwaters at bay. Yet, as any seasoned captain will tell you, the best way to survive a storm is by reinforcing the barriers and making the ship seaworthy.

In Florida's case, this means constructing homes that can wink at a hurricane and withstand its fury.

Enter the world of enhanced construction techniques, a realm where building codes don't just meet minimum standards but exceed them, where homes are not just shelters but fortresses against the elements.

It's the equivalent of outfitting your ship with the best sails, the sturdiest hull, and a skilled crew that even the Kraken thinks twice before attacking.

Yet, as we navigate these waters, we must maintain sight of the humor in our situation. We're armoring our castles against dragons that, instead of breathing fire, huff and puff and try to blow our houses down.

It's a modern-day fairy tale, where the big bad wolf is the hurricane, and the three little pigs are architects, builders, and homeowners working together to ensure their homes are the ones made of bricks.

Enhanced Building Standards: Lessons from Hurricane Charley

As a member of the Florida House of Representatives, I had the sobering opportunity to witness firsthand the devastation wrought by Hurricane Charley in 2004. As we toured the affected areas of Charlotte County, the impact of the hurricane was evident in the debris of mobile homes and the damaged structures that once housed families and businesses.

Hurricane Charley, a Category 4 storm, struck with ferocity, bringing 150 mph winds that caused unprecedented damage, particularly to mobile homes and older structures. The hurricane not only uprooted lives but also provided critical insights into the effectiveness of our building standards.

The Case for "Code Plus" Standards

Walking through the communities hit hardest by Charley, the advantages of newer, robust building codes were unmistakable. Homes adhering to updated standards showed remarkable resilience compared to their older counterparts. This stark contrast was a lesson observed and a call to action. Clearly, "Code Plus" standards—those that exceed the minimum requirements—could significantly mitigate the impact of such catastrophic events.

Strategic Responses and Recovery Efforts

The federal and state response to Hurricane Charley involved significant efforts in disaster relief and infrastructure reconstruction. However, the real takeaway was the undeniable need for a preemptive approach to building and community planning, especially in areas prone to hurricanes.

Building a Resilient Future

1. Vulnerability of Mobile Homes: The destruction of mobile homes underscored their vulnerability to high winds. Despite improvements,

better anchoring systems and compliance with stringent building codes are critical.

2. Importance of Updated Building Codes and Standards: The resilience of buildings constructed under newer codes highlighted the necessity for continuous updates and rigorous enforcement of building regulations.
3. Enhanced Tie-down Strategies and Regular Inspections: Charley showed the importance of secure tie-downs for mobile homes, calling for innovative anchoring techniques and frequent inspections to ensure compliance with safety standards.
4. Public Awareness and Education: Educating residents about the risks associated with mobile homes and the importance of evacuation plans is vital for community safety.
5. Community Planning and Zoning: Thoughtful zoning laws that consider the placement of mobile home parks can significantly reduce risk alongside integrating safer housing solutions.
6. Emergency Response and Evacuation Procedures: The storm emphasized the need for specific evacuation strategies for mobile home residents, underscoring the importance of efficient communication and early warning systems.

The narrative of Hurricane Charley is a powerful reminder of nature's force and the imperative to adapt our building practices. By incorporating "Code Plus" standards, we protect physical structures and safeguard the lives of those who call Florida home. This proactive approach to building and community planning is a testament to what we can achieve in disaster readiness and resilience.

In conclusion, while reducing future losses or claims is a cornerstone of lowering insurance premiums, it's a goal that requires more than just wishful thinking.

It demands action, innovation, and a willingness to build homes that stand not just on the sand but on a foundation of resilience. By doing so, Florida can transform from a state perpetually bracing for the next big storm to one that faces hurricane season with a confident smile, knowing its homes are built to weather any storm. And as for the homeowners?

They can enjoy their lighthouses, knowing they're not just beacons in the storm but bastions of safety, come what may.

While Florida's building code stands among the nation's best, a compelling opportunity exists for enhancement. Elevating it from a baseline of minimum standards to a more robust "Code Plus" model could set a new benchmark in building resilience, underscoring a proactive commitment to safeguarding properties and lives against the unpredictable fury of hurricanes.

In navigating these turbulent waters, my experience as a state representative focusing on insurance reform has illuminated the dire need for a shift towards more resilient risk assessment and management frameworks. The lessons from the past beckon us to a future where the emphasis is on safeguarding communities and economies against the inevitable storms that lie ahead.

Now that we've got a solid grip on "Code Plus" and why it's crucial to beef up the strength of Florida's buildings, let's shift gears a bit.

Summary of Chapter 16:

Chapter 16 presents the concept of "Code Plus," advocating for the enhancement of building codes and standards in Florida to elevate the state's defense against hurricanes. It begins by contextualizing the necessity of minimizing future losses, particularly in light of past catastrophic events like Hurricane Andrew, which exposed vulnerabilities in the insurance industry and underscored the inadequacy of existing risk models.

The chapter introduces the term "Code Plus," which refers to the augmentation of building codes and standards beyond minimum requirements to create more resilient structures capable of withstanding severe weather events, particularly hurricanes. It emphasizes the importance of implementing these enhanced standards to reduce damage and losses incurred during such disasters, ultimately leading to more affordable insurance premiums for homeowners.

Drawing on historical data and research, the chapter examines the evolution of hurricane activity and its impact on Florida's insurance market. It highlights the exponential growth in coastal populations and development as a significant factor exacerbating the state's susceptibility to hurricane risks and emphasizes the need for adaptive strategies to address these challenges.

The chapter presents insights from a pivotal report by the University of Florida's Engineering School of Sustainable Infrastructure and Environment, which explores optional enhanced construction techniques for wind, flood, and storm surge provisions of the Florida Building Code. These techniques aim to strengthen building resilience against hurricanes by addressing vulnerabilities in building envelope systems and enhancing wind and water intrusion resistance.

Key proposed enhancements include updates to design wind load standards, improvements in roof sheathing attachment, requirements for impact-resistant coverings for windows and doors, and enhancements to roofing materials and wall coverings. These measures are designed to fortify building structures against hurricane-induced forces and reduce the risk of damage and loss during severe weather events.

While the implementation of enhanced building standards presents challenges such as increased construction costs and ensuring consistent enforcement across jurisdictions, the potential benefits in terms of reducing losses and stabilizing the insurance market are significant. By investing in more resilient construction practices, Florida can mitigate the impact of future hurricanes, protect homeowners' investments, and create a more sustainable insurance environment.

The chapter concludes by emphasizing the importance of proactive measures, such as "Code Plus," in fortifying Florida's resilience against hurricanes and ensuring the long-term viability of its insurance market. It underscores the need for collaborative efforts from homeowners, insurers, policymakers, and communities to prioritize building resilience and mitigate the financial strains of future disasters.

Overall, Chapter 16 provides a comprehensive analysis of the role of enhanced building standards in reducing losses and stabilizing Florida's homeowners' insurance market. It highlights the importance of proactive measures in mitigating hurricane risks and underscores the need for adaptive strategies to address the evolving challenges facing the state's insurance landscape.

Transition to Chapter 17:

Next is Chapter 17, "Risk vs Uncertainty - According to Dr. Frank H. Knight." Sounds a bit daunting. But don't worry, it's going to be interesting. We're going from the practical stuff – like bricks and mortar – to the brainy world of theoretical economics. We'll explore how the insurance world juggles the things we know can go wrong (those pesky risks) and the stuff we can't even see coming (those mysterious uncertainties). It's all about understanding the fine line between the predictable and the unpredictable in the realms of insurance and keeping our homes safe. Ready to dive in?

Chapter 17

Risk vs. Uncertainty: Insights from Dr. Frank H. Knight

Dr. Frank H. Knight, an influential American economist, laid the foundation for what would later become known as the Chicago School of Economics with his seminal work, "*Risk, Uncertainty, and Profit*," published in 1921. This book challenged existing economic theories and introduced a critical distinction between risk and uncertainty that has profoundly impacted economic thought and practice.

Knight was born in 1885 in McLean County, Illinois, and grew up in a farming community. He attended the University of Tennessee and later earned his Ph.D. from Cornell University in 1916. Knight commenced his academic career at the University of Chicago in 1917, where he spent the majority of his professional life. He was a central figure in the development of the Chicago School of Economics, known for its emphasis on free-market principles and the role of prices in allocating resources.

Beyond his contributions to economic theory, Knight was a formidable figure who resisted many of the prevailing economic shifts of his time, including Keynesianism and theories of monopolistic competition.

Despite his foundational role in the Chicago School, Knight remained an eclectic thinker, often challenging and refining his ideas. His skepticism of government intervention in economics and his belief in individualism and political liberty underscore his broader philosophical stance on economics as intertwined with freedom and the complexities of human decision-making under uncertainty.

"Risk, Uncertainty, and Profit" remains a cornerstone of economic literature, celebrated for its innovative approach to understanding the dynamics of markets and the function of profit within them. Knight's rigorous analysis and the distinctions he drew between risk and uncertainty have enriched economic theory and provided valuable insights for entrepreneurs navigating the unpredictable terrains of the market.

Measurability

Knight argued that risk refers to situations where the probability of outcomes can be known or calculated, making them quantifiable and insurable. This measurability allows businesses to manage risk through insurance or hedging strategies. For example, the probability of a dice roll or the risk of a warehouse fire can be statistically assessed based on past data, allowing for the calculation of insurance premiums to cover such risks.

In contrast, uncertainty, or what Knight termed "true uncertainty" or "Knightian uncertainty," cannot be measured or quantified because it pertains to events with unknown probabilities. This unquantifiable nature of uncertainty makes it impossible to insure against or hedge similarly to calculable risks.

Predictability

Under Knight's framework, risk predictability is relatively high since it can be assessed and managed through statistical and mathematical models. Firms can allocate resources and adjust their strategies based on the known probabilities of different risks, integrating these factors into their business planning and capital allocation processes.

However, uncertainty presents a challenge to predictability because it involves rare, unique events or have no prior history to inform their likelihood. Decisions made under conditions of uncertainty are based on judgment and intuition rather than calculable odds. This unpredictability necessitates a different approach to decision-making, where entrepreneurs must rely on their insights and expertise to navigate these uncharted waters.

Impact on Capital Adequacy

Knight's distinction between risk and uncertainty has significant implications for capital adequacy—the amount of capital a firm needs to sustain its operations and absorb unexpected losses. In the case of risks, firms can plan and set aside capital based on the expected loss probabilities and insurance costs, allowing for a more straightforward calculation of the necessary capital reserves to maintain financial stability.

On the other hand, uncertainty complicates capital adequacy assessment because it's challenging to predict the capital required to cover unknown and unmeasurable events. This unpredictability may lead firms to maintain higher capital levels as a buffer against unforeseen outcomes or invest in flexibility and adaptability as strategic assets in uncertain environments.

Humor Alert

For such a complicated subject, I thought I'd start with some humor before getting back to a serious note. If one explanation doesn't hit the mark, maybe the other one will.

When I first started learning about the differences between risk and uncertainty, according to Dr. Frank H. Knight, I thought I had it all figured out. 'Oh sure,' I told myself, 'This is a piece of cake!' But just as the saying goes, 'It's easy until the ducks start quacking in a different language,' and that's exactly how I felt after trying to wrap my head around the intricacies of these concepts."

Let's look at an example to shed some light on the situation. Take hurricanes: We all know they can strike, and we even know when and where they might appear. We can estimate their paths and anticipate potential impacts thanks to years of scientific modeling. So, we're clearly dealing with risk here—a quantifiable uncertainty. In other words, we know the chips will be down eventually; we just don't know exactly when or how many.

But uncertainty? Now, that's a different beast. Imagine you're sailing down the insurance stream, and suddenly, an angry bear jumps out of the water and starts rowing your boat backward (stay with me here). That's uncertainty: You didn't see it coming, and the usual models are just as perplexed.

So, I was sitting in my office, trying to unravel this tangled mess of risks and uncertainties. I remember calling up an old colleague, hoping for some guidance. "Well, think of it this way," he said, "Risk is like playing poker with cards face up, and uncertainty is playing poker with no cards at all. Either way, you're still gonna lose a lot of money if you're not careful."

That might sound cynical, but it's actually a great way to view risk management in the face of Florida's catastrophic hurricane exposure. You can try to predict and quantify risks all you want, but uncertainty will always find a way to keep you guessing.

And that brings us back to Dr. Frank H. Knight's original work on the topic, where he differentiated risk as something you can calculate with data, while uncertainty is anything you can't predict with reasonable accuracy. In this sense, the two are fundamentally different, which is why every risk manager worth their salt needs to develop both a Plan A and a Plan B (and sometimes a Plan C, just for good measure).

So, when I looked at my risk management strategy again, I felt a little like I was back at the poker table. But this time, I knew when to fold 'em. "Risk vs. uncertainty," I muttered under my breath, "if that ain't a pair of aces and eights, I don't know what is."

In the end, understanding the difference between the two helps us prepare better for the uncertainties we can't anticipate. But that doesn't mean I've got it all figured out yet. Just like the buffalo ran empty, I'll have to stay on my toes, because in the world of risk management, there's always another surprise lurking around the corner.

And that brings us back to the serious reality of Dr. Frank H. Knight's work. Understanding the difference between risk and uncertainty can help us prepare better for the unexpected challenges we can't anticipate. But it's not foolproof, and we need to stay vigilant to respond effectively. With that in mind, let's explore further how distinguishing between risk and uncertainty shapes our understanding and approach to Florida's insurance market.

To better understand Knight's distinction between risk and uncertainty, let us propose a series of questions and consider how his work might respond.

Question:

If risk and uncertainty are viewed as opposite extremes on a spectrum, would it be fair to say that to the same extent one moves across that spectrum from risk toward uncertainty is the same extent to which capital will flee?

Uncertainty

Risk

Answer:

Yes, it is generally fair to say that as you move across the spectrum from risk toward uncertainty, the tendency for capital to flee or become more reluctant to invest increases. This concept aligns with the principle of risk aversion in financial markets and investment decisions.

Let's delve into a more detailed explanation:

1. **Risk Aversion**: Investors and capital providers are typically risk-averse, preferring investments with more predictable and quantifiable outcomes. These investments, characterized by lower levels of uncertainty, generally attract more comfortable capital allocation from investors.

2. **Risk vs. Uncertainty**: When confronting well-defined risks that can be measured, managed, and have historical data (e.g., traditional insurance risks like car accidents or property damage), investors can evaluate the potential losses and allocate suitable capital reserves. There is a degree of comfort in this predictability.

3. **Moving Toward Uncertainty**: As you progress along the spectrum towards uncertainty, you encounter less predictable events that may have

unknown probabilities or lack historical data for reference. (e.g., "black swan" events or rare catastrophes). In these cases, investors and capital providers become more cautious because they cannot accurately assess the level of risk or potential losses.

4. **Capital Flight**: When faced with increased uncertainty, investors may respond by becoming risk-averse and reducing their exposure to investments with higher uncertainty. They may seek safer assets or move capital to more stable and predictable market areas.

In the context of catastrophe insurance, if an insurer faces catastrophic events that are highly uncertain and lack historical precedent, attracting and maintaining capital becomes challenging. Investors and reinsurers may hesitate to provide capital support because they cannot accurately gauge the potential losses. This can lead to difficulties in securing sufficient capital to cover catastrophic risks.

So, the movement across the risk-uncertainty spectrum influences the behavior of capital providers, with capital becoming more elusive as uncertainty increases. Insurers and other organizations managing catastrophic risks must carefully consider this dynamic when planning for capital adequacy and risk management.

Question:

Catastrophe insurance, by its very nature, is a highly regulated industry. The risk vs uncertainty question pertaining to natural catastrophes, i.e., hurricanes, is challenging enough, but how is it complicated further by the political uncertainty created when legislative bodies rush to enact laws to "fix" the insurance system? This question is based on the proposition that high insurance premiums are the symptom. The problem, instead, is hurricanes and the tendency of people to build their homes in very vulnerable locations.

Answer:

You're absolutely right that catastrophe insurance is inherently complex due to the nature of the risks it covers, such as hurricanes, earthquakes, wildfires, and the like. Political and legislative actions can further complicate the landscape, particularly when lawmakers attempt to address the challenges created by high insurance premiums and vulnerabilities in the system. Here's how political uncertainty can affect the catastrophe insurance industry:

1. **Legislative Interventions**: When lawmakers rush to enact laws to address issues related to high insurance premiums, it can lead to various outcomes, some of which may not effectively solve the underlying problems. For example, legislators might impose price controls on insurance premiums to make coverage more affordable. While this may provide short-term relief for policyholders, it can create long-term challenges for insurers who must adequately price risk to remain financially stable.

2. **Moral Hazard**: If government intervention reduces the cost of insurance for individuals who choose to live in high-risk areas (e.g., hurricane-prone coastal regions), it can inadvertently encourage more people to build in these vulnerable locations. This phenomenon is known as "moral hazard," where individuals take on more significant risks because they believe they will be bailed out in the event of a catastrophe. This, in turn, exacerbates the underlying problem of people building in vulnerable areas.

3. **Subsidies and Risk Transfer**: Governments may create programs to provide subsidies or reinsurance (*insurance that an insurance company purchases to limit its risk by sharing some of its potential losses with other insurers*) for catastrophe insurance coverage. While these programs can help make insurance more affordable for homeowners and insurers, they also involve significant political and budgetary considerations. Changes in

political leadership or budget priorities can introduce uncertainty into the stability of such programs.

4. **Regulatory Changes**: Legislative actions can introduce new regulations or alter existing ones, affecting how insurance companies operate and price policies. These regulatory changes can introduce uncertainty about insurers' compliance, reporting, and capital requirements, potentially affecting their willingness to underwrite catastrophic risks.

5. **Funding and Resources**: The government's role in disaster response and recovery and its ability to provide financial aid to affected areas can influence the insurance industry's dynamics. Insurance companies may factor in government assistance when assessing the economic impact of catastrophic events.

Political uncertainty stemming from legislative responses to high insurance premiums and vulnerabilities in the catastrophe insurance system can complicate matters. While these interventions may be well-intentioned, they often have unintended consequences and can introduce unpredictability into the insurance industry.

Striking a balance between addressing affordability concerns and maintaining the financial stability of the insurance sector is a challenging task, and it requires careful consideration of both risk and uncertainty factors associated with catastrophic events and the behavior of insured parties.

Question:

So, catastrophe risk in Florida may be between Knight's description of risk and uncertainty. One strategy to reduce hurricanes' uncertainty is to build more substantial homes. However, that strategy has limits when people build in coastal areas, where tidal surges, or flooding is likely. Recognizing that Florida represents the peak catastrophe risk in the world makes it even more critical that policymakers use great care not to create political uncertainty by enacting radical changes in the law that displace the private market in favor of government programs.

Answer:

Absolutely, let's thoroughly explore that with a refreshed narrative that includes the dynamics of catastrophe risk in Florida, the impact of building strategies, and the critical role of policymaking.

1. **Navigating the Risk-Uncertainty Spectrum in Florida**: Imagine Florida as a board game on Knight's risk-uncertainty spectrum. You're playing a high-stakes game where hurricanes are regular, albeit unpredictable, players. It's not quite Russian roulette (where you know the odds) and not entirely a roll of cosmic dice (total uncertainty). It's in the murky middle, making it a challenging game for insurers and homeowners alike.

2. **Building Stronger Homes – The First Line of Defense**: One strategy in our game is building sturdier homes – think of it as upgrading your armor in a battle game. This move is wise, like choosing an umbrella over a newspaper to weather a storm. It's effective against typical hurricanes, but when you're building on the coast, it's like setting up a lemonade stand in a splash zone – there's only so much your umbrella can do against a tidal wave.

3. **The Coastal Conundrum – Risky Real Estate Roulette**: Building in coastal areas or flood-prone zones is like betting on a high-risk slot in the game. You might hit the jackpot with a beautiful ocean view, but the stakes are high. It's like hosting a picnic on an active volcano – scenic, but is it worth the risk?

4. **Florida's Peak Catastrophe Risk – Walking on Eggshells**: Florida isn't just playing any game; it's on the world's peak catastrophe risk board. This means every move and every policy decision is like tiptoeing on a tightrope over a gator-infested swamp. The balance is crucial, and one wrong step could have dire consequences.

5. **The Role of Policymakers – The Game Masters**: Here's where policymakers come in – they're like game masters. Their role is pivotal in balancing private market dynamics and government intervention. Radical changes in law, especially those displacing the private market with government programs, are like throwing a wild card into an already volatile game. It's essential they navigate these waters with the precision of a chess grandmaster, understanding that every move affects the stability and attractiveness of Florida's insurance market.

6. **Conclusion—The Art of Playing it Smart**: To wrap up, Florida's situation is a complex puzzle in Knight's spectrum of risk and uncertainty. The key is playing it smart—building stronger but wiser, understanding the limits of where and how we build, and having policymakers who don't shake the board too hard. It's about finding that sweet spot where the sun shines bright, but the foundations are strong enough to weather any storm.

In these questions and answers, we see how catastrophe risk in Florida is a delicate balance, requiring thoughtful strategies and prudent policy-making to navigate the challenging waters of risk and uncertainty.

As we wrap up our exploration of risk and uncertainty through the lens of Frank H. Knight's seminal work, it's pivotal to highlight one of the pragmatic strategies he indirectly alludes to for mitigating such uncertainties: the construction of sturdier homes. Knight's distinction between risk and uncertainty illuminates the challenges inherent in predicting and preparing for natural catastrophes and underscores the importance of proactive measures in building resilience against such events.

In the context of reducing future catastrophe losses, particularly in hurricane-prone areas like Florida, the role of solid building codes cannot be overstated. These codes serve as a critical bridge between Knight's theoretical insights and practical, on-the-ground strategies for risk management. Strong building codes effectively translate Knight's concept of reducing uncertainty into tangible action by mandating construction standards that can withstand the forces of nature.

Summary of Chapter 17:

In Chapter 17, I undertake a careful analysis of the foundational work of Dr. Frank H. Knight, an eminent American economist whose groundbreaking book "Risk, Uncertainty, and Profit" reshaped economic theory. Knight's work introduced a pivotal distinction between risk and uncertainty, shedding light on their profound implications for economic decision-making.

Knight, a towering figure in the Chicago School of Economics, challenged prevailing economic theories and emphasized the critical role of individual judgment in navigating uncertain terrains. His distinction between risk, which can be quantified and managed, and uncertainty, which defies measurement and prediction, provided valuable insights for understanding market dynamics and the function of profit.

I explore Knight's concepts of measurability and predictability, illustrating how they apply to economic decision-making and capital adequacy. While risks can be assessed and managed through statistical models, uncertainties require a different approach, relying on judgment and intuition rather than calculable odds.

Furthermore, I delve into the impact of political uncertainty on catastrophe insurance, highlighting the challenges posed by legislative interventions and government policies. Political uncertainty complicates the landscape, affecting insurers, homeowners, and policymakers alike, and requires careful navigation to strike a balance between addressing affordability concerns and maintaining financial stability.

Through a series of questions and answers, I elucidate the nuanced interplay between risk and uncertainty, particularly in the context of catastrophe risk in Florida. I emphasize the importance of prudent policymaking and proactive measures, such as strong building codes, in mitigating uncertainties and building resilience against natural disasters.

Ultimately, Chapter 17 underscores the intricate dynamics of risk and uncertainty in economic decision-making, offering valuable insights for policymakers, insurers, and individuals navigating uncertain environments. It serves as a testament to Knight's enduring legacy and his profound contributions to economic theory and practice.

Transition to Chapter 18:

We've just tackled the tricky task of untangling the difference between risk and uncertainty in all that economic jargon. Now, let's bring it back down to earth. In Chapter 18, "Storms and Stability - Crafting Equitable Strategies in Residential Property Insurance," we will see how all these high-flying ideas actually play out in the real world. We're closely examining how these elements influence the strategies behind residential property insurance, which is a big deal in Florida, especially with all the natural disasters we face. It's all about figuring out how to make insurance fair and keep it going strong in the face of Mother Nature's curveballs. Let's get into it!

Part 4

ESSAYS ON INSURANCE AND PUBLIC POLICY

Chapter 18

Storms and Stability: Crafting Equitable Strategies in Residential Property Insurance

In residential property insurance, categorizing risks is akin to organizing a wardrobe: you wouldn't store your beach shorts and ski jackets in the same drawer, just like you wouldn't lump coastal and inland homes under the same insurance umbrella. This differentiation is crucial because, much like deciding between flip-flops or snow boots, the location of your property dramatically influences the insurance risks – and premiums.

Risk Classification: A Kaleidoscope of Factors

Consider the insurance industry's approach to risk classification as the meticulous art of sorting a jigsaw puzzle. Each piece symbolizes a risk factor, such as geographic location, construction material, proximity to fire stations, and the likelihood of experiencing a hurricane or a wildfire.

Inland properties, snuggled far from the wrath of Poseidon, might only flirt with the occasional flood or fire, offering a relatively stable and predictable risk profile. It's like living in a place where the most exciting event is the annual bake sale.

Coastal properties, however, dance on the edge of nature's fury. They face the full spectrum of coastal joys - from sunsets that paint the sky in hues of gold to hurricanes that decide to remodel entire neighborhoods without permission.

Insuring these properties is like playing roulette with Mother Nature, where she, unfortunately, spins the wheel.

The Art of Avoiding Cross-Subsidization

The principle of not letting the inland homeowners subsidize the high-stakes coastal insurance game is a testament to fairness and financial prudence. Imagine if buying groceries worked the same way, and your bill randomly doubled because your neighbor decided to buy a yacht's worth of caviar. Not the ideal communal spirit, right?

Insurance company regulators use this principle to ensure everyone pays their fair share based on the risk their property presents. It's about providing the guy with a beachfront villa, and the lady in the mountain cabin isn't paying into the same risk pot. After all, it wouldn't be fair for the mountain cabin's owner to subsidize the villa's dance with hurricanes. I'll admit that analogy was not the best – we live in Florida, after all, but you get my point.

Market Distortions: When Politics Plays Insurance Broker

However, when regulators, pushed by political winds, decide to cap rates in high-risk areas and hike them in safer zones, the market contorts like a pretzel. This well-intentioned but misguided approach leads to scenarios where risk and premiums are as mismatched as socks on laundry day.

High-risk areas become underpriced all-you-can-eat buffets of insurance coverage, while low-risk areas foot the bill despite dining on a much more modest menu of risks.

This distortion undermines the essence of risk-based pricing and encourages risky behavior, like building more properties in areas where even the bravest seagulls hesitate to land. It's akin to offering discounts for tightrope walking without a net; thrilling, but you wouldn't want your retirement plan dependent on it.

A Balancing Act in Insurance Cuisine

Navigating the nuanced culinary art of insurance pricing, especially in the context of residential properties, requires a balance between risk appetite and financial seasoning. The goal is to serve a fair and sustainable premium pie, where each slice is proportionate to the risk ingredients baked into it. So, as we ponder the future of insurance cuisine, let's aim for recipes that encourage resilience, fairness, and a touch of humor to digest the inevitable complexities life serves.

In essence, the insurance landscape, with its blend of risk, regulation, and real estate, mirrors the complexity and unpredictability of life itself. Yet, with a dash of humor and a spoonful of wisdom, navigating it becomes not just manageable but intriguingly enjoyable.

The Serious Business of Spreading Risk vs. Pooling Risk

Adding to the vivid tapestry of our discussion on residential property insurance, let's delve into the serious distinction between spreading risk and pooling risk, two foundational strategies that ensure the insurance industry remains afloat amidst the unpredictable seas of risk.

While our journey through insurance landscapes has been sprinkled with humor and analogies, the concepts of spreading risk and pooling risk warrant a focused discussion due to their critical importance in insurance underwriting (*the process of evaluating the risks involved in insuring a person or asset and determining appropriate premium rates*) and risk management.

Spreading Risk

This strategy involves diversifying the insurer's portfolio by covering various risks across geographic areas, property types, and policyholder demographics. Much like a chef ensuring a balanced diet by incorporating different food groups, insurers spread risk to avoid overexposure to a single kind of claim.

While this lighthearted analogy captures the essence of the balancing act insurers must perform, the serious business of spreading and pooling risk is crucial to maintaining stability in the face of storms.

In residential property insurance, this means insuring coastal properties prone to hurricanes and covering inland homes, city apartments, and countryside cottages. The goal is to mitigate the financial impact of a disaster striking any one category of insured properties.

Pooling Risk

On the other side of the coin, pooling risk is about aggregating premiums from a large group of policyholders to pay for the losses of a few within that group. It's akin to a communal potluck where everyone brings a dish (premiums) to share, ensuring there's enough food (funds) to feed anyone who ends up hungry (suffers a loss).

In practice, this means that homeowners in both high-risk and low-risk areas contribute to the same pool, with the understanding that while not everyone will need to claim for a loss, the pool will cover those who do.

Distinguishing the Two

While both strategies aim to mitigate financial risk for insurers, their approaches are markedly different. Spreading risk is about the insurer managing its risk exposure across a broad spectrum, ensuring no single event can capsize the ship. Pooling risk is more about the collective sharing of risk among policyholders, underpinned by the principle that there's strength in numbers.

The critical difference lies in their application: spreading risk is an insurer-centric strategy for financial stability, while pooling risk is a policyholder-centric model that ensures claims can be paid. When properly balanced, these strategies allow insurers to provide affordable, equitable coverage without succumbing to the potential financial devastation of large-scale disasters.

Understanding the Dynamics: The Global Catastrophe Market's Influence on Florida's Homeowners Insurance

As we delve into the nuanced landscape of Florida's insurance market, we must consider the broader influences that shape our local insurance dynamics. One critical aspect often questioned by homeowners revolves around the escalating insurance costs. We turn to a question-and-answer format that breaks down complex factors into digestible insights to address these concerns. This section highlights how global market trends directly impact Florida's homeowners' insurance cost, particularly within the catastrophe market. By understanding these global influences, homeowners can better navigate the complexities of their insurance needs and make more informed decisions.

Question:

I am an average Florida homeowner concerned about the rising cost of homeowner's insurance. I want to understand better what factors drive that cost. I understand one of those factors is the status of the global catastrophe market, including the impact on reinsurance (insurance for insurance companies) and other risk transfer vehicles and the cost of capital. Please help me understand what is driving the cost of my insurance.

Answer:

As an average Florida homeowner, it's understandable to be concerned about the rising cost of homeowner's insurance. Several factors contribute to this increase, and one significant factor is the status of the global catastrophe market, which includes the impact on reinsurance, other risk transfer vehicles, and the cost of capital. This essay will explore these factors to help you better understand what is driving the cost of your insurance.

Reinsurance is a crucial component of the insurance industry. It is essentially insurance for insurance companies, allowing them to transfer a portion of their risk to other insurers. In the event of a catastrophic occurrence, such as a hurricane, insurance companies depend on reinsurance to assist in paying claims and maintaining financial stability. However, the global catastrophe market has been under pressure in recent years due to natural disasters' increased frequency and severity.

Climate change has contributed to more intense hurricanes, wildfires, and floods worldwide. As a result, insurance companies face higher claims payouts, affecting the reinsurance market. Reinsurers are raising their prices or reducing their capacity to take on risk as they reassess the potential losses they could incur. This trend directly impacts primary insurers, who must pay more for reinsurance coverage or absorb more risk themselves.

The cost of capital is another factor influencing the price of reinsurance and, consequently, homeowners' insurance. When reinsurers face increased risks and potential losses, they require a higher return on their capital to justify the risk they are taking. This higher cost of capital is passed down to primary insurers, who then incorporate it into the premiums they charge homeowners.

In addition to reinsurance and the cost of capital, other risk transfer vehicles, such as catastrophe bonds (also known as cat bonds), have an impact on the cost of homeowner's insurance. Cat bonds are financial instruments that allow insurers to transfer a portion of their catastrophe risk to investors. If a specified catastrophic event occurs, investors lose their principal, and the insurer uses the funds to pay claims. However, if the catastrophe does not occur, investors receive their principal back plus interest.

The demand for cat bonds has grown in recent years as insurers seek alternative ways to manage their risk. However, the increased frequency and severity of natural disasters have made investors more cautious, leading to higher yields on cat bonds. This increased cost is ultimately passed on to homeowners through higher insurance premiums.

Florida, in particular, is a high-risk area for hurricanes, which makes it more challenging for insurers to manage their risk and secure affordable reinsurance and risk transfer options. The state has also faced issues with fraudulent or exaggerated claims, contributing to the rising cost of insurance.

In conclusion, the rising cost of homeowners insurance in Florida is influenced by several factors, including the status of the global catastrophe market, its impact on reinsurance and other risk transfer vehicles, and the cost of capital. Climate change, the increased frequency and severity of natural disasters, and the demand for higher returns by reinsurers and investors all contribute to the increased cost of insurance.

As a Florida homeowner, understanding these factors can help you better navigate the insurance market and make informed decisions about protecting your home.

Question:

Please focus on and expand your discussion on the impact of the global catastrophe market on the cost of homeowners insurance in Florida.

Answer:

The global catastrophe market plays a significant role in determining the cost of Florida homeowners' insurance. This market involves buying and selling insurance and reinsurance policies that cover catastrophic events such as hurricanes, earthquakes, and wildfires. When the global catastrophe market is strained, it directly impacts the cost of homeowners insurance in high-risk areas like Florida.

One of the primary drivers of the global catastrophe market is the frequency and severity of natural disasters. In recent years, the world has seen an increase in the number and intensity of catastrophic events, particularly hurricanes. This trend is especially relevant to Florida, which is prone to hurricanes due to its location. As the frequency and severity of hurricanes increase, insurance companies face higher potential losses, which in turn affects the global catastrophe market.

Reinsurance companies, which provide insurance for insurance companies, are particularly sensitive to changes in the global catastrophe market. When the risk of catastrophic events increases, reinsurers must reassess their exposure and adjust their prices accordingly. If reinsurers perceive the risk as too high, they may reduce their capacity or withdraw from certain markets altogether. This reduced capacity and increased cost of reinsurance directly impact primary insurers, who rely on reinsurance to manage their risk.

As reinsurance becomes more expensive or less available, primary insurers either absorb more risk or pass the increased costs on to policyholders through higher premiums. In Florida, where the risk of hurricanes is high, insurers heavily depend on reinsurance to manage their exposure. When reinsurance costs rise, Florida insurers must raise their rates to maintain financial stability.

Another aspect of the global catastrophe market that affects Florida homeowners' insurance is using alternative risk transfer vehicles, such as catastrophe bonds (cat bonds). Cat bonds are financial instruments that allow insurers to transfer a portion of their catastrophe risk to investors. When catastrophic events occur more frequently or with greater severity, investors demand higher yields on cat bonds to compensate for the increased risk. This higher cost of capital is ultimately passed on to policyholders, contributing to the rising cost of homeowners insurance in Florida.

The overall capacity of the insurance and reinsurance industries also influences the global catastrophe market. When major catastrophic events occur, such as a series of powerful hurricanes, the global catastrophe market can experience a temporary capacity shortage. This shortage can lead to increased competition for the remaining capacity, driving up prices for insurance and reinsurance.

In recent years, Florida has seen several insurance companies become insolvent or leave the state due to the challenges posed by the global catastrophe market and the state's high-risk environment. This reduction in competition can also contribute to higher prices for homeowners' insurance, as the remaining insurers have less incentive to keep prices low.

In conclusion, the global catastrophe market significantly impacts Florida's homeowners' insurance cost. The increased frequency and severity of natural disasters, particularly hurricanes, strain the global catastrophe market, leading to higher reinsurance costs and reduced capacity. These factors, combined with the use of alternative risk transfer vehicles and the overall capacity of the insurance industry, contribute to the rising cost of homeowners insurance in Florida. As a Florida homeowner, understanding the role of the global catastrophe market can provide valuable insight into the factors driving the cost of your insurance.

Having explored the broader global influences that shape our insurance costs, it's crucial to examine how local regulatory actions align—or misalign—with these dynamics. The following section, "The Impact of Misaligned Regulatory Actions," delves into the consequences of regulatory decisions that do not fully consider these global pressures. As we transition from a global perspective back to state-specific issues, we'll explore these regulatory choices' ripple effects on insurers and homeowners alike. This analysis will help us understand the intricate balance needed between managing immediate local challenges and responding to global market conditions.

The Impact of Misaligned Regulatory Actions

As mentioned, when regulatory actions force rates in high-risk areas down and bump up rates in low-risk areas, the delicate balance of risk spreading and pooling is disturbed. This distorts the market and undermines the principles that keep the insurance ecosystem healthy and equitable. Ensuring that premiums accurately reflect the risk is not just about fairness; it's about maintaining the integrity and sustainability of the insurance model.

Wrapping up (yes, I know I've already pulled the 'conclusion' card before, only to ramble on—much like a preacher declaring "In closing," which, let's face it, is code for "Buckle up, we're going on another loop of this sermon"), understanding, and effectively implementing the strategies of spreading and pooling risk is paramount for the insurance industry to thrive.

As we navigate the complexities of insuring properties from serene inland retreats to storm-swept coastal havens, the industry must continue to innovate and adapt these strategies to meet the ever-changing risk landscape. This ongoing evolution ensures that the umbrella of protection offered by insurers remains wide, welcoming, and wise to the world's ways.

Summary of Chapter 18:

In Chapter 18, I investigate the dynamic world of residential property insurance, likening the process of risk classification to organizing a wardrobe where each garment finds its place based on its unique characteristics. From the tranquil inland abodes to the tempestuous coastal havens, the location of a property plays a pivotal role in determining its insurance risks and premiums.

I explore the art of avoiding cross-subsidization in insurance, emphasizing the importance of fairness and financial prudence in ensuring that each homeowner pays their fair share based on the risk their property presents. However, I also caution against market distortions caused by political interventions that disrupt the delicate balance of risk-based pricing, leading to mismatches between risk and premiums.

Through a series of vivid analogies and humorous illustrations, I highlight the complexities of insurance pricing and the challenges of navigating regulatory actions in high-risk areas. I underscore the need for equitable strategies that balance risk appetite and financial seasoning to serve a fair and sustainable premium pie to policyholders.

Furthermore, I explore the serious business of spreading risk and pooling risk, two foundational strategies that ensure the insurance industry remains resilient amidst the unpredictable seas of risk. I distinguish between these approaches, emphasizing their respective roles in insurer-centric financial stability and policyholder-centric risk sharing.

However, I also caution against misaligned regulatory actions that disturb the delicate balance of risk spreading and pooling, undermining the integrity and sustainability of the insurance model. I stress the importance of accurately reflecting risk in premiums to maintain fairness and ensure the industry's continued viability.

In conclusion, Chapter 18 underscores the intricate interplay between storms and stability in residential property insurance, offering insights into the challenges and opportunities inherent in crafting equitable strategies to navigate the ever-changing risk landscape. It serves as a testament to the resilience and adaptability of the insurance industry in providing protection and peace of mind to homeowners across diverse geographic areas.

Transition to Chapter 19:

So, we've been talking about risk, markets, and that precarious balance of residential property insurance. Next, we're stepping back from the nitty-gritty and casting an eye over the bigger picture in "The Inevitable Storm - Unmasking the True Cost of Paradise." It's a tale as old as time in Florida - the allure of living in paradise, with that ever-present risk of nature's wrath. Here, we peel back the layers of comfort we've built up and look at what it really costs us when the heavens open and the winds howl.

CHAPTER 19

The Price of Paradise: Unmasking the True Cost of Living in Hurricane-Prone Florida

Introduction

This chapter explores the multifaceted impact of hurricanes in Florida, a paradise frequently disturbed by nature's fury. We begin by recounting the historical impacts of these storms, which have shaped the state's infrastructure, economy, and community life. A comprehensive case study on Hurricane Michael demonstrates the immediate impact and recovery strategies employed in the aftermath of recent hurricanes.

We further discuss the evolution of insurance policies in response to escalating hurricane damages, and the advancements in technology that now aid in better predicting and mitigating these storms. The role of federal disaster relief is critiqued, leading into a discussion on comprehensive preventative measures aimed at reducing future impacts.

The chapter concludes with a reflection on the broader economic and social implications of living under the constant threat of hurricanes, urging a proactive approach to disaster management.

My experiences as a State Representative grappling with these issues reflect the long-standing challenges Florida has faced in the wake of hurricanes, as evidenced by the historical impact of these storms on the state.

Having set the stage with the ongoing battle against hurricanes, let us delve into the historical impacts that have defined Florida's response to these natural disasters.

Historical Impact of Hurricanes in Florida

Historically, hurricanes have sculpted Florida's infrastructure, economy, and community life. The state has witnessed the fury of storms like Hurricane Andrew and Hurricane Irma, which have collectively reshaped our understanding of disaster preparedness and response. These events provide a backdrop for discussing the evolving challenges of managing hurricane impacts.

With a foundational understanding of past hurricanes, we now turn to a more recent event. Hurricane Michael's devastation provides a vivid lens through which we can examine the immediate and lingering challenges of storm recovery.

Case Study: Hurricane Michael

Hurricane Michael, a Category 5 storm, made landfall in the Florida Panhandle in October 2018. The storm's high winds and heavy rainfall caused extensive damage to the region, with an estimated cost of $25 billion. The long-term recovery from Hurricane Michael involved a multifaceted approach, prioritizing infrastructure repairs, such as roads and bridges, alongside the reconstruction of homes. Economic initiatives were crucial to revitalizing the affected areas, and comprehensive social support services addressed the broader human impacts, aiding in the psychological and physical recovery of the residents.

The extensive damage wrought by Hurricane Michael bring us to an essential aspect of hurricane recovery: insurance. Let's explore how this disaster has reshaped insurance policies in Florida, aiming for resilience in the face of increasing risks.

Changes in Insurance Policies

Post-Charley, significant changes in insurance policies were necessary. The storm highlighted the limitations of existing coverage frameworks, leading to increased premiums and a push for stricter building codes. These changes aim to ensure that both residential and commercial properties are better equipped to withstand future hurricanes, balancing affordability with comprehensive coverage.

As we consider the evolving landscape of insurance, it's crucial to recognize the role of technology in shaping our preparedness. Advances in hurricane prediction and mitigation technologies have transformed our approach to managing these storms.

Technological Advancements in Hurricane Prediction and Mitigation

Advancements in technology have revolutionized hurricane prediction and mitigation. Enhanced satellite imagery and sophisticated computer models now provide more accurate forecasts, allowing for timely evacuations and preparedness measures.

Additionally, innovations in building materials and construction techniques have significantly improved the resilience of new structures.

Equipped with better technology, our attention shifts to the federal response. How effective is FEMA in coordinating and supporting state and local disaster relief efforts? This section evaluates the strengths and shortcomings of federal aid.

The Role of Federal Disaster Relief

The Federal Emergency Management Agency (FEMA) plays a pivotal role in coordinating disaster relief efforts. Post-hurricane responses involve deploying aid, assessing damage, and supporting recovery operations. This federal support is crucial, yet it also highlights the need for state and local strategies to complement these efforts, ensuring a cohesive approach to disaster management.

Acknowledging the mixed results of federal intervention, we now consider a broader strategy. Preventative measures offer a proactive approach to reduce the impact of future hurricanes, enhancing Florida's resilience.

Comprehensive Approach to Preventative Measures

A comprehensive strategy to address the challenges posed by hurricanes involves both reactive and proactive measures. Preventative planning includes enhancing public awareness, improving community infrastructure, and enforcing stricter zoning laws. These efforts aim to reduce the overall impact of hurricanes and enhance the state's capacity to recover and thrive after events.

Having explored practical measures and strategies to mitigate hurricane impacts, we conclude with a reflection on the economic and social implications these storms have on our paradise. It's time to reassess our preparedness and commitment to resilience.

The persistence in underpricing the risk of residing in a hurricane-prone paradise serves to postpone the reckoning rather than deter it. It's akin to building a sandcastle at the water's edge, marveling at its beauty even as the tide encroaches.

The efforts to legislate away the economic realities of disaster risk or to cap insurance rates in the name of consumer protection are equivalent to adding more turrets to our sandcastle, ignoring the rising tide that threatens to wash it all away.

The dialogue surrounding the cost of hurricanes and the role of insurance needs a paradigm shift. It's time to peel away the layers of political expedience and regulatory inhibition to confront the heart of the issue.

At its core, insurance is a mechanism of risk distribution, a collective fund to which we all contribute, hoping never to require a withdrawal but appreciative of its presence when calamity strikes. Yet, this system falters when the premiums collected do not accurately reflect the risk assumed.

It's an economic imbalance that no legislative creativity or regulatory restraint can rectify.

In addressing this challenge, the focus must shift from vilifying insurance companies to enhancing our collective resilience. This includes embracing actuarially sound premiums that accurately reflect the risk of coastal living, investing in infrastructure that can withstand the onslaught of hurricanes, and fostering a community ethos that prioritizes preparedness and sustainability over short-term gains.

Before we conclude this discussion on how to finance the cost of catastrophic Florida hurricanes and to support the notion that governments are not always the wisest councilors, let's consult with a voice from our past:

Adam Smith was an 18th-century Scottish economist, philosopher, and author who is considered the father of modern economics. He was a proponent of free markets and emphasized minimizing the role of government intervention in private markets.

Adams famously wrote: "The statesman who should attempt to direct private people in what manner they ought to employ their capitals, would not only load himself with a most unnecessary attention, but assume an authority which could safely be trusted to no council and senate whatever, and which would nowhere be so dangerous as in the hands of a man who had folly and presumption enough to fancy himself fit to exercise it."

The wisdom of Adam Smith was very much in view in 2011 when I delivered a presentation to the Florida Senate Banking and Insurance Committee. Excerpts from my presentation follow:

"Senators:

Thank you for the opportunity to present on this very timely subject.

You have asked for and received many ideas on improving the Florida residential property insurance market. The proposal Associated Industries of Florida prepared is in your packet, and we encourage you to reference that information for our detailed recommendations.

I will briefly summarize some of our most essential recommendations…

Florida's problem is NOT "insurance."

The problem is Florida's extraordinary vulnerability to Hurricanes. All the insurance challenges we face are a result of our Hurricane problem. We should not allow all the details to divert our focus from this simple fact:

- Florida's exposure concentration in our coastal counties is higher than any of the other Gulf Coast states.
- Our total wind exposure is more significant than all our Gulf Coast neighbor states combined.
- In fact, Florida has about half of the total hurricane exposure of the entire nation.

We should NOT allow our differing opinions…to cause us to lose sight of these facts.

Also, we CAN NOT afford to "self-insure" all that exposure.

Generally speaking, there are two strategies available to you when thinking about how to manage this enormous hurricane risk:

- On the one hand, you can finance this risk with private capital.
- Or, on the other hand, you can finance the risk with public debt.

If you choose the capital option, you will realize a risk transfer in exchange for the cost of that capital. By utilizing a more market-based approach, you also reduce our exposure to hurricane taxes and assessments.

If you choose post-event debt, the risk is retained in exchange for lower premiums now but with extreme exposure to hurricane taxes and assessments after the storm.

It is my opinion that in the past, you have chosen options that rely too heavily upon a redistribution of the cost of our exposure from a) lower-risk regions of our state to the higher-risk regions and b) from employers, working families, and other individuals to a subsidized group of individuals.

We also request that you give careful attention to one additional fact:

- Citizens represents approximately 23% of the Florida residential property insurance market. That means that approximately 77% of Florida's homeowners are not insured by Citizens.

Notwithstanding this fact, these non-citizens homeowners and all auto policyholders, businesses, charities, churches, not-for-profits and local governmental entities must shoulder the burden of any Citizens or Cat Fund funding shortfalls…

Now that you have all the requested information, you must decide how to use it.

May I suggest that before specific ideas are considered, a critical question should be asked, and the answer to that question should measure all proposed ideas:

'Is the ultimate goal to provide insurance with real risk transfer, or is the goal to provide the best 'self-insurance' program possible?' Depending upon the answer to that question, each idea can be judged based on how well it accomplishes the desired goal.

We hope you will see the need to attract more capital, transfer more risk out of Florida, and rely much less upon risk retention.

The status quo prompted Howard Troxler, columnist for the St. Petersburg Times on April 4th, 2010, to write:

'We have the worst of all possible worlds in Florida - a weak private sector, a public sector bearing enormous risk, and a plan to borrow money and sock it to everybody on the back end... we ought to try something different.'

In summary, Florida citizens currently pay high homeowners insurance premiums and are subject to post-event hurricane taxes/assessments. By design, we rely heavily upon public debt rather than private capital to finance our exposure to hurricanes.

In closing, please allow me a point of personal privilege.

Having sat on your side of the legislative desk, I know how difficult it is to correctly identify the real problem, sort through all the distractions, and focus on a solution. I also know that, at times, we become so confident in our abilities that we begin to believe that because we are so bright, we can suspend the laws of nature and the laws of economics.

The reality is that even the most well-crafted plans in HB1A (previous legislation) have proven ineffective. Despite good intentions, they have not achieved the desired results.

We should consider a different strategy, one that has been proven successful in Louisiana, rather than resorting to short-term fixes.

AIF would welcome the opportunity to discuss the contents of our reform proposal further and provide additional details upon request.

Thank You"

The actual cost of living in paradise is not just the price of admission but the commitment to stewardship it demands. It's an agreement with nature, recognizing its power and preparing with respect rather than defiance.

As Florida faces the certainty of the next $50 billion storm, the question is not who will pay but how we can collectively mitigate the impact.

The answer lies not in the sandcastles of policy and rhetoric but in the bedrock of preparedness, resilience, and a realistic appraisal of the risks we face. Only then can we truly safeguard our paradise for generations to come.

As we dissect the financial repercussions of hurricane impacts in Florida, it's crucial to examine the macroeconomic landscape and the individual behaviors that reflect and influence this broader context. Let's shift our focus momentarily to a parable that, while seemingly distant from hurricane economics, offers poignant insights into the perilous allure of deferred costs and the illusion of affordability.

Humor Alert

"Keeping Up with the Joneses: A Cautionary Tale of Dining and Disaster"

Once upon a time, in a suburban paradise, I lived next to the most ostentatious neighbors, Mr. and Mrs. Jones. Every evening, like clockwork, the Joneses would gather their picture-perfect family, hop into their gleaming SUV, and announce to the entire neighborhood that they were off to indulge in yet another night of fine dining.

As I stood there, watching them back out of their driveway with a wave, my own wife turned to me with a raised eyebrow. "Why don't we ever go out to eat like the Joneses?" she asked a hint of envy in her voice.

Now, I'm a sensible man. I know dining out every night is a recipe for financial indigestion. But with my wife's challenge ringing in my ears and the Joneses' taillights disappearing into the night, I found myself at the bank the next day, applying for a shiny new credit card.

To my surprise (and perhaps my downfall), the bank happily issued me a card with a limit that could feed a small country. Armed with this plastic ticket to gastronomic glory, I set out to give the Joneses a taste of their own medicine.

As the Joneses prepared for their nightly culinary excursion the following evening, I beat them to the punch. With a cheerful wave and a grin, I announced that my wife and I were heading out for a night in town. And so began our own delicious adventure, fueled by the magic of credit.

We dined like royalty each night, sampling the city's finest cuisine. And each night, I blissfully swiped my card, paying only the minimum monthly balance. It was a delightful dance of instant gratification, with the bill conveniently pushed to the back of my mind.

But alas, all good things must come to an end. At the close of the year, I was drowning in a sea of debt, with the credit card company demanding payment in full. My card was canceled, and I was left with a mountain of bills and a wife who had grown accustomed to the finer things in life.

The worst part? I had nothing to show for my extravagant spending, save for a few extra pounds round my waistline and a lingering sense of regret. The delicious meals had long been digested and forgotten (In fact, I had flushed them out of sight), leaving me with nothing but a financial hangover.

And so, dear friends, let this be a cautionary tale. Just as dining out on credit can lead to a bitter end, artificially low homeowners' insurance rates are a recipe for disaster. When regulators and policymakers bow to political pressure and set rates below actuarially sound levels, it's like handing out credit cards without regard for the consequences.

Sure, it might feel good now, like savoring a gourmet meal on someone else's dime. But when the storm hits, and the true costs come due, homeowners are left with a bill they can't afford to pay. Post-storm assessments and financial ruin become the unappetizing reality, leaving a bitter taste in everyone's mouth.

So, the next time you're tempted by the siren song of artificially low insurance rates, remember the tale of the Joneses and their envious neighbor. It's better to pay a fair price upfront than to be left with an empty wallet and a sinking feeling when disaster strikes. After all, in the grand buffet of life, it's always wise to make sure you can afford the bill before you take a bite.

This tale of fiscal imprudence mirrors the broader narrative of Florida's property insurance market. Just as the protagonist was seduced by the immediate gratification of opulent dining, underpinned by the deceptive comfort of credit, Florida's approach to property insurance has sometimes been marred by a similar short-sightedness. The artificial suppression of insurance rates, much like the reckless accumulation of credit card debt, creates an illusion of affordability. At the same time, the looming storm of financial reality gathers strength in the shadows.

Conclusion

Florida's experience with hurricanes offers critical lessons in resilience and preparedness. As we face the reality of more frequent and severe storms, it is imperative to adopt a holistic approach that encompasses improved regulations, community engagement, and innovative technologies. Only through such a comprehensive strategy can we hope to protect our paradise from the inevitable storms.

Call to Action

This chapter serves as a call to action for lawmakers, community leaders, and residents to forge a resilient future. It is a collective responsibility to embrace these strategies and implement them effectively, ensuring Florida remains a safe and thriving state for generations to come.

Summary of Chapter 19:

Chapter 19, "The Inevitable Storm: Unmasking the True Cost of Paradise," offers a comprehensive exploration of Florida's challenges in managing the impact of hurricanes. It addresses the economic, social, and policy ramifications of living in a hurricane-prone paradise. By weaving together historical data, case studies, and advancements in hurricane prediction and mitigation, the chapter paints a detailed picture of the state's ongoing battle against these natural disasters.

The discussion highlights how underpriced risk, driven by political and regulatory pressures, fails to prepare the state for inevitable future storms. Through a compelling narrative that includes a critical examination of insurance policies and disaster relief efforts, the chapter calls for a paradigm shift towards more sustainable and economically sound disaster management strategies. This reflection urges policymakers, insurers, and residents to reevaluate and strengthen their approach to building a resilient future for Florida.

Transition to Chapter 20:

Now that we've had a heart-to-heart talk about the actual costs of living in our sunny paradise, let's roll up our sleeves and get down to the brass tacks of handling what Mother Nature throws our way. Chapter 20, titled "Risk Management in the Face of Florida's Catastrophic Hurricane Exposure," delves into the complexities of balancing risk retention and transfer, drawing insightful comparisons and lessons from international events. Join me as we navigate the nuanced landscape of risk management and explore its profound implications for Florida's economic resilience in the wake of natural disasters.

Part 4

Essays on Insurance and Public Policy

CHAPTER 20

Risk Management in the Face of Florida's Catastrophe Hurricane Exposure

In addressing the complexities of risk management, especially in the context of Florida's hurricane exposure, we can draw insightful comparisons and lessons from international events like the February 2011 Christchurch, New Zealand earthquake[24] and Japan's earthquake and tsunami[25] in March 2011.

These events ranked among the most significant and devastating natural disasters of the early 21st century.

---

[24] https://nzhistory.govt.nz/page/christchurch-earthquake-kills-185
[25] https://en.wikipedia.org/wiki/2011_T%C5%8Dhoku_earthquake_and_tsunami

Florida's approach to handling hurricane risks offers a compelling case study in balancing risk retention and risk transfer, a balance that significantly impacts post-catastrophe economic recovery.

The Five Principles of Risk Management & Florida's Hurricane Exposure

1. **Risk Identification:**

Florida, notorious for its hurricane exposure, identifies this as a primary risk. The state's Enhanced State Hazard Mitigation Plan and the Hurricane Loss Mitigation Program focus on understanding and preparing for these catastrophic events.

2. **Risk Analysis:**

Florida's Division of Emergency Management employs advanced GIS analysis to understand the impacts of hurricanes. This involves assessing potential hurricanes' likelihood and potential severity, considering factors like climate change and urban development.

3. **Risk Control:**

Strategies include retrofitting buildings and infrastructure, enhancing drainage systems, and implementing comprehensive evacuation plans. These measures aim to reduce the damage and disruption caused by hurricanes.

4. **Risk Financing and Claims Management:**

The state funds initiatives like the Hurricane Loss Mitigation Program, demonstrating an investment in risk control measures.

5. **Continuous Monitoring and Improvement:**

Florida continually updates its hazard mitigation strategies using the latest data and technology, ensuring the state remains prepared for future challenges.

Why is Risk Management Important in Florida?

1. **Protects Reputation and Economy:**

Effective risk management is crucial for maintaining Florida's reputation as a safe place to live and do business. Economically, risk management is essential to protect the economy and its ability to finance the state's infrastructure.

2. **Facilitates Decision Making:**

Informed decisions on land use, building codes, and emergency response are critical for minimizing hurricane impact.

3. **Ensures Regulatory Compliance:**

Adhering to federal and state guidelines for hurricane preparedness.

4. **Financial Stability:**

Florida can reduce the economic impact of these events by mitigating hurricane risks.

Florida's Hurricane Risk Management

The Challenge: Balancing Immediate Relief with Long-term Sustainability

The Florida Hurricane Catastrophe Fund (FHCF), established in November 1993, serves a critical role in the state's approach to managing the financial risks of hurricanes.[26] This tax-exempt state trust fund was created in response to the devastating impact of Hurricane Andrew, which caused over $15 billion in losses.[27]

---

[26] Florida Hurricane Catastrophe Fund: https://fhcf.sbafla.com/about-the-fhcf/#:~:text=The%20coverage%20provided%20by%20the,up%20to%20a%20maximum%20of%20payout.

[27] National Oceanic and Atmospheric Administration: "Hurricane Andrew: South Florida and Louisiana: August 23-26, 1992" https://repository.library.noaa.gov/view/noaa/7252

The fund's primary objective is to protect and advance Florida's interest in maintaining insurance capacity by providing reimbursements to insurers for a portion of their catastrophic hurricane losses.

The FHCF operates under the direction and control of the State Board of Administration (SBA) and is mandatory for all residential property insurance companies in Florida.

These companies are required to enter into a reimbursement contract with the FHCF. The coverage provided by FHCF is akin to private reinsurance (*insurance that an insurance company purchases to limit its risk by sharing some of its potential losses with other insurers*). Still, it typically comes at a lower cost than what is available in the private market. It covers a percentage of an insurance company's losses exceeding their retention level (like a deductible) up to a maximum payout.

Regarding funding, the FHCF is primarily supported by reimbursement premiums paid by participating insurers. It also generates funds from investment income, proceeds from pre-event bonding, recoveries from reinsurance and other risk-transfer transactions, and, in some situations, proceeds from post-event revenue bonds.

The fund is designed to be self-supporting, except in extraordinary circumstances, and does not rely on legislative appropriations for its operations.

As of 2023, the FHCF had an estimated $12.3 billion in claims-paying capacity,[28] which is vital for Florida's property-insurance system, especially in providing low-cost reinsurance.

The fund's maximum potential liability for claims is capped at $17 billion. After significant losses from Hurricane Ian, the fund projected to have about $3.7

---

[28] Florida Hurricane Catastrophe Fund – Financial Reports https://fhcf.sbafla.com/reports/

billion to pay claims in the upcoming year, supplemented by an estimated bonding capacity of $8.6 billion. The fund was estimated to have suffered a $10 billion loss from Hurricane Ian alone.

The establishment and operation of the FHCF underscore Florida's proactive approach to addressing the financial challenges posed by hurricanes, ensuring that insurance companies can meet their obligations to homeowners and maintain the state's economic stability in the face of these natural disasters.

For years, proposals have been discussed to temporarily adjust the Florida Hurricane Catastrophe Fund (FHCF), but they present a complex challenge.

The argument is that these proposed changes are designed to offer swift financial aid to insurance companies by easing the threshold for claiming reimbursements from the FHCF. Initially, this move may garner widespread support; insurance companies would welcome the relief, policyholders would appreciate the reinforced security of their insurers, and the state government would be lauded for its prompt action to stabilize the tumultuous insurance market.

However, the implementation of this temporary measure could lead to several unintended and potentially detrimental consequences:

1. **Increased Financial Burden on FHCF**:

The surge in claims resulting from the lowered retention levels, for example, could impose an unprecedented financial strain on FHCF. The fund might struggle to meet these unexpected demands, surpassing the initial projections established when the measure was implemented.

It should also be noted that (at the time of this writing), according to the FHCF's October 24, 2023, Claim-Paying Capacity Estimates Report (available at FHCF Report), the fund is currently more financially vulnerable than it has been since 2006.

Weakening its position or altering its operations (such as lowering the retention or eliminating the cash build-up factor) could be detrimental.

2. **Market Distortion**:

The intended short-term relief could inadvertently skew the insurance market. Tempted by the lowered retention levels, insurers might alter their risk models and pricing strategies, thereby shifting the market dynamics and increasing reliance on the FHCF. This reliance could undermine the fund's original purpose of serving as a safety net rather than a primary source of claims reimbursement.

3. **Dependency and Hardening Expectations**:

As this temporary measure expires, insurance companies and stakeholders might push for an extension. They could argue that the market remains unstable and that reverting to the original structure of the FHCF could be disastrous. Consequently, what was meant as a temporary fix might start to resemble a permanent solution.

4. **Challenges in Reversion**:

Returning to the original purpose of the FHCF could face resistance fueled by fears of market instability. The temporary adjustment, now deeply embedded in the operational frameworks of insurers and the expectations of policyholders, could prove challenging to retract.

5. **Long-Term Financial Risks**:

The escalated exposure of the FHCF raises concerns about its enduring viability and capacity to respond to future catastrophic events. This situation could trigger debates over the necessity for structural reforms and the introduction of additional financial safeguards.

In essence, what was conceived as a short-term, well-intentioned amendment to support the insurance market in the aftermath of a crisis could spiral into a complex issue with extensive implications. This underscores the intricate nature of policymaking, where temporary solutions can inadvertently pave the way for long-term challenges if not judiciously managed and monitored.

Ironically, the real crux of Florida's property insurance market issues isn't primarily catastrophic hurricanes but years of unbridled litigation. In 2022 and 2023, the legislature has aptly addressed this issue through significant legal changes.

Now, allowing time for these changes to manifest their intended effects is imperative. Altering the Cat Fund might be an answer, but perhaps to the wrong question.

Summary of Chapter 20:

In Chapter 20, I examine the multifaceted world of risk management in the context of Florida's vulnerability to catastrophic hurricanes. Drawing parallels with international events like the Christchurch earthquake and Japan's earthquake and tsunami, I underscore the importance of proactive risk mitigation strategies in safeguarding against the economic fallout of natural disasters.

The chapter outlines the Five Principles of Risk Management and their application to Florida's hurricane exposure. From risk identification to continuous monitoring and improvement, Florida's approach emphasizes preparedness, resilience, and informed decision-making.

I highlight the critical role of the Florida Hurricane Catastrophe Fund (FHCF) in managing the financial risks associated with hurricanes. Established in the aftermath of Hurricane Andrew, the FHCF serves as a vital safety net for insurers, ensuring their ability to meet obligations to homeowners and maintain economic stability.

However, I caution against the temptation to enact temporary adjustments to the FHCF in response to immediate crises. While such measures may offer short-term relief, they pose significant long-term risks, including increased financial burden, market distortion, and dependency.

Furthermore, I address the underlying issues plaguing Florida's property insurance market, emphasizing the need for structural reforms and the prudent implementation of legal changes to mitigate litigation-related challenges.

Chapter 20 underscores the importance of proactive risk management in building resilience against the inevitable storms that threaten Florida's prosperity. By embracing sound risk mitigation strategies and resisting short-term fixes, the state can navigate the complexities of hurricane exposure and emerge stronger in the face of adversity.

Transition to Chapter 21:

Having explored the intricacies of risk management in the face of Florida's catastrophic hurricane exposure let's turn our attention to a new way of referring to an old principle - "The Joseph Principle." Building on our deepened understanding of the market's complexities, we focus on how foresight and prudence, encapsulated in the Joseph Principle, can inform strategies to fortify Florida's insurance landscape against future uncertainties. This exploration offers a segue into the broader discussions of risk management and economic stability and underscores the importance of strategic planning in an ever-evolving insurance environment.

Chapter 21

The Joseph Principle: Navigating the Storms of Florida's Property Insurance Market

Joseph's ancient wisdom illuminates the path to resilience in a world of uncertainty. As Florida faces the tempests of natural disasters and the complexities of its insurance landscape, the Joseph Principle emerges as a beacon of hope, guiding insurers and policyholders alike through the trials of modern times. Discover how this timeless tale of foresight and preparedness holds the key to weathering the storms that lie ahead.

Prudence and Provision:

The Lesson of Joseph for Modern Insurance - A Florida Perspective

Introduction - The Timeless Tale of Joseph

Picture this: a young man, beloved by his father but betrayed by his brothers, sold into slavery, and cast into a foreign land. This is the story of Joseph, a tale that has echoed through the ages, from the pages of the Book of Genesis to the heart of Florida's property insurance industry.

You might wonder what an ancient biblical narrative possibly has to do with the complex world of insurance in the Sunshine State. As it turns out, everything. In Joseph's journey from prisoner to prophet, from forgotten son to savior of nations, lies a powerful lesson about the importance of foresight, prudence, and preparedness.

It's a lesson that resonates deeply in a state like Florida, where the forces of nature can strike with sudden and devastating fury. From the hurricane-battered coast of the Panhandle to the flood-prone streets of Miami, Floridians know all too well the importance of being prepared for the worst.

Yet, in the face of such challenges, the people of Florida have shown remarkable resilience, a determination to rebuild and recover no matter the odds. This spirit echoes the story of Joseph, a man who faced unimaginable adversity and yet emerged stronger, wiser, and more compassionate than before.

The Wisdom of Joseph - Building Reserves

Imagine the scene: Pharaoh, the mighty ruler of Egypt, haunted by a pair of perplexing dreams: seven lean cows devouring seven fat ones, seven withered ears of grain consuming seven healthy ones. Perplexed and troubled, Pharaoh seeks the counsel of a wise man, a prisoner with an uncanny gift for interpreting dreams. This man is Joseph, and his words will change the course of history.

With divine insight, Joseph reveals the meaning of Pharaoh's dreams: seven years of abundance will be followed by seven years of devastating famine. But Joseph doesn't stop there. He offers a solution, a plan so daring and visionary that it will save countless lives. Pharaoh must store a portion of the harvest during the plentiful years, building a reserve to sustain Egypt through the lean times ahead.

This, my friends, is the essence of the Joseph Principle: the wisdom of building reserves during times of plenty to weather the storms of adversity. And it is a lesson that Florida's property insurers have taken to heart.

Take the story of Florida Peninsula Insurance Company, a homegrown insurer that has navigated the tempests of the Sunshine State since 2005. When Hurricane Irma struck in 2017, Florida Peninsula's robust financial reserves allowed it to respond swiftly and effectively to over 15,000 claims, providing a lifeline to policyholders in their darkest hour (Florida Peninsula Insurance Company, 2018).

It's a testament to the power of prudence, to the wisdom of setting aside resources during good times to ensure survival during bad times. This principle extends far beyond the realm of insurance into the very fabric of our lives.

Think about it: how often do we neglect to save for a rainy day to build up our own personal reserves against the uncertainties of life? How often do we live for the moment without a thought for thinking about the future? The story of Joseph reminds us of the folly of such short-sightedness and the wisdom of planning ahead.

The Human Impact: Stories of Resilience

But the Joseph Principle is about more than just numbers and balance sheets. Behind every insurance policy lies a human story—a tale of individuals and families seeking protection and support amid life's uncertainties. For Floridians, insurance is more than a mere financial transaction; it promises resilience and a beacon of hope in times of crisis.

In the aftermath of Hurricane Michael in 2018, the story of Dina and George Soper showcased the crucial role of insurance in recovery. The Soper's, residents of Lynn Haven, Florida, saw their home severely damaged by the Category 5 storm. "If it wasn't for insurance, we wouldn't have been able to rebuild," Dina Soper told the Panama City News Herald. "It's been a long process, but we're finally getting back to normal" (Reeves, 2020)[29].

---

[29] Reeves, T. (2020, October 10). Two years after Hurricane Michael, Florida Panhandle residents still struggling to recover. Panama City News Herald. Retrieved from https://www.newsherald.com/story/news/2020/10/10/two-years-after-hurricane-michael-florida-panhandle-residents-still-struggling-recover/3635527001/

And then there's the story of Jeff and Kathy Faide, residents of Fort Myers Beach, Florida. Their story exemplifies insurance's vital role in the aftermath of a disaster. When Hurricane Ian made landfall in September 2022, the Faide's home was among the many damaged by the storm's fierce winds and flooding. "We lost everything on the first floor," Jeff told the Tampa Bay Times. "But we're thankful to be alive and to have insurance to help us rebuild." The Faides, like countless other Floridians, relied on their insurance coverage to begin the process of recovery and restoration. "It's going to be a tough road ahead, but we know we'll get through it with the help of our insurance and our community," Kathy added (Frago, 2022).

Stories like the Sopers and the Faides underscore the insurance industry's tangible, human impact in Florida. By embodying the principles of prudence and foresight exemplified by Joseph, insurers become more than just financial entities; they become guardians of dreams and enablers of resilience.

And they are not alone. Across the state, countless others have faced nature's fury with courage and determination. There's the story of the Robinsons, a family of four who huddled in their bathroom as Hurricane Michael tore the roof from their home. Or the tale of the Garcias, who waded through chest-deep water to escape the floods of Hurricane Irma.

These inspire us and remind us of the indomitable human spirit that lies at the heart of the Joseph Principle. They are the stories of ordinary people facing extraordinary circumstances and emerging stronger, more resilient, and more united than ever before.

Navigating the Challenges: Fraud and Climate Change

But the path to resilience is never easy, and Florida's insurers must navigate a perilous landscape of fraud and climate change. This complex web of challenges includes the increasing frequency and severity of natural disasters and the ever-present specter of fraud.

Insurance fraud has been a scourge on the industry. A 2020 report by the Florida Association of Public Insurance Adjusters found that fraudulent claims related to Assignments of Benefits (AOB) increased by 70% between 2017 and 2019, costing insurers an estimated $1.6 billion (FAPIA, 2020).

In response, insurers have had to develop sophisticated fraud detection systems, leveraging advanced data analytics and artificial intelligence to identify and prevent fraudulent activities. This problem costs insurers billions of dollars each year and drives up premiums for honest policyholders.

Take the example of artificial intelligence, which is used to detect fraudulent behavior patterns and flag suspicious claims. Or using drones and satellite imagery to assess damage and verify the legitimacy of claims. These are just a few of the tools in the modern insurer's arsenal, tools that are helping to level the playing field.

And then there's the specter of climate change, looming on the horizon like a gathering storm. A 2020 study by the First Street Foundation projected that the number of Florida properties at risk of flooding will increase by 69% over the next 30 years due to sea-level rise (First Street Foundation, 2020)[30].

As sea levels rise, hurricanes intensify, and flooding becomes more frequent, Florida's insurers must continually refine their risk models and pricing strategies. Some companies are exploring innovative solutions, such as parametric insurance, which ties payouts to specific, measurable events rather than actual damages.

---

[30] First Street Foundation. (2020). The First National Flood Risk Assessment: Defining America's Growing Risk. Retrieved from https://assets.firststreet.org/uploads/2020/06/first_street_foundation__first_national_flood_risk_assessment.pdf

Others invest in resilient infrastructure, such as storm-resistant buildings and flood-control systems. Still, others are working with policymakers and community leaders to develop comprehensive plans for mitigating the impacts of climate change.

It's a multifaceted approach, one that recognizes the complexity and urgency of the challenge before us. It draws inspiration from the story of Joseph, who faced the impending famine with a bold and visionary plan that saved countless lives.

The Regulatory Landscape: Balancing Protection and Innovation

Amidst these challenges, Florida's insurers must also navigate a complex regulatory landscape that seeks to balance consumer protection with market stability. This delicate dance requires a keen understanding of the law and a willingness to adapt to changing circumstances. However, these regulations can sometimes create unintended consequences.

For instance, Florida Statute 627.0629(1)(b) requires property insurers to notify policyholders if their renewal premium is set to increase by more than 10% for any reason (The 2022 Florida Statutes, 2022)[31]. This provision, while intended to promote transparency and consumer protection, can sometimes hinder insurers' ability to adjust prices in response to changing risk profiles.

Similarly, the "assignment of benefits" (*a practice where a policyholder transfers their insurance claim rights to a third party, typically a contractor or service provider*) law, while intended to streamline the claims process, has led to a proliferation of fraudulent claims and litigation, driving up costs for both insurers and policyholders.

---

[31] The 2022 Florida Statutes. (2022). Chapter 627: Insurance Rates and Contracts. Retrieved from http://www.leg.state.fl.us/statutes/index.cfm?App_mode=Display_Statute&URL=0600-0699/0627/Sections/0627.0629.html

In 2019, the Florida Legislature passed HB 7065, a bill to curb AOB abuse and reduce frivolous litigation. The bill introduced several key reforms, including limiting attorney fees and requiring written notice before filing a lawsuit (Florida House of Representatives, 2019)[32]. It was a hard-fought victory for insurers, requiring months of lobbying and negotiation. But it was also a reminder of the vital role that policymakers play in shaping the industry's future.

While the long-term impact of these changes remains to be seen, they represent a step towards balancing consumer protection with market stability.

At the same time, regulators are grappling with the rapid pace of technological change as insurtech startups and established players alike seek to innovate and disrupt the traditional insurance model. It's a balancing act that requires a nimble and forward-thinking approach to regulation.

On the one hand, regulators must ensure that consumers are protected from fraud and abuse and that insurers are held to the highest standards of transparency and accountability. On the other hand, they must create a regulatory environment that encourages innovation and allows insurers to adapt to changing market conditions.

It's a challenge that requires collaboration and communication between insurers, regulators, and policymakers. It's a challenge that draws inspiration from the story of Joseph, who worked closely with Pharaoh to implement a plan that balanced the people's needs with the realities of the impending famine.

The Future of Insurance: Personalization and Insurtech

As we gaze into the crystal ball of Florida's insurance future, we see a world of endless possibilities. With the rise of smart home technologies, telematics, and big

---

[32] Florida House of Representatives. (2019). HB 7065 - Insurance Assignment Agreements. Retrieved from https://www.myfloridahouse.gov/Sections/Bills/billsdetail.aspx?BillId=66380

data, insurers are poised to offer more personalized, usage-based products that reflect the unique needs and risk profiles of each policyholder.

Imagine a world where your insurance premiums are based not on broad demographic categories but on your individual behavior and lifestyle. Your smart home sensors can detect a leak before it becomes a flood, and your insurance company can dispatch a repair crew before you even know there's a problem.

This is the world of Insurtech, where technology and insurance collide to create something entirely new. It's a world of sleek apps, chatbots, artificial intelligence, and machine learning. And it's a world that is already taking shape, with companies like Honey Quote using satellite imagery and AI to provide personalized flood insurance quotes (Gallin, 2020)[33].

But Insurtech is about more than just cool gadgets and cutting-edge algorithms. It's about fundamentally reimagining the relationship between insurers and policyholders, creating a more transparent, collaborative, and customer-centric insurance experience.

In this brave new world, insurers are not just financial safety nets but true partners in risk management and loss prevention. They are trusted advisors, helping policyholders navigate the complexities of an ever-changing risk landscape. And they are innovators, constantly pushing the boundaries of what's possible and finding new ways to deliver value to their customers.

It's a vision that draws inspiration from the story of Joseph, who used his wisdom and foresight to not just survive the famine but thrive in its aftermath. It's a vision

---

[33] Gallin, J. (2020, November 10). This insurtech startup is using AI to lower your flood insurance rates. Forbes. Retrieved from https://www.forbes.com/sites/joshgallin/2020/11/10/this-insurtech-startup-is-using-ai-to-lower-your-flood-insurance-rates/?sh=7c4b8f5f6f1a

that has the power to transform the insurance industry as we know it, creating a more resilient, more sustainable, and more customer-centric future for us all.

Conclusion

As we come to the end of our journey, we find ourselves back where we started, with the story of Joseph. In this ancient tale of foresight and resilience, we find a timeless lesson for Florida's property insurers.

Like Joseph, insurers must be wise and prudent, building reserves during times of plenty to weather the storms of adversity. They must be vigilant and adaptable, navigating the treacherous waters of fraud and climate change. And they must be creative and innovative, embracing new technologies and ways of thinking to meet the challenges of tomorrow.

But most of all, they must never lose sight of the human stories that lie at the heart of their work. For in the end, insurance is about more than just policies and premiums. It's about the resilience of the human spirit, the power of community, and the unshakable belief that, together, we can weather any storm.

So let us take inspiration from the story of Joseph, and from the stories of countless Floridians who have faced the tempests of life with courage and determination. Let us build a future where every policyholder can sleep soundly, knowing that they are protected by the wisdom and foresight of their insurers.

In this way, we can all become part of the Joseph Principle, part of a timeless legacy of resilience and hope that will endure long after the storms have passed. In doing so, we can create a brighter, more resilient future for ourselves, our communities, and future generations.

Summary of Chapter 21:

Chapter 21 introduces the timeless tale of Joseph, drawing parallels between his journey of foresight and resilience and the challenges faced by Florida's property insurance market. It begins by contextualizing the significance of Joseph's story within the modern insurance landscape, highlighting the relevance of his principles of prudence, provision, and preparedness.

The chapter explores the wisdom of Joseph's approach to building reserves during times of plenty, drawing parallels with the importance of financial stability and risk management for insurers in Florida. Through examples like Florida Peninsula Insurance Company, the chapter illustrates how robust reserves enable insurers to respond effectively to disasters, providing a lifeline to policyholders in their time of need.

Moving beyond financial considerations, the chapter delves into the human impact of insurance, recounting stories of resilience and recovery in the aftermath of natural disasters. Through the experiences of families like the Sopers and the Faides, the chapter underscores the tangible, human impact of insurance, emphasizing its role as a beacon of hope amidst adversity.

However, the path to resilience is fraught with challenges, including the specter of fraud and the looming threat of climate change. The chapter examines the industry's efforts to combat fraud through advanced analytics and artificial intelligence, highlighting the role of technology in leveling the playing field.

Moreover, it confronts the urgent imperative of addressing climate change, exploring innovative solutions such as parametric insurance and resilient infrastructure. By drawing inspiration from Joseph's visionary approach to crisis management, insurers in Florida are striving to adapt and innovate in the face of evolving risks.

Amidst these challenges, the chapter navigates the complexities of the regulatory landscape, balancing consumer protection with market stability. It examines key legislative reforms like HB 7065 and the regulatory implications of technological disruption, emphasizing the need for collaboration and adaptability in shaping the industry's future.

Looking ahead, the chapter envisions a future of personalized, technology-driven insurance products that reflect policyholders' unique needs. Drawing inspiration from the story of Joseph, insurers are reimagining their role as trusted advisors and innovators, fostering a more resilient and customer-centric insurance experience.

In conclusion, Chapter 21 calls upon insurers to embrace the timeless legacy of the Joseph Principle, embodying the values of foresight, prudence, and resilience in their pursuit of a brighter future. By learning from the wisdom of the past and confronting the challenges of the present, insurers can navigate the storms of uncertainty with confidence, ensuring a legacy of protection and hope for future generations.

Chapter 22

Hurricane Models: Imperfect Yet Indispensable Tools in Risk Management

Florida, a state perennially dancing on the razor's edge with nature's fury, finds a beacon of hope in the science of hurricane catastrophe modeling. This field, perpetually evolving against a backdrop of technological advancement and climatic unpredictability, provides a crucial tool for understanding and mitigating the impact of hurricanes.

These models, scientific and mathematical tools, help insurers, regulators, and rating agencies evaluate risk. Likewise, reinsurers—insurance providers for insurance companies—are also subject to assessment and evaluation by these entities. Catastrophe risk is measured, often with the help of various models, and stress and scenario testing are performed to ensure solvency in the face of unexpected loss events.

However, several significant consequences can emerge when political considerations override scientific evidence and suppress adequate rate-setting.

Firstly, insurers may be forced to underprice the risk associated with specific policies, leading to inadequate reserves for covering losses, especially in areas prone to natural disasters. This underpricing increases the risk of insolvency for insurance companies, as they may lack sufficient funds to cover large-scale claims following catastrophic events.

Additionally, insurers might withdraw from markets where they cannot charge rates commensurate with the risk, leading to a scarcity of insurance options for consumers in high-risk areas. In such scenarios, low-risk policyholders might end up subsidizing the premiums of high-risk policyholders due to artificial rate suppression.

This situation could necessitate government intervention, resulting in state-backed insurance pools or other mechanisms at a significant cost to taxpayers.

Adverse selection, where higher-risk individuals are more likely to purchase insurance than lower-risk individuals, can further exacerbate insurers' financial strain.

Property values may decline when insurance becomes unaffordable or unavailable, discouraging new development or encouraging development in less risky areas, impacting local economies.

Additionally, if primary insurers are not collecting adequate premiums, reinsurers may become reluctant to underwrite certain risks, compounding availability and affordability issues in the insurance market.

Consequently, the financial burden of disaster relief often falls more heavily on government resources, leading to increased public spending and strain on government budgets, especially following major disaster events.

These consequences highlight the delicate balance between political considerations and the economic realities of risk management in the insurance industry, underscoring the importance of allowing insurers to set rates that accurately reflect risk to ensure financial stability and availability of coverage in the market.

While hurricane catastrophe models and chemotherapy remain imperfect, they are based on the best current science. Disregarding the most up-to-date science, whether in the context of chemotherapy or hurricane catastrophe modeling, is nonsensical.

Lookout - I See a Rabbit Chase Coming Up

Sometimes, policymakers struggle with conflicting beliefs when crafting insurance legislation, resulting in actions that don't align with intentions. These situations often result in unintended consequences. Here's a story to illustrate this point.

When insurance regulation reforms are the subject of legislative debate, lawmakers often find themselves trapped in the tricky space between doing what's right and appeasing their constituents. We all know that hurricanes and stubborn human behavior are major problems, yet legislators can't resist tinkering with regulatory laws to show they're taking action. However, this often leads to what psychologists' call "cognitive dissonance," a term for the discomfort experienced when holding two conflicting beliefs or desires.

This image of the vintage car and the bedraggled chicken captures that sense of indecision perfectly. Legislators know they need to go right—to create sensible, long-term solutions for mitigating hurricane risk. But as the political car veers left, influenced by the demands and pressures of politics, they find themselves stuck in the muddy road of mixed intentions.

Picture a policy meeting where legislators are ready to discuss bold reforms to stabilize insurance rates and help homeowners weather future storms. But as the conversation deepens, familiar political pressures come into play. One lawmaker argues for keeping rates low, while another pushes for stricter building standards to reduce hurricane damage. Meanwhile, others clamor to safeguard constituents from immediate rate hikes, leading to a convoluted tangle of proposals that ultimately results in more regulations and less clarity.

In the end, they wind up making compromises that try to go both ways but satisfy neither side fully. The legislation becomes a patchwork of half-measures, a result of cognitive dissonance that leaves insurers and homeowners equally frustrated. The lawmakers want to do the right thing, but political pressure keeps pulling them left—toward short-term fixes that may win favor with voters but fail to address the underlying problems.

The bedraggled chicken illustrates the effect of cognitive dissonance on these policies. It's like trying to navigate a vintage car that has its wheels pointed in two directions at once. The result? A wobbly journey that leaves everyone involved feeling disoriented and a little worse for wear.

In the end, it's not just a matter of legislative intentions or political will. True reform requires a recognition of this cognitive dissonance and a willingness to stay the course in spite of competing interests. Lawmakers must resist the urge to let the car steer them into the potholes of expedience and instead focus on crafting long-term, effective insurance policies that will truly protect constituents, even if the political journey is a little rocky.

This illustrates how cognitive dissonance leads us down the wrong path when policy changes don't address the root problems or align with initial goals. As we work to create a healthier insurance market, it's crucial that we maintain our focus on crafting practical solutions based on a clear understanding of the challenges, free from external pressures. Let's now return to exploring specific ways to ensure our insurance strategies align with the ultimate objective of market stability."

That Wasn't a Rabbit Chase at all – it was a Plucked Chicken Chase
Back to our Narrative

The following discussion spans various models, each contributing uniquely to our understanding of these natural phenomena.

The Florida Public Hurricane Loss Model (FPHLM) stands out for its comprehensive approach. It integrates meteorological data with structural engineering and financial assessments to accurately predict hurricane impacts.

Moody's RMS North Atlantic Hurricane Models leverage recent hurricane data to enhance predictive accuracy and risk assessment.

AIR Worldwide's Hurricane Model emphasizes consistent catastrophe modeling standards and offers robust risk management tools in the Florida insurance landscape.

ARA's HurLoss Model incorporates climate-conditioned perspectives, acknowledging the evolving nature of hurricane threats in a changing climate.

The field grapples with balancing the complexity of scientific models against their practical application. The intersection of political influence and scientific accuracy complicates policymaking and insurance practices.

Hurricane models significantly influence policy decisions, shaping insurance rates, building codes, and informing emergency preparedness strategies. They are pivotal in the public and private sector's response to hurricane risks.

Catastrophe models are instrumental in risk assessment, underwriting (*the process of evaluating the risks involved in insuring a person or asset and determining appropriate premium rates*), and strategic decision-making in insurance. They provide a framework for understanding potential loss scenarios, aiding in developing more resilient insurance products and policies.

Research indicates a trend toward integrating AI and machine learning in hurricane modeling. This evolution promises more accurate, real-time predictions, transforming disaster management strategies not just in Florida but globally.

In conclusion, catastrophe models are not flawless, but their significance should not be understated. Like chemotherapy in cancer treatment—imperfect yet indispensable—hurricane models are crucial in our fight against natural disasters. They provide a foundation for informed decision-making, ultimately safeguarding lives, and properties.

As we navigate an era marked by climatic uncertainties, these models are testaments to human ingenuity and adaptability.

Summary of Chapter 22:

In Chapter 22, I illuminate the pivotal role of hurricane catastrophe models in Florida's ongoing battle against nature's fury. These models serve as indispensable tools for insurers, regulators, and policymakers, enabling them to evaluate risk, enhance resilience, and inform strategic decision-making.

The chapter begins by underscoring the consequences of political considerations overriding scientific evidence in rate-setting, leading to underpricing of risk and inadequate reserves for insurers. This imbalance can result in insolvency, market withdrawal, and scarcity of insurance options, ultimately burdening taxpayers and straining government resources.

Against this backdrop, I delve into the landscape of hurricane catastrophe models, highlighting their diverse methodologies and contributions to risk assessment. From the comprehensive approach of the Florida Public Hurricane Loss Model to the predictive accuracy of Moody's RMS North Atlantic Hurricane Models, each model offers unique insights into hurricane impacts and risk management strategies.

I emphasize the evolving nature of catastrophe modeling, with a trend toward integrating AI and machine learning for more accurate predictions and real-time insights. This technological evolution promises to revolutionize disaster management strategies not only in Florida but globally, enhancing our ability to safeguard lives and properties in the face of climatic uncertainties.

In conclusion, I underscore the indispensability of catastrophe models in our fight against natural disasters, likening them to chemotherapy in cancer treatment—imperfect yet indispensable. As we navigate the challenges of an increasingly unpredictable climate, these models stand as testaments to human ingenuity and adaptability, guiding us toward a more resilient future.

Transition to Chapter 23:

Have you ever considered the thin line between taking risks and being reckless? Well, "Gambling vs Insurance" has some thoughts on that – and spoiler alert, it's quite a balancing act. We'll see how living in Hurricane Alley is a bit like playing poker against Mother Nature – sometimes you hold 'em, sometimes you fold 'em, and sometimes you wonder why you sat down to play in the first place.

Chapter 23

Gambling vs Insurance

Imagine if life were a casino, where every sunrise brought the shuffle of cards or the spin of a roulette wheel. In this grand casino, gambling, and insurance sit at opposite ends of the vast floor, playing entirely different games under the same dazzling lights.

Gambling, our first player, is the bold risk-taker, always chasing the thrill of the unknown. Picture it as the high roller rolling dice on a craps table, where each throw is a flirtation with fortune.

Gambling creates a risk where none existed, like deciding to cross a busy highway blindfolded for the chance of finding a $100 bill on the other side. It's the financial equivalent of seeking treasure in a dragon's lair, where the dragon is just as likely to incinerate you as to let you leave with gold.

We find Insurance, the prudent protector, at the other end of the floor. Imagine insurance as a thoughtful chess player, carefully planning each move with foresight and strategy.

Insurance steps in like a superhero, caped in actuarial data, swooping down to shield you from the fiery breath of life's dragons—be it illness, accident, or natural disaster. Rather than seeking a thrill, it's about installing a safety net beneath your tightrope, ensuring that if you slip, you won't plummet into financial despair.

While gambling relies on luck and often ends in tales of "what could have been," insurance is grounded in the mathematics of probability and the certainty of "what is." It's akin to the difference between betting on a horse because you like its name and wearing a helmet because you know the ground is hard.

The humor in comparing the two comes from imagining insurance as the responsible adult at a Vegas bachelor party, constantly reminding everyone to drink water and keep track of their hotel key, while gambling is the friend egging you on to bet it all on black because "what happens in Vegas..."

Yet, despite their differences, gambling, and insurance are fascinated with the future's uncertainty. One revels in its unpredictability, while the other seeks to master it for our peace of mind.

The Social and Economic Impact of Pathological Gambling

The negative impacts of gambling extend far beyond the individual, affecting both society and the economy in profound ways.

Research into the social and economic effects of pathological gambling highlights several key areas of concern, including employment costs, bad debts, criminal justice system costs, therapy costs, and welfare costs.

For instance, the annual cost of lost working hours due to gambling is estimated to be substantial per problem gambler, with additional significant costs attributed to unemployment compensation, bad debts associated with bankruptcy proceedings, and criminal justice expenses.

These estimates underscore the broad financial implications of gambling on individuals and society.[34]

Moreover, the personal and social health outcomes related to gambling are alarming. Gambling disorder is associated with increased mortality, suicidality, and a range of comorbid conditions, indicating a significant public health concern.

Studies have linked problem gambling to a higher risk of suicide, highlighting the severe mental health implications for affected individuals. This evidence suggests that gambling disorders not only have a financial impact but also profoundly affect individuals' psychological and physical health, leading to a decrease in quality of life and even life-threatening situations.[35]

These findings are critical for understanding the full scope of gambling's impact and underscore the necessity for effective intervention strategies to mitigate these adverse outcomes. The research suggests a need for a more comprehensive approach to gambling regulation and support services for those affected by

---

[34] https://www.ncbi.nlm.nih.gov/books/NBK230628/

[35] https://www.nature.com/articles/s41562-020-01045-w

gambling disorders, highlighting the importance of addressing this issue not just from an individual perspective but as a significant societal challenge.

The Social and Economic Impact of Insurance

The insurance industry fosters positive personal, social, and economic impacts, addresses a broad spectrum of societal challenges, and offers tangible benefits beyond financial protection.

Research and analyses highlight the multifaceted ways in which insurance contributes to societal well-being and economic stability.

Insurance companies are uniquely positioned to address social issues through financial inclusion and the promotion of economic well-being. By embracing these roles, insurers can generate significant business benefits, including increased revenue, improved shareholder returns, higher employee morale, and a more substantial, more trusted brand reputation.

The approach involves prioritizing social initiatives that align with the company's overall strategy, establishing clear accountability, empowering businesses to act on these initiatives, tailoring projects to the needs of local markets and customers, and measuring and reporting progress.

This strategic focus on social impact not only addresses the growing societal challenges but also presents a substantial opportunity for insurers to do well by doing good, as highlighted by Boston Consulting Group's survey, which shows many insurers recognizing the reputational benefits of addressing social issues, with many still exploring how to quantify the business value of their programs

The concept of "impact underwriting" further illustrates how the insurance industry can contribute positively to society while pursuing business opportunities. Impact underwriting involves creating insurance products that provide financial protection and contribute to societal goals, such as mitigating the effects of climate change, supporting renewable energy investments, and promoting sustainable lifestyles.

This approach offers a "double dividend" by generating revenue in a growing market and realizing positive societal externalities, such as reducing the physical and transition risks associated with environmental challenges and supporting the transition to sustainable energy and mobility solutions.

Furthermore, tackling social challenges can unlock vast, untapped growth opportunities for insurance companies. Initiatives that address these challenges can lead to the creation of shared value, benefiting both the insurers and the broader community.

By finding the business case in addressing social issues, insurance companies can build success stories that contribute to social well-being and economic stability, setting examples for how the industry can play a transformative role in promoting health, equity, and environmental sustainability.[36]

In summary, the insurance industry's engagement in social impact initiatives and sustainable underwriting (*the process of evaluating the risks involved in insuring a person or asset and determining appropriate premium rates*) practices represents a significant avenue for promoting financial inclusion, enhancing economic well-being, and contributing to environmental and societal resilience.

These efforts help mitigate risks, address global challenges, and open new avenues for business growth and innovation, demonstrating insurance's decisive role in shaping a more sustainable and equitable future.

---

[36] https://www.fsg.org/blog/insurance-social-impact-and-profit/

Balancing Risk: Lessons from Gambling for Hurricane Risk Management

In view of the well documented negative societal impacts of gambling, why would policymakers ever consider embracing the element of risk, akin to gambling, when devising strategies to combat the formidable force of hurricanes? This question strikes at the heart of a paradox that unfolds within the realm of policymaking, particularly when confronting natural disasters.

Our previous discussion sheds light on the dire consequences of pathological gambling, illustrating not just its individual toll but its broader societal and economic fallout. It articulates how gambling's repercussions ripple through various facets of society, from inflating employment costs to straining the criminal justice system. The stark revelations about gambling's linkage to severe mental health outcomes, including an elevated suicide risk, add layers to the urgency for comprehensive regulation and intervention.

Drawing parallels between the risks associated with gambling and those entailed in hurricane risk management, one can't help but ponder: If the hazards of gambling, a largely controllable human activity, are so profound, why would policymakers entertain similar risks in the high-stakes arena of hurricane preparedness?

The answer might lie in the nuanced nature of risk itself. In the context of hurricanes, risk management involves a delicate balance between risk avoidance, mitigation, and transfer. Unlike gambling, where risk is often unnecessary and predominantly negative, the calculated risks in hurricane strategies are a form of proactive engagement with uncertainty. Here, policymakers weigh the potential costs and benefits, aiming to minimize losses while optimizing resource allocation.

Moreover, the concept of risk retention in hurricane strategies might stem from the pragmatic acknowledgment that not all risks can be eliminated. Instead, they must be managed judiciously, with contingency plans in place. This approach does not glorify risk-taking but recognizes it as an inherent aspect of dealing with unpredictable natural phenomena.

In conclusion, while the negative impacts of gambling serve as a cautionary tale about the perils of unchecked risk, the strategic embrace of risk in hurricane management reflects a nuanced acknowledgment of its inevitability. Policymakers are tasked with the complex challenge of distinguishing between unnecessary, detrimental risk-taking and essential, calculated risks that strive to safeguard communities against the ravages of nature.

As a former state representative known for addressing complex issues with nuanced understanding, particularly in the realm of insurance and risk management, I recognize the critical importance of informed, thoughtful policymaking in this domain. The lessons learned from the study of gambling's impacts can indeed inform broader policy decisions, guiding us toward strategies that mitigate risk without succumbing to its temptations.

In the grand scheme of things, gambling might win you a fortune, but insurance ensures you won't lose everything chasing it.

As we wrap up this exploration, remember in the casino of life, it's wise to know when to bet and when to insure. Just as car insurance is not meant for intentional damage, like in a demolition derby, relying on superstition rather than proper insurance is ineffective in protecting your home from hurricanes. The distinction is as clear as the difference between playing to win and playing not to lose.

As we look to the horizon, let's watch how technology and innovation continue to shuffle the deck of risk management. In this ever-evolving game, the only sure bet is that understanding the rules will always be your best strategy.

Summary of Chapter 23:

In Chapter 23, I discuss the fascinating dichotomy between gambling and insurance, two distinct approaches to navigating life's uncertainties. I liken gambling to the thrill-seeking venture of a high-stakes casino player, while insurance emerges as the prudent protector, offering a safety net against life's unpredictable twists and turns.

Through vivid analogies and insightful comparisons, I illuminate the stark differences between gambling and insurance, showcasing how each approach embodies a unique philosophy towards risk. While gambling thrives on chance and the allure of fortune, insurance operates on principles of probability and foresight, providing a shield against financial ruin.

The chapter delves into the profound societal and economic impacts of gambling, highlighting its adverse effects on individuals, communities, and economies. From employment costs to mental health implications, the repercussions of pathological gambling are far-reaching, underscoring the urgent need for comprehensive regulation and intervention.

In contrast, insurance emerges as a force for social good, fostering financial inclusion, economic stability, and societal resilience. By embracing impact underwriting and social impact initiatives, insurance companies can not only protect against financial risks but also address pressing social challenges, contributing to a more equitable and sustainable future.

Drawing parallels between the risks inherent in gambling and those involved in hurricane risk management, I explore the nuanced nature of risk in policymaking. While gambling epitomizes unnecessary risk-taking, hurricane risk management embodies a calculated approach to uncertainty, aiming to minimize losses and safeguard communities against natural disasters.

As a former state representative deeply versed in insurance and risk management issues, I underscore the critical importance of informed policymaking in navigating the complexities of risk. By learning from the lessons of gambling's impacts, policymakers can devise strategies that mitigate risk without succumbing to its pitfalls, ensuring the well-being of individuals and communities alike.

In conclusion, the chapter emphasizes the importance of understanding the distinctions between gambling and insurance, reminding us that in the casino of life, strategic risk management is key. As technology and innovation continue to shape the landscape of risk management, it is essential to grasp the rules of the game and make informed decisions that protect against life's uncertainties.

Transition to Chapter 24:

With our heads still spinning from the gambling table, it's time to get honest about those storms we just can't seem to quit. "The Comedy of Stubborn Human Behavior: Insights into Florida's Property Insurance Market" isn't just a fancy title – it's a look at how we keep building our sandcastles even though we know the tide's coming in. There's a bit of humor, a dash of stubbornness, and a whole lot of truth about what happens when we ignore the writing on the weather radar.

Chapter 24

The Comedy of Stubborn Human Behavior:

Insights into Florida's Property Insurance Market

It is a scarcely acknowledged truth that we, the high-minded citizens of Western Cultures, tend to dance around the symptoms of our problems rather than confront the root cause(s) head-on. This peculiar dance is akin to attempting to tiptoe through a hurricane, naively hoping to remain dry.

This weakness for skirting around the issues extends its tendrils into various facets of our society, including the mirthful realm of "Public Policy." And so, dear reader, we waltz into the heart of our tale - the Florida property insurance market. In 2007, Florida's leaders, bless their hearts, with the very best of intentions, crafted a solution (HB1A) to the wrong problem (high homeowners' premiums). It's akin to George Burns trying to win an Oscar by singing instead of acting - noble but misguided.

So, if high homeowners' premiums are not the heart of the hurricane, what is? The problem, dear friends, is threefold: 1) the severity of hurricanes, which, unlike George Bernard Shaw, do not gracefully age; 2) stubborn human behavior, which insists on building castles on the sand; and 3) excessive litigation, a sport more beloved in Florida than croquet at a garden party.

We all pay more than a jester's ransom to shield our abodes from hurricanes. Yet, the price of our insurance is merely the tip of the iceberg, with the Titanic-sized problem being Florida's prodigious vulnerability to hurricanes. Until we can tame these tempestuous beasts, we're simply performing a rain dance in a monsoon.

 Each "solution" attempting to treat the hurricane problem as an insurance conundrum is doomed as a Shakespearean tragedy. High insurance rates are the mere symptoms. The true protagonist in this drama is the severity of hurricanes, coupled with our obstinate behavior of building in hurricane-prone zones while expecting to pass the bill like a hot potato to someone else – now that's the plot twist!

In the wise words of one of my favorite quips, "It's difficult to leave footprints in the sand when you're sitting on your butt. And who wants to leave butt prints in the sand?" In other words, unless we take action to mitigate the high cost of hurricanes, we'll find ourselves with nothing but an expensive, sandy mess.

When it comes to the stubborn human behavior in the face of these meteorological monsters, it's as if Florida has become America's prime stage for a performance of catastrophic proportions. If a hurricane were to audition for a role on the eastern coast of the USA, there's a 41% chance it would land a starring role in Florida.[37] The stakes are high and rising, like the plot of a gripping novel.

According to AIR Worldwide, the total value of insured coastal exposure in Florida in 2018 was a staggering $3.6 trillion, representing a $733B increase since 2012 (up 25.6%). Florida's coastal exposure was more bloated than the collective

---

[37] https://www.statista.com/statistics/1269483/number-of-hurricanes-that-made-landfall-in-the-us-state/

egos at a Hollywood after-party, $1439B larger than that of Texas, Louisiana, Mississippi, and Alabama combined.[38]

The situation, as dramatic as a soap opera, has escalated even further. A report by Insurance Business America reveals that as of 2023, Florida's insurance market faces significant challenges, with insurers retreating faster than bashful suitors from high-risk areas. This retreat leads to a dwindling number of coverage options and a surge in property insurance rates, predicted to skyrocket by as much as 40% in 2023.

It's like watching the plot thicken in a mystery novel, but the mystery is how much more one will have to pay to live in paradise.

Furthermore, recent events, like the star-studded cast of a disaster movie, have spotlighted the volatile nature of Florida's property insurance exposure. Take Hurricane Idalia, for instance, which placed Citizens Property Insurance Corp. in a dangerous spotlight with around 190,700 policies in eight coastal counties facing potential exposure of $72B.[39]

This figure, mind you, is just a slice of the hurricane pie, with counties like Lee and Pinellas facing storm surge threats to homes valued at a jaw-dropping $83.7B and $49.4B, respectively. The overall property insurance exposure during this event surpassed $238B, a stark reminder of the escalating drama and potential for damage in the Sunshine State.[40]

---

[38] https://www.air-worldwide.com/press-releases/air-worldwide-estimates-insured-value-of-u-s--coastal-properties-continues-to-grow/
[39] https://www.citizensfla.com/news/citizens-prepares-for-hurricane-idalia-urges-policyholders-to-be-ready
[40] https://www.corelogic.com/intelligence/corelogic-2023-hurricane-report-reveals-nearly-8-million-homes-and-over-2-trillion-at-risk-from-damaging-winds/

Even more alarming is that Florida's insured coastal exposure, as a percentage of statewide-insured exposure, was 79% more than any other state in 2018.[41] According to the University of Florida Bureau of Economic and Business Research, Florida will continue adding millions of new residents in the coming years, further straining the state's fragile property insurance market.[42]

Managing catastrophe risk requires financial discipline and careful planning. Otherwise, it's easy to fall into the trap of accumulating debt with dire consequences.

Early in my professional career, while working for the First National Bank of DeFuniak Springs, I often overheard the advice my boss, the bank president, gave to prospective borrowers: "You can't drink yourself sober, and you can't spend yourself out of debt." That wisdom had a clear application when someone was on the verge of incurring more debt than they could afford to repay.

I've never forgotten those words, and over the years, that sage advice often resurfaced in my mind, especially during debates over public policy relating to homeowners' insurance. Every time the topic of debt-financed catastrophe risk came up, I would share this quote with my colleagues. It became my way of emphasizing that debt is a precarious way to manage the financial fallout from catastrophic events like hurricanes.

Picture this: a legislative session where we're all earnestly discussing solutions to keep homeowners' insurance rates reasonable. One policy proposal suggested addressing hurricane losses through borrowing via the Florida Hurricane Catastrophe Fund (FHCF). I leaned over to a fellow legislator and said, "You

---

[41] https://www.air-worldwide.com/press-releases/air-worldwide-estimates-insured-value-of-u-s--coastal-properties-continues-to-grow/
[42] https://www.bebr.ufl.edu/population/publications/projections-florida-population-county-2025-2050-estimates-2022

know, borrowing money to pay for hurricane losses is like trying to drink yourself sober after a three-day bender—it just doesn't work."

He laughed, nodding in agreement. "True, but politics wins over sobriety every time."

But that was precisely the issue. Despite good intentions, relying on debt to cover catastrophe risk creates a shaky financial stool—much like sitting on a two-legged chair after one too many drinks. The FHCF's initial goal was to help manage excess losses by maintaining a pool of funds to backstop insurers after a storm. But over time, it became the go-to solution for covering shortfalls, leading to ballooning debt obligations that could easily collapse the entire system if a string of major hurricanes struck.

I remember one instance vividly when a policy debate raged on for hours over whether increasing borrowing limits was the best solution to handle future storms. Finally, one lawmaker stood up and quipped, "If we don't address the debt problem now, we might as well start printing money and pray that the next hurricane season forgets Florida exists!"

Though the comment was made in jest, it struck a chord. The reality is that debt can make the whole system wobbly, threatening to leave homeowners and insurers in the lurch. It's a dangerous game, relying on borrowing to cover catastrophe risk, because ultimately, those debts have to be repaid.

Managing catastrophe risk requires a steady hand, a realistic understanding of financial resources, and strategic planning that involves more than quick fixes. Lawmakers and insurers must heed that old advice from my banking days: "You can't drink yourself sober, and you can't spend yourself out of debt." Crafting equitable insurance strategies should involve a more sustainable approach that recognizes the limits of debt-financing.

After all, you wouldn't try to prop up a two-legged stool, would you?

This principle holds particularly true when considering how to fund insurance companies after natural disasters. Just like a heavy drinker can't sober up by consuming more alcohol, relying on excessive borrowing to manage catastrophe risk will only make matters worse. Instead, comprehensive reforms and proper planning are necessary to strengthen Florida's insurance market, ensuring that we're resilient and prepared when the next storm hits.

As we conclude this tale, it's clear that a new approach to solving the problems in Florida's property insurance market is needed. As the quip goes, "The key to success is elusive, but the key to failure is trying to please everyone." It's time for strong leaders to face the storm head-on, not just what we want to hear. For once, we need to "count the cost" before continuing to build in treacherous places.

And so, in the immortal words of William Shakespeare, we find that the quality of living is not merely a chronological affair. Before deciding we are too old to tackle the hurricane of challenges, it might be wise to remember, "You can hide from reality, but you cannot hide from the consequences of hiding from reality."

To close this essay, I have paraphrased a version of a presentation I made to the Florida Senate in 2010. You will recognize the theme. The first challenge is correctly identifying the problem, i.e., hurricanes, not insurance. Secondly, decide whether we will retain the risk and finance it with debt or transfer it to avoid post-loss assessments.

"Ladies and gentlemen, I stand before you today, not just as a presenter, but as a Floridian deeply concerned about our state's future amidst the relentless fury of hurricanes. As we delve into discussions on our residential property insurance market, let's not lose sight of the core issue at hand: our battle is not merely with insurance but with Florida's undeniable vulnerability to hurricanes.

Our state's exposure to these natural calamities is unparalleled, bearing the weight of half the nation's hurricane risk. This reality demands our immediate attention, not just as policymakers but as stewards of our state's well-being. We're at a crossroads, faced with choices that could redefine our approach to this persistent threat.

We've heard numerous proposals, including insightful recommendations from Associated Industries of Florida. Yet, amidst this wealth of ideas, a fundamental truth echoes through the real adversary: our state's hurricane exposure, not the intricacies of insurance policy.

The question we face is stark in its simplicity yet profound in its implications: Should we lean on private capital or public debt to shoulder this risk? The choice is ours, and it's a decision that will echo through the lives of every Floridian.

As we ponder these paths, let's remember the lessons of the past, where choices made in legislative halls reverberated through communities, shaping the destinies of countless families and businesses. The distribution of risk and the balance between immediate relief and long-term sustainability are not just policy decisions; they are moral imperatives that define our legacy.

So, as we gather our collective wisdom to confront this challenge, let's ask ourselves: Are we merely seeking a band-aid solution, or are we aiming for a transformative shift that genuinely transfers risk, safeguarding our state's future against the capricious whims of nature?

Our state's resilience hinges on these decisions. It's a call to action that resonates with the urgency of now, urging us to forge a path that is sustainable, equitable, and reflective of the indomitable spirit of Florida.

As we embark on this journey, let's do so knowing that our choices will shape the horizon for generations to come, a testament to our courage, wisdom, and unwavering commitment to the welfare of our beloved state."

Summary of Chapter 24:

Chapter 24 relates to the very heart of Florida's property insurance market, exposing the stark realities of our state's vulnerability to hurricanes and the comedy of stubborn human behavior that exacerbates this perilous situation. Through poignant analogies and insightful observations, I shed light on the root causes of Florida's property insurance crisis, urging policymakers and citizens alike to confront the underlying challenges head-on.

At its core, Florida's property insurance dilemma is not merely a matter of high premiums or insurance complexities but a fundamental battle against the relentless fury of hurricanes. Despite our best intentions, legislative efforts to address high homeowners' premiums have often missed the mark, resembling a futile attempt to dance around the symptoms rather than tackle the root cause.

The chapter identifies <u>three primary factors</u> driving Florida's property insurance crisis: the severity of hurricanes, stubborn human behavior, and excessive litigation. Unlike a Shakespearean tragedy, where the plot unfolds with tragic inevitability, Florida's insurance conundrum is marked by a series of misguided solutions that fail to address the underlying challenges.

Through compelling anecdotes and data-driven analysis, I paint a vivid picture of Florida's precarious position in the face of hurricane risks. The staggering growth of insured coastal exposure in recent years, coupled with insurers' retreat from high-risk areas, paints a grim picture of our state's vulnerability to catastrophic losses.

Furthermore, recent events, such as Hurricane Idalia, serve as stark reminders of the escalating drama and potential for damage in the Sunshine State. As insurers withdraw from high-risk areas and property insurance rates skyrocket, Floridians are left to grapple with the harsh realities of living in paradise amidst nature's fury.

In light of these challenges, the chapter calls for a new approach to solving Florida's property insurance crisis. Rather than seeking band-aid solutions or placing undue emphasis on insurance complexities, policymakers must confront the core issue at hand: our state's undeniable vulnerability to hurricanes.

Drawing upon lessons from the past and insights from industry experts, I advocate for a transformative shift in our approach to hurricane risk management. Whether leaning on private capital or public debt, the choice we make will reverberate through the lives of every Floridian, shaping the destiny of our state for generations to come.

In closing, the chapter serves as a rallying cry for bold action and visionary leadership in confronting Florida's property insurance crisis. As we stand at a crossroads, faced with choices that will define our state's resilience and sustainability, let us rise to the occasion with courage, wisdom, and unwavering commitment to the welfare of our beloved Sunshine State.

Transition to Chapter 25:

Speaking of sandcastles, let's discuss the big kahuna of Florida's property insurance market—Citizens Property Insurance Company. We're talking big bucks, big risks, and some very big decisions about who picks up the tab when those stormy skies roll in. Chapter 23, I disclose the complexities surrounding Citizens, examining its history, purpose, and financial standing. Join me as we unravel the enigma of Citizens and explore the implications of its role as an insurer of last resort in a state vulnerable to hurricanes.

CHAPTER 25

Citizens Property Insurance Company: The Big Gamble

Is Florida's approach to property insurance, specifically through the Florida Citizens Property Insurance Company, prudent or risky? This question gains particular relevance when considering the company's history, purpose, and financial standing.

Florida Citizens Property Insurance Corporation, commonly called "Citizens", was established in 2002 and has emerged as a prominent player in Florida's insurance landscape. It was formed through the merger of the Florida Residential Property and Casualty Joint Underwriting Association and the Florida Windstorm Underwriting Association.[43]

Citizens operates as a not-for-profit, tax-exempt government corporation. Its primary role is to function as an insurer of last resort, providing coverage to those who have no other options. However, Citizens' existence is not without controversy.

Some argue it distorts the market by offering rates that do not fully reflect the risk, potentially leading to a situation where the company might not have sufficient funds to cover claims after a major disaster.

The financial health of "Citizens" is a continual concern, especially given Florida's susceptibility to hurricanes. This concern was particularly evident around the time of the passage of House Bill 1A in 2007. HB1A aimed to tackle the escalating

---

[43] https://www.citizensfla.com/about

insurance costs in the state following the active hurricane seasons of 2004 and 2005.[44] This legislation had a profound impact on "Citizens."

House Bill 1A included several reforms, such as freezing "Citizens'" rates, expanding its ability to offer coverage, and reducing the risk exposure of private insurers by increasing the capacity of the Florida Hurricane Catastrophe Fund. The bill responded to the Florida homeowners' insurance market crisis, where many insurers were either leaving the state or significantly raising premiums due to the high risk of hurricanes.

The rate freeze and expansion of coverage meant that "Citizens" grew rapidly in size, as it became a more affordable option for many homeowners. However, this growth also increased the financial risk for the corporation. If a major hurricane were to strike, "Citizens" could face enormous claims, potentially leading to significant financial deficits.

This situation raised questions about the model's sustainability and the potential burden on Florida taxpayers and policyholders.

Capital vs Debt Financing of Hurricane Catastrophe Risk

In a previous chapter titled "Risk Management in the Face of Florida's Catastrophe Hurricane Exposure," we discussed lessons that should be learned from comparing New Zealand's and Japan's different strategies related to natural catastrophes.

New Zealand effectively transferred risk and benefitted from capital inflows after its devastating earthquakes. On the other hand, Japan chose to retain its earthquake risk, resulting in crushing post-catastrophe debt, the effects of which are still observable today.

---

[44] https://www.flsenate.gov/Session/Bill/2007A/1A

Policymakers in Florida have likewise chosen to embrace hurricane catastrophe risk and to use post-storm debt to finance losses. (Does this sound a little like gambling to you?)

Broad-based "assessments" serve as the primary mechanism to fund the future losses of "Citizens" when premiums collected from its policyholders prove inadequate to cover losses."

Regular Assessments can be imposed on "Citizens" policyholders. Emergency Assessments can be levied on "Citizens" and all Florida policyholders in the property and casualty insurance market with few exceptions. This approach raises questions about the fairness and sustainability of such a model.

(A more in-depth description of Citizens Assessment can be found in the next chapter)

It's akin to walking a tightrope. On one hand, Citizens provides a crucial safety net for homeowners who would otherwise be uninsured. On the other hand, it operates in a challenging environment that balances offering affordable insurance with maintaining financial solvency.

Considering this, one might ask: Is relying on a government entity like Citizens a viable long-term solution for high-risk insurance, or does it merely postpone an inevitable financial reckoning? Further discussions could delve into alternative models of property insurance in high-risk areas or the impact of climate change on insurance markets.

Why the Financial Stability of Citizens is Critical

The financial stability of Citizens is crucial because high premiums are a concern, but nothing is worse than relying on an insurer that cannot fulfill its obligations. Picture this:

As an experienced independent insurance agent with over 35 years in the industry, I've had countless conversations with policyholders regarding their homeowner's insurance premiums. It's understandable that many find the cost of coverage to be a source of frustration, and the prospect of a premium increase or policy non-renewal can be daunting.

However, the true concern should not be solely focused on the dollar amount of the premium, but rather on the financial stability and solvency of the insurance companies themselves. While high premiums are certainly an inconvenience, the consequences of an insolvent insurer can be far more devastating.

Consider the following scenario: A policyholder comes into your office, their face blackened with soot, having just experienced a devastating house fire. They had dutifully paid their renewal premium, only to learn that the insurance company had filed for bankruptcy. In this situation, the customer's claim may not be fully covered, leaving them in a precarious position.

This hypothetical, while not one I've personally encountered, illustrates the stark contrast between concerns over high premiums and the critical importance of insurer solvency. While the regulation of insurance rates is important, the regulation of insurance companies to ensure their financial stability is paramount.

Policyholders must understand that the risk of an insurer becoming insolvent and unable to fulfill their obligations is far more consequential than the temporary discomfort of a premium increase. The financial well-being and long-term protection of their homes and assets should be the primary concern.

As an insurance professional, my role was to not only assist clients in managing their premium costs, but also to educate them on the importance of working with financially sound insurance providers. By maintaining a clear focus on insurer solvency, we can help policyholders make informed decisions and ensure they have the coverage they need when they need it most.

This underscores the importance of maintaining the solvency of Citizens and ensuring it can deliver on its promises to policyholders, rather than leaving them exposed to the most expensive form of insurance—one that can't pay out claims.

"Citizens" Reform: Should it return to an Insurer of Last Resort?

Reforming Citizens to ensure it remains an insurer of last resort while increasing its ability to pay claims involves several considerations:

1. **Actuarial Adequacy**: Setting rates to be actuarially adequate would reflect the true risk of insuring properties, especially in high-risk areas. This could make insurance more expensive for policyholders but improve Citizens' financial stability.

2. **Subsidization**: Continuing to subsidize rates through assessments on non-citizen policyholders raises questions of equity and sustainability. While it lowers rates for Citizens' policyholders, it places a financial burden on others and may not be a long-term solution.

3. **Rate Comparison**: Reverting to the original requirement that Citizens' rates be higher than those of the top ten private market insurers in a given territory could drive more policyholders to the private market, reducing Citizens' risk exposure. However, this could also leave some high-risk homeowners without affordable insurance options.

In conclusion, the Florida Citizens Property Insurance Corporation is essential in providing insurance to homeowners in high-risk areas of Florida. However, legislative actions such as the passage of House Bill 1A in 2007 have significantly impacted its operations, raising concerns about its financial sustainability and risk management strategies. The ongoing challenge for Citizens is to balance the need to provide affordable insurance with maintaining financial solvency in a state prone to natural disasters.

Summary of Chapter 25:

Chapter 25 scrutinizes the Florida Citizens Property Insurance Company, shedding light on its establishment, function, and financial stability in the tumultuous landscape of Florida's insurance market. With a keen eye for detail and a commitment to informed analysis, I dissect the multifaceted nature of Citizens and the implications of its operations on homeowners, policymakers, and taxpayers alike.

Established in 2002 as a response to the escalating insurance costs in Florida, Citizens emerged as a pivotal player in the state's insurance market, providing coverage to homeowners deemed uninsurable by private insurers. However, its existence has been mired in controversy, with critics arguing that it distorts the market by offering rates that fail to fully reflect the risk, potentially jeopardizing its financial solvency in the event of a major disaster.

The chapter navigates through the intricacies of Citizens' financial health, particularly in light of Florida's susceptibility to hurricanes. The passage of House Bill 1A in 2007, aimed at addressing the state's insurance crisis, had significant ramifications for Citizens, freezing its rates and expanding its coverage, thus increasing its risk exposure amidst a volatile market.

Delving deeper, the chapter explores the mechanisms used to finance Citizens' losses, highlighting the reliance on assessments imposed on policyholders and the broader insurance market. This approach raises questions about its fairness and sustainability, prompting discussions on alternative models of property insurance and the long-term viability of Citizens as an insurer of last resort.

Furthermore, the chapter examines proposed reforms for Citizens, emphasizing the need for actuarial adequacy in setting rates, addressing issues of subsidization, and exploring rate comparison strategies to mitigate risk exposure. These considerations underscore the delicate balance between providing affordable insurance and maintaining financial stability in a state prone to natural disasters.

In conclusion, Chapter 25 underscores the pivotal role of the Florida Citizens Property Insurance Company in providing insurance to homeowners in high-risk areas. However, it also underscores the inherent challenges in its operations and urges policymakers to enact reforms that ensure its long-term sustainability and effectiveness as a safety net for Florida homeowners.

Transition to Chapter 26:

And if you thought the plot was thickening, wait till you hear about "Citizens Assessment." It's all about the dollar bills - who's paying them, where they're going, and how we're all pitching in to keep our roofs over our heads when the wind blows. It's a bit like going Dutch on a date with a hurricane – everyone's got to chip in.

Top of Form

Chapter 26

Citizens Assessments

The Intricacies of Funding Florida's Insurance Safety Net

Imagine this: Florida is hit by a hurricane, and the damage is astronomical. The entity at the heart of the financial aftermath? Citizens Property Insurance Corporation. This scenario extends beyond the theoretical; it is a stark reality for many Floridians.

Citizens, a state-run "insurer of last resort," steps in when the unthinkable happens. But what happens when the funds run dry, and the claims exceed what's in the bank? Enter the world of assessments.

Assessments are essentially financial safety nets woven into the fabric of Florida's insurance landscape to ensure Citizens can meet their obligations.

The process starts when Citizens faces a deficit, where the claims costs surpass the available capital and reinsurance recoveries. To bridge this gap, Citizens can levy assessments on all Florida's policyholders, not just its own. This mechanism is structured in layers designed to be activated under specific conditions.

First, we have the Citizens Policyholder Surcharge, a measure directly impacting Citizens' policyholders. In a scenario where all accounts are in deficit, this could mean an additional charge of up to 45% across different accounts. But this is just the first layer.

Should the surcharge not suffice, Citizens turns to Regular Assessments. These are broader in scope, targeting a more comprehensive range of policies across the state, excluding workers' compensation, medical malpractice, crop, or federal flood insurance. This move can generate significant funds, aiming to stabilize the financial quagmire.

And if that's still not enough, we enter the realm of Emergency Assessments. This last resort can impact many policyholders, including Citizens' own, spreading the financial responsibility even further and for a longer duration, typically over a decade.

The figures involved are staggering. Imagine needing to cover a shortfall of billions, with various assessments potentially raising funds in the double-digit billions over time. The financial implications for policyholders are profound, impacting annual payments and overall cost burdens.

You might wonder, "Why does this matter to me?" Well, it's a vivid illustration of how interconnected our financial safety nets are and the domino effect a catastrophic event can have on an entire state's economy. It also sheds light on the intricate balancing act between providing support and managing financial risk in the insurance sector.

This narrative isn't just about insurance policies and assessments; it's a story of preparedness, resilience, and collective responsibility. As we navigate the uncertainties of nature and economics, understanding mechanisms like Citizens' assessments becomes crucial.

It's a reminder that a well-thought-out financial strategy can be as vital as the immediate response to the crisis in the face of disaster.

As someone who has navigated the complex world of insurance, witnessing firsthand the impact of policy decisions on communities and individuals, I cannot overstate the importance of transparency and the need for robust financial planning. The story of Citizens and its assessments is a testament to the challenges and responsibilities of managing risk in a state prone to natural disasters.

It's a narrative that underscores the importance of foresight, collaboration, and commitment to resilience in the face of adversity.

Summary of Chapter 26:

Chapter 26 examines the intricate process of funding Florida's insurance safety net through Citizens Assessments. It provides insights into the mechanisms to bridge the financial gap when Citizens Property Insurance Corporation faces deficits beyond its available capital and reinsurance recoveries.

The chapter begins by vividly describing the aftermath of a hurricane in Florida, highlighting the pivotal role of Citizens as the insurer of last resort in providing financial support to affected homeowners. However, when the magnitude of claims surpasses available funds, assessments become a crucial financial safety net.

Assessments are structured in layers, each activated under specific conditions to generate funds for Citizens. The process starts with the Citizens Policyholder Surcharge, impacting Citizens' policyholders directly with additional charges of up to 45% across different accounts. If this proves insufficient, Regular Assessments broaden the scope to include a comprehensive range of policies across the state, excluding certain categories. Finally, Emergency Assessments serve as a last resort, spreading financial responsibility even further across policyholders, including Citizens' own, over an extended period.

The chapter emphasizes the staggering figures involved in funding deficits, with assessments potentially raising funds in the double-digit billions over time. This has profound financial implications for policyholders, affecting annual payments and overall cost burdens. It highlights the interconnectedness of financial safety nets and the collective responsibility in managing risks.

Beyond insurance policies and assessments, the narrative underscores the importance of preparedness, resilience, and collective responsibility in navigating the uncertainties of nature and economics. It emphasizes the need for transparency and robust financial planning to mitigate the impact of catastrophic events on communities and individuals, echoing the challenges and responsibilities inherent in managing risk in a state prone to natural disasters.

In conclusion, Chapter 26 serves as a poignant reminder of the vital role assessments play in ensuring financial stability and support in the aftermath of disasters, underscoring the importance of foresight, collaboration, and commitment to resilience in safeguarding the well-being of communities and the economy.

Transition to Chapter 27:

Having explored the intricacies of funding Florida's insurance safety net through Citizens Assessments, we now focus on broader international perspectives on economic recovery and risk management. In Chapter 27, I draw parallels between the post-disaster experiences of New Zealand and Japan, offering valuable insights into Florida's approach to disaster resilience. Join me as we examine the contrasting strategies employed by these nations and reflect on the implications for Florida's risk management framework.

CHAPTER 27

Economic Recovery Post Canterbury Earthquake in New Zealand Versus Japan

Florida can learn valuable lessons from the contrasting approaches to economic recovery and risk management taken by New Zealand in the aftermath of the Canterbury earthquakes and by Japan following its earthquake and tsunami.

New Zealand's Recovery Post Canterbury Earthquake[45]

The Canterbury earthquake in New Zealand, notably the devastating February 2011 quake, presented significant challenges. However, the country's high insurance penetration, mainly due to the partnership between the insurance industry and the Earthquake Commission (EQC), played a critical role in the recovery process.

New Zealand benefited from being covered by three of the world's top six reinsurance programs, which helped mitigate the economic impact of the disaster. The losses from the earthquake were approximately equivalent to 20% of New Zealand's GDP, showcasing the significant financial burden placed on the country.

The Earthquake Commission (EQC) was pivotal in managing and improving the claims process, especially after the 2016 Kaikoura earthquake, which generated another 40,000 claims. The EQC embraced digital technologies for efficient and

---

[45] Britannica Christchurch earthquakes of 2010-11
https://www.britannica.com/event/Christchurch-earthquakes-of-2010-2011

unified claims processing, partnering with private insurers to manage the end-to-end claims journey.

This new operating model and technological implementation significantly enhanced disaster recovery, setting a precedent for a coherent and integrated approach.

Property insurance claims from the earthquakes amounted to about $38 billion, with 72%, the most significant portion, funded by existing reinsurance. This mix of funding sources, including after-the-event reinsurance and additional capital, underscored the importance of robust funding mechanisms for future disasters.

Research has shown that the type and timing of insurance payouts significantly influenced the recovery of residential areas and businesses in Christchurch.

For every 1% increase in insurance payment for building damage, economic recovery increased by 0.36%. This empirical link between post-catastrophe insurance payments and local economic recovery highlights the critical role of timely and effective insurance responses in disaster recovery.

Japan's Post-Disaster Economic Recovery[46]

In contrast to New Zealand, Japan's decision to retain risk following its earthquake and tsunami led to a more sluggish and painful economic recovery. The lack of substantial outside capital to finance rebuilding damaged infrastructure slowed the recovery process. This situation in Japan illustrates the potential drawbacks of a risk retention strategy, especially in large-scale natural disasters where the financial burden can be overwhelming.[47]

---

[46] The Great East-Japan Earthquake and devastating tsunami: an update and lessons from the past Great Earthquakes in Japan since 1923 https://pubmed.ncbi.nlm.nih.gov/23583960/
[47] Summary - Lessons Learned from the Fukushima Nuclear Accident for Improving Safety of U.S. Nuclear Plants https://www.ncbi.nlm.nih.gov/books/NBK253923/

Applying the Lessons to Florida

Florida can draw critical insights from these contrasting approaches. New Zealand's experience underscores the value of risk transfer, mainly through insurance and reinsurance, in facilitating swift and effective post-disaster recovery. The integration of digital technology and collaboration with private insurers, as seen in New Zealand, can also enhance the efficiency and effectiveness of disaster recovery efforts.

In contrast, Japan's experience highlights the potential challenges associated with risk retention, particularly the difficulty in mobilizing sufficient resources for recovery without external financial support.

Florida can benefit from a balanced approach to risk management that leverages the strengths of risk transfer and retention. This entails maintaining adequate insurance coverage and investing in technology and collaborative frameworks to optimize recovery processes. Such an approach can enhance the state's resilience to catastrophe events like hurricanes, ensuring a more robust and swift economic recovery.

One Final Thought Experiment

Consider yourself a financial advisor. Your client is a 40-year-old married couple whose home is currently appraised for $400,000. They are both employed and have two teenage children. Early in their married life, they decided to focus their financial resources on paying off their mortgage early. They chose not to buy expensive automobiles or to take vacations. Rather, they singularly focused on paying off the mortgage.

Today, the mortgage has been paid in full. Now they have a question for you: Homeowners insurance is expensive, and now that there is no mortgage, they are not required to buy insurance. Should they continue to pay insurance or retain those premium dollars and create a fund to accumulate them solely to pay future losses? In other words, should they self-insure and invest the money they would have paid for insurance?"

Homeowners' Insurance vs. Self-Insuring: A Deep Dive

At first glance, the idea of self-insuring may sound appealing, especially to a couple who has demonstrated remarkable financial discipline by paying off their mortgage early. However, this decision should not be taken lightly and requires a thorough understanding of the risks involved.

The Case for Homeowners' Insurance:

1. **Comprehensive Protection:** Homeowners' insurance covers the structure itself, protection for personal belongings, and, in many cases, additional living expenses if your home becomes uninhabitable.

2. **Risk Pooling:** Insurance is based on the concept of risk pooling, where the financial risk of home repairs or rebuilds is shared among many policyholders. This significantly lowers the cost burden for any single individual.

3. **Peace of Mind:** Knowing you're protected in unforeseen events, such as natural disasters or theft, can provide invaluable peace of mind.

The Case for Self-Insuring:

1. **Potential Savings:** Without monthly or annual insurance premiums, you could potentially save money, especially <u>if you're fortunate enough to avoid major incidents</u>.

2. **Control Over Funds:** By setting aside money for potential damage, you can directly control the funds and potentially invest them for growth.

However, self-insuring carries significant risks:

1. **Financial Vulnerability:** The cost of rebuilding a home can quickly surpass the average savings or investment growth from the money that would have been spent on insurance premiums.

2. **Unexpected Magnitude of Losses:** Major disasters can result in losses far exceeding what one can reasonably save or accumulate over time.

3. **Lack of Additional Protections:** Homeowners' insurance often includes coverage that is hard to quantify but immensely valuable, such as liability protection and additional living expenses coverage.

Recommendation:

Given the potential for catastrophic losses and the comprehensive protection offered by homeowners' insurance, the prudent choice for this client is to maintain their coverage.

While the appeal of saving on premiums is understandable, the magnitude and unpredictability of potential losses render self-insuring a risky proposition. Moreover, as a retired insurance agent with extensive experience in risk management and an understanding of the nuanced benefits of insurance, I'd emphasize to this client that insurance isn't just about what's likely to happen but also about being prepared for unlikely yet possible catastrophic events.

One Final Iteration

What if your client was the State of Florida? What if they were considering self-insurance? What advice would you give them? What if Florida's leaders thought they were smarter than Mother Nature and wanted you to participate in a scheme to retain the risk of catastrophic hurricanes over and above the high premiums you already pay? What if they wanted to concentrate the risk in Florida rather than spread it across the global catastrophe market?

Do you realize that decision has already been made for you? Today, after you pay your homeowners' insurance premium, you are still liable for post-loss assessments, even if your property was not damaged, to fund the wager that has already been made.

The next time you hear a proposal that claims to reduce homeowners' insurance premiums by expanding the Florida Hurricane Catastrophe Fund or lowering the premiums for Citizens Property Insurance Company, I hope you will remember this thought experiment.

Momma always told me, "When something sounds too good to be true, it usually is!" One more quip from Ronald Reagan seems apropos, *"The nine most terrifying words in the English language are: I'm from the Government, and I'm here to help."* Don't fall for the gimmick of government insurance. It always concentrates risk rather than transfer risk, and when the wind blows, you are on the hook whether your property is damaged or not.

In conclusion, navigating risk management in hurricane-prone areas like Florida can be as tricky as predicting the weather with a broken barometer. On the other hand, Florida has science and technology on its side, together with an array of tools, not the least of which is hurricane catastrophe models (see Chapter 20 for a quick refresher).

For a deeper dive into Florida's risk management strategies and how they compare to international cases, you might find the Florida Disaster [State Hazard Mitigation Plan](), [Hurricane Loss Mitigation Program](), and [Esri's report]() particularly enlightening.

Summary of Chapter 27:

Chapter 27 opens a conversation into the contrasting approaches to economic recovery and risk management observed in the aftermath of the Canterbury earthquakes in New Zealand and the earthquake and tsunami in Japan, offering valuable lessons for Florida's disaster resilience strategies.

New Zealand's recovery post-Canterbury earthquake demonstrated the effectiveness of risk transfer mechanisms, particularly insurance and reinsurance, in facilitating swift and effective disaster recovery. The partnership between the insurance industry and the Earthquake Commission played a crucial role, highlighting the importance of robust funding mechanisms and integrated approaches to claims processing.

In contrast, Japan's decision to retain risk following its earthquake and tsunami led to a more sluggish and challenging economic recovery, underscoring the potential drawbacks of risk retention strategies in large-scale disasters.

Applying these lessons to Florida, I emphasize the value of a balanced approach to risk management that leverages the strengths of risk transfer and retention. Integrating digital technology and collaborative frameworks, as seen in New Zealand, can enhance the efficiency and effectiveness of disaster recovery efforts, while acknowledging the potential challenges associated with risk retention, as evident in Japan's experience.

Furthermore, I engage readers in a thought experiment, challenging the notion of self-insurance for homeowners and extending the analogy to the state level. Highlighting the risks and implications of concentrating risk within the state, I caution against overlooking the benefits of insurance and risk transfer mechanisms in mitigating catastrophic losses.

In conclusion, Chapter 27 underscores the importance of drawing insights from international cases to inform Florida's risk management strategies. By learning from past experiences and adopting a comprehensive approach to disaster resilience, Florida can enhance its preparedness and ensure a more robust and swift recovery in the face of future catastrophes.

Transition to Chapter 28:

Let's return our globetrotting hats and hop from one international lesson to another. With the insights from New Zealand and Japan in our pocket, Chapter 28 beckons us to keep one eye on the horizon and another on the history books. "Ellsberg Paradox vs. Dr. Frank Knight's Risk vs. Uncertainty" isn't just a mouthful—it's a brain full, too. Here, we'll unpack how understanding different risks can help us navigate Florida's stormy insurance waters. And, trust me, with hurricanes around, that's knowledge worth having.

Chapter 28

Ellsberg, Knight, and the Florida Investor: A Tale of Risk and Uncertainty

Imagine you're a capital investor looking at Florida's sunny, hurricane-prone shores. You aim to make intelligent investments that won't get blown away by the next big storm or tangled up in unexpected political changes.

Understanding the Ellsberg Paradox and Dr. Knight's theory of risk vs. uncertainty can be your compass to navigate these waters.

As articulated by Daniel Ellsberg and Frank Knight, the concepts of risk and uncertainty have significant implications for investors in Florida's property insurance market. Understanding these concepts can help investors make more informed decisions and better manage their exposure to both catastrophe and political risk.

The Ellsberg Paradox: A Closer Look

The Ellsberg Paradox is like choosing between two jars of jellybeans for a chance to win a prize. One jar has 50 red and 50 black jellybeans. The other jar also has 100 jellybeans mixed with red and black, but you don't know the exact numbers. You win if you pick the color that gets drawn from the jar.

Given the choice, most people prefer betting on the jar with the known 50/50 split. Even though both jars could potentially offer the same chances, we're more comfortable when we know the odds.

This quirk in our decision-making is at the heart of the Ellsberg Paradox. We tend to avoid options with unknown risks (ambiguity) even when they might offer the same or better chances of winning. It's like choosing a familiar path through the woods rather than venturing onto an unknown trail, even if the unknown could be a shortcut.

In the context of Florida's property insurance market, this means that investors may be more comfortable with the quantifiable risks associated with hurricanes (e.g., the probability of a Category 3 storm making landfall in a given year) than with the uncertain risks associated with changing political and regulatory environments.

Dr. Knight's Risk vs. Uncertainty

Dr. Knight takes this a step further by differentiating between risk (where the odds are known, like the first jar of jellybeans) and uncertainty (where the odds are unknown, reminiscent of the second jar).

In the world of investing, risk can be managed, measured, and even insured against. Uncertainty, however, is a wild card. It represents situations where we can't calculate the odds because we deal with unknowns. It's like preparing for a hurricane when you know its path and strength versus suddenly finding out a storm is coming without any details.

Practical Effects for Capital Investors in Florida

When considering hurricane risk in Florida, an investor equipped with the understanding of the Ellsberg Paradox and Knight's theory would look at catastrophe risk (like hurricanes) and political risk (like changes in insurance regulation or property laws) through different lenses.

- **Catastrophe Risk**: Historical data and models can give us probabilities of a hurricane hitting and its potential impact. This risk is more quantifiable and insurable, much like choosing the jar with a known 50/50 split of jellybeans. Investors can use this data to weigh their options and decide if the risk is worth taking.

- **Political Risk**: This falls more into the realm of uncertainty. It's like the jar with an unknown mix of jellybeans. You don't know how political landscapes will shift or how those changes might affect your investments. Will new laws increase insurance costs? Will zoning changes affect property values? These unknowns make it harder to assess the potential impact on your investment.

In both cases, an investor's decision-making process would be influenced by their comfort level with ambiguity and their strategies for managing or embracing uncertainty. Understanding these concepts helps investors recognize their own biases towards risk and uncertainty, encouraging more informed and potentially less emotionally driven investment decisions.

For investors in Florida's real estate or insurance markets, grappling with these concepts means balancing the knowns and unknowns of hurricane impacts with the unpredictable nature of political changes. It's a bit like deciding whether to invest in a sturdy, well-insured beachfront property with a known flood history or a new development in an area without a clear regulatory future.

In essence, navigating investment decisions with the Ellsberg Paradox and Knight's differentiation in mind is about understanding not just the risks you can measure, but also being aware of and prepared for the uncertainties you can't. It teaches investors to be as prepared as possible for hurricanes and the unpredictable winds of political change alike.

So, political uncertainty appears to be the "weak link" when considering capital investment by insurance and reinsurance companies in Florida. This would suggest that policymakers should carefully consider sudden changes in laws and regulations governing property insurance, recognizing that to the extent uncertainty is created will be the extent to which capital will flee.

For insurance and reinsurance (*insurance that an insurance company purchases to limit its risk by sharing some of its potential losses with other insurers*) companies, a stable and predictable regulatory environment is predicated on their ability to accurately price risk and, therefore, offer products at competitive rates.

Sudden changes in property insurance laws and regulations can introduce uncertainty that complicates these calculations. This is not just about the immediate financial impact of such changes but also about the ability to plan for future risks and allocate capital accordingly.

When policymakers contemplate adjustments to the regulatory framework, the potential impact on the investment climate should be paramount. The introduction of uncertainty, especially when it is sudden and significant, can deter investment.

This is because investors, including insurance and reinsurance companies, tend to favor environments where the game's rules are clear and stable. Uncertainty, especially in regulatory terms, introduces an additional layer of risk that can be difficult to quantify and manage.

To maintain and attract capital investment in Florida's insurance market, a concerted effort should be made to ensure that any changes in laws and regulations are communicated clearly, implemented with sufficient lead time, and, where possible, done in consultation with industry stakeholders.

This approach not only aids in maintaining a stable investment environment but also ensures that the insurance sector remains robust and capable of serving Floridians' needs, particularly in the face of natural disasters.

By carefully considering the impact of regulatory changes and striving to minimize uncertainty, policymakers can help sustain a healthy investment climate. This, in turn, ensures that capital does not flee due to sudden shifts in the regulatory landscape, thereby securing the state's economic stability and the well-being of its residents.

The lessons of Ellsberg and Knight are not unique to Florida. Still, they are perhaps uniquely relevant given the state's outsized exposure to catastrophe risk and insurance regulation vagaries. As the state grapples with the challenges of maintaining a stable and affordable property insurance market, investors who can navigate the known risks and the uncertain terrain will be best positioned for long-term success.

Summary of Chapter 28:

Chapter 28 explores the nuanced interplay of risk and uncertainty in Florida's investment landscape, particularly within the property insurance market. Drawing on the concepts of the Ellsberg Paradox and Dr. Knight's differentiation between risk and uncertainty, I offer insights for investors seeking to make informed decisions amid Florida's hurricane-prone shores and dynamic regulatory environment.

The Ellsberg Paradox is a framework for understanding investors' preference for known risks over unknown uncertainties. Investors can better assess their comfort levels with ambiguity by examining familiar probabilities, such as hurricane impacts, against unpredictable political landscapes and make more informed investment decisions.

Dr. Knight's theory distinguishes between risk, where probabilities are known and manageable, and uncertainty, where probabilities are unknown and inherently unpredictable. This differentiation is crucial for investors grappling with the quantifiable risks of hurricanes alongside the unpredictable nature of political changes.

In practical terms, investors in Florida's real estate and insurance markets must balance the knowns of hurricane impacts with the unknowns of regulatory shifts. Catastrophe risk, backed by historical data and models, can be quantified and managed, akin to choosing a jar of jellybeans with a known split. However, political uncertainty introduces ambiguity, complicating investment decisions and potentially deterring capital.

Political uncertainty emerges as a significant weak link in the decision-making process for capital investment, particularly within sectors sensitive to regulatory changes like insurance and reinsurance. Sudden shifts in property insurance laws and regulations can introduce uncertainty, challenging investors' ability to accurately price risk and plan for future contingencies.

To maintain a stable investment climate in Florida's insurance market, policymakers must prioritize clear and transparent regulatory frameworks. Clear communication, sufficient lead time for implementation, and stakeholder consultation are essential to mitigate uncertainty and sustain investor confidence.

Ultimately, the lessons of Ellsberg and Knight underscore the importance of navigating known risks and uncertain terrains in Florida's investment arena. By understanding the complexities of risk and uncertainty, investors can position themselves for long-term success amid the Sunshine State's unique challenges and opportunities.

Transition to Chapter 29:

Sailing from the theoretical to the concrete, Chapter 29, "Florida's Shifting Paradigms," is where the rubber meets the road—or, should I say, where the storm surge meets the shore. We've seen paradigms shift like sands on a windy beach, and this chapter is all about the ever-changing landscape of Florida's policies and how they aim to withstand nature's tests. It's a tale of adaptation and, sometimes, a bit of stubborn defiance.

Chapter 29

Florida's Shifting Paradigms: Navigating Through the Storms of Change

In Florida's vibrant narrative, a story of transformation unfolds, marked by the state's evolving battle against its most relentless adversary: hurricanes. This story, "Florida's Shifting Paradigms," is not just about weathering storms; it's a deeper exploration of how Florida's strategies and attitudes toward these natural phenomena have changed, shedding light on human resilience as much as meteorological challenges.

The pre-Andrew era, which we might call the "Paradise Paradigm," was characterized by rapid growth and development, particularly along the coast. There was a prevailing sense of optimism and invincibility, with little recognition

of the potential for catastrophic losses. Insurance was relatively cheap and readily available, and building codes were lax by today's standards.

Hurricane Andrew's devastating impact in 1992 shattered this paradigm and ushered in a new era of risk awareness and mitigation efforts. The "Andrew Paradigm" saw a significant strengthening of building codes and a recognition of the need for more rigorous hurricane modeling and risk assessment. Insurers and reinsurers also reassessed their exposure to Florida hurricane risk, leading to a hardening of the market and higher premiums for many policyholders.

The mid-2000s saw another shift, which we might call the "Charlie Crist Paradigm," named after the former Governor who championed a series of insurance market reforms. These reforms, such as the expansion of Citizens Property Insurance Corporation and the freezing of its rates, were politically popular but had significant unintended consequences.

Amidst a backdrop of political platitudes and short-term fixes, the state grappled with insurance reforms that totally missed the mark. Rather than addressing Florida's underlying vulnerability to hurricanes and the imprudent trend of coastal development, these reforms seemed to play a game of financial hot potato, shuffling responsibilities without sealing the cracks in the system.

By suppressing rates and crowding out private insurers, these policies significantly increased Citizens' exposure and left the state vulnerable to massive post-hurricane assessments. The Charlie Crist Paradigm also prioritized short-term affordability over long-term stability and risk management.

In retrospect, it was "Florida's Grand Experiment" – nothing less than gambling with the people's money. This gamble was fueled by the arrogant assumption that we could have borrowed enough money to cover our losses. History informs us that if Mother Nature had called our bluff, Florida and its citizens could have faced financial devastation.

Mother Nature, choosing to wink at our ignorance, spared us a storm for nearly a decade, granting us sufficient time to partially rectify Charlie Crist's mess. This era underscored the necessity of a more astute and foresighted approach to fortify the state against its turbulent challenges.

Entertainment Alert

This whole debacle, which I call the Charlie Crist Paradigm, was made possible because the Governor and Legislature chose to ignore the three basic principles of problem solving: Rule #1: Properly identify the problem. Rule #2: Properly identify the problem. Rule #3: Refer to Rules #1 and #2 before proceeding.

Ignoring this wisdom resulted in a solution crafted for the wrong problem, namely, high homeowners' insurance premiums. High homeowners' insurance premiums were the symptom. The problem was Florida's exposure to hurricanes and human behavior of building in very dangerous places. The solution to the problem would have been very different.

As I observed the gradual unfolding of this disastrous situation, I became increasingly frustrated.

During one particularly animated debate, I felt the conversation had slipped into the ditch and needed a little help to get back on track. So, I asked to be recognized. The chairman, sensing what was coming, gave me a knowing look as I said, "Members, let me tell you a story about something that happened a long time ago."

That was a dead giveaway that what was to follow would not necessarily be directly related to the issue in debate but rather a lesson in country wisdom. I continued, "Now, back in Freeport, Florida, we used to have a Rattlesnake Rodeo every year. Weeks before the big day, the community men would start searching for gopher holes in the woods, where rattlers often make themselves at home.

I'm not talking about a little furry rodent when I say gopher holes. I'm talking about a land tortious, a powerful creature that can dig a hole 15 feet deep into the sandy soil of Northwest Florida, seeking a cooler place to live on the hot summer days of mid-July. The men hunting these gopher holes would take bullis vines from the creeks swamps, tie a hook to one end, and run it down the gopher holes, hoping to snag a tortoise or two. Of course, tortoises are protected these days, but back then, they were pretty good with dumplings and rice.

Now, about those rattlesnakes. The men would run a garden hose down the gopher holes, pour in some gasoline, and wait for the snake to slither out. Then, with a long stick with a string on the end, they'd catch the snake by the head and drop it in a Crocker sack or drum in preparation for the big event.

On Saturday, hundreds of folks would come from all around to enjoy the food, music, and games before the main event—the rattlesnake handler. We kids would gather around the fence and watch as the handler blew up balloons for the snakes to pop, milked their venom for medicine, and showed how to skin them for cooking. But the most important lesson I learned from that whole ordeal was simple: when you catch a rattlesnake, you've got to grab it by the head. If you catch it by the tail, you're gonna end up getting bit.

You may ask, what's this got to do with insurance? Well, just like that rattlesnake handler would tell us back then, you've got to catch the problem by the head, not the tail. If you don't properly identify the real issue, you'll be bitten by unintended consequences. So, as we tackle policy challenges here in Florida's homeowners' insurance market, let's make sure we identify the core problems and address them carefully, ensuring we're not catching the wrong end of this snake.

While this amusing tale highlights the importance of properly identifying the problem, a similar principle applies when examining the stubborn human behaviors that contribute to the challenges facing Florida's property insurance market.

Now, moving forward, let's examine how our current proposals align with these principles and ensure we're crafting reforms that accurately solve the problems at hand."

In the years since, there has been a gradual recognition of the need for a new paradigm, one that balances affordability with sound risk management and encourages private market participation.

This "Resilience Paradigm" is still emerging, but its key features include:

1. A renewed focus on mitigation and resilience, including continued strengthening of building codes and investments in infrastructure hardening.
2. Gradual depopulation of Citizens and return of policies to the private market, aided by the clearinghouse program.

3. More risk-based pricing for insurance would allow premiums to reflect actual hurricane exposure better and encourage policyholders to invest in mitigation.

4. Greater use of private reinsurance and alternative risk transfer mechanisms to spread Florida's hurricane risk globally.

5. Improved data analytics and modeling will help us better understand and price hurricane risk and inform land-use planning and development decisions.

Implementing this Resilience Paradigm will require a sustained commitment from policymakers, insurers, and other stakeholders. It will also require a willingness to make difficult choices and to prioritize long-term stability over short-term political expediency.

One key challenge will be balancing the need for affordable coverage with the imperative to charge risk-based rates. This may require targeted subsidies or other assistance for low-income policyholders rather than the broad-based rate suppression of the Charlie Crist era.

Another challenge will be maintaining the political will to stay the course, even in the face of future hurricanes and the inevitable pressure to provide immediate relief. This will require education and outreach to help stakeholders understand the benefits of a resilience-focused approach.

As we conclude this chapter, I invite you to continue with us into the upcoming sections, where we'll delve deeper into the specifics of Charlie Crist's dangerous policies and identify where they missed the mark. Yet, our exploration doesn't just dwell on past missteps; we'll also look forward to examining how tackling the core issues, rather than merely their manifestations, can lead us toward a more promising future.

So, prepare for an insightful journey as we dissect these complex matters and discover how a focused approach can illuminate the path to a brighter, more prosperous tomorrow.

Summary of Chapter 29:

Chapter 29, "Florida's Shifting Paradigms," traces the historical evolution of Florida's strategies in mitigating hurricane risk, highlighting key paradigm shifts and their implications for the state's resilience. Beginning with the pre-Andrew era of rapid growth and lax building codes, I explore how Hurricane Andrew's devastation in 1992 catalyzed a newfound awareness of risk and the implementation of stricter building codes and risk assessment measures.

The narrative then transitions to the "Charlie Crist Paradigm," characterized by short-term fixes and politically popular reforms that exacerbated Florida's vulnerability to hurricanes. The chapter critically examines the unintended consequences of these policies, prioritizing affordability over long-term stability and risk management, exposing the state to financial devastation.

Amidst this retrospective analysis, the chapter introduces the "Florida's Grand Experiment" concept, highlighting the perilous gamble of overlooking systemic vulnerabilities in favor of short-term financial gains. Mother Nature's temporary reprieve from major storms provided a window for corrective action, prompting a gradual shift towards a more resilient paradigm.

The emergence of the "Resilience Paradigm" signals a renewed commitment to sound risk management and private market participation. Key features of this paradigm include continued investments in mitigation and infrastructure hardening, depopulation of Citizens Property Insurance Corporation, risk-based pricing for insurance, and enhanced data analytics and modeling.

However, implementing the Resilience Paradigm presents challenges, including balancing affordability with risk-based rates and maintaining political will amidst future hurricanes. The chapter underscores the need for sustained commitment from policymakers, insurers, and stakeholders to prioritize long-term stability over short-term expediency.

As the chapter concludes, it invites readers to delve deeper into exploring past policy missteps while looking forward to a more promising future guided by a focused approach to hurricane resilience. Through critical analysis and forward-thinking strategies, Florida can navigate the storms of change and emerge stronger and more resilient than ever before.

Transition to Chapter 30: Now, ever wondered about the financial wizardry that keeps insurers from keeling over when the winds blow a bit too hard? Enter Chapter 30, "Beyond the Storm - How Reinsurance Protects Florida's Homeowners." Reinsurance might seem like the insurance world's behind-the-scenes magic, but it's got more spotlight moments than you'd think—especially in a hurricane-prone place like Florida.

CHAPTER 30

Beyond the Storm: How Reinsurance Protects Florida's Homeowners

Reinsurance, the insurance for insurance companies, plays a critical role in Florida's insurance landscape, particularly given the state's vulnerability to hurricanes.

In Florida, a state celebrated for its sunny days and sandy beaches, homeowners face a lurking menace: hurricanes. These natural disasters can cause catastrophic damage, leading to significant financial strain on insurance companies and, by extension, homeowners. Here, reinsurance (*insurance that an insurance company purchases to limit its risk by sharing some of its potential losses with other insurers*)

plays a pivotal role, acting as a financial safety net for insurance companies, ensuring they can fulfill claims after disasters strike.

This discussion delves into the intricate role of reinsurance in safeguarding Florida's homeowners and stabilizing the insurance market.

The Foundation of Reinsurance

Reinsurance plays a crucial role in the insurance world, providing a financial safety net for companies facing the devastating consequences of hurricanes. It's a system in which insurance companies purchase insurance to mitigate their risk exposure. For Florida, with its high propensity for hurricanes, this isn't just a safety measure; it's a necessity. Reinsurance provides a buffer that absorbs the shock of massive claims, ensuring that insurance companies don't buckle under the financial pressure of a natural disaster.

Why Reinsurance Matters to Florida Homeowners

Understanding reinsurance is crucial for homeowners. This mechanism ensures insurance companies remain solvent and capable of paying out claims in the aftermath of a hurricane.

Without reinsurance, insurers might hesitate to operate in such a high-risk area, limiting availability and driving up consumer costs. By spreading the risk globally, reinsurance makes it financially viable for insurers to offer coverage in hurricane-prone areas.

Interestingly, the reinsurance market is complex, featuring mechanisms like "sidecars" to manage specific risks. A sidecar is a separate financial entity allowing external investors to partner with a reinsurer to take on specific risks and share in the potential profits. This structure provides reinsurers with additional capacity to cover risks and gives investors an opportunity to participate directly in the reinsurance market. Sidecars are frequently employed for high-risk, high-return segments of the market, such as catastrophe reinsurance, enabling reinsurers to spread their risk and access additional capital.

The global nature of reinsurance markets enables more effective risk distribution and cost management. Examples like the Caribbean Catastrophe Risk Insurance Facility (CCRIF) and the African Risk Capacity (ARC) demonstrate how spreading risk across multiple countries or regions can lead to more affordable coverage and faster payouts in the event of a disaster.

The global reinsurance market's response to Hurricane Katrina in 2005 highlights the economic efficiencies of international risk spreading. When Katrina caused an estimated $41 billion in insured losses, reinsurers from Europe, Bermuda, and other regions stepped in to absorb a significant share of the claims. This helped stabilize the US insurance market and ensure that claims could be paid without causing widespread insolvencies.

The flow of risk and capital in the reinsurance market can be visualized as follows: risk is transferred from primary insurers to reinsurers and then to retrocession Aires (reinsurers for reinsurers), with capital flowing in the opposite direction from investors to support these risk transfers. This dynamic underlies the reinsurance market's ability to manage and distribute risk on a global scale.

The debate over keeping reinsurance funds within Florida versus utilizing global reinsurance markets highlights the economic efficiencies gained from spreading risk internationally. While there might be an instinctive appeal to retaining funds within the state, the global nature of reinsurance markets enables more effective risk distribution and cost management.

Reinsurance is not merely an accounting trick or a financial abstraction; it's a vital part of the insurance industry's infrastructure, particularly in risk-prone areas like Florida. By understanding the nuances of reinsurance, stakeholders can better navigate the complexities of the insurance market, ensuring stability and affordability for policyholders.

Understanding Reinsurance Through Three Everyday Analogies

Imagine you're planning the construction of a massive, intricate domino setup that sprawls across an entire gymnasium floor. Each domino represents an insurance policy issued by an insurance company, meticulously placed with precision and care.

The goal is to create a mesmerizing show where, with a flick of the first domino (a claim), a cascading effect ensues, demonstrating the interconnectedness and impact of each policy.

But there's a catch: in this setup, you want to ensure that if a section unexpectedly topples due to an unforeseen bump (a natural disaster like a hurricane), the entire masterpiece doesn't come crashing down, ruining the show (financial stability of the insurance company).

Enter reinsurance, akin to strategically placed safety gates within your domino masterpiece. These gates are designed to stop the falling dominos (claims) from triggering a complete collapse, protecting sections of the setup (the insurance company's capital) from being overwhelmed by a chain reaction.

This setup allows the spectacle (insurance coverage) to continue, even if parts of it face disruption. In Florida, the threat of hurricanes acts like a ball rolling across our domino setup, threatening to topple large sections in a single swoop. The stakes are high; these aren't just dominos but people's homes, businesses, and livelihoods.

Reinsurance acts as a crucial intervention, ensuring that even in the face of such disruption, the insurance companies can absorb the impact without jeopardizing their ability to serve all policyholders.

Another way of looking at the issue is to imagine a hurricane as a rogue wave crashing into a carefully built sandcastle—the sandcastle representing an insurance company's financial stability. Reinsurance is like the seawall that absorbs the shock, protecting the sandcastle from being washed away.

Finally, you can also think of reinsurance as the safety net in a circus. Just as these nets catch acrobats if they fall, reinsurance catches insurance companies, preventing financial disaster after major claims, like those from hurricanes.

The Competitive Edge

Reinsurance injects healthy competition into the insurance market. Like multiple lemonade stands popping up in a neighborhood, reinsurance allows more players to enter the market. This competition benefits homeowners by providing more options and helping to keep insurance rates competitive. It enables smaller and mid-sized insurers to participate in the market, offering policyholders a broader range of choices.

Navigating the Financial Seas

The cost of capital is a significant factor in the insurance industry. Reinsurance can be seen as a financial lighthouse, guiding insurers through the turbulent waters of risk and capital management. Reinsurers can optimize their capital by pooling risks, including those from hurricanes in Florida with less correlated risks globally. This optimization helps reduce the cost of insurance, which, in turn, benefits homeowners through more affordable premiums.

Demystifying Costs and Benefits

There's a common misconception about reinsurance, and that is that it only adds to consumer costs. It's akin to thinking that adding more kitchen chefs will slow meal preparation. In reality, just as more skilled chefs can create a feast more efficiently, reinsurance distributes risk globally, keeping costs down for consumers.

Reinsurance spreads risk like a potluck dinner distributes the effort of cooking. Everyone brings a dish (or in this case, risk coverage) to the table, ensuring no one person (or company) bears the entire burden of a disaster.

Historical Examples of How Reinsurance Enhanced Florida Storm Recovery

The historical examples of reinsurance's impact on Florida's storm recovery underscore the vital role that risk transfer plays in ensuring financial stability and resilience in the face of natural disasters.

When Hurricane Andrew struck Florida in 1992, causing $15.5 billion in insured losses, it was a wake-up call for the insurance industry. Many primary insurers found themselves overexposed and undercapitalized, leading to a wave of insolvencies and a crisis in the Florida insurance market.

However, reinsurers stepped in to absorb a significant portion of these losses, helping to stabilize the market and ensure that claims could be paid. This risk transfer allowed the Florida insurance market to recover and rebuild, demonstrating the critical importance of reinsurance in managing catastrophic risk.

Similarly, when Hurricane Irma struck Florida in 2017, causing an estimated $50 billion in total economic losses, reinsurers again played a vital role in supporting the Florida insurance market. By absorbing a significant share of these losses, reinsurers helped to maintain the solvency and stability of primary insurers, ensuring that policyholders could be compensated for their losses.

After Hurricane Ian, Florida's Citizens Property Insurance Corp. (Citizens) significantly utilized private reinsurance to manage its losses. Citizens reported direct losses, litigation, and other expenses from Hurricane Ian, reaching $3.8 billion.

However, this figure was below the threshold that would trigger an assessment of policyholders. Of the $3.8 billion, Citizens anticipated that $1.4 billion would be ceded (transferred) to the Florida Hurricane Catastrophe Fund and private reinsurance, demonstrating the vital role of private reinsurance in mitigating financial impacts on the insurer's surplus. This move highlights how reinsurance arrangements can provide substantial financial relief to insurers, ensuring they remain solvent and capable of fulfilling claims post-disaster.

For a detailed review of Hurricane Ian Insurance and Reinsurance company losses as of 10/20/2022, please see "Carrier Management: Critical Information for P/C Carrier Executives" at:

https://www.carriermanagement.com/news/2022/10/21/241543.htm

The case of Citizens underscores the broader industry reliance on reinsurance to manage catastrophic losses and maintain market stability, particularly in high-risk areas like Florida where natural disasters such as hurricanes are prevalent.[48]

Moreover, the Florida insurance market's unique structure, characterized by a significant presence of small-to-medium-sized, Florida-focused insurers (often referred to as "take-out companies"), emphasizes the critical role of reinsurance.

These companies heavily depend on reinsurance, ceding (transferring) nearly two-thirds of their premium and risk to reinsurers to manage the outsized risk associated with operating in Florida. This dependency underscores reinsurance's importance in providing a safety net that allows these insurers to offer coverage in a high-risk state.

---

[48] https://www.insurancejournal.com/news/southeast/2022/11/15/695108.htm

The aftermath of Hurricane Ian further highlighted the cautious approach of reinsurers like Swiss Re, which adjusted its Florida exposure by raising rates and reducing commissions to insurer partners. This scenario reflects the broader market dynamics where the supply and demand for reinsurance directly influence insurance rates for homeowners.

The careful management of risk and the strategic use of reinsurance are essential for maintaining insurers' solvency and competitiveness in Florida's challenging market.[49]

These examples highlight the broader theme of how reinsurance supports financial stability and resilience in the face of major disasters. By transferring risk to well-capitalized global reinsurers, primary insurers can manage their exposure and ensure they have the financial resources to weather even the most severe storms. This risk transfer is essential for maintaining the stability of the insurance market and protecting policyholders in the aftermath of a catastrophe.

What are the Alternatives to Reinsurance?

Insurance companies have several avenues to access capital beyond their own balance sheets, which is crucial for expanding their ability to underwrite more policies, especially in high-risk areas like Florida. Beyond reinsurance, these methods include:

1. Letters of Credit: A letter of credit from a bank guarantee that the insurance company can access a specified amount of money when needed. This can be particularly useful for covering claims in the short term or as a form of collateral.

---

[49] https://www.insurancejournal.com/news/southeast/2022/10/25/691475.htm

2. Sale of Company Stock: An insurance company can raise equity capital directly from investors by issuing new stock. This provides immediate funds and distributes ownership and risk among a broader base.
3. Bank Loans: Insurance companies can also take out loans directly from banks or other financial institutions. These loans provide immediate liquidity but must be repaid with interest, which can affect the company's financial health over time.
4. Catastrophe Bonds and Insurance-Linked Securities (ILS): These financial instruments transfer insurance risk to the capital markets. Catastrophe bonds, for instance, are designed to raise money in case of a specific disaster, with investors losing their principal if the disaster occurs. The ILS market has grown significantly in recent years, providing insurers with an alternative source of capacity for managing catastrophe risk. However, these instruments can be complex and expensive to issue, and their capacity may be limited compared to reinsurance.
5. Collateralized Reinsurance: This is a form of reinsurance where the reinsurer provides collateral to cover its potential obligations. The collateral, often in the form of trust funds or letters of credit, provides an additional layer of security for the ceding insurer. Collateralized reinsurance has become increasingly popular, particularly for covering catastrophe risks, as it allows reinsurers to isolate specific risks and attract investors who may not want exposure to an entire reinsurance portfolio.
6. Industry Loss Warranties (ILWs): These are a type of reinsurance contract that pays out based on the total loss experienced by the insurance industry from a specific event, rather than the losses of the individual insurer. ILWs can be a cost-effective way for insurers to protect against catastrophic events, as they are typically triggered only by very large industry losses. However, they provide less specific coverage than traditional reinsurance contracts.
7. Contingent Capital: These are arrangements where an insurer can access additional capital in the event of a significant loss event, often in the form of a pre-arranged debt facility or a put option on the insurer's stock. Contingent capital can provide insurers with an additional layer of

financial protection, but it can be expensive and may come with restrictive covenants or trigger events.

8. Surplus Notes: Issued by insurers, these debt instruments are subordinated to all other claims, including policyholder claims. They provide a flexible form of capital that can be used under regulatory constraints. However, the issuance of surplus notes is subject to regulatory approval, and their use may be limited by factors such as the insurer's financial strength and the overall market conditions.

Despite these alternatives, reinsurance remains the preferred source of outside capital for several reasons:

- Risk Transfer Efficiency: Reinsurance is designed to transfer risk from the primary insurer. This allows insurance companies to manage their exposure to significant losses more effectively than through financial instruments that may still leave them bearing a significant portion of the risk.
- Capital Management Flexibility: Reinsurance agreements can be customized to cover specific risks, territories, or types of insurance, providing insurers with tailored solutions that other forms of capital cannot offer.
- Regulatory Favor: Regulatory frameworks often view reinsurance more favorably than other forms of capital. Reinsurance can be treated as a reduction in liability, directly lowering the amount of capital insurers need to hold against potential claims.
- Market Dynamics: The reinsurance market is global and highly competitive, allowing insurers to find cost-effective coverage for their risks. This competition helps keep reinsurance prices relatively attractive compared to capital costs through equity or debt markets.
- Operational Continuity: Reinsurance agreements often come with expertise and support from the reinsurer. This can help insurers manage claims and recover from large events more efficiently than if they had to rely on their resources or those provided through financial markets.

In practice, insurers often use a combination of reinsurance and other risk transfer mechanisms to manage their exposure. The optimal mix will depend on factors such as the insurer's size, risk profile, regulatory environment, and overall business strategy. For Florida property insurers, reinsurance will likely remain a key component of their risk management strategy, given the state's unique exposure to hurricane risk and the proven track record of reinsurance in absorbing losses from past storms.

Real-world examples demonstrate the use of these alternatives in managing catastrophe risk:

- After Hurricane Andrew in 1992, several Florida insurers turned to the catastrophe bond market to access additional capacity as the reinsurance market hardened after the massive losses.
- In the aftermath of the 2008 financial crisis, collateralized reinsurance grew in popularity as investors sought alternative investment opportunities outside of traditional financial markets.
- Large global insurers, such as AIG and Allianz, have used contingent capital arrangements to manage their exposure to systemic risks, such as pandemics or financial crises.

As the risk transfer landscape evolves, insurers may increasingly look to complement reinsurance with other forms of capital to build more resilient and diversified risk management programs. Innovations such as blockchain and smart contracts could potentially streamline the issuance of ILS and other risk transfer instruments in the future, making these alternatives more accessible and cost-effective.

However, it's important to note that these alternatives are not a panacea and come with their own challenges and limitations. Catastrophe bonds, for instance, can be expensive to issue and may not provide the same level of coverage as reinsurance. Collateralized reinsurance, while providing additional security, can be complex to structure and may tie up significant amounts of capital. ILWs, while cost-effective, may not provide the specific coverage an insurer needs.

While reinsurance remains the preferred risk transfer mechanism for many insurers, alternatives such as catastrophe bonds, collateralized reinsurance, ILWs, contingent capital, and surplus notes can play a valuable role in a comprehensive risk management strategy.

As the risk landscape evolves, insurers will need to continually assess their risk transfer options to find the optimal mix of reinsurance and alternative capital sources. For Florida property insurers, this will likely involve a combination of traditional reinsurance, which has a proven track record in the state, and newer alternatives that can provide additional capacity and diversification.

By carefully considering the pros and cons of each alternative and how they fit into their overall risk management strategy, insurers can build more resilient and adaptable businesses that are better prepared to weather the storms ahead.

In summary, while there are multiple ways for insurance companies to access capital, reinsurance is preferred due to its direct impact on risk management, flexibility, regulatory treatment, and overall cost-effectiveness in supporting the core operations of insurance underwriting (*the process of evaluating the risks involved in insuring a person or asset and determining appropriate premium rates*) and claims management.

Conclusion: The Unseen Guardian

Reinsurance might seem like an industry buzzword, but for Florida homeowners, it's the unseen guardian that fortifies the insurance market against the tempest of hurricanes. It ensures that when the skies clear after a storm, the financial infrastructure of their insurance coverage remains intact, ready to rebuild and restore. Understanding reinsurance is not just about recognizing its role in risk management; it's about appreciating the peace of mind it brings to homeowners in the Sunshine State, ensuring that their homes and futures are protected against the unpredictable fury of nature.

Summary of Chapter 30:

Chapter 30, "Beyond the Storm: How Reinsurance Protects Florida's Homeowners," explorers the indispensable role of reinsurance in Florida's insurance landscape, particularly in mitigating the financial impact of hurricanes. The chapter begins by elucidating the foundational role of reinsurance, likening it to a superhero that swoops in to protect insurance companies from the aftermath of natural disasters, ensuring they can fulfill claims and maintain stability.

Reinsurance serves as a financial safety net for insurance companies, especially in high-risk areas like Florida, where hurricanes pose significant threats to homeowners. By spreading risk globally, reinsurance makes it financially viable for insurers to offer coverage in hurricane-prone regions, ensuring availability and affordability for policyholders.

The chapter explores the complex mechanisms of the reinsurance market, including sidecars and global risk distribution facilities like the Caribbean Catastrophe Risk Insurance Facility (CCRIF) and the African Risk Capacity (ARC). These mechanisms demonstrate how reinsurance enables effective risk management and cost mitigation on a global scale, benefiting insurers and policyholders alike.

Historical examples, such as the response to Hurricane Katrina in 2005 and Hurricane Irma in 2017, underscore the critical role of reinsurance in stabilizing the insurance market and ensuring claims can be paid promptly after catastrophic events. The chapter also examines the specific impact of reinsurance on Florida's insurance market, highlighting the reliance of small-to-medium-sized insurers on reinsurance to manage their exposure to hurricane risk.

The chapter elucidates reinsurance through everyday analogies, such as domino setups, sandcastles, and circus safety nets, making the concept accessible to readers. These analogies illustrate how reinsurance acts as a crucial intervention, protecting insurers from financial disaster and ensuring policyholders' homes and livelihoods remain safeguarded.

Furthermore, the chapter explores the competitive edge that reinsurance injects into the insurance market, enabling more players to enter and offering homeowners a broader range of choices. It navigates the financial seas, demystifying the costs and benefits of reinsurance and highlighting its role in optimizing insurers' capital management.

In addition to reinsurance, the chapter examines alternative risk transfer mechanisms, including letters of credit, catastrophe bonds, and industry loss warranties (ILWs). While these alternatives offer flexibility and diversification, reinsurance remains the preferred source of outside capital for insurers due to its efficiency, regulatory favor, and operational continuity.

As we conclude this chapter, I emphasize the unseen yet crucial role of reinsurance in fortifying Florida's insurance market against the unpredictable fury of hurricanes. Understanding reinsurance goes beyond risk management; it's about ensuring peace of mind for homeowners, knowing that their homes and futures are protected even in the face of nature's most formidable challenges.

Transition to Chapter 31:

Finally, after delving deep into reinsurance, Chapter 31, "Navigating the Complexities of Florida," extends our discourse, inviting readers to delve deeper into the twisting intricacies of Florida's property insurance market, where the theoretical meets the practical, and the economic intertwines with the fundamental.

So, as we turn the pages from one chapter to the next, let's remember that every bit of history and every slice of knowledge tucks another sandbag against the floodwaters of future storms. Onward we go, with a keen eye on the past and a ready mind for what lies ahead.

Chapter 31

Navigating the Complexities of Florida's Property Insurance Market

In prior chapters, we examined the writings of Daniel Ellsberg, Dr. Frank Knight, and Frederic Bastiat. Before we leave this part of our story, let's examine the ideas of these three brilliant minds one final time.

The Ellsberg Paradox and Ambiguity Aversion

First up, let's talk again about Daniel Ellsberg and his paradox. You will remember that Ellsberg found that people prefer known risks over ambiguous ones, even when the expected outcomes are the same. In the context of the Florida property insurance market, this means that both insurers and policyholders may gravitate towards situations where risks are quantifiable and well-understood. This

preference for clarity and predictability highlights the importance of <u>accurate data collection</u>, <u>sophisticated modeling techniques</u>, and <u>transparent communication</u> in the insurance industry.

From a policy perspective, encouraging the use of advanced analytics and climate models could help reduce ambiguity in insurance pricing and coverage decisions. Providing a clearer picture of the risks involved could make insurance products more attractive to consumers and more manageable for insurers, ultimately contributing to a more stable and efficient market.

Knight's Risk-Uncertainty Distinction and the Role of Reinsurance

Next, we discussed Frank Knight and his distinction between risk and uncertainty. While risk refers to situations where probabilities can be quantified, uncertainty describes scenarios where probabilities are unknown or unmeasurable. In a state prone to natural disasters like Florida, the inherent uncertainty surrounding the frequency and severity of events like hurricanes poses significant challenges for insurers.

Private reinsurance emerges as a potential solution to this Knightian uncertainty. By spreading risk globally, reinsurance allows insurers to transfer portions of their risk to international markets, ensuring that no single entity bears a disproportionate share of the potential losses. This global distribution of risk aligns with Knight's principles of effective risk management, promoting a more competitive and resilient insurance market.

The 2005 hurricane season provides a compelling example of the effectiveness of the private reinsurance model, with losses distributed across a diverse range of insurers and reinsurers worldwide. In contrast, government-created catastrophe funds, which concentrate risk within a single jurisdiction, may inadvertently transform quantifiable risks into uncertainties, particularly regarding the fund's long-term solvency and the potential burden on taxpayers.

Bastiat's Cautionary Tale and the Unintended Consequences of Regulation

Finally, let's consider Frédéric Bastiat's observations on human nature and the unintended consequences of government intervention. Bastiat argues that people tend to pursue their own interests, sometimes at the expense of others, and that well-intentioned government policies can often lead to unforeseen negative outcomes.

In the context of insurance regulation, overly prescriptive policies, such as strict rate-setting or coverage mandates, could inadvertently stifle competition, discourage innovation, and ultimately undermine the market's stability and affordability. Policymakers must, therefore, strike a delicate balance between protecting consumers and fostering a competitive, innovative insurance market.

Bastiat's insights suggest that regulatory frameworks should prioritize transparency, consumer protection, and solvency requirements while allowing market forces to play a significant role in pricing and coverage decisions. By creating an environment that encourages competition and innovation, policymakers can harness the power of the private sector to develop creative solutions to the unique challenges posed by the Florida property insurance market.

The Principles of Effective Risk Management

So, what can we learn from these insights? In this context, let's take a look at the principles of effective risk management:

1. **<u>Quantifying and managing risk</u>**: Effective risk management involves accurately quantifying risks, allowing insurers to price their products

appropriately and make informed decisions about coverage. This principle aligns with Ellsberg's Paradox, which highlights the importance of reducing ambiguity in decision-making.

2. **Diversifying risk exposure**: Spreading risk across various parties and geographies is a central tenet of effective risk management. This principle is exemplified by the global reinsurance model, which distributes risk internationally, ensuring that no single entity bears a disproportionate share of potential losses. This approach aligns with Knight's distinction between risk and uncertainty, as it helps transform unquantifiable uncertainties into manageable risks.

3. **Promoting market competition**: A competitive insurance market is essential for effective risk management, as it encourages innovation, efficiency, and customer choice. Bastiat's observations on the unintended consequences of government intervention underscore the importance of fostering a competitive market environment, where private sector actors are incentivized to develop creative solutions to complex risk management challenges.

4. **Ensuring transparency and solvency**: Effective risk management requires transparency in risk assessment and communication and insurers' financial solvency. Regulatory frameworks prioritizing transparency and solvency requirements can help build trust in the insurance market and protect consumers from potential losses.

5. **Encouraging risk mitigation**: Effective risk management should also involve incentives for risk mitigation, such as encouraging the adoption of resilient building practices or implementing disaster preparedness measures. These strategies can help lower the overall insurance cost and promote long-term sustainability by reducing the underlying risks.

6. **Continuous learning and adaptation**: Given the dynamic nature of risks, particularly in the context of climate change, effective risk management requires continuous learning and adaptation. This involves regularly updating risk models, incorporating new data and insights, and adjusting strategies as needed to respond to changing circumstances.

The Florida Hurricane Catastrophe Fund Debate

Now, let's address the debate surrounding the expansion of the Florida Hurricane Catastrophe Fund (FHCF). Some argue that expanding the FHCF will reduce homeowners' insurance premiums, but there are some important concerns to consider.

Cautionary Note: *A catastrophe fund violates one of the fundamental tenets of insurance – spreading the risk. It also supplants private-sector reinsurance, which is fully paid for in advance.*

Private reinsurance spreads the risk globally, and the cost of that reinsurance is paid upfront. A state catastrophe fund concentrates that risk in one jurisdiction and shifts the financial risk of catastrophic losses from private sector insurers to insurance buyers and taxpayers.

On the other hand, private reinsurance promotes the spreading of risk and loss. Results from the 2005 hurricanes indicate that the losses were borne as follows: 41% in the private insurer market, 24% among Bermuda reinsurers, 11% for U.S. reinsurers, 13% among European reinsurers, 9% in Lloyds, and 1% for other. Risk spreading fosters a viable competitive market; risk concentration among a few insurers and state funds inhibits a competitive market.

So, let's break down the concerns:

1. Violating the fundamental tenet of risk spreading: As the cautionary note states, the FHCF concentrates risk within a single jurisdiction rather than

spreading it globally. This approach violates a core principle of insurance and effective risk management. By expanding the FHCF, Florida would further concentrate risk, potentially increasing the state's and its taxpayers' financial vulnerability in the event of a major catastrophe.

2. Supplanting private reinsurance: The expansion of the FHCF would likely supplant private reinsurance, which is fully paid for in advance and spreads risk globally. Data from the 2005 hurricanes demonstrates the effectiveness of private reinsurance in distributing losses across a wide range of entities and geographies. By replacing private reinsurance with a state-run catastrophe fund, Florida would forego the benefits of global risk spreading and potentially expose itself to greater financial risk.

3. Shifting risk to insurance buyers and taxpayers: The cautionary note highlights that the FHCF shifts the financial risk of catastrophic losses from private insurers to insurance buyers and taxpayers. This means that the financial burden would fall on Floridians in the event of a major catastrophe, rather than being spread across a global network of reinsurers. This concentration of risk could lead to significant financial strain for the state and its residents.

4. Inhibiting a competitive market: As noted, risk spreading fosters a viable competitive market, while risk concentration among a few insurers and state funds inhibits competition. The expansion of the FHCF would likely reduce the role of private reinsurance and concentrate risk within the state, potentially leading to a less competitive and less innovative insurance market in Florida.

5. Potential for unintended consequences: Drawing from Bastiat's observations, the expansion of the FHCF could lead to unintended consequences, such as reduced market competition, decreased incentives for risk mitigation, and increased moral hazard (the risk that a party protected by insurance will take greater risks because the financial consequences are borne by the insurer). Policymakers should carefully consider these potential drawbacks before pursuing an expansion of the state-run catastrophe fund.

While the goal of reducing homeowner insurance premiums in Florida is understandable and important, the expansion of the FHCF may not be the most effective or sustainable solution. Instead, policymakers should focus on promoting a competitive and innovative private insurance market, encouraging risk mitigation efforts, and developing targeted assistance programs for vulnerable homeowners.

Florida can work towards a more resilient and equitable property insurance system without compromising the fundamental principles of effective risk management by strengthening the private reinsurance market, improving building codes and land-use planning, and providing targeted support to those in need. This approach, guided by the insights of Ellsberg, Knight, and Bastiat, would prioritize the long-term stability and sustainability of the Florida property insurance market while also addressing the pressing need for affordable coverage.

Florida's Property Insurance Market: The Three-Legged Stool

Florida's property insurance market functions like a three-legged stool, supported by three main components that provide balance and stability: the Citizens Property Insurance Company, the Florida Hurricane Catastrophe Fund (FHCF), and the Florida Insurance Guaranty Fund. Each one plays a crucial role in protecting Florida homeowners and providing financial stability to the market. But what happens when one leg becomes impaired or goes missing altogether?

Have you ever tried to sit on a two-legged stool? Imagine perching yourself atop one of these unstable contraptions, teetering back and forth while trying to find balance. It's almost impossible to remain upright, and the effort to stay steady becomes exhausting. In the same way, managing Florida's property insurance market becomes incredibly challenging when one of these three governmental institutions is impaired or absent.

1. **A Balanced Market:** In a well-functioning insurance market, all three components work harmoniously. Citizens Property Insurance ensures that all homeowners, including those who can't secure private insurance, have access to coverage. The Florida Hurricane Catastrophe Fund (FHCF) provides additional financial support to insurers by covering excess losses from hurricanes. Finally, the Florida Insurance Guaranty Fund steps in to protect policyholders when an insurer becomes insolvent. Together, these components create a balanced system that keeps Florida's insurance market stable and functional.

2. **A Broken Leg:** If one of the three components' falters, such as if the FHCF were weakened by self-serving policy changes, the stool begins to wobble. Any modification that undermines the FHCF's ability to fulfill its financial obligations destabilizes the entire market, leaving it imbalanced and prone to collapse. Just as it's challenging to maintain balance on a stool with only two legs, a weakened insurance market quickly becomes untenable.

3. **Missing a Leg:** If one of these supports is entirely absent, like a stool with only two legs, the market can no longer stand upright. The absence of the FHCF, for example, would create a dangerous gap, leaving insurers exposed and policyholders without proper protection. In such a scenario, managing Florida's property insurance market becomes nearly impossible, and homeowners are left vulnerable to coverage gaps and skyrocketing rates.

Maintaining balance in Florida's property insurance market requires that all three pillars remain strong and work together. Weakening or removing any of them creates an unstable system, putting the entire market at risk. Just as you wouldn't dare trust yourself to sit on a two-legged stool, we can't afford to let one of these crucial supports falter or disappear. Lawmakers should prioritize keeping each institution stable and fully functional to safeguard Florida's insurance market and ensure comprehensive protection for homeowners.

Now, let's conclude with a summary of these fundamental principles.

Conclusion

The Florida property insurance market is undoubtedly complex, with numerous economic, behavioral, and political factors at play. By understanding Ellsberg, Knight, and Bastiat's insights and adhering to the principles of effective risk management, policymakers, insurers, and consumers can work together to create a more resilient, sustainable, and equitable property insurance market.

Ultimately, the success of Florida's property insurance market depends on collaboration, adaptability, and a commitment to long-term stability. By embracing these principles and learning from experience, Florida can better protect its citizens and economy from the impacts of natural disasters while promoting a healthy and vibrant insurance market.

Summary of Chapter 31:

Chapter 31 examines the intricacies of Florida's property insurance market, drawing insights from the theories of Daniel Ellsberg, Dr. Frank Knight, and Frédéric Bastiat. It begins by revisiting Ellsberg's paradox and its implications for insurance decision-making, emphasizing the importance of clarity and predictability in risk assessment. Moving on to Knight's distinction between risk and uncertainty, the chapter explores how private reinsurance serves as a solution to the inherent uncertainties of natural disasters like hurricanes, promoting a more competitive and resilient insurance market.

Bastiat's cautionary observations on the unintended consequences of government intervention provide a lens through which to evaluate insurance regulation. The chapter argues for a balanced approach that prioritizes transparency, consumer protection, and market competition while avoiding overly prescriptive policies that stifle innovation.

The principles of effective risk management, including quantifying and diversifying risk, promoting market competition, and ensuring transparency and solvency, are highlighted as guiding principles for policymakers and insurers. The chapter also examines the debate surrounding the expansion of the Florida Hurricane Catastrophe Fund (FHCF), cautioning against the potential drawbacks of concentrating risk within a single jurisdiction and supplanting private reinsurance.

Ultimately, the chapter advocates for a collaborative approach that embraces the insights of Ellsberg, Knight, and Bastiat to create a more resilient, sustainable, and equitable property insurance market in Florida. By fostering innovation, promoting risk mitigation efforts, and prioritizing long-term stability, policymakers can navigate the complexities of the insurance landscape while safeguarding the interests of homeowners and taxpayers alike.

Chapter 32

Behavioral Economics and Decision Making Under Uncertainty: A Comprehensive Analysis

Introduction

Behavioral economics and the study of decision-making under uncertainty form a critical juncture at which human psychology intersects with economic theory. Traditional economic models assume that individuals act rationally, seeking to maximize utility in a predictable, quantifiable manner. However, behavioral economics challenges this assumption, presenting a nuanced view incorporating psychological, cognitive, and emotional factors affecting decisions.

This Chapter explores the principles of behavioral economics, examines how individuals make decisions in conditions of uncertainty, and applies these insights to the complex challenges facing Florida's property insurance market, as detailed in several previous Chapters of this book.

Core Principles of Behavioral Economics

Behavioral economics integrates insights from psychology into economic analysis to understand why people sometimes make irrational decisions, behave in ways that deviate from standard economic predictions, or delay gratification in a manner that conflicts with their long-term goals.

Key concepts include:

1. Bounded rationality: People have limited cognitive abilities and often use mental shortcuts (heuristics) to make decisions rather than optimizing.

2. Loss aversion: Losses loom larger than equivalent gains. People tend to strongly prefer avoiding losses to acquiring gains.
3. Framing effects: Different ways of presenting the same information can evoke different emotions and lead to different decisions.
4. Status quo bias: People tend to prefer things to stay the same and exhibit inertia in decision making.
5. Availability heuristic: People tend to overestimate the likelihood of events that easily come to mind.
6. Prospect Theory: Developed by Daniel Kahneman and Amos Tversky, this theory suggests that people value gains and losses differently, leading to decision-making asymmetries.

Decision Making Under Uncertainty

Decision-making under uncertainty involves scenarios where the outcomes of decisions are unknown or where probabilities cannot be precisely assigned.

Key aspects include:

1. Ambiguity aversion: People prefer risks with known probabilities over those with unknown probabilities (Ellsberg paradox).
2. Knightian uncertainty: In some situations, probabilities are unknowable, not just unknown. This causes challenges for optimization frameworks.
3. Risk Aversion: In the face of uncertainty, individuals tend to prefer avoiding losses rather than acquiring equivalent gains.
4. Impact of Emotions: Emotional responses to uncertainty can lead to decisions that deviate from what is expected under traditional economic theory. Stress and fear can cause individuals to make more conservative choices or avoid decision-making altogether.

Narrative and Support from Previous Chapters

Previous Chapters illustrates these principles in action within the context of Florida's property insurance market.

Chapter 14 highlights how consumers underestimate risks and make irrational decisions when not faced with the true costs, in line with bounded rationality and availability heuristic ideas.

Chapter 23 showcases framing effects, with people dancing around symptoms rather than confronting root causes directly. It also discusses the legislative tendency to focus on immediate gratification over long-term benefits, mirroring the concepts of loss aversion and prospect theory.

Chapter 27 dives into ambiguity aversion and Knightian uncertainty, highlighting how uncertainty about political/regulatory changes generates challenges distinct from measurable hurricane risks. The Ellsberg Paradox is particularly pertinent here, illustrating how people's avoidance of ambiguous options leads to conservative decision-making.

Strategies for Effective Decision-Making

Chapter 14 of the manuscript outlines several strategies for overcoming the impediments to effective decision-making, including:

1. A tutorial on problem-solving: This provides a structured approach to addressing complex issues by breaking them down into manageable steps. By clearly defining the problem, gathering relevant data, and analyzing the root causes, policymakers can develop a more comprehensive understanding of the challenges and identify targeted solutions.
2. Guiding principles for insurance legislation: These principles serve as a powerful antidote to the status quo bias and ambiguity aversion hindering meaningful reform. They provide a clear set of values and objectives to anchor decision-making, helping legislators overcome the temptation to maintain the current state of affairs or avoid difficult choices in the face of uncertainty.
3. Evaluating future legislation: This framework provides a structured approach to assessing proposed policies against the guiding principles and

key objectives of insurance reform. It encourages a more rigorous and evidence-based approach to policymaking, mitigating the influence of bounded rationality and the availability heuristic.

Conclusion

Behavioral economics and the study of decision-making under uncertainty reveal the complexity of human behavior in economic contexts. The insights from these fields provide a powerful lens through which to understand the seemingly irrational decisions and behaviors that shape the challenges facing Florida's property insurance market. By acknowledging and understanding the psychological underpinnings of decision-making, policymakers can develop more effective strategies for managing risk, promoting responsible behavior, and ensuring the long-term resilience of communities in the face of an ever-changing climate and an increasingly complex insurance market.

The strategies outlined in this book including the tutorial on problem-solving, the establishment of guiding principles for insurance legislation, and the framework for evaluating future legislation, offer valuable tools for overcoming the behavioral and cognitive biases that often impede effective decision making. By consistently applying these tools and principles over time, and by building a broad coalition of stakeholders committed to meaningful reform, Florida can gradually shift the landscape of insurance policymaking towards a more sustainable and equitable future.

As I reflect on the journey that led me to write this book, I am struck by the depth and complexity of the issues at hand. From my early days as an insurance agent to my tenure as a state representative, I have seen firsthand the devastating impact that natural disasters can have on communities and the critical role that insurance markets play in promoting resilience and recovery.

At the same time, I have also witnessed the unintended consequences that can arise when well-intentioned policies fail to account for the complex incentives and feedback loops that shape market dynamics. Too often, policymakers have sought to provide short-term relief without considering the long-term implications of their actions, creating perverse incentives that undermine the very goals they seek to achieve.

It is my hope that by sharing my experiences and insights in this book, I can contribute to a more informed and nuanced dialogue about the challenges facing Florida's insurance markets and the broader implications for risk management in an uncertain world. By drawing on the wisdom of leading economic thinkers and grounding my analysis in real-world examples, I have sought to provide a framework for thinking about these issues that is both intellectually rigorous and practically relevant.

For a deeper understanding of Behavioral economics and the study of decision-making under uncertainty, please see the links to additional resources shown below:

Citations:

1. "The Undoing Project: A Friendship That Changed Our Minds" by Michael Lewis (Book)

    https://www.goodreads.com/book/show/35631386-the-undoing-project

2. "Behavioral Economics: Past, Present, and Future" by Richard H. Thaler (Paper)

    https://www.bbvaopenmind.com/en/articles/behavioral-economics-past-present-and-future/?utm_source=views&utm_medium=article1019&utm_campaign

=MITcompany&cid=dis:::----mitcompany:--:views::::::sitlnk:techreview:art1019

3. "Prospect Theory: An Analysis of Decision Under Risk" by Daniel Kahneman and Amos Tversky (Paper)

   https://web.mit.edu/curhan/www/docs/Articles/15341_Readings/Behavioral_Decision_Theory/Kahneman_Tversky_1979_Prospect_theory.pdf

4. "Judgment Under Uncertainty: Heuristics and Biases" by Amos Tversky and Daniel Kahneman (Paper)

   https://www2.psych.ubc.ca/~schaller/Psyc590Readings/TverskyKahneman1974.pdf

5. "The Framing of Decisions and the Psychology of Choice" by Amos Tversky and Daniel Kahneman (Paper)

   https://www.academia.edu/36011398/The_Framing_of_Decisions_and_the_Psychology_of_Choice

6. "Risk, Uncertainty, and Profit" by Frank H. Knight (Book)

   https://cdn.mises.org/Risk,%20Uncertainty,%20and%20Profit_4.pdf

7. Why are we Satisfied by "Good Enough?": Bounded Rationality Explained

   https://thedecisionlab.com/biases/bounded-rationality

8. What Is Status Quo Bias? |Definition & Examples

   https://www.scribbr.com/research-bias/status-quo-bias/

9. A Holistic Review of Framing Effect: Theories and Applications

   https://www.atlantis-press.com/article/125982166.pdf

10. Loss Aversion – Everything You Need to Know – Inside BE

https://insidebe.com/articles/loss-aversion/

11. Behavioral Economics and Public Policy: A Pragmatic Perspective by Raj Chetty (Paper)

    https://dash.harvard.edu/bitstream/handle/1/34330194/behavioral_ely.pdf

12. Behavioral Economics to Insurance: A Brief Guide by Roberto Rizzo

    https://www.rgare.com/knowledge-center/article/behavioral-approach-to-insurance

13. Choice Under Uncertainty: Problems Solved and Unsolved by Mark J. Machina (Paper)

    https://econweb.ucsd.edu/~mmachina/papers/Machina_Problems_Paper.pdf

14. Behavioral Economics and Insurance Law by Tom Baker and Peter Siegelman (Paper)

    https://scholarship.law.upenn.edu/cgi/viewcontent.cgi?referer=&httpsredir=1&article=1654&context=faculty_scholarship

Transition to Chapter 33:

Chapter 33, "The History of Florida Hurricanes," promises to be a nostalgic ride—not the fun kind, but the kind that teaches us something. We'll trace the paths of hurricanes that have danced across Florida's skies, some leaving little more than a few turned leaves, others rewriting the story of entire communities. It's like flipping through an old family album, except instead of Aunt Marge's 80s hairdos, we're looking at the echoes of past storms and the marks they left on the Sunshine State's memory.

CHAPTER 33

The History of Florida Hurricanes: The Apex of Catastrophe

Florida, often referred to as the Sunshine State, paradoxically stands as the peak catastrophe zone in the world, particularly when it comes to hurricanes. This narrative unveils the turbulent history of hurricanes in Florida, a state that has weathered the brunt of some of the most devastating storms in history.

(The hurricanes in this list occurring before 1900 are not exhaustive, and their descriptions are derived from non-official, anecdotal sources. These accounts are included for informational purposes only and may not represent definitive historical records.)

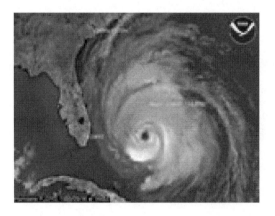

The Chronology of Chaos

The Early Years: 1500s to 1800s

1. 1559: The Unnamed Terror - In September 1559, a formidable hurricane wreaked havoc on the Pensacola Bay Area of Florida, a grim reminder of

nature's fury. Details are scarce, but the impact was significant enough to be recorded in history.

See: https://floridatravel.blog/history-of-florida-hurricanes-10-worst/

See: https://hurricanescience.org/history/storms/pre1900s/1559/index.html

2. 1599: The Repeat Onslaught - History repeated itself four decades later in 1599, with another unnamed hurricane lashing at St. Augustine, Florida's shores. The recurring pattern of these storms began to paint a picture of a state in the eye of nature's wrath.

See: https://floridatravStel.blog/history-of-florida-hurricanes-10-worst/

3. 1622: The Atlantic Fury - 1622 marked another chapter in Florida's hurricane history. A hurricane in the Atlantic Ocean passed through the Florida Keys and left a trail of destruction, signaling the unpredictable power of these natural phenomena.

See: https://floridatravel.blog/history-of-florida-hurricanes-10-worst/

4. 1752: The Santa Rosa Island Calamity—On November 3, 1752, a hurricane struck Santa Rosa Island. The storm's impact was profound, reshaping the island's geography and leaving a lasting imprint on the local communities. https://floridatravel.blog/history-of-florida-hurricanes-10-worst/

See also: A History Shaped by Hurricanes - "Pensacola Maritime Heritage Trail" https://www.hmdb.org/m.asp?m=130814;

See also: Legends of America - "Presidio Isla Santa Rosa Punta de Siguenza, Florida" https://www.legendsofamerica.com/presidio-isla-santa-rosa/

5. 1760: The Pensacola Havoc - August 1760 witnessed a hurricane that hit Pensacola with such force that it destroyed much of the settlement. This event underscored the vulnerability of coastal cities to hurricane threats.

See: https://floridatravel.blog/history-of-florida-hurricanes-10-worst/

6. 1811 - The St. Augustine Storm: October 5, 1811, brought a hurricane to St. Augustine, causing considerable damage and contributing to the city's long history with hurricanes.

See: https://floridatravel.blog/history-of-florida-hurricanes-10-worst/

7. 1811—Pensacola Hurricane: On October 11, 1811, a hurricane struck Pensacola, FL, and Fort Stoddard, Alabama. The specific details of this storm

are limited. However, historical records classify it as a significant hurricane during the 1811 Atlantic hurricane season.
See: https://en.wikipedia.org/wiki/1810s_Atlantic_hurricane_seasons

8. 1821 - The Northeast Florida Hurricane struck with vengeance, particularly impacting Northeast Florida. Its intensity and destruction were a grim reminder of the region's vulnerability.

9. 1831 - The Central Florida Hurricane: In 1831, a hurricane swept through Central Florida, demonstrating that no part of the state is immune to the wrath of these storms.

10. 1831 - The Escambia County Hurricane: In 1831, a severe hurricane struck Escambia County, highlighting the susceptibility of Florida's panhandle to these devastating natural disasters.

11. 1834 - The Northern Florida Hurricane: This hurricane focused its fury on Northern Florida, reinforcing that hurricanes are a statewide concern.

12. 1841 - The Great Tampa Bay Hurricane: The 1841 hurricane that hit Tampa Bay was significant, emphasizing the area's vulnerability to severe storms. This hurricane set a precedent for the need for better preparedness in the region. This catastrophic hurricane wreaked havoc across Tampa Bay, a stark example of the unpredictable fury of these storms.

13. 1841 - Hurricane destroys Fort Dulany at Punta Rassa (near Ft. Myers) on the Caloosahatchee River.
https://floridatravel.blog/history-of-florida-hurricanes-10-worst/

14. 1844 - The Havana Hurricane: Striking in October 1844, this hurricane, known as the Havana Hurricane, also affected Florida significantly, underscoring the interconnected weather patterns of the Caribbean and Florida.

15. 1846 - The Key West Hurricane AKA The Great Havana Hurricane: The Key West Hurricane of 1846 left a trail of destruction, particularly impacting the Florida Keys, an area frequently in the path of these relentless storms.
See: https://en.wikipedia.org/wiki/1846_Havana_hurricane

16. 1848 - The Tampa Bay Hurricane: Another severe hurricane struck Tampa Bay in 1848, reinforcing the region's vulnerability to tropical cyclones.
See: https://en.wikipedia.org/wiki/1848_Tampa_Bay_hurricane

17. 1852 – No Name Storm: Storm ID – 1852278N14293. Max Cat H2. Landfall 10/09/1852, Apalachicola, FL.
    See: https://ibtracs.unca.edu/index.php?name=v04r00-1852278N14293

18. 1856 – No Name Storm: Storm ID – 1856235N13302 Max Cat H3. Landfall 08/24/1856, Bay County, FL.
    See: https://ibtracs.unca.edu/index.php?name=v04r00-1856235N13302

19. 1858 – No Name Storm: Storm ID – 1858254N21273 Max Cat H2. Landfall 09/16/1858, Tampa Bay, FL.
    See: https://ibtracs.unca.edu/index.php?name=v04r00-1858254N21273

20. 1859 – No Name Storm: Storm ID – 1859297N20267 Max Cat H1. Landfall 10/28/1859, Tampa Bay, FL.
    See: https://ibtracs.unca.edu/index.php?name=v04r00-1859297N20267

21. 1865 – No Name Storm; Storm ID – 1865287N11303 Max Cat H2. Landfall 10/15/1865, Marco Island, FL.
    See: https://ibtracs.unca.edu/index.php?name=v04r00-1865287N11303

22. 1870 – No Name Storm; Storm ID – 1870278N18286 Max Cat H3. Landfall 10/05/1870, Key West, FL.
    See: https://ibtracs.unca.edu/index.php?name=v04r00-1870278N18286

23. 1870 – No Name Storm; Storm ID – 187029N15279 Max Cat H2. Landfall 10/20/1870, Naples, FL.
    See: https://ibtracs.unca.edu/index.php?name=v04r00-1870290N15279

24. 1871 – No Name Storm: Storm ID – 1871224N26291 Max Cat H3. Landfall 08/17/1871 St. Lucie County, FL.
    See: https://ibtracs.unca.edu/index.php?name=v04r00-1871224N26291

25. 1871 – No Name Storm: Storm ID - 1871229N11329 Max Cat H3. Landfall 08/25/1871, Palm Beach, FL
    See: https://ibtracs.unca.edu/index.php?name=v04r00-1871229N11329

26. 1871 – No Name Storm: Storm ID – 1871247N28277 Max Cat H1. Landfall 09/06/1871, Levy County, FL.
    See: https://ibtracs.unca.edu/index.php?name=v04r00-1871247N28277

27. 1871 – No Name Storm: Storm ID – 1871271N19269 Max Cat H1. Landfall 10/05/1871, Apalachicola, FL.
    See: https://ibtracs.unca.edu/index.php?name=v04r00-1871271N19269

28. 1872 - No Name: Storm ID - 1872296N23271 Max Cat H1. Landfall Oct 23, 1872, Pinellas County, FL.
See: https://ibtracs.unca.edu/index.php?name=v04r00-1872296N23271

29. 1873 – No Name: Storm ID - 1873256N13296 Max Cat H1. Landfall Sep 19, 1873, Apalachicola, FL.
See: https://ibtracs.unca.edu/index.php?name=v04r00-1873256N13296

30. 1873 - No Name: Storm ID - 1873269N13303 Max Cat H3. Landfall Sep 29, 1873, Fort Myers, FL.
See: https://ibtracs.unca.edu/index.php?name=v04r00- 1873269N13303

31. 1874 - No Name: Storm ID - 1874268N18274 Max Cat H1. Landfall Sep 25, 1874, Levy County, FL
See: https://ibtracs.unca.edu/index.php?name=v04r00-1874268N18274

32. 1876 – No Name: Storm ID - 1876285N11279 Max Cat H3. Landfall Oct 19, 1876, Naples, FL.
See :https://ibtracs.unca.edu/index.php?name=v04r00-1876285N11279

33. 1877 - No Name: Storm ID - 1877257N22268 Max Cat H1. Landfall Sep 18, 1877, Fort Walton Beach, FL.
See: https://ibtracs.unca.edu/index.php?name=v04r00-1877257N22268

34. 1877 - No Name: Storm ID - 1877260N17327 Max Cat H3. Landfall Sep 23, 1877, Panama City, FL.
See: https://ibtracs.unca.edu/index.php?name=v04r00-1877260N17327

35. 1878 - No Name: Storm ID - 1878244N09306 Max Cat H2. Landfall Sep 4, 1878, Monroe County, FL.
See: https://ibtracs.unca.edu/index.php?name=v04r00-1878244N09306

36. 1878 – No Name: Storm ID - 1878282N24269 Max Cat H1. Landfall Oct 10, 1878, Port St. Joe, FL.
See: https://ibtracs.unca.edu/index.php?name=v04r00-1878282N24269

37. 1878 – No Name: Storm ID - 1878287N19283 Max Cat H2. Landfall Oct 21, 1878, Florida Keys, FL.
See: https://ibtracs.unca.edu/index.php?name=v04r00-1878287N19283

38. 1879 - No Name: Storm ID - 1879297N20275 Max Cat H1. Landfall Oct 27, 1879, Levy County, FL.
See: https://ibtracs.unca.edu/index.php?name=v04r00-1879297N20275

39. 1880 - No Name: Storm ID - 1880230N15342 Max Cat H2. Landfall Aug 29, 1880, Brevard County, FL.
    See: https://ibtracs.unca.edu/index.php?name=v04r00-1880230N15342
40. 1880 – No Name: Storm ID - 1880250N24271 Max Cat H1. Landfall Sep 8, 1880, Perry, FL.
    See: https://ibtracs.unca.edu/index.php?name=v04r00-1880250N24271
41. 1880 – No Name: 1880279N18275 Max Cat H1. Landfall Oct 6, 1880, Citrus County, FL.
    See: https://ibtracs.unca.edu/index.php?name=v04r00-1880279N18275
42. 1881 – No Name: Storm ID - 1881228N20273 Max Cat H1. Landfall Aug 22, 1881, Key West, FL.
    See: https://ibtracs.unca.edu/index.php?name=v04r00-1881228N20273
43. 1882 – No Name: Storm ID - 1882244N19296 Max Cat H3. Landfall Sep 5, 1882, Fort Walton Beach, FL
    See: https://ibtracs.unca.edu/index.php?name=v04r00-1882244N19296
44. 1882 – No Name: Storm ID - 1882278N11279 Max Cat H4. Landfall Oct 9, 1882, Perry, FL
    See: https://ibtracs.unca.edu/index.php?name=v04r00-1882278N11279
45. 1885 – No Name: Storm ID - 581885233N21293 Max Cat H2. Landfall Aug 25, 1885, Jacksonville, FL.
    See: https://ibtracs.unca.edu/index.php?name=v04r00-1885233N21293
46. 1885 – No Name: Storm ID - 1885264N28268 Max Cat H2. Landfall Sep 21, 1885, Bay County, FL.
    See: https://ibtracs.unca.edu/index.php?name=v04r00-1885264N28268
47. 1885 – No Name: Storm ID - 1885260N22265 Max Cat H1. Landfall Sep 28, 1885, Pensacola, FL.
    See: https://ibtracs.unca.edu/index.php?name=v04r00-1885260N22265
48. 1886 – No Name: Storm ID - 1886195N19277 Max Cat H1, Landfall Jun 19, 1886, Hernando County, FL.
    See: https://ibtracs.unca.edu/index.php?name=v04r00-1886195N19277
49. 1886 – No Name: Storm ID - 1886168N19275 Max Cat H2. Landfall Jun 21, 1886, Wakulla County, FL.
    See: https://ibtracs.unca.edu/index.php?name=v04r00-1886168N19275

50. 1886 – No Name: Storm ID -1886178N17286 Max Cat H2. Landfall Jun 27, 1886, Apalachicola, FL.
    See: https://ibtracs.unca.edu/index.php?name=v04r00-1886178N17286

51. 1887 – No Name: Storm ID - 1887201N12302 Max Cat H2. Landfall Jul 25, 1887, Fort Walton Beach, FL.
    See: https://ibtracs.unca.edu/index.php?name=v04r00-1887201N12302

52. 1887 – No Name: Storm ID - 1887282N19300 Max Cat H. Landfall Oct 11, 1887, Pensacola, FL.
    See: https://ibtracs.unca.edu/index.php?name=v04r00-1887282N19300

53. 1888 – No Name: Storm ID - 1888283N22267 Max Cat H2. Landfall Oct 11, 1888, Levy County, FL.
    See: https://ibtracs.unca.edu/index.php?name=v04r00-1888283N22267

54. 1889 – No Storm: Storm ID - 1889255N16301 Max Cat H2. Landfall Sep 18, 1889, Pensacola, FL.
    See: https://ibtracs.unca.edu/index.php?name=v04r00-1889255N16301

55. 1891 – No Name: Storm ID - 1891229N11313 Max Cat H3. Landfall Aug 24, 1891, Homestead, FL.
    See: https://ibtracs.unca.edu/index.php?name=v04r00-1891229N11313

56. 1893 – No Name: Storm ID - 1893163N20265 Max Cat H1. Landfall Jun 15, 1893, Apalachicola, FL.
    See: https://ibtracs.unca.edu/index.php?name=v04r00-1893163N20265

57. 1893 – No Name: Storm ID - 1893271N16278 Max Cat H4. Landfall Sep 29, 1893, Mobile, AL/Pensacola, FL.
    See: https://ibtracs.unca.edu/index.php?name=v04r00-1893271N16278

58. 1893 – No Name: Storm ID - 1893268N12335 Max Cat H3.Landfall Oct 13, 1893, Jacksonville, FL.
    See: https://ibtracs.unca.edu/index.php?name=v04r00-1893268N12335

59. 1894 – No Name: Storm ID - 1894261N13311 Max Cat H3. Landfall Sep 22, 1894, Tampa, FL.
    See: https://ibtracs.unca.edu/index.php?name=v04r00-1894261N13311

60. 1894 – No Name: Storm ID - 1894270N12284 Max Cat H3. Landfall Oct 9, 1894, Bay County, FL.
    See: https://ibtracs.unca.edu/index.php?name=v04r00-1894270N12284

61. 1896 – No Name: Storm ID - 1896187N21279 Max Cat H2. Landfall Jul 7, 1896, Fort Walton Beach, FL,
    See: https://ibtracs.unca.edu/index.php?name=v04r00-1896187N21279
62. 1896 - Cedar Keys Hurricane: Storm ID - 1896266N17298 Max Cat H3. Landfall Sep 29, 1896.. Cedar Keys was devastated by this powerful hurricane, marking one of the earliest recorded storms to have such a catastrophic impact on this area.
    See: https://ibtracs.unca.edu/index.php?name=v04r00-1896266N17298
    See Also:
    https://floridatravel.blog/history-of-florida-hurricanes-10-worst/
    See also: Alabama Wx Weather Blog - "The Cedar Keys Hurricane of 1896" https://www.alabamawx.com/?p=3726
    See also: Florida Travel Blog - "Historic Cedar Key Florida Road Trip on the Gulf Coast" https://floridatravel.blog/cedar-key-oyster-business-and-clams/
63. 1898 – No Name: Storm ID - 1898214N27280 Max Cat H1. Aug 2, 1898, Stuart, FL. And Aug 3, 1898, Apalachicola, FL.
    See: https://ibtracs.unca.edu/index.php?name=v04r00-1898214N27280
64. 1898 – No Name: Storm ID - 1898268N16302 Mac Cat H4. Landfall Oct 2, 1898, Fernandina Beach, FL.
    See: https://ibtracs.unca.edu/index.php?name=v04r00-1898268N16302
65. 1899 – No Name: Storm ID - 1899210N17291 Max Cat H2. Landfall Jul 28, 1899, Florida Keys, FL. Jul 30, 1899, Apalachicola, FL.
    See: https://ibtracs.unca.edu/index.php?name=v04r00-1899210N17291

The Turn of the Century: 1900s to 1950s

As Florida entered the 20th century, the state continued to face the relentless fury of hurricanes. This period saw some of the most devastating storms in Florida's history, leaving indelible marks on the state's landscape and psyche.

66. **1901 – No Name**: Storm ID - 1901214N33322 Max Cat H1. Landfall Aug 10, 1901, Fort Lauderdale, FL.
    See: https://ibtracs.unca.edu/index.php?name=v04r00-1901214N33322
67. **1901 – No Name**: Storm ID - 1901252N18309 Max Cat H1. Sep 12, 1901, Fort Walton Beach, FL
    See: https://ibtracs.unca.edu/index.php?name=v04r00-1901252N18309
68. **1902 – No Name**: Storm ID - 1902276N14266 Max Cat H2. Landfall Oct 4, 1902, Pensacola, FL.
    See: https://ibtracs.unca.edu/index.php?name=v04r00-1902276N14266

69. **1903 – No Name**: Storm ID -1903252N21288 Max Cat H1. Landfall Sep 13, 1903, Panama City, FL.
See: https://ibtracs.unca.edu/index.php?name=v04r00-1903252N21288

70. **1904 – No Name**: Storm ID - 1904286N15284 Max Cat H1. Landfall Oct 16, 1904, Homestead, FL.
See: https://ibtracs.unca.edu/index.php?name=v04r00-1904286N15284

71. **1906 – No Name**: Storm ID - 1906165N23284 Max Cat H2. Landfall Jun 17, 1906, Key West, FL.
See: https://ibtracs.unca.edu/index.php?name=v04r00-1906165N23284

72. **1906 – No Name**: Storm ID - 1906281N11284 Max Cat H3. Landfall Oct 10, 1906, Florida Keys, FL.
See: https://ibtracs.unca.edu/index.php?name=v04r00-1906281N11284

73. **1909 – No Name**: Storm ID - 1909280N11284 Max Cat H3. Landfall Oct 11, 1909, Key West, FL.
See: https://ibtracs.unca.edu/index.php?name=v04r00-1909280N11284

74. **1910 – No Name**: Storm ID - 1910282N11281 Max Cat H4. Landfall Oct 14, 1910, Fort Myers, FL.
See: https://ibtracs.unca.edu/index.php?name=v04r00-1910282N11281

75. **1915 – No Name**: Storm ID - 1915244N15281 Max Cat H2. Landfall Sep 3, 1915, Port St. Joe, FL.
See: https://ibtracs.unca.edu/index.php?name=v04r00-1915244N15281

76. **1916 – No Name**: Storm ID - 1916283N19284 Max Cat H2. Landfall Oct 15, 1916, Pensacola, FL.
See: https://ibtracs.unca.edu/index.php?name=v04r00-1916283N19284

77. **1917 – No Name**: Storm ID - 1917263N13303 Max Cat H4. Landfall Sep 23, 1917, Destin, FL.
See: https://ibtracs.unca.edu/index.php?name=v04r00-1917263N13303

78. **1919 - Florida Keys Hurricane**: Storm ID - 1919246N16299 Max Cat H4. Landfall Sep 3, 1919. This devastating hurricane in 1919 caused significant destruction in the Florida Keys, a stark reminder of the region's susceptibility to these natural disasters.
https://ibtracs.unca.edu/index.php?name=v04r00-1919246N16299
See Also:

https://hurricanescience.org/history/storms/1910s/FloridaKeys/index.html

79. **1920 – No Name**: Storm ID - 1920269N25277 Max Cat H1. Landfall Sep 30, 1920, Levy County, FL.
See: https://ibtracs.unca.edu/index.php?name=v04r00-1920269N25277

80. **1921 – No Name**: Storm ID - 1921293N13280 Max Cat H4. Landfall Oct 25, 1921, Pasco County, FL.
See: https://ibtracs.unca.edu/index.php?name=v04r00-1921293N13280

81. **1924 – No Name**: Storm ID - 1924257N24276 Max Cat H1. Landfall Sep 15, 1924, Apalachicola, FL.
See: https://ibtracs.unca.edu/index.php?name=v04r00-1924257N24276

82. **1924 – No Name**: Storm ID - 1924288N16277 Max Cat H5. Landfall Oct 12, 1924, Naples, FL.
See: https://ibtracs.unca.edu/index.php?name=v04r00-1924288N16277

83. **1926 – No Name**: Storm ID - 1926203N13304 Max Cat H4. Landfall Jul 28, 1926 Titusville, FL.
See: https://ibtracs.unca.edu/index.php?name=v04r00-1926203N13304

84. **1926 - Great Miami Hurricane**: Storm ID - 1926255N15314 Max Cat H4. Landfall Sep 18, 1926. The Great Miami Hurricane of 1926 stands as one of the most significant hurricanes of the 20th century, causing extensive damage and loss of life in Miami.
See: https://ibtracs.unca.edu/index.php?name=v04r00-1926255N15314
See Also:
https://hurricanescience.org/history/storms/1920s/GreatMiami/index.html

85. *Personal Story: The Great Miami Hurricane's impact was felt across all strata of society. Julia Tuttle, the "Mother of Miami," had passed away just a year before the hurricane. Her legacy, the thriving city of Miami, was left in ruins. The storm surge inundated the city, destroying homes and businesses alike. Many residents were forced to take shelter in public buildings, such as schools and churches, which were themselves not immune to the storm's wrath.*

86. **1926 – No Name**: Storm ID - 1926287N12279 Max Cat H4. Landfall Oct 20, 1926, Key West, FL.

See: https://ibtracs.unca.edu/index.php?name=v04r00-1926287N12279

87. **1928 – No Name:** Storm ID - 1928216N19296 Max Cat H2. Landfall Aug 8, 1928, Ft. Pierce, FL.
    See: https://ibtracs.unca.edu/index.php?name=v04r00-1928216N19296

88. **1928 – No Name:** Storm ID - 1928221N12300 Max Cat H1. Landfall Aut 11, 1928, Key West, FL.
    See: https://ibtracs.unca.edu/index.php?name=v04r00-1928221N12300

89. **1928 - Okeechobee Hurricane:** Storm ID - 1928250N14343 Max Cat H5. Landfall Sep 13, 1928. One of the deadliest hurricanes in United States history, the 1928 Okeechobee Hurricane caused catastrophic damage, particularly around Lake Okeechobee.
    See: https://ibtracs.unca.edu/index.php?name=v04r00-1928250N14343
    See Also: https://hurricanescience.org/history/storms/1920s/Okeechobee/index.html

90. *Personal Story: The Okeechobee Hurricane's impact was particularly devastating for the migrant farm workers in the area. Many of these workers, primarily of African American and Caribbean descent, lived in flimsy, makeshift housing near the lake. When the hurricane struck, the storm surge from the lake inundated these settlements, leading to numerous drownings. The exact death toll among these communities was never fully accounted for, a tragic reflection of the social inequalities of the time.*

91. **1929 – No Name:** Storm ID - 1929262N23296 Max Cat H4. Landfall Sep 26, 1929, Florida Keys, FL
    See: https://ibtracs.unca.edu/index.php?name=v04r00-1929262N23296

92. **1930 – No Name:** Storm ID - 1930241N13317 Max Cat H4. Landfall Sep 3, 1930, Tampa, FL.
    See: https://ibtracs.unca.edu/index.php?name=v04r00-1930241N13317

93. **1933 – No Name:** Storm ID -1933206N14306 Max Cat H1. Landfall Jul 39, 1933, Stuart, FL.
    See: https://ibtracs.unca.edu/index.php?name=v04r00-1933206N14306

94. **1933 – No Name:** Storm ID - 1933243N18304 Max Cat H4. Landfall Sep 4, 1933, Palm Beach County, FL.

See: https://ibtracs.unca.edu/index.php?name=v04r00-1933243N18304

95. **1935 – Labor Day Hurricane**: Storm ID - 1935241N23291 Max Cat H5. Landfall on Sep 2, Labor Day, 1935. This hurricane raced through the Keys with winds near 185 MPH. Over 400 workmen on Flagler's Overseas Railroad were killed. The railroad never ran again, selling the right of way to the state of Florida. This storm also impacted Ernest Hemingway and his writing. One of the Strongest in the History of Hurricanes in Florida.
See: https://ibtracs.unca.edu/index.php?name=v04r00-1935241N23291
See Also: https://hurricanescience.org/history/storms/1930s/LaborDay/index.html

96. **1935 – No Name**: Storm ID - 1935303N32299 Max Cat H2. Landfall Nov 4, 1935, Miami, FL.
See: https://ibtracs.unca.edu/index.php?name=v04r00-1935303N32299

97. **1936 – No Name**: Storm ID - 1936209N24286 Max Cat H2. Landfall Jul 28, 1936, Homestead, FL and July 29, 1936 Fort Walton Beach, FL.
See: https://ibtracs.unca.edu/index.php?name=v04r00-1936209N24286

98. Daddy was caught in this storm

99. **1939 – No Name**: Storm ID - 1939220N19296 Max Cat H1. Landfall Aug 11, 1939, Fort Pierce, FL and Aug 13, 1939, Fort Walton Beach, FL
See: https://ibtracs.unca.edu/index.php?name=v04r00-1939220N19296

100. **1941 – No Name**: Storm ID - 1941277N21298 Max Cat H3. Landfall Oct 6, 1941, Miami, FL and Oct 7, 1941, Apalachicola, FL.
See: https://ibtracs.unca.edu/index.php?name=v04r00-1941277N21298

101. **1944 – No Name**. Storm ID - 1944287N16280 Max Cat H4. Landfall Oct 18, 1944, Sarasota, FL
See: https://ibtracs.unca.edu/index.php?name=v04r00-1944287N16280

102. **1945 – No Name**. Storm ID - 1945172N19274 Max Cat H2. Landfall Jun 24, 1945, Hernando County, FL.
See: https://ibtracs.unca.edu/index.php?name=v04r00-1945172N19274

103. **1945 – Homestead Hurricane**: Storm ID - 1945255N19302 Max Cat H4. Landfall Sep 15, 1945, Homestead/Key Largo, FL. Key Largo took a

direct hit with winds of more than 145 MPH. Four people died in the aftermath. One of the Strongest in the History of Hurricanes in Florida
See: https://ibtracs.unca.edu/index.php?name=v04r00-1945255N19302

104. **1946 – No Name. Storm ID** - 1946279N18273 Max Cat H2. Landfall Oct 7, 1946, Tampa, FL.
See: https://ibtracs.unca.edu/index.php?name=v04r00-1946279N18273

105. **1947 – The Fort Lauderdale Hurricane**: Storm ID - 1947247N15340 Max Cat H4. Landfall Sep 17, 1947, Fort Lauderdale, FL. This was a category 4 hurricane at 145 MPH. As it hit Florida's east coast and raced across the state. The storm killed 34 people and the damages on Florida's west coast as it exited the state were significant with flooding in the Tampa Bay area. One of the Strongest in the History of Hurricanes in Florida.
See: https://ibtracs.unca.edu/index.php?name=v04r00-1947247N15340

106. **1947 – No Name**: Storm ID - 1947282N13278 Max Cat H2. Landfall Oct 11, 1947, Monroe County, FL.
See: https://ibtracs.unca.edu/index.php?name=v04r00-1947282N13278

107. **1948 – No Name**: Storm ID - 1948262N18281 Max Cat H4. Landfall Sep 21, 1948, near Boca Chica in the Florida Keys on September 21, 1948, as a Category 2 hurricane. It strengthened after leaving the Keys and hit on the peninsula of Florida near Chokoloskee the next day as a Category 4 hurricane with 145 MPH winds. Crop damage along with the destruction of several hundred buildings was a result. One of the Strongest in the History of Hurricanes in Florida.
See: https://ibtracs.unca.edu/index.php?name=v04r00-1948262N18281

108. **1948 – No Name**: Storm ID - 1948278N17277 Max Cat H3. Landfall Oct 15, 1948, Florida Keys, FL
See: https://ibtracs.unca.edu/index.php?name=v04r00-1948278N17277

109. **1949 – Delray Beach Hurricane**: Storm ID - 1949235N18300 Max Cat H4. Landfall Aug 27, 1949, Delray Beach, FL. This Hurricane hit the eastern coast of Florida with 130 MPH winds. The storm ripped north along the beaches from Miami to St. Augustine with hurricane-force winds.

Estimates of over $50 million in damages were reported. One of the Strongest in the History of Hurricanes in Florida

See: https://ibtracs.unca.edu/index.php?name=v04r00-1949235N18300

110. **1950 – Hurricane Easy**: Storm ID - 1950244N20277 Mac Cat H3. Landfall Sep 3, 1950, Cedar Key, FL. Hurricane Easy was the first of two major hurricanes of the 1950 Atlantic hurricane season. Landing on September 5, 1950, the storm lingered causing waves to batter Florida's coastline from Homosassa to the panhandle.

See: https://www.weather.gov/media/tbw/paig/PresAmHurricane1950.pdf

See Also: https://ibtracs.unca.edu/index.php?name=v04r00-1950244N20277

111. **1950 – Hurricane King**: Storm ID - 1950286N16276 Max Cat H4. Little known Hurricane King landed in downtown Miami on October 18, 1950. This was the sixth hurricane of the season, and it was the worst Florida hurricane of the year with 130 MPH wind. There were 4 fatalities. Damages included crops throughout south Florida which were estimated at $30 million. One of the Strongest in the History of Hurricanes in Florida.

See: https://fcit.usf.edu/florida/maps/pages/12300/f12369/f12369.htm

See Also: https://ibtracs.unca.edu/index.php?name=v04r00-1950286N16276

112. **In 1953 the weather service started giving hurricanes female names. That ended in 1978 when both male and female names began being used. The history of naming hurricanes is here.**

113. **1956 – Hurricane Flossy**: Storm ID - 1956265N18274 Max Cat 1. Flossy began as a well-developed circulation over the Yucatan Peninsula on September 21st. The disturbance continued to organize and grow as it moved northward into the Gulf of Mexico. Flossy continued to strengthen and gained hurricane status on the 23rd of September in 1956. Flossy made a second landfall as a Category 1 Hurricane near Fort Walton Beach and Destin in far southeastern Okaloosa County, FL late in the evening on September 24th, 1956.

See: https://www.weather.gov/mob/flossy

Also See: https://en.wikipedia.org/wiki/Hurricane_Flossy_(1956)

Also See: https://www.weather.gov/lch/1956Flossy

114. The Modern Era: 1960s to Present

115. As Florida continued to grow and develop in the latter half of the 20th century, the impact of hurricanes became increasingly complex. With more people and property in harm's way, the state's vulnerability to these storms was amplified.

116. **1960 – Donna**: Storm ID - 1960243N10337 Max Cat H4. Landfall Sep 10, 1960, Florida Keys, FL. Hurricane Donna hit the Florida peninsula on September 10, 1960, after going through the Keys near Naples. 13 deaths and $300 million in damages were attributed to Donna. Winds were estimated at 145 MPH. One of the Strongest in the History of Hurricanes in Florida.
See: https://www.weather.gov/mfl/donna
See Also:
https://www.weather.gov/media/tbw/paig/PresAmHurricane1960.pdf
See Also:
https://fcit.usf.edu/florida/maps/pages/12300/f12340/f12340.htm
See Also:
https://hurricanescience.org/history/storms/1960s/donna/index.html

117. **1964 - Hurricane Cleo**: Storm ID - 1964234N13316 Max Cat H4. Landfall Aug 24, 1964, Miami, FL. Hurricane Cleo, striking in 1964, unleashed its fury across Southeast Florida. With its powerful winds and heavy rains, Cleo caused significant damage, particularly in Miami, underscoring the area's vulnerability to strong Atlantic hurricanes.
See: https://fcit.usf.edu/florida/maps/pages/12300/f12334/f12334.htm
See Also: https://www.wpc.ncep.noaa.gov/tropical/rain/cleo1964.html

118. **1964 - Hurricane Dora**: Storm ID - 1964242N14343 Max Cat 4. Landfall Sep 10, 1964, Jacksonville, FL. Following Cleo in the same year, Hurricane Dora made landfall near St. Augustine, bringing with it a trail of destruction. Dora's impact was notable for its intensity and the extent of damage along the northeast coast of Florida.
See: https://www.wpc.ncep.noaa.gov/tropical/rain/dora1964.html

119. **1964 - Hurricane Isbell**: Storm ID - 1964283N15277 Max Cat H3. Landfall Oct 14, 1964, Naples, FL. Capping off a particularly active hurricane season for Florida, Hurricane Isbell also struck in 1964. Isbell affected the Florida eys and the western part of the state, bringing heavy rains and strong winds, and highlighting the relentless hurricane challenges faced by Floridians that year.
See: https://en.wikipedia.org/wiki/Hurricane_Isbell
See: https://www.wpc.ncep.noaa.gov/tropical/rain/isbell1964.html
See: https://www.weather.gov/mfl/isbell

120. **1965 - Betsy**: Storm ID - 1965239N11310 Max Cat H4. Landfall Sep 10, 1965, Florida Keys, FL. Hurricane Betsy was a destructive hurricane that brought widespread damage to areas of Florida. Landing on September 8,1965, Betsy battered the Florida Keys and the storm surge flooded the islands, and cut off the only road through the Keys. It was the strongest storm in the Keys since 1926.
See: https://www.weather.gov/lch/1965Betsy
See: https://hurricanescience.org/history/storms/1960s/betsy/

121. **1966 - Inez**: Storm ID – 1966265N10325 Max Cat H5. Inez did not make a Florida Landfall but impacted the Florida Keys. Hurricane Inez was a powerful Category 5 major hurricane that affected the Caribbean, Bahamas, Florida, and Mexico, killing over 1,000 people in 1966. In the Straits of Florida, Inez capsized a boat of Cuban refugees, killing 45 people. In the northern Gulf of Mexico, a helicopter crashed after carrying evacuees from an oil rig, killing 11 people.
See: https://en.wikipedia.org/wiki/Hurricane_Inez

122. **1966 - Alma**: Storm ID – 1966156N16275 Max Cat H3. Hurricane Alma landed on June 13, 1966, near Apalachee Bay (St. Marks, Florida). It was a rare (and the most recent) June major hurricane in the 1966 Atlantic hurricane season. It was the earliest Atlantic hurricane in the calendar year in fifteen years, as well as the earliest continental U.S. hurricane strike since 1825.
See: https://en.wikipedia.org/wiki/Hurricane_Alma_(1966)

123. **1975 - Eloise**: Storm ID 1975256N18306 Max Cat H3. Landfall – Sep 17, 1975, Santa Rosa Beach, FL. Hurricane Eloise was the most destructive hurricane of the 1975 Atlantic hurricane season landing on September 24, 1975 near Panama City, Florida.
See: https://ibtracs.unca.edu/index.php?name=v04r00-1975256N18306
See Also: https://en.wikipedia.org/wiki/Hurricane_Eloise

124. **1979 - David**: Storm ID - 1979238N12324 Max Cat H5. Landfall Aug 31, 1979, Fort Lauderdale, FL. Hurricane David was the strongest and deadliest hurricane of the 1979 Atlantic hurricane season, but not the costliest. This hurricane caused a lot of damage as it slammed into Dominican Republic as a category 5 hurricane and was it struck Florida as a category 2 hurricane.
See: https://ibtracs.unca.edu/index.php?name=v04r00-1979238N12324
See Also: https://en.wikipedia.org/wiki/Hurricane_David

125. **1992 - Andrew**: Storm ID - 1992230N11325 Max Cat H5. Landfall Aug 24, 1992, Homestead, FL. Hurricane Andrew pounded south Florida on August 24, 1992. As the worst Florida hurricane to date, 65,000 homes were destroyed and 175,000 people were left homeless in this Category 5 storm. Only four category 5 hurricanes had hit the continental United States at this time. One of the Strongest in the History of Hurricanes in Florida
See: https://ibtracs.unca.edu/index.php?name=v04r00-1992230N11325
See Also: https://en.wikipedia.org/wiki/Hurricane_Andrew

126. *Personal Story: For many residents of South Florida, Hurricane Andrew was a life-altering event. John Smith, a homeowner in Homestead, recalls the terror of huddling in his bathroom with his family as the storm tore the roof off his house. "It sounded like a freight train was coming through the walls," he remembers. In the aftermath, John and his family, like countless others, were left to rebuild their lives from the rubble.*

127. **1995 - Elena**: Hurricane Elena blasted the western Florida gulf coast for days beginning on August 30, 1985. Elena was unique in the fact it never made landfall in Florida but remained just offshore battering the coastline with wind and waves. The flooding, erosion, and beaches were hammered by this lingering Category 3 hurricane.

See: https://en.wikipedia.org/wiki/Hurricane_Elena

128. **1995 - Opal**: Storm ID - 1995271N19273 Max Cat H4. Landfall Sep 28, 1995, near Pensacola, FL. Hurricane Opal was a large and powerful Category 4 hurricane that caused severe and extensive damage along the northern Florida Gulf Coast after landing on October 4 1995, near Pensacola with 120 MPH winds.

    See: https://ibtracs.unca.edu/index.php?name=v04r00-1995271N19273
    See Also: https://en.wikipedia.org/wiki/Hurricane_Opal

129. **1998 - Georges**: Storm ID - 1998259N10335 Max Cat H4. Landfall Sep 21, 1998, Key West, FL. Hurricane Georges formed on September 15, 1998 as a tropical depression 300 miles south-southwest of the Cape Verde Islands in the far eastern Atlantic. Georges strengthened to a hurricane on September 17th and reached Category 4 intensity on September 19th. Georges tracked across Puerto Rico, the island of Hispaniola, and eastern Cuba from the evening of the 21st through the 24th. The track over the mountainous terrain weakened Georges to a Category 1 hurricane. However, Georges began to re-intensify as it trekked north of the Cuban coast and tracked west-northwest toward the Gulf of Mexico.

    See: https://ibtracs.unca.edu/index.php?name=v04r00-1998259N10335
    See Also: https://en.wikipedia.org/wiki/Hurricane_Georges

130. **1998 - Earl**: Storm ID - 1998244N22267 Max Cat H2. Landfall Sep 3, 1998, Panama City, FL. On September 1, 1998, Earl became a tropical storm as it moved northeast (east of a sharp upper level trough, which was not forecast well by the short range models at that time according to NWS WPC) across the Gulf of Mexico. Hurricane Hunter reconnaissance aircraft data showed Earl strengthening to a hurricane in the late morning hours on September 2. Earl continued to strengthen and peaked as a Category 2 Hurricane on the morning of September 3rd. Hurricane Earl weakened as it made landfall just east of our area (near Panama City, FL) on September 3, 1998 and quickly transitioned into a subtropical cyclone in southern Georgia on September 3. Earl caused only minor damage across the area from Dauphin Island, AL to Destin, FL.

    See: https://ibtracs.unca.edu/index.php?name=v04r00-1998244N22267

See Also: https://en.wikipedia.org/wiki/Hurricane_Earl_(1998)

131. Recent Devastations (2000 - 2023):

132. **2004 - Charley**: Storm ID - 2004223N11301 Max Cat H4. Landfall Aug 13, 2004, Punta Gorda, FL. Hurricane Charley was the first of four separate hurricanes to impact or strike Florida during 2004, along with Frances, Ivan and Jeanne, as well as one of the strongest hurricanes ever to strike the United States. It was the third named storm, the second hurricane, and the second major hurricane of the 2004 Atlantic hurricane season.
See: https://ibtracs.unca.edu/index.php?name=v04r00-2004223N11301
See Also: https://en.wikipedia.org/wiki/Hurricane_Charley

133. **2004 - Frances**: Storm ID - 2004238N11325 Max Cat H4. On September 5, 2004, Hurricane Frances struck Hutchinson Island near Stuart, Florida with 120 MPH winds. The storm cut across central Florida in a path that will be mimicked three weeks later by hurricane Jeanne.
See: https://ibtracs.unca.edu/index.php?name=v04r00-2004238N11325
See Also: https://en.wikipedia.org/wiki/Hurricane_Frances

134. **2004 - Ivan**: Storm ID - 2004247N10332 Max Cat H5. Hurricane Ivan battered the panhandle near Pensacola on September 16, 2004. What made Ivan so dangerous was the breadth of the wind field and its slow-moving path. It was a category 3 but was degraded to a 2.
See: https://ibtracs.unca.edu/index.php?name=v04r00-2004247N10332
See Also: https://en.wikipedia.org/wiki/Hurricane_Ivan

135. **2004 - Jeanne**: Storm ID - 2004258N16300 Max Cat H3. Hurricane Jeanne struck Hutchinson Island near Stuart, Florida on September 25, 2004. Jeanne was the fourth hurricane of the year. Jeanne also landed within a couple of miles of where hurricane Frances hit less than three weeks earlier. Winds achieved 120 MPH as the storm raced across Florida.
See: https://ibtracs.unca.edu/index.php?name=v04r00-2004258N16300
See Also: https://en.wikipedia.org/wiki/Hurricane_Jeanne

136. The year 2004 was particularly traumatic for Florida, with four major hurricanes - Charley, Frances, Ivan, and Jeanne - striking the state in quick succession.

137. *Personal Story: The 2004 hurricane season left many Floridians reeling. Sarah Johnson, a small business owner in Orlando, remembers the stress of repeatedly boarding up her shop and evacuating. "It was like a never-ending nightmare," she recalls. "Every time we thought we had recovered from one storm, another one was on the way." The cumulative impact of these storms was a testament to the resilience of Florida's communities.*

138. **2005 - Dennis**: Storm ID - 2005186N12299 Max Cat H4. Hurricane Dennis pummels the panhandle with Category 3 winds on July 10, 2005. Landing on Santa Rosa Island in the panhandle, the storm was narrow and fast. The damage was moderated in Florida as compared to Ivan the previous year that also landed in the panhandle.
See: https://ibtracs.unca.edu/index.php?name=v04r00-2005186N12299
See Also: https://en.wikipedia.org/wiki/Hurricane_Dennis

139. **2005 - Katrina**: Storm ID - 2005236N23285 Max Cat 5. Before devastating the Gulf Coast, particularly New Orleans, Hurricane Katrina made its first landfall in Florida as a Category 1 hurricane on August 25 near the Miami-Dade/Broward County line. It brought heavy rains and winds, causing flooding and power outages.
See: https://ibtracs.unca.edu/index.php?name=v04r00-2005236N23285
See Also: https://en.wikipedia.org/wiki/Hurricane_Katrina

140. **2005 - Rita**: Storm ID - 2005261N21290 Max Cat H5. Rita did not make landfall in Florida, it's impact was felt in the Florida Keys. While Rita is more known for its impact on Texas and Louisiana, it also affected Florida. As a tropical depression, it produced heavy rainfall over portions of southeastern Florida, causing some flooding and wind damage.
See: https://ibtracs.unca.edu/index.php?name=v04r00-2005261N21290
See Also: https://en.wikipedia.org/wiki/Hurricane_Rita

141. **2005 - Wilma**: Storm ID - 2005289N18282 Max Cat H5. Landfall Oct 24, 2005, Naples, FL. Hurricane Wilma was a powerful Category 3 hurricane when it made landfall on October 24 near Cape Romano, Florida. Wilma caused widespread damage across southern Florida, particularly in the Florida Keys, the Miami metropolitan area, and the western parts of Palm Beach County.

See: https://ibtracs.unca.edu/index.php?name=v04r00-2005289N18282
See Also: https://en.wikipedia.org/wiki/Hurricane_Wilma

142. **2017 - Hurricane Irma**: Storm ID - 2017242N16333 Max Cat H5. Landfall Sep10, 2017, Naples, FL. In 2017, Hurricane Irma, a Category 5 storm, caused widespread devastation across the state, marking it as one of the most powerful hurricanes to strike Florida in recent history.
See: https://ibtracs.unca.edu/index.php?name=v04r00-2017242N16333
See Also: https://en.wikipedia.org/wiki/Hurricane_Irma

143. **2018 - Hurricane Michael**: Storm ID - 2018280N18273 Max Cat H5. Landfall Oct 6, 2018, Mexico Beach, FL. Hurricane Michael in 2018, another Category 5 storm, brought catastrophic damage to the Florida Panhandle, highlighting the increasing intensity of recent hurricanes.
See: https://ibtracs.unca.edu/index.php?name=v04r00-2018280N18273
See Also: https://en.wikipedia.org/wiki/Hurricane_Michael

144. **2020 – Hurricane Isaias**: Storm ID - 2020211N13306 Max Cat H1. No Florida Landfall. Approached Miami, FL, Jul 30, 2020.
See: https://ibtracs.unca.edu/index.php?name=v04r00-2020211N13306

145. **2020 - Hurricane Sally**: Storm ID - 2020256N25281 Max Cat H2. Landfall Sep 12, 2020, Homestead, FL/Sep 16, 2020, West of Pensacola, FL. In 2020, Hurricane Sally's slow movement resulted in significant flooding and damage, particularly in the western Florida Panhandle.
See: https://en.wikipedia.org/wiki/Hurricane_Sally

146. **2022 - Hurricane Ian**: Storm ID - 2022266N12294 Max Cat H5. Landfall Sep 28, 2022, Cayo Costa, FL. Hurricane Ian, striking in 2022, caused severe destruction across southwest Florida, emphasizing the relentless challenge posed by these natural disasters.
See: http://ibtracs.unca.edu/index.php?name=v04r00-2022266N12294
See Also: https://en.wikipedia.org/wiki/Hurricane_Ian

147. **2023 - Hurricane Idalia**: The most recent, Hurricane Idalia in 2023, serves as a reminder that Florida's struggle with hurricanes is an ongoing saga, with each storm writing a new chapter in the state's history.
See: https://www.weather.gov/mhx/IdaliaReview2023
See Also: https://en.wikipedia.org/wiki/Hurricane_Idalia

Summary:

The tapestry of Florida's history is richly embroidered with the narratives of hurricanes, each one adding its unique pattern of resilience and renewal. From the early records of the 16th century to the present day, Florida's history is deeply intertwined with the story of hurricanes.

These powerful storms, from the earliest days to the modern era, have shaped the state's culture, economy, and landscape. It has further influenced its development and impacted the lives of its residents. The chronicle of these hurricanes not only serves as a record of past events but also as a stark reminder of the ongoing challenges faced by Floridians in the face of nature's fury.

As we look to the future, understanding this history is vital for preparing and adapting to the inevitable challenges posed by these natural phenomena.

In my professional journey as an insurance agent and state representative, the impact of these hurricanes has been a constant reminder of the importance of resilience, preparedness, and community support. Florida's history with hurricanes teaches us about strength, adaptability, and the unyielding human spirit in the face of nature's most formidable challenges.

Looking Ahead: Resilience in the Face of Climate Change

As Florida looks to the future, the specter of climate change looms large. With rising sea levels and the potential for more intense hurricanes, the state is taking proactive steps to enhance its resilience.

1. Statewide Mitigation Strategies: The Florida Division of Emergency Management has developed a comprehensive mitigation strategy that includes strengthening building codes, improving infrastructure resilience, and enhancing flood protection measures. These efforts aim to reduce the physical vulnerability of communities to hurricane impacts.

2. Climate Adaptation Planning: Many Florida cities and counties are developing climate adaptation plans that take into account the projected impacts of climate change, including sea-level rise and more intense hurricanes. These plans often involve strategies such as elevating critical infrastructure, creating green spaces to absorb floodwaters, and encouraging development away from high-risk areas.

3. Community Resilience Initiatives: Recognizing that resilience starts at the community level, Florida is investing in programs to empower local residents and organizations. For example, the Florida Resilient Coastlines Program provides funding and technical assistance to help coastal communities assess their vulnerability and develop adaptation strategies.

4. Improving Hurricane Forecasting: Florida is also investing in advanced hurricane forecasting technologies, such as improved computer modeling and enhanced satellite imagery. These tools can provide earlier and more accurate warnings, giving residents more time to prepare and evacuate if necessary.

Conclusion: A Testament to Resilience

The history of hurricanes in Florida is a testament to the resilience of the state and its people. From the early Spanish settlers to the modern-day residents, Floridians have faced the challenges of these storms with courage and determination.

As we look to the future, it is clear that Florida will continue to face the threat of hurricanes. However, by learning from the past, investing in resilience measures, and fostering a culture of preparedness, the state can be better equipped to weather whatever storms may come.

Personal Reflection: As a long-time resident of Florida and a former insurance agent, I have seen firsthand the devastation that hurricanes can bring. But I have also seen the incredible strength and spirit of our communities in the face of these challenges. It is their response to tragedy that gives me hope for the future, knowing that together, we can build a Florida that is stronger, safer, and more prepared for whatever nature may bring.

Humor in the Eye of the Storm

They say every cloud has a silver lining, but in Florida, it seems every hurricane has a story to tell. Here's to hoping the next chapter is a little less windy!

Future Discussions: In the future, it would be enlightening to explore the evolving technologies in hurricane prediction and tracking, the impact of urban development on vulnerability to hurricanes, and the role of government policies in shaping disaster response and recovery efforts. These discussions are crucial for fortifying Florida against the inevitable storms of the future.

The years 1964, 2004 and 2005 stand out in Florida's hurricane history as a reminder of how multiple powerful storms can strike in quick succession, testing the resilience and preparedness of communities and the state's disaster management systems.

The events from the late 19th and early 20th centuries mark some of the most devastating chapters in Florida's hurricane history, underscoring the relentless challenge these natural disasters pose to the state.

Other Online Resources:

National Hurricane Center and Central Pacific Hurricane Center
The Deadliest Atlantic Tropical Cyclones, 1492-1996
https://www.nhc.noaa.gov/pastdeadlyapp2.shtml?

Wikipedia

List of Florida Hurricanes (pre-1900)

https://en.wikipedia.org/wiki/List_of_Florida_hurricanes_(pre-1900)

Hurricane History for East Central Florida – Flhurricane

https://flhurricane.com/wiki/Hurricane_History_for_East_Central_Florida

100 Year of Hurricanes Hitting and Missing Florida, Visualized

The Washington Post

https://www.washingtonpost.com/graphics/national/one-hundred-years-of-hurricanes/

Florida Travel Blog

History of Florida Hurricanes Since 1559 – 10 Worst Florida Hurricanes

https://floridatravel.blog/history-of-florida-hurricanes-10-worst/

Chronological Listing of Tropical Cyclones Affecting North Florida and Coastal Georgia 1565-1899

https://www.aoml.noaa.gov/hrd/Landsea/history/index.html

As we synthesize the diverse aspects of Florida's insurance landscape, we prepare to conclude our exploration with a summary chapter that draws together the key themes and lessons from the preceding discussions.

Summary of Chapter 33:

Chapter 33 delves into the rich tapestry of Florida's history, woven with the narratives of hurricanes that have shaped the state's identity. From the early records of the 16th century to the recent devastations of the 21st century, Florida's history is deeply intertwined with the story of hurricanes. The chapter chronicles the chronology of chaos, detailing significant hurricanes from the 1500s to the present day. It highlights how these storms have impacted Florida's culture, economy, and landscape, leaving indelible marks on its residents.

The chapter not only serves as a historical record but also as a stark reminder of the ongoing challenges faced by Floridians in the face of nature's fury. It emphasizes the importance of resilience, preparedness, and community support in mitigating the impacts of hurricanes. Furthermore, it looks ahead to the future, discussing proactive measures taken by the state to enhance its resilience in the face of climate change.

As a former insurance agent and state representative, the impact of hurricanes has been a constant reminder of the importance of resilience and preparedness. The chapter concludes with a personal reflection, acknowledging the strength and spirit of Florida's communities in the face of adversity. It also hints at future discussions, inviting exploration into evolving technologies in hurricane prediction, the impact of urban development on vulnerability, and the role of government policies in disaster response and recovery efforts.

In essence, Chapter 32 serves as a comprehensive exploration of Florida's tumultuous relationship with hurricanes, offering insights into the state's past, present, and future challenges and opportunities.

Transition to Chapter 34:

As I reflect on the complexities of insurance and the challenges posed by natural disasters like hurricanes, I can't help but feel a sense of urgency. In the previous chapter, we discussed the intricacies of policy interventions and market dynamics shaping Florida's insurance landscape. Now, as we step into Chapter 34, the culmination of our exploration, I invite you to join me in synthesizing our journey thus far. Together, let's navigate the storm of Florida's insurance landscape, weaving together the threads of understanding, resilience, and preparedness that will define our path forward.

CHAPTER 34

Navigating the Storm - Synthesizing Florida's Insurance Landscape

In this pivotal section of our exploration, we've journeyed through the multifaceted world of Florida's insurance landscape, especially in the context of its vulnerability to hurricanes. Through twenty-three insightful chapters, we've unpacked the complexities, challenges, and strategic responses that define this dynamic field. As we culminate this section, let's distill the essence of our exploration, weaving together the key points, lessons learned, and visions for a resilient future.

1. **Foundational Understanding of Insurance and Reinsurance:** We began with a foundational understanding of insurance and reinsurance, illustrating how these mechanisms are not merely financial tools but lifelines that uphold the stability and resilience of Florida's communities. Reinsurance, in particular, serves as a critical buffer, ensuring that insurance companies can withstand the financial aftermath of hurricanes, thereby safeguarding homeowners and the broader economy.

2. **The Role of Citizens Property Insurance:** Citizens Property Insurance Company emerged as a central figure in our narrative, embodying the challenges and responsibilities of serving as an insurer of last resort. Its evolution, influenced by legislative actions and market pressures, reflects the broader themes of adaptability and the continuous search for equilibrium in a market perpetually under the threat of natural disasters.

3. **Financial Mechanisms and Market Dynamics:** We delved into the financial underpinnings that sustain this sector, from Citizens' assessment mechanisms to the broader reinsurance market dynamics. These chapters illuminated the interconnectedness of various stakeholders and the critical

importance of maintaining financial solvency to ensure continuous protection for policyholders.

4. **Lessons from Global Perspectives:** By comparing Florida's disaster management strategies with those of New Zealand and Japan, we extracted valuable lessons on risk transfer, economic recovery, and the imperative of adopting a forward-thinking approach to disaster preparedness and financial planning.

5. **Theoretical Insights:** The Ellsberg Paradox and Dr. Frank Knight's distinction between risk and uncertainty provided a theoretical lens through which we examined the decision-making processes that influence policy and investment in Florida's hurricane-prone context. These insights underscore the need for clarity, predictability, and strategic foresight in managing the state's insurance landscape.

6. **Historical Context and Future Implications:** The rich history of Florida's encounters with hurricanes, documented in a chronological narrative, serves as a sobering reminder of the state's vulnerability and the indispensable role of effective insurance and risk management strategies. This historical perspective reinforces the urgency of learning from the past to navigate the future more adeptly.

7. **The Joseph Principle**

    In a world of uncertainty, the ancient wisdom of Joseph illuminates the path to resilience. As Florida faces the tempests of natural disasters and the complexities of its insurance landscape, the Joseph Principle emerges as a beacon of hope, guiding insurers and policyholders alike through the trials of modern times. Discover how this timeless tale of foresight and preparedness holds the key to weathering the storms that lie ahead.

8. **A Call for Resilience and Adaptation:** Florida's evolving paradigms regarding hurricane risk and insurance culminate in a call for a resilience paradigm. This forward-looking perspective advocates for a holistic approach that integrates comprehensive risk assessments, sustainable development, community engagement, and proactive legislative frameworks to build a future where Florida survives and thrives in the face of its climatic challenges.

As we wrap-up Part 4 of this book, our journey through these twenty-three insightful chapters underscores a fundamental truth: the insurance landscape in Florida is a microcosm of broader societal, economic, and environmental interplays. As we look to the future, fostering a resilient, adaptive, and financially robust insurance market is pivotal for Florida's continued prosperity. This endeavor requires a concerted effort from all stakeholders—policymakers, insurance professionals, homeowners, and the community—to craft strategies that are responsive to current challenges and anticipate future risks.

We have also learned that the rising cost of homeowner's insurance due to hurricane exposure is a significant challenge for many Floridians. Despite the risks associated with living in hurricane-prone areas, the popularity of these areas remains high. This is due in part to the natural beauty and appeal of Florida's coastal communities, as well as the economic opportunities they offer. However, the high cost of insurance can be a significant burden for homeowners, particularly those with limited resources. This reminds me of the following quip: "Despite the cost of living, have you noticed how living remains so popular?" This is a testament to the enduring appeal of Florida's coastal communities, but it also highlights the need for effective solutions to address the challenges faced by homeowners in these areas.

In synthesizing these insights, we equip ourselves with the knowledge and perspective needed to forge a path toward a more resilient and insured Florida, ready to face tomorrow's storms with confidence and preparedness.

This journey towards resilience is not just about external aid or expecting others to prepare for us. Reflecting on different societal models of support, we see: "If you want your father to take care of you, that's paternalism… If you want your mama to take care of you, that's maternalism… If you want Uncle Sam to take care of you, that's socialism… If you want your comrades to take care of you, that's communism... But, if you want to take care of yourself, that's Americanism!!!"

Embracing this spirit of Americanism, we recognize the importance of self-reliance and personal preparedness in shaping a secure future.

Before we leave this final chapter of Part 4 – Essays on Insurance and Public Policy, I think it would be fitting to take a retrospective look at how Florida's insurance landscape has changed over the decades – and how much has stayed the same.

When I first entered this field, the insurance market was a vastly different place. Hurricanes and storms weren't just weather events; they were monumental disruptors that could send shockwaves through the entire state's economy.

One of the most significant shifts came in the form of legislation designed to stabilize the property insurance market after the devastation of Hurricane Andrew in 1992. This hurricane served as a wake-up call that our market was underprepared and overexposed. It was a critical turning point that prompted the establishment of the Florida Hurricane Catastrophe Fund (FHCF), which provided reinsurance support to insurers to help them weather future storms. I was fortunate to work with some of the lawmakers and insurance professionals who recognized the need for this safety net.

Dr. Jack Nicholson, the Chief Operating Officer of the Florida Hurricane Catastrophe Fund, managed and defended the Fund's mission from September 1994 until February 2016, ensuring that it remained a strong bulwark against catastrophic losses and continued to serve as a vital backstop for the state's insurance market.

Then there's the Citizens Property Insurance Company, which emerged from the merger of two state-run insurers in 2002. The purpose was clear: provide coverage for those who couldn't secure it in the private market, particularly in coastal regions prone to storms. Barry Gilway, the former CEO of Citizens, did a Herculean job of managing one of the largest insurance enterprises in the nation during the critical years following the 2006 financial crisis. During my time advocating for homeowners' rights, I often found myself caught between defending the affordability of Citizens and ensuring that the company didn't become a crutch that distorted the market.

Governor Jeb Bush also played a pivotal role, providing leadership and direction following the back-to-back storms of 2004 and 2005. His administration prioritized proactive responses and recovery strategies that bolstered Florida's resilience in the face of subsequent disasters.

In 2007, I stood as one of only two legislators to vote against HB1A, which significantly expanded the state's involvement in private markets. At the time, my opposition wasn't popular, but I believed it would lead to unintended consequences by further distorting the market and increasing the state's liability. Today, many of my concerns have come to pass as rising premiums and financial instability have led to further reform efforts.

Key figures like former Florida Insurance Commissioner Kevin McCarty shaped the regulatory framework that sought to balance consumer protection and market health. His leadership through periods of crisis, such as multiple hurricane seasons and the global financial downturn, helped navigate turbulent waters. Other influential voices included Tom Gallagher, who, as Chief Financial Officer, oversaw regulatory initiatives and worked to modernize the insurance landscape.

I've had the privilege of working alongside colleagues who pushed for transparency and fairness in policy drafting and implementation. These efforts aimed to ensure that while companies remained solvent, policyholders were also adequately protected. I've also seen how shifting political climates have played a role in whether reforms succeeded or stalled.

The insurance landscape in Florida will continue to evolve as we face new challenges in the form of climate change, rising sea levels, and evolving risk models. But through it all, the principles of balance and preparation remain as important as ever. Moving forward, our greatest successes will hinge on learning from our past missteps and ensuring that we're adapting thoughtfully, not just hastily reacting to the storm on the horizon.

Summary of Chapter 34:

In Chapter 34, "Navigating the Storm - Synthesizing Florida's Insurance Landscape," I encapsulate the essence of our exploration. We embarked on a journey through the multifaceted world of Florida's insurance landscape, particularly in the context of its vulnerability to hurricanes. Here's a breakdown of the key points:

1. **Foundational Understanding of Insurance and Reinsurance:** We started by understanding the vital roles of insurance and reinsurance in stabilizing Florida's communities' post-disaster.
2. **The Role of Citizens Property Insurance:** Citizens Property Insurance Company emerged as a central figure, highlighting the challenges of being an insurer of last resort.
3. **Financial Mechanisms and Market Dynamics:** We explored the financial mechanisms that sustain the insurance sector, emphasizing the importance of financial solvency.
4. **Lessons from Global Perspectives:** Drawing comparisons with disaster management strategies of other nations, we learned valuable lessons on risk transfer and economic recovery.
5. **Theoretical Insights:** The Ellsberg Paradox and Dr. Frank Knight's concepts helped us understand decision-making processes in Florida's hurricane-prone context.

6. **Historical Context and Future Implications:** By examining Florida's history with hurricanes, we gained insights into the state's vulnerability and the importance of effective risk management.
7. **The Joseph Principle:** Drawing from ancient wisdom, we discussed how foresight and preparedness can guide us through modern-day challenges.
8. **A Call for Resilience and Adaptation:** We concluded with a call for a resilience paradigm, advocating for comprehensive risk assessments and sustainable development.
9. **A Retrospective Look at How Florida's Insurance Landscape Has Changed:** We covered some of the Florida insurance marketplace defining moments over the last several decades and mentioned a few key figures who have shaped its evolution.

In conclusion, our journey through these chapters revealed that Florida's insurance landscape mirrors broader societal, economic, and environmental interplays. To ensure Florida's continued prosperity, stakeholders must collaborate on responsive and anticipatory strategies. By synthesizing these insights, we equip ourselves to build a more resilient and insured Florida, ready to face the storms of tomorrow with confidence.

Transition to Chapter 35:

As I reflect on the milestones and challenges outlined in the previous chapter, it becomes clear that my legislative journey has been shaped by the individuals with whom I've had the privilege to work. From navigating complex policy debates to forging bipartisan alliances, each encounter has left an indelible mark on my understanding of public service and the legislative process. Now, as I delve into Chapter 35, I invite you to join me on a journey of reflection and tribute, as we honor the influential figures who have shaped my legislative path.

Chapter 35

From Roots to Realization: Honoring the Influential Figures of My Legislative Journey

Introduction:

In my eight years serving in the Florida House of Representatives, I worked alongside some of the most remarkable individuals in the state's political landscape. These people, from governors and speakers to fellow representatives, staff members, and lobbyists, left an indelible mark on my personal and professional life, shaping my understanding of public service, leadership, and the intricacies of the legislative process.

"The ultimate result of shielding men from the effects of folly is to fill the world with fools."

--Herbert Spencer, English Philosopher (1820-1903)

This quote serves as a reminder that over-regulation and excessive protectionism can have unintended consequences, hindering growth and innovation.

This chapter is a tribute to those individuals who profoundly impacted me during my time in the House. It is an attempt to capture the essence of their personalities, the depth of their knowledge, and the breadth of their contributions to the state of Florida.

Through these tributes, I aim to share my experiences, insights, and the invaluable lessons I learned from each of these extraordinary people.

The individuals featured in this chapter come from diverse backgrounds and hold various positions, but they all share a common dedication to serving the people of Florida. Some were mentors, guiding me through the complexities of the legislative process, while others were collaborators, working alongside me to craft policies and navigate the challenges we faced. Some were friends, offering support and encouragement during the most trying times, and others were simply inspiring figures, leading by example and setting the standard for what it means to be a public servant.

Reflecting on my time in the Florida House, I am grateful for the opportunity to have known and worked with each of these remarkable individuals. Their influence extends far beyond the halls of the legislature, and their legacies continue to shape the state of Florida to this day.

Through this chapter, I hope to offer readers a glimpse into the human side of the legislative process and showcase the passion, dedication, and hard work that goes into serving the people of Florida. These tributes are not just a record of my personal experiences but a testament to the enduring impact that one person can have on another and the power of collaboration, mentorship, and friendship in the realm of public service.

As you read through these tributes, I invite you to join me in honoring these extraordinary individuals and their indelible mark on the state of Florida and my life. Their stories remind me of the importance of leadership, integrity, and the power of human connection in the face of even the most daunting challenges.

Governor Jeb Bush

Jeb Bush, the 43rd Governor of Florida from 1999 to 2007, was a beacon of policy expertise and a unique political force. His deep knowledge of a broad area of public policy inspired his staff and those he worked with, including myself. Governor Bush's leadership and profound impact on Florida's political landscape were evident in our collaboration on various issues, particularly legal reform. His commitment to public service and his ability to navigate complex policy matters left a lasting impression on me. I am grateful for the opportunity to have worked with such an exceptional leader.

Governor Charlie Crist

Governor Charlie Crist was known for his centrist and sometimes unpredictable political stances and served as the Governor of Florida from 2007 to 2011. Compared to Governor Bush, I found him to have a shallow understanding of many public policy issues. He reminds me of this quip: "Light travels faster than sound. This is why some people appear bright until you hear them speak." His tan and charisma made up for what he lacked in public policy expertise. I believe he fits the stereotypical definition of a "politician."

"A government big enough to give you everything you want, is strong enough to take everything you have." –*Thomas Jefferson*

This quote could serve as a commentary on the perceived lack of depth in Governor Crist's policy understanding and the potential dangers of relying too heavily on charisma in politics.

Speaker of the Florida House – Tom Feeney

Tom Feeney, a respected colleague in the Florida House, demonstrated a strong commitment to conservative values and a strategic political insight. As Speaker, Tom's leadership was marked by decisiveness and a talent for bringing people together. His dedication to promoting conservative ideals was pivotal in shaping Florida's political landscape, and his impact extended well beyond his tenure in the state legislature.

I admire Tom's political acumen, integrity, sense of humor, and sincere commitment to public service. Working alongside him was an enriching experience that left a lasting impact on my own approach to legislating.

Speaker of the Florida House – Johnnie Byrd

My time serving with Speaker Johnnie Byrd in the Florida House was a period filled with significant learning and shared efforts. Being appointed by Byrd to lead key committees such as the Select Committee on Florida's Economic Future and the Subcommittee on Insurance Regulation was both a challenge and an honor. It was a clear sign of his confidence in me, which was pivotal in my growth and understanding of Florida's economic and regulatory issues.

Johnnie Byrd was deeply knowledgeable and dedicated to his role, always pushing us to do our best. His leadership from 1996 to 2004, especially as Speaker, was focused on creating policies that truly met the needs of Floridians. His work didn't stop in the political arena; he also made significant contributions to the community, like establishing the Johnnie B. Byrd Sr. Alzheimer's Institute, demonstrating his commitment to tackling pressing health issues.

I greatly respect and admire Speaker Byrd, not just for his political expertise but also for his real dedication to the well-being of Florida's residents. His enduring impact on the state and his lasting influence on the community are a testament to his meaningful and dedicated service.

Speaker of the Florida House – Allen Bense

Remembering my time with Speaker Allen Bense in the Florida House of Representatives brings back memories of a leader who was adept at navigating the complexities of public policy and embodied the essence of leadership and respect.

From his humble beginnings in Panama City, where he worked his way through school in various jobs, to his ascent to becoming the Speaker of the House, Allen's journey is a testament to his perseverance, dedication, and commitment to service.

Allen's time in the Florida House was marked by a clear vision and a unyielding commitment to the principles he believed in. His experience in business was evident in his approach to governance—pragmatic, insightful, and always aimed at fostering growth and prosperity for Florida.

His leadership extended beyond his business achievements. As Speaker from 2004 to 2006, Allen's ability to guide discussions, build consensus, and drive legislation was instrumental in shaping Florida's legislative landscape. His influence was felt in every committee he was a part of and in every decision that was made under his leadership.

His involvement with the James Madison Institute, Triumph Gulf Coast, and numerous other boards and commissions underscores his commitment to contributing to Florida's growth and well-being.

Beyond his political achievements, Allen's personal dedication to his family and community speaks volumes about his character. I am honored to have served alongside Speaker Allen Bense and to call him a dear friend. His legacy of integrity, leadership, and service continues to inspire all who had the privilege of knowing him.

Speaker of the Florida House – Marco Rubio

Working with Representative and later Speaker Marco Rubio was a highlight of my time in the Florida House. Marco's rise from modest beginnings to becoming a key political figure in Florida underscored his resilience and commitment to public service.

His "100 Innovative Ideas for Florida's Future" was a standout moment, drawing people statewide into the legislative process and leading to significant policy advancements.

As Speaker, Marco steered the House with a progressive stance, focusing on key areas like education and healthcare, and was respected by peers across the political spectrum. My personal interactions with him were based on shared respect and a mutual goal to serve Florida effectively.

Marco's path from the state to the national stage reflects his ongoing dedication to public service and his ability to influence change.

I admire him for his remarkable skill and ambition and as a public servant who remains deeply committed to his roots and values.

His legacy in the Florida House and his ongoing contributions to our nation are a testament to the enduring impact one individual can have on the fabric of our society

State Representative Dennis Ross

Having worked alongside Dennis Ross during his tenure in the Florida House of Representatives, I have come to know him not only as a legislator but as a dedicated public servant whose commitment to his constituents was always his top priority. From his early days in the Florida House of Representations to his impactful years in the U.S. Congress, Dennis consistently demonstrated his dedication to effective governance and policy improvements, particularly in the realms of insurance reform and community initiatives.

Dennis Ross's political approach was always rooted in practical solutions and a deep understanding of the legislative process. His ability to work effectively across the aisle made him a respected figure among his peers. Known for his articulate and well-reasoned debates, he brought clarity and insight to complex issues, making a lasting impact on those of us fortunate enough to work with him.

Beyond his professional accomplishments, Dennis's integrity stood out. He deliberated carefully, always aiming to act in the best interest of those he represented. His thoughtful consideration of each issue and his unwavering commitment to his principles earned him admiration from both colleagues and constituents.

As a fellow legislator, I admired his collaborative spirit and knack for fostering bipartisanship, which was instrumental in driving legislative success in Florida. Working with Dennis, I was consistently impressed by his keen intellect and ability to convey complex ideas in an accessible manner. His contributions during our sessions were informative and often pivotal in guiding our decisions.

Reflecting on his career, Dennis Ross exemplifies the qualities of a true leader—dedicated, thoughtful, and always eager to serve. His legacy in Florida politics is marked by his significant contributions to improving the systems and policies that affect everyday Floridians, from his home district to the broader state landscape.

As I look back on our time together in the legislature, I am grateful for his friendship, partnership and deeply respect the enduring impact of his service.

State Representative Jeff Atwater

Jeff Atwater's journey through Florida politics and beyond is a testament to his dedication and skill. Serving first in the Florida House and then the Senate, where he was President, Jeff demonstrated a deep commitment to public service and a keen understanding of finance and policy. His tenure as Florida's Chief Financial Officer further showcased his expertise and dedication to the state's fiscal health.

Choosing to continue his journey at Florida Atlantic University, Jeff has been applying his vast experience to education and strategic projects, impacting future generations.

Having worked alongside Jeff, I've seen his dedication to Florida and its people firsthand. His career is a series of positions and a continuous effort to make a positive difference. I'm proud to call him a friend and a colleague, and I'm confident his contributions will leave a legacy in Florida's history.

State Representative David Simmons

I have known David H. Simmons for many years, and I can say without hesitation that he is remarkable. As a lawyer and legislator, David has dedicated his life to serving the people of Florida with integrity, intelligence, and unwavering commitment.

David's journey began in Nashville, Tennessee, where he developed a strong foundation in mathematics at Tennessee Technological University. He then pursued his passion for law at Vanderbilt University Law School, earning his Juris Doctor in 1977. With his education and determination, David moved to Florida and co-founded the DSK Law Firm in Orlando, where he continues to serve as the financial managing partner.

Throughout his legislative career, first in the Florida House of Representatives from 2000 to 2008 and then in the Florida Senate from 2010 to 2020, David tirelessly worked to improve the lives of Floridians. His focus on law reform, education, and healthcare has made a lasting impact on our state. As President Pro Tempore in the Senate, David's leadership skills shone through as he navigated complex issues with grace and wisdom.

David's expertise in civil trial and business litigation has been recognized by The Florida Bar, which has board-certified him in both areas. The National Board of Trial Advocacy has also certified him in Civil Trial. His excellence in legal practice has earned him the highest ranking (AV) from the Martindale-Hubbell Law Directory, a testament to his skill and reputation among his peers.

Beyond his professional accomplishments, David is a man of character and compassion. He enjoys participating in triathlon events and cherishes time spent with his friends and family. I am proud to know David and to have witnessed his unwavering commitment to making a positive difference in the lives of others.

State Representative Frank Attkisson

Frank Attkisson was a dedicated public servant who made significant contributions to the state of Florida. Serving in the Florida House of Representatives from 2000 to 2008 and as the mayor of Kissimmee from 1996 to 2000, Frank left a lasting impact on his constituents and colleagues alike.

His exceptional oratory skills and genuine friendship were just a few of the qualities that made him stand out as a leader. Frank's involvement in key legislative matters, such as "Terri's Law" and property tax reform, showcased his commitment to addressing the needs of Floridians. His service on various committees, including Education K-20, Education Appropriations, and the Government Efficiency & Accountability Council, demonstrated his diverse expertise and dedication to good governance.

In 2010, Attkisson was elected to the Osceola County Commission and, in 2012, was elected as the board's chairman. He also served as the Chairman of the Small Business Regulatory Advisory Council, which reviews state agency rules and their impact on small businesses. He was also the Vice-Chairman of the American Board Certification for Teachers of Excellence, a national alternative teacher certification board established by Congress in 2001.

Beyond his legislative achievements, Frank was a devoted family man and a community pillar. His untimely passing in 2017 left a void in the hearts of those who knew him, but his legacy as a committed public servant and friend will endure. I feel privileged to have known Frank Attkisson and witnessed his unwavering dedication to serving the people of Florida. I will always remember him as an accomplished orator and a great friend.

State Representative Jack Seiler

A respected colleague, Jack Seiler, was an exceptional debater and a dedicated public servant. From 2000 to 2008, when he represented District 92 in Broward County in the Florida House of Representatives, Jack consistently demonstrated his commitment to his constituents and his ability to work effectively with his fellow legislators.

Following his time in the Florida House, Jack served as the 41st Mayor of Fort Lauderdale from 2009 to 2018, further showcasing his dedication to public service.

Jack's ability to engage in thoughtful, well-reasoned debate was one of his greatest strengths. He had a keen intellect and a talent for articulating his positions clearly and persuasively. His colleagues, me included, always looked forward to hearing his perspective on the issues we faced, knowing that he would bring valuable insights to the table.

Beyond his skills as a debater, Jack was also known for his integrity and his commitment to doing what was right for his constituents. He carefully considered every decision, always striving to find solutions to benefit the people he served.

As a fellow legislator, I had the privilege of working closely with Jack on several key issues. His collaborative spirit and willingness to reach across the aisle were instrumental in helping us achieve meaningful progress for the people of Florida

State Representative Ralph Arza

I enjoyed serving alongside Ralph Arza in the Florida House of Representatives, where he represented District 102 from 2000 to 2006. During his tenure, Ralph was known for his fun-loving personality and ability to bring a sense of levity to even the most serious situations.

One of Ralph's most memorable pranks involved his uncanny ability to copy Speaker Tom Feeney's signature. He would send notes to other members, requesting their presence in the Speaker's office, causing a bit of confusion and concern until the truth was revealed. Thankfully, Speaker Feeney had a good sense of humor and would dismiss each "victim" with a smile.

Despite his playful nature, Ralph was a highly capable legislator who made significant contributions to Florida's educational reform. As Chair of the PreK-12 Education Committee and Vice Chair of the Education Council, he worked tirelessly to improve the state's education system and ensure access to quality education for every child.

While Ralph's career was not without its controversies, I choose to focus on his positive impact during his time in the legislature. His ability to build relationships, even across party lines, and his willingness to tackle tough issues head-on were admirable qualities that served him well in his role as a representative.

Reflecting on my time serving with Ralph Arza, I am grateful for the experiences we shared and the lessons I learned from him. His fun-loving spirit and his dedication to public service made him a memorable and effective legislator, and I am proud to have called him a colleague and friend.

State Representative Dwight Stansel

Dwight Stansel, a true common-sense country boy, was an outstanding public servant who always put the needs of his constituents first during his time in the Florida House of Representatives from 1998 to 2006.

Growing up in a farming family and continuing to work in agriculture throughout his life, Dwight's deep roots in the industry shaped his legislative priorities. He consistently advocated for the interests of farmers and rural communities.

As a member of the State Agriculture Committee, where he served as Vice Chairman, Dwight's expertise and passion for agriculture, property rights, and education were evident in his work. He sponsored and co-sponsored numerous bills related to land ownership, property rights, and hunting regulations, demonstrating his commitment to these critical issues.

Beyond his legislative work, Dwight was known for his engaging personality and his ability to connect with people from all walks of life. He was famous for cracking the whip during the Florida House's annual "Boot Day" while explaining the historical significance of the term "Florida Cracker" and its connection to the state's cattle-driving past.

Dwight Stansel's dedication to public service, his deep understanding of the issues facing his constituents, and his unwavering commitment to promoting the interests of farmers and rural communities made him an invaluable member of the Florida House. I am honored to have served alongside him and witnessed his positive impact on our state firsthand.

State Representative Holly Benson

Holly Benson was a smart, effective legislator with a contagious smile. She was part of the 2000 Florida House class and served until 2006. She was the first Republican to win District 3.

Holly's legislative work, particularly as Chair of the Health and Families Council and Co-Chair of the Select Committee on Medicaid Reform, showcased her deep understanding of the issues and her commitment to fostering meaningful change. Her leadership on the Select Committee on Article V, which implemented a vital constitutional amendment, further demonstrated her capability to navigate complex legal and governmental structures to achieve substantial outcomes.

Holly's subsequent roles as Secretary of the Florida Department of Business and Professional Regulation and the Agency for Health Care Administration were marked by her adeptness at steering these significant

entities, reflecting her broad expertise and unwavering dedication to Florida's welfare.

Beyond her public service, Holly's ventures into affordable housing and contributions to cultural tourism in Pensacola highlight her versatile engagement with the community and her enduring impact on Florida's social and economic fabric.

Holly Benson's legacy is a testament to her skillful leadership, deep commitment to public service, and enduring impact on Florida.

State Representation Rob Wallace

Rob Wallace is a passionate fiscal conservative. I really miss Rob. He was elected to the Florida House in 1994 as a professional engineer and president/founder of Environmental Engineering Consultants, Inc.

In the Florida State House, Rob Wallace was a fiscal conservative, not just by title but through his impassioned advocacy for prudent financial stewardship. His colleagues and constituents knew him as a man who could artfully blend humor with earnestness, bringing a unique vibrancy to the often-dry debates on state budgeting and spending.

His dedication to conservative fiscal policy was more than just political posturing; it was a deeply held belief, a principle he lived by in his professional and personal life. As a business owner and engineer, Wallace applied the same rigorous standards to his company, ensuring that every decision was economically sound and beneficial to the community he served.

Beyond the legislature, Wallace was a family man and community stalwart. His love for his family was evident, and his commitment to his community was unwavering. In times of triumph and controversy alike, he remained a figure of respect and admiration, his integrity unquestioned, his legacy enduring.

Rob Wallace's story is one of conviction and compassion, a testament to a dedicated individual's impact on the world around them. In remembering him, we recall not just a fiscal conservative but a man of humor, heart, and unwavering dedication to the ideals he held dear.

State Representative Gaston Cantens

Gaston Cantens, a statesman and legislative leader, played a pivotal role in my political journey and left an indelible mark on the Florida House of Representatives. As the Republican Majority Whip, Gaston's influence extended beyond marshaling votes; he was instrumental in shaping the legislative narrative, a role he embraced with a unique blend of tenacity and finesse.

My appointment as a deputy whip by Speaker Johnny Byrd, delivered by Gaston with an insistence that brooked no argument, was a testament to his persuasive prowess and commitment to the collective cause.

Gaston Cantens' legacy in the Florida House is one of strong leadership, strategic brilliance, and a dedication to advancing the legislative agenda. His impact on my own political journey and the lessons I learned from observing his approach to governance will forever shape my understanding of  what it means to be an effective leader and legislator.

State Representative Charlie Dean

Charlie Dean, a man whose stature was matched only by his charisma, brought a unique blend of law enforcement experience and legislative prowess to the Florida House of Representatives. As a former sheriff, Charlie's transition to the legislative arena was marked by a sense of decisiveness and a palpable warmth that drew people to him.

My first formal meeting with Charlie, initiated under the guise of my new deputy whip duties, quickly evolved from a formal introduction to a moment of genuine

camaraderie, as my playful jest of becoming his "Whippor" and he my "Whippee" was met with his booming laughter and a bear-like hand on my shoulder, this moment exemplified Charlie's ability to bridge gaps between backgrounds and experiences, fostering a sense of unity and shared purpose among his colleagues.

His contributions to policymaking and relationship-building left a lasting impact on the chamber and those who worked alongside him.

Charlie Dean's legacy in the Florida House is one of leadership through connection, reminding us of the importance of balancing legislative duties with the human element of governance.

State Representative Leslie Waters

Leslie Waters, a remarkable mentor and an extraordinary leader, played a pivotal role in shaping my early experiences as a member of the Florida House of Representatives. As chair of the Insurance Committee, Leslie's infectious energy and commitment to inclusivity, particularly toward freshman members like myself, created an environment that fostered growth, learning, and meaningful contributions.

From the very beginning, Leslie empowered me and my colleagues to dive deep into the committee's work, encouraging a sense of ownership and engagement that laid the foundation for my future leadership roles.

Leslie's encouragement was pivotal in my early days at the House. She encouraged me to attend a leadership training program conducted by the esteemed Griffin Institute under the auspices of NCOIL. This event, set against the backdrop of Columbus, Ohio, in early September 2001, was meant to be a moment of learning and growth. However, it became etched in my memory for a far different reason.

On the morning of September 11, as the conference was winding down, the unimaginable news of the national tragedy struck us all. Amidst the confusion and chaos, my planned return home was upended, leading to an unexpected extended stay and a solitary drive back in a rental car as the nation grappled with the shock and sorrow of the attacks.

In 2003, buoyed by Leslie Waters's confidence in me, I was appointed Chairman of the House Subcommittee on Property Casualty Insurance. This appointment was a reflection of Leslie's insightful leadership and her knack for recognizing and nurturing talent.

Leslie Waters wasn't just a chairperson or a colleague; she was a friend and an inspiration. Her impact extended beyond the confines of committee meetings or legislative sessions; it was felt in her guidance, the opportunities she facilitated, and the example she set as a dedicated public servant and trailblazer. Keep the "Water Wave" going.

State Representative Dudley Goodlette

My encounters with Representative Dudley Goodlette revealed a man of profound integrity and wisdom, characteristics that resonated deeply with me from our very first meeting. His demeanor was not just that of a seasoned statesman but a dedicated mentor and friend whose guidance was insightful and invaluable.

Dudley's background is as diverse as it is impressive. As a West Point cadet and a U.S. Army Military Intelligence captain, his service commitment was evident early on. His legal and political careers are marked by significant achievements, including serving as a Representative in the Florida House, where he chaired crucial councils and demonstrated exemplary leadership.

His community involvement is equally notable. Recognized as a "pioneer" of business leadership in Collier County, Dudley's influence extends beyond the political arena. His service on various boards and commissions, including the Naples Ethics Commission, underscores his dedication to public service and ethical governance.

His accolades, including being named the 2014 Humanitarian of the Year by Hodges University, reflect a life dedicated to improving his community and the state of Florida. His induction into the Junior Achievement Business Leadership Hall of Fame and other honors speaks volumes of the respect and admiration he has garnered over the years.

In Dudley Goodlette, I found a leader who had indeed earned the respect of his colleagues, a mentor whose advice was both sage and sincere and a friend whose camaraderie was genuine.

State Representative – JD Alexander

From my earliest interactions with JD Alexander, he was a formidable presence in the Florida House of Representatives. His tenure as Chairman of the Council for Competitive Commerce marked him as a leader whose fervor and commitment were palpable, qualities that commanded respect even from a distance.

When JD transitioned to the Florida Senate, his passion for public service and dedication to the issues we both cared about in the House became even more evident. He wasn't just a politician; he was a vocal advocate, a strategist, and, in many ways, a mentor from whom I gleaned considerable insight.

His work on significant projects, like the controversial Heartland Parkway and the establishment of Florida Polytechnic University, demonstrated his willingness to champion bold initiatives, undeterred by the complexities or the opposition he faced. These endeavors were not just political statements but reflections of a man who was deeply invested in the future of Florida.

His tenacity and unwavering dedication stand out as I reflect on JD's legacy. His ability to navigate the legislative landscape, advocate passionately for his beliefs, and effect tangible change left an indelible mark on those privileged to work alongside him. JD Alexander will be long remembered for his contributions, leadership, and the indomitable spirit with which he served the state of Florida.

State Representative – Jim Kallinger

Reflecting on my time with Jim Kallinger in the Florida House of Representatives from 2000 to 2004 brings back vivid memories of a legislator who was my colleague and someone I grew to respect deeply. During his tenure, Jim, representing Districts 35 and 69, was a formidable presence in debates, standing his ground with unwavering conviction, even when faced with contentious issues.

I recall a specific instance when Jim sponsored a controversial proposal. His ability to stand in debate, articulating his points with clarity and resolve, was truly impressive. In moments like these, Jim's depth of knowledge and commitment to his principles shone through, distinguishing him as a leader in our legislative community.

Another memorable event is our visit to the Florida Supreme Court with a select group of legislators. During our discussions with several justices, Jim's insights into American history and government were enlightening. His references to the Federalist Papers were not just quotations but reflections of his profound understanding of our nation's foundational principles.

Beyond the legislature, Jim's stance on the Constitution Revision Commission, advocating for its abolishment to preserve the integrity of our state constitution, and his leadership roles in various campaigns and coalitions underscore his active participation in civic matters.

In the years following his service in the House, Jim's involvement with organizations like the Florida Faith and Freedom Coalition and Consumers for Smart Solar demonstrates his continued influence in state politics, advocating for causes he believes in.

To this day, I consider Jim Kallinger a former colleague and a personal friend whose dedication and service to Florida inspire me.

State Representative – Ralph Poppell

During my time in the Florida House of Representatives, I had the privilege of working closely with Ralph Poppell, especially during the period from 2007 to 2008 when I chaired the House Insurance Committee, and he served as Vice-Chair. Ralph was a determined lawmaker, deeply rooted in agriculture, and equipped with a pragmatic approach to business, which he brought into his legislative work.

Ralph's dedication was evident in his active participation on the committee, where his input was invaluable. His hard work and insightful contributions significantly aided our efforts to navigate complex insurance issues, demonstrating his commitment to serving the interests of Floridians.

Beyond our committee work, one of Ralph's notable legislative endeavors was his proactive stance on an environmental issue that hit close to home for many in South Florida – the problem of invasive Burmese pythons. Ralph spearheaded a bill to regulate these snakes, aiming to mitigate their impact on native wildlife and prevent potential risks to human safety. His initiative to introduce regulations for python ownership underscored his multifaceted approach to solving the state's challenges, blending environmental stewardship with public safety concerns.

Working alongside Ralph, I witnessed his ability to tackle diverse issues with a practical and informed perspective. Whether addressing insurance matters or environmental threats, Ralph consistently demonstrated his capability as a legislator.

His efforts, particularly on the Python regulation bill, showcased his proactive and thoughtful approach to governance, leaving a lasting impact on our state's legislative landscape and its natural environment.

State Representative – Jeff Kottkamp

Beginning in 2000, my journey with Jeff Kottkamp in the Florida House of Representatives was a shared path through some of the most pivotal moments in recent history, including the contentious presidential election of 2000 and the unforgettable tragedy of 9/11. Despite occasionally differing viewpoints, our friendship and mutual respect were constant, reflecting the collaborative spirit of public service.

Jeff's tenure in the Florida House was marked by leadership roles on various committees, demonstrating his commitment to impactful legislation. His advocacy for tax reduction and his sponsorship of significant legislation, like the Dr. Marvin Davies Civil Rights Act, underscored his dedication to justice and fiscal responsibility. Our discussions and collaborations, even when we saw issues from different perspectives, were always grounded in a shared goal of serving the people of Florida with integrity and diligence.

Ascending to Florida's 17th Lieutenant Governor role, Jeff continued his public service with a broadened scope, chairing Space Florida and the Children and Youth Cabinet, among other responsibilities.

His efforts in drug control, especially the push for the Prescription Drug Monitoring Program, and his leadership in aerospace and children's services were a testament to his versatile and committed approach to governance.

Even after his tenure in public office, Jeff's journey continued to reflect a blend of public service and private sector engagement, shaping his legacy as a multifaceted leader and advocate for Florida. My friendship with Jeff, rooted in our shared experiences in the Florida House, remains a valued connection, embodying the enduring bonds formed in the crucible of public service.

State Representative – David Mealor

In 2000, David Mealor and I were first elected to the Florida House of Representatives. From the moment I met David, I sensed his distinctive nature. Unlike many in politics, who often bask in their own spotlight, David exhibited refreshing humility and a genuine interest in others.

David's demeanor wasn't just pleasant but emblematic of a true public servant. His approach to politics was never about grandstanding but about meaningful engagement and creating impactful change. As a professor and an educator with a rich background, his contributions to the Committees on Schools & Learning and Postsecondary Education reflected his commitment to shaping a brighter future through education.

Throughout his tenure, David's dedication to his community was obvious. Whether through his service on various committees or his recognition with awards like the Christian Coalition of Florida's Faith and Family Award, his efforts were always geared toward uplifting others. His work, particularly in education and mental health, showcased his deep understanding of the issues and his unwavering dedication to service.

David's involvement extended beyond the legislative chambers. As a mayor and city commissioner, he was deeply rooted in his community, consistently advocating for local issues and ensuring that the voices of his constituents were heard. His leadership in local governance was just another chapter in his commendable journey of public service.

Remembering David Mealor is to recall a man of integrity, a dedicated public servant, and one of the kindest individuals I've had the privilege to meet. His legacy in the Florida House, his local community, and the lives he touched are testaments to the profound impact one person can have when they serve with sincerity and a heart for others.

State Representative – Bryan Nelson

In my tenure alongside Representative Bryan Nelson in the Florida House, I observed firsthand his unwavering dedication and insightful contributions, particularly in insurance and small business advocacy. Our shared background in the insurance industry provided a common ground, yet Bryan's profound understanding and commitment set him apart.

With his deep-rooted knowledge of the insurance sector, Chairman Nelson brought invaluable perspectives to our legislative discussions. His legislative work, particularly his leadership of the Insurance & Banking Subcommittee, was a testament to his expertise and dedication to rectifying legislative oversights. His approach was meticulous and driven by a genuine desire to serve the interests of Floridians, especially when correcting previous legislative missteps.

Bryan's work extended beyond the confines of our shared industry, touching various facets of state governance and impacting numerous lives through his thoughtful, informed decision-making.

I hold Chairman Nelson in high esteem for his professional achievements, character, and integrity. His ongoing contributions to our state are a beacon of public service excellence, reflecting a commitment to the greater good that continues to inspire his colleagues and constituents alike.

State Representative – Jerry Maygarden

Reflecting on my time with Jerry Maygarden in the Florida House brings a sense of nostalgia and admiration for a man whose tenure was defined by leadership, integrity, and a deep commitment to public service. Serving alongside Jerry, I witnessed a legislator who commanded respect for his position and the wisdom and earnest dedication he brought to every debate and decision.

Jerry's leadership roles, particularly as Majority Leader and Floor Leader, showcased his ability to guide and influence with a sense of purpose and vision. His contributions to the legislative process were profound, addressing various issues from tax legislation to civil rights, demonstrating his multifaceted approach to governance.

His memorable remarks during the Florida election recount, in which he passionately defended the integrity of our voting system, encapsulate his spirit and resolve. His post-legislative career advocating in the healthcare sector further exemplifies his ongoing commitment to public advocacy and community welfare.

Jerry's educational achievements and military service, complementing his political career, paint a picture of a man dedicated to lifelong service and leadership. His recognition, like the PACE Pioneer and Community Leader of the Year awards, is a testament to his impact and legacy.

In sum, Jerry Maygarden's legacy in the Florida House is a testament to his commitment to his principles, his community, and the state of Florida, making him not just an esteemed politician but a true statesman in every sense of the word.

State Representative – Alan Hays

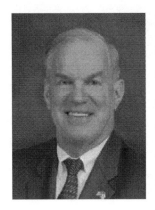

His remarkable tenacity and dedication marked my time with Representative Alan Hays in the legislature. From our first meeting after his election in 2004, Alan's deep commitment to the insurance sector, particularly through our collaborative efforts on the insurance committee I chaired in 2007 and 2008, was evident. His insights were not just valuable—they were instrumental in driving forward meaningful reforms aimed at improving the lives of Florida homeowners.

Alan's dedication to the issues he cared about did not waver when he transitioned to the Florida Senate. His continued advocacy for legal reforms to make insurance more affordable for Floridians reflected his unwavering commitment to this crucial issue. As a vocal member of a team of Senators pushing for these changes, Alan's contributions were integral to the progress made in this area.

'Beyond his work on insurance and homeowners' rights, Alan's legislative contributions were remarkably diverse, touching upon a wide range of issues that impacted the lives of Floridians. From his efforts to raise awareness about prescription drug abuse to his advocacy for public transportation reforms, Alan's approach to legislating was always proactive, thoughtful, and centered on the needs of his constituents.

In a metaphorical fight for justice and progress within the halls of the Florida legislature, Alan Hays is undoubtedly the person you'd want on your side. His firm resolve and strategic and thoughtful approach to legislation made him an invaluable ally in pursuing positive change.

Alan's tenure in various legislative capacities, his recognition for leadership, and his ongoing commitment to public service define a career dedicated to the betterment of Florida. His legacy is a testament to his dedication, making him an esteemed politician and a true statesman whose impact will be felt for years.

State Representative – Perry McGriff

Serving alongside Representative Perry McGriff in the Florida House of Representatives was an insightful experience.

I recall a particular moment on the State Administration Committee when Perry, deeply engrossed in the legislative rules, surprised us all by strategically using them. His strategic use of a motion to "reconsider and leave pending" during a bill vote was a lesson in the nuanced power of procedural knowledge.

This instance, while unexpected, highlighted Perry's understanding of legislative intricacies and his commitment to thoughtful governance. His approach, balancing keen insight with a judicious application of rules, made a lasting impression on me and underscored the importance of being well-versed in the mechanics of legislation.

Perry's legacy, marked by his service and astute engagement in the legislative process, remains a testament to his dedication to effective representation and the thoughtful application of procedural knowledge for the benefit of Floridian governance.

State Representative – Jimmy Patronis

Reflecting on my time with Jimmy Patronis, I remember our unique journey in Florida's political landscape. Initially, our paths crossed under the competitive circumstances of the 2006 elections, where, admittedly, my support lay with one of his opponents. However, the subsequent years have not only dissolved that initial rivalry but also fostered a deep, mutual respect and genuine friendship between us.

Observing Jimmy's service from the Gulf Coast Community College Foundation Board, Bay County EDA, Restaurateur – Captain Anderson's to the Florida House of Representatives, the Florida Elections Commission, the Public Service Commission, and now as Florida's Chief Financial Officer, has been nothing short of inspiring.

His trajectory in public service is marked by an unwavering dedication to the people of Florida, showcasing an admirable and impactful passion.

Beyond his professional achievements, what truly stands out is Jimmy's devotion to his faith, family, and community. These personal commitments resonate deeply with me, illustrating a man who, despite his vast responsibilities, places immense value on his foundational principles.

As I look back on the journey that Jimmy and I have shared, from those early days of political rivalry to the deep friendship we share today, I am struck by the realization that his impact on my life extends far beyond the realm of politics. Jimmy's example of leadership, his commitment to his values, and his dedication to serving others have profoundly influenced my approach to public service and my understanding of what it truly means to be a servant of the people.

State Representative – Jerry Melvin

Jerry Melvin was an energetic Dean of the Florida House. He was known for his high energy and tireless advocacy for education and good government. He served in the Florida House from 1968 to 1978 and again from 1994 until 2002.

As I reflect on my time in the Florida Legislature, one of the most unforgettable and impactful colleagues I had the privilege of serving with was Jerry Melvin. From the moment I first met Jerry, even before we began serving together from 2000 to 2002, I was struck by his infectious energy, unwavering positive outlook, and deep commitment to public service.

Jerry's enthusiasm for life and his work as a legislator was contagious. I will never forget when he invited me to join him on a talk radio show in Fort Walton Beach. His excitement was palpable, and his decision to stand and "dance in his tracks" throughout the two-hour broadcast perfectly encapsulated his lively spirit and unbridled passion for engaging with his constituents.

Jerry's legislative career, marked by his dedication to various causes, particularly elder care and animal welfare, showcased his compassionate nature and commitment to making a tangible difference in the community. His leadership and advocacy left a significant impact, not only on policy but on the lives of countless Floridians.

Beyond his public service, Jerry's personal qualities—his approachability, genuine interest in others, and infectious enthusiasm—made him a beloved figure. His ability to uplift those around him, to inspire action, and to face challenges with a positive attitude was truly remarkable.

While I could say, "Rest in Peace," I know that Jerry wouldn't have it any other way than to keep on dancing, even in Heaven. His spirit, energy, and love for life and serving others will live on in the hearts and minds of those who had the privilege of knowing him. Jerry Melvin was a true original, a one-of-a-kind legislator, and a friend that I will never forget.

State Representative – Garrett Richter

Garrett Richter is one of my favorite legislators. Reflecting on my experiences with Representative Garrett Richter makes me smile, especially recalling our brief time as seatmates in the Florida House of Representatives. Garrett, who succeeded my good friend Dudley Goodlette, brought a unique blend of seriousness and humor to his role, a refreshing and impactful balance.

During our organizational session, the festive atmosphere, amplified by the holiday season, provided a backdrop for camaraderie and lighthearted moments. One such instance was when Garrett, new to the legislative protocols, inadvertently brought a pastry onto the House floor, a moment that led to a discreet but humorous exchange between us. His willingness to adapt, tucking away the treat for later, was a testament to his adaptability and good nature.

Another memorable moment involved my unwitting musical tie performance, which Garrett, the considerate colleague, tactfully mitigated by tucking the tie into my shirt pocket. This saved our colleagues from further unintended musical interludes and me from being unknowingly embarrassed.

From his term in the Florida House to his distinguished service in the Florida Senate, Garrett's legislative journey was marked by dedication and a commitment to addressing key issues like housing, insurance, and even the complexities of hydraulic fracturing legislation. His approach to public

service, characterized by thoughtful legislation and a proactive stance on economic and environmental matters, demonstrated his deep commitment to Florida's well-being.

Beyond the halls of the legislature, Garrett's background, from his military service to his contributions to banking and community development, painted a picture of a man deeply invested in his community and state. His leadership in various civic and economic organizations reflected his broader commitment to fostering growth and opportunity in Florida.

In tribute to Garrett Richter, I celebrate not only being a dedicated public servant and legislator but also a friend whose warmth, wit, and dedication enriched the lives of those around him and left an indelible mark on the state he served so diligently.

Florida House – Impressive Staff
Tom Cooper

During my time in the Florida House of Representatives, Tom Cooper, an incredible lawyer and public policy expert, played a crucial role in shaping the legislative landscape. His deep understanding of the law and keen insight into public policy's intricacies made him an invaluable asset to our legislative team.

Katrina Calloway

Katrina Calloway's talent and hard work were evident when she joined our legislative staff. Her dedication to the legislative process and ability to easily navigate complex policy issues made her an indispensable team member. Katrina's contributions to our legislative successes cannot be overstated, and I am grateful for the opportunity to have worked alongside such a talented and committed individual.

John Bussey

John Bussey, a true "amicus fidelis" or faithful friend, was a constant source of support and guidance during my time in the Florida House. His unwavering loyalty and deep commitment to the legislative process made him an invaluable team member. John's friendship and dedication to serving the people of Florida will always hold a special place in my heart.

John Phelps

John Phelps, a distinguished authority on the rules of the Florida House, played a critical role in ensuring the smooth functioning of the legislative process. His deep understanding of parliamentary procedure and ability to navigate the complexities of the House rules made him an indispensable resource for members and staff alike. John's contributions to the Florida House and his dedication to upholding the integrity of the legislative process will always be remembered and appreciated.

Bob Ward

Bob Ward, a solid and devoted member of the Florida House staff, was a true asset to the institution and its members. His commitment to the legislative process and his unwavering support for the members he served made him a beloved figure in the House. Bob's dedication to the institution and his tireless work on behalf of the people of Florida will always be remembered and admired.

Don Rubottom

Don Rubottom, a man who challenges others to do their best and an incredible legal scholar, inspired all who worked with him. His deep understanding of the law and commitment to excellence in all aspects of his work made him an invaluable resource for members and staff. Don's contributions to the legislative process and his unwavering dedication to serving the people of Florida will always be remembered and appreciated.

Extraordinary Lobbyist
Larry Williams

Larry Williams, a lobbyist full of wit and charm, was a joy to work with during my time in the Florida House. His quick wit and ability to bring a smile to even the most stressful situations made him a beloved figure in the legislative process. Larry's contributions to the legislative process and his unwavering commitment to serving the people of Florida will always be remembered and appreciated.

Richard Coats

Richard Coats, a lobbyist with impressive knowledge, was a valuable resource during my time in the Florida House. His expertise on various policy issues and his ability to effectively communicate complex ideas made him a respected figure in the legislative process. Richard's contributions to the legislative process and his dedication to serving the people of Florida will always be remembered and appreciated.

James Massie

James Massie, a subject matter expert and a true friend, was an invaluable asset to the legislative process during my time in the Florida House. His deep understanding of the issues and ability to provide insights and guidance on even the most complex policy matters made him a respected figure among members and staff. James' friendship and his unwavering commitment to serving the people of Florida will always hold a special place in my heart.

Paul Hamilton

Paul Hamilton, a fun-loving lobbyist with a heart of gold, was a joy to work with during my time in the Florida House. His infectious enthusiasm and ability to bring a sense of levity to even the most challenging situations made him a beloved figure in the legislative process. Paul's contributions to the legislative process and his unwavering commitment to serving the people of Florida will always be remembered and appreciated.

Herb Morgan

Herb Morgan, a former Representative, and a true friend was a constant source of encouragement and support during my time in the Florida House. His deep understanding of the legislative process and ability to provide guidance and advice on even the most complex policy issues made him an invaluable resource for members and staff. Herb's friendship and his unwavering commitment to serving the people of Florida will always hold a special place in my heart.

Gerald Wester

Gerald Wester, an influential policy expert with a keen understanding of the legislative process, was a valuable asset to the Florida House during my time as a member. His ability to navigate complex policy issues and his deep commitment to crafting effective legislation made him a respected figure among members and staff alike. Gerald's contributions to the legislative process and his unwavering dedication to serving the people of Florida will always be remembered and appreciated.

Mark Delegal

Mark Delegal, a respected policy expert with a wealth of knowledge and experience, was an invaluable resource during my time in the Florida House. His deep understanding of the issues and ability to provide insights and guidance on even the most complex policy matters made him a respected figure among members and staff. Mark's contributions to the legislative process and his unwavering commitment to serving the people of Florida will always be remembered and appreciated.

Jim Cardaro

Jim Cardaro, a friendly and helpful lobbyist who invited me to my first college football game, holds a special place in my memory. His kindness, generosity, and deep commitment to the legislative process made him a beloved figure in the Florida House. Jim's contributions to the legislative process and his unwavering dedication to serving the people of Florida will always be remembered and appreciated.

Lisa Miller

Lisa Miller & Associates

I have known and worked with Lisa Miller for many years. She is one of the most dedicated and passionate legislative advocates I have ever met. Her energy is contagious, and her unwavering loyalty to her clients and friends is truly admirable.

Lisa's extensive experience in the public sector has equipped her with a deep understanding of disaster recovery, insurance and financial services regulations, real estate, and emergency management. But what I admire most about Lisa is her selflessness. She devotes a substantial portion of her time to volunteer advocacy, helping consumers and supporting various causes. Her commitment to giving back to the community is inspiring, and her involvement with charities and organizations has made a tangible difference in the lives of many.

Chris Doolin

I have had the pleasure of working alongside Chris Doolin, a dedicated lobbyist who represents the Small County Coalition and the Small School District Council Consortium. Chris is known for his unwavering commitment to his clients, and I have witnessed firsthand his tireless efforts to level the playing field for small counties and school districts in Florida.

Chris brings a unique perspective to his work, shaped by his extensive experience in various fields. He is always on the lookout for opportunities to support his clients, and I have personally benefited from his expertise on many occasions. One notable instance was when he drew me into a legislative dispute that ultimately turned out well for small counties. What impresses me most about Chris is his exceptional knowledge of local government funding programs. He is a subject matter expert, and his preparation is always thorough. I am grateful to have had him as a colleague.

Tom "T.K." Kovel

Tom "T.K." Kovel, a workers' compensation expert with a wealth of knowledge and experience, was an invaluable resource during my time in the Florida House. His deep understanding of the complex issues surrounding workers' compensation and his ability to provide insights and guidance on policy matters made him a respected figure among members and staff. T.K.'s contributions to the legislative process and his unwavering commitment to serving the people of Florida will always be remembered and appreciated.

Tim Meenhan

Tim Meenhan, a charismatic lobbyist with a diverse knowledge base and a love for Machiavelli, was a fascinating figure during my time in the Florida House. His ability to engage in deep, philosophical discussions while navigating the practical realities of the legislative process made him a unique and respected presence in the Capitol. Tim's contributions to the legislative process and his unwavering commitment to serving the people of Florida will always be remembered and appreciated.

Paul Sanford

Paul Sanford's unparalleled life and health insurance expertise made him an invaluable resource during my time at the Florida House. His deep understanding of the complex issues surrounding these critical policy areas was truly remarkable, and his contributions to the development of Florida's insurance statutes cannot be overstated.

As a legislator, I had the privilege of working closely with Paul numerous times. His wealth of knowledge and ability to navigate even the most intricate policy matters easily impressed me. His guidance and insights were instrumental in shaping many of the key insurance reforms that were enacted during my tenure, and his impact on Florida's insurance landscape will be felt for generations to come.

I will always be grateful for the opportunity to have worked alongside Paul Sanford and to have learned from his incredible depth of knowledge and experience. His contributions to the legislative process and his dedication to serving the people of Florida will forever be remembered and appreciated.

Jim Brainard

Jim Brainard's early and consistent support was a key factor in my success as a member of the Florida Legislature. From the moment I arrived in Tallahassee, Jim was there to offer his guidance, expertise, and friendship. I will always be grateful for his role in helping me navigate the complex world of state government.

Jim was a subject matter expert. His knowledge and insights were invaluable to me and to many other members of the Legislature. He deeply understood various policy issues and was always willing to share his expertise with those who sought his counsel. His ability to break down complex topics and to provide clear, concise analysis was truly remarkable, and his contributions to the legislative process were immeasurable.

Mark Trafton

When I was once asked to offer a lighthearted observation about Mark Trafton, I thought, "Well, that'll be easy. He's such a likable guy." But the more I tried, the more my thoughts turned serious. At the time, I had only known Mark for about seven years, and only a small fraction of his time was devoted to an industry he knows so well. He has my total respect. All of us would be wise to learn from his example.

I can only imagine what it must have been like when Mark started his career in the insurance industry. I believe the printing press had already been invented, but typewriters and computers were invented much later. I am convinced He reads every word of every bill and every amendment. He even reads that "Title" stuff.

Unlike most of the "big shots" in Tallahassee today, Mark got where he was the old-fashioned way: "He Earned It!"!" Honest," Hardworking," and "A Man of Integrity" are just a few of the words I would use to describe him.

One final observation: Having had the benefit of such a long career of legislative involvement, I am sure that Mark has "seen it all." In view of this, I couldn't understand how Mark could retain his composure when he saw the butchery the "Johnny come lately's" had made of the insurance system in Florida in recent years. But composed and dignified, he remained.

Mark Trafton is a man I hope to emulate when I grow up. He reminds me of my Daddy.

Stephen Weinstein

Stephen Weinstein is a remarkable individual who has left an indelible mark on me and the lives of countless others in the business and insurance world. His influence extends far beyond his professional accomplishments; he is a mentor, a visionary, and, most importantly, a dear friend.

One of Stephen's most admirable qualities is his innate ability to encourage and inspire those around him. Known for his "gift of encouragement," he has been a beacon of hope and support for many, including myself, during times of uncertainty.

Over the years, I have had the great privilege of getting to know Stephen well, and I can say with absolute certainty that he is one of the most talented and principled individuals I have ever encountered. His contributions to both the business world and public policy are nothing short of extraordinary.

During his two-decade tenure at RenaissanceRe, Stephen demonstrated exceptional leadership as chief legal officer, navigating the company through complex legal and regulatory matters. His dedication to researching and developing risk mitigation techniques through the RenaissanceRe Risk Sciences Foundation has undoubtedly touched the lives of countless individuals. As I reflect on Stephen's impact on me and the lives of so many others, I am filled with gratitude and admiration. His guidance was instrumental in my continued involvement in public policy, a field where his wisdom and moral clarity have made a lasting impact. I know his legacy will continue to inspire and guide us all for years.

Dr. Jack Nicholson

I have known Dr. Jack Nicholson for many years, and his contributions to addressing Florida's hurricane insurance challenges cannot be overstated. As the former COO of the Florida Hurricane Catastrophe Fund (FHCF), Dr. Nicholson was vital in proposing reforms to stabilize the fund financially, particularly considering its significant liabilities.

While in the Florida House of Representatives, I relied on Dr. Nicholson's expertise and insights into the Florida insurance market. His attention to detail and depth of knowledge were always impressive.

I recall a conversation with him about how Florida could best plan for the cost of hurricanes, and he wisely stated, "It's always best to pay for catastrophe risk with capital rather than debt."

Dr. Nicholson's wisdom and candor were especially evident during the lead-up to the passage of House Bill 1A in the special session of January 2007. When asked for his opinion on changes to the FHCF, his views were unfortunately rejected. He later remarked about legislators who seemed to lack understanding of the issue, "This is like watching a bunch of shade tree mechanics perform brain surgery." While said in jest, his words proved more accurate than we realized then.

I have come to value Dr. Nicholson as a wise counselor and a dear friend. His tireless efforts to mitigate the risks associated with potential funding shortfalls following major hurricanes have been crucial in safeguarding Florida's fiscal future. By working to ensure the sustainability and effectiveness of the FHCF he has helped keep insurance costs more manageable for Florida residents.

Dr. Jack Nicholson's dedication, expertise, and unwavering commitment to serving the people of Florida have made a lasting impact on our state. I am grateful for his friendship and his invaluable contributions throughout his career.

Cecil Pearce

In the ever-evolving landscape of Florida's insurance industry, where hurricanes and property claims pose relentless challenges, one figure has stood out for his unwavering dedication and strategic foresight—Cecil Pearce, President and CEO of the Florida Insurance Council. Under his leadership, the Council has navigated these turbulent waters and set a benchmark for excellence and ethical conduct in the insurance sector.

Cecil's tenure has been marked by key legislative reforms and proactive measures addressing some of Florida's most pressing insurance issues. His advocacy efforts have helped craft policies that mitigate risks and reduce fraud and have also contributed to sustaining a stable market environment essential for economic growth and consumer trust.

It's noteworthy that Cecil's leadership style is complemented by his personal charm and wit. Known among colleagues and friends for his sense of humor, Cecil has a knack for lightening serious discussions with his timely stories, making complex policy discussions more accessible and engaging. This unique blend of professionalism and personability has earned him respect and deep admiration within the industry.

Summary of Chapter 35:

Chapter 35 of my book serves as a heartfelt tribute to the influential figures who have left a lasting impression on my legislative journey in the Florida House of Representatives. From esteemed governors to dedicated colleagues, staff members, and lobbyists, each individual has contributed in unique ways to my growth as a legislator and a person.

The chapter begins with an introduction emphasizing the significance of these individuals in shaping my understanding of public service, leadership, and the legislative process. It underscores the diversity of backgrounds and positions held by these figures, united by their shared dedication to serving the people of Florida.

The tributes commence with a focus on Governor Jeb Bush highlighting his leadership style and his impact on Florida's political landscape. Each tribute provides insight into the strengths and challenges faced by these leaders, offering a nuanced perspective on their contributions to governance.

Following the gubernatorial tributes, the chapter turns to recognize speakers of the Florida House, such as Tom Feeney, Johnnie Byrd, Allen Bense, and Marco Rubio. These sections delve into the leadership qualities and policy priorities of each speaker, illustrating their influence on legislative outcomes and the state's trajectory.

The tributes extend beyond elected officials to encompass state representatives and extraordinary staff members. Profiles of individuals like Dennis Ross, Jimmy Patronis, Garrett Richter, and Tom Cooper highlight their dedication to effective governance and their impact on legislative achievements.

The chapter also pays homage to remarkable lobbyists who have played pivotal roles in shaping policy debates and facilitating collaboration among stakeholders. Profiles of lobbyists such as Larry Williams, Richard Coats, and James Massie showcase their expertise, professionalism, and contributions to the legislative process.

Additionally, the chapter features tributes to individuals outside the realm of politics, including Dr. Jack Nicholson, Stephen Weinstein, and Cecil Pearce. These profiles underscore the interdisciplinary nature of policymaking and the invaluable insights offered by experts in various fields.

Overall, Chapter 35 offers a comprehensive tribute to the influential figures who have contributed to my legislative journey. Through these profiles, readers gain a deeper understanding of the collaborative and multifaceted nature of governance, as well as the enduring impact of mentorship, friendship, and dedicated public service.

Personal Credentials:

As a retired insurance agent and former State Representative in the Florida House, my legislative journey has been marked by a steadfast commitment to advocating for smaller government, market-based solutions, and the well-being of Florida residents. My experiences have shaped my perspective on governance and inspired me to honor the individuals who have played significant roles in my legislative endeavors. Through this chapter, I hope to convey the profound impact of these influential figures on my personal and professional growth, while also highlighting the importance of collaboration and mentorship in the realm of public service.

Transition to Chapter 36:

In the wake of profound loss and tragedy, the tapestry of our lives continued to unfold, revealing threads of resilience and unwavering love. As I reflect on the challenges we've faced, there emerges a truth that shines brightly amidst the darkness—a truth embodied by my steadfast, loving wife, Diane. Please join me in Chapter 33 as I tell her incredible life story.

Chapter 36

My Steadfast, Loving Wife

The revelation came unexpectedly—a truth about Diane, my future wife—that seemed almost mythical in its scale. It wasn't an achievement she sought; instead, it was a testament to her extraordinary resilience. With her unwavering strength, Diane might be a candidate for the Guinness Book of World Records.

Reflecting on the tapestry of my life, woven through with trials and triumphs, it becomes clear that Diane's challenges dwarfed my own. Her story is not just about enduring but also about thriving against the odds.

Early Struggles

Before she agreed to marry me, Diane had an unusual request. She wanted me to meet her doctor. At first, I was perplexed. "Why this sudden need for a doctor's approval?" I wondered. But it wasn't about approval; it was about understanding.

In the muted light of the doctor's office, a narrative unfolded. Diane had a congenital heart defect, a ventral septal defect—simply put, a hole in her heart. It was a condition that offered few remedies back in her childhood.

Yet, at the age of six, Diane underwent pioneering open-heart surgery, a procedure rare and experimental at the time. Whether or not to have the risky surgery was a monumental decision for Diane's parents and one they struggled considerably over.

One thing was sure: Diane's life would be short without the surgery. On the other hand, if the surgery was successful, the doctors could not assure them how long her life might be extended or how much the quality of her life would be improved. The outcome would not be sure.

Unfortunately, another child in their community was diagnosed with the same condition, and his parents faced a similar dilemma. After many tears and prayers, the decision was made. Diane would have the surgery with the hope of a normal life. Tragically, the other child's parents made a different choice, and the inevitable outcome was realized in his early 40's.

In 1979, when I proposed to her, I discovered that she was facing another health challenge—a leaking aortic valve. Her decision not to share this information with me earlier spoke to her strength of character, as she didn't want her condition to influence my feelings. Through this experience, I learned that love grows stronger when faced with adversity.

We believed our journey was divinely guided. Despite the doctors' reservations, we married, embracing our faith and the shared path before us.

Diane and I were married on April 15, 1979. A cardiac catheterization was scheduled two months later, and it confirmed the doctors' diagnosis. The surgery could not be delayed.

Diane's second open heart surgery was performed on July 9, 1979, only slightly short of three months after we were married. Diane's medical team faced many choices, not the least of which was the replacement valve type. The one that held the prospect of the longest useful life was a St. Jude's prosthetic valve made of metal and plastic.

However, it would require anticoagulants (warfarin, also known as coumadin) if used. This would make Diane's lifelong dream of motherhood highly risky and not advisable.

Alternatively, a porcine valve (pig valve) offered advantages and disadvantages. One disadvantage was that its projected useful life was shorter. A significant benefit was that a porcine valve did not require anticoagulants and consequently did not rule out Diane's dream of motherhood.

Again, difficult decisions were made, and Diane's dream survived. A few years later, we were both significantly rewarded.

As I ventured into entrepreneurship, founding an insurance firm, Diane was my cornerstone. Her energy was infectious, and her resolve was unyielding. Even as she managed our home [cooking and canning summer vegetables] and business, life presented us with a new miracle—our daughter, Lori Callista, a name chosen for its meaning, "Most Beautiful."

A Mother's Love and Laughter

Having a baby to care for increased Diane's workload, but she joyfully accomplished every new task.

Before Lori was one year old, she slept late one morning, which allowed Diane to do some laundry and other chores around the house. Some noise from the bedroom alerted Diane to the fact that Lori was finally awake.

As she entered the room, she discovered the source of the noise. Lori had managed to reach over the rail of her bed and open a jar of Vaseline from a nearby nightstand. She had emptied the jar and was covered from head to toe with Vaseline, so much so that it was nearly impossible to hold onto her.

With an initial cry of laughter, Diane exclaimed," Lori made a mess." Ironically, one of Lori's first phrases was "Momma made a mess" after Diane spilled milk on the kitchen table.

This anecdote, while messy, perfectly encapsulates the joy and laughter that Diane brought to our family, even in the face of daily challenges. Her ability to find humor and light in every situation was a testament to her resilient spirit and the depth of her love for our daughter.

Facing Tragedy Together

Life was good in the Browns' little home. 1988 was made much happier due to some newfound but unlikely friends. Rex and Pat Brogdale were much older than Diane and me. Both were originally from upstate New York, in Rex's case, and New Hampshire, in Pat's case. Rex retired from the military, and I never had the honor to serve in that role.

Rex and Pat were highly respected in their community, most notably for their commitment to their faith in the face of tremendous tragedy.

Several years before we met them, their teenage son and a friend were killed in an automobile accident. How they "lived their faith" in the months and years after the accident was remarkable.

Their faithful witness of the goodness of God and His sovereignty in human affairs was amazing. There is much more to this story that I will share later.

An exciting turn took place in our marriage in the late 1980s. Diane and I attended a Christian conference focusing on "Strengthening Families" and "Basic Youth

Conflict." During the meeting, men and women were encouraged to respect and honor their spouses.

One simple but practical strategy suggested to accomplish the goal of respecting and honoring one another was that men should open doors for their wives. Wives should patiently wait for their husbands to open doors for them.

It's such a simple concept, but I can tell you from the perspective of forty-five-plus years of marriage that it can make a powerful difference.

Diane and I agreed that when she is in my presence, she will not walk through any door I do not open first. This requires the commitment of the husband to be faithful and the wife to be patient.

Not many weeks after we made this simple commitment to one another, we were invited to a social function with a group of friends. The function was held at a beautiful lake venue. We saw that many of our friends had already arrived as we approached. Not wanting to delay joining our friends, I parked the car and promptly joined the party.

After several minutes, someone asked if Diane would be joining the party. I immediately realized that I had failed to honor my commitment. Rushing to the car, I opened the door with great embarrassment to a disappointed wife who felt forgotten.

Diane forgave me for that incident, and we have enjoyed years of comments, particularly from younger couples, as they observe our little ritual. This simple act of respect and consideration has not only strengthened our bond but has also served as an inspiration to others, reminding them of the importance of cherishing and honoring one's partner in the daily moments of life.

I cannot begin to tell you how this has impacted our marriage. We have taken countless opportunities to share this simple principle with those younger couples in hopes that they will honor and respect one another.

The ensuing years presented additional challenges. In 1989, Diane's porcine heart valve failed, requiring the third open heart surgery. This time, St. Jude's prosthetic value was used, which required introducing anticoagulants and managing their use.

If you or a member of your family has been required to use this family of medications, you will know how difficult it can be.

Notwithstanding our new reality, Diane demonstrated a resilience that seemed superhuman. Her courage wasn't just in facing the surgeries but in living fully between them.

A tragedy struck in 1993. My son from a previous marriage passed away, leaving me in a chasm of grief. Diane kept our world turning, managing our business with unwavering dedication. She was my rock, my anchor in a sea of despair.

Jamie had been missing for five days, nowhere to be found. I had driven 60 miles from home to be with one of my sisters the night I received the call informing me that Jamie and a friend of his had been found at the scene of an automobile accident. They had not survived the 300-foot plunge down the side of a steep mountain. My world crashed.

As we drove home that night, word of the tragedy had spread among our friends, many of whom had made their way to our home to greet us and offer comfort. When we arrived, 20 or 30 cars were parked in our front yard. As I looked into that sea of faces, two stood out immediately. It would become evident why the unlikely friendship of Rex and Pat Brogdale was preordained.

Among so many loving friends, they were the only ones who did not need to speak. They had lived an example that said more than any words. In retrospect, the power of their example is illustrated by one instance among many.

A year or two before Jamie's accident, Rex called me one day to invite Diane, Jamie, Lori, and me to join him and Pat for a day of fellowship and a meal in their home. We commonly shared a meal at least once a week. While the invitation was routine, what happened that day was not.

While Daine, Lori, and Pat were happily making bread and preparing a meal, Rex requested that Jamie and I help with a chore that was a little more than he could do alone. The chore was to improve his son's gravesite. It was a hot day that required frequent breaks for water and rest in the shade.

During our work and rest, Rex and Jamie had a deep conversation. Due to the nature of our task, compelling questions about the meaning of life and what happens when we die came to the surface.

Even today, the care and wisdom Rex displayed in response to Jamie's questions amazes me. We could not have known the profound nature of this conversation on that hot day in a rural cemetery. Jamie and Rex developed a much deeper bond because of it. Pat, too, was like a second grandmother to Jamie, not to mention she was Diane's BFF (Best Friends Forever).

The Power of Friendship

In 1995, there was more tragedy. In August, Diane's father passed away suddenly. Then, in September, my mother died unexpectedly. The untimely deaths of our parents compounded the grief from Jamie's accident.

For me, coping was difficult, but Diane found strength in her faith and did her job and much of mine.

1995 was also a good year. We found a new church home and became friends with the pastor and his family, Ron and Shirley Meade. As our friendship grew, so did the time we spent together. We could not have known how impactful this friendship with the Meade family would be.

I'll share more about this new friendship in a moment.

During this period, another friend suggested I run for political office. I ran and lost by a few hundred votes. The loss was very disappointing, but it challenged me to try again.

In 2000, I was elected to the Florida House of Representatives. My passion for responsive government found a new outlet, and Diane was there, encouraging me and believing in me when I couldn't.

She was my campaign's unsung hero, managing both our business and my political aspirations with unparalleled grace.

On April 6, 2003, our dear friend Pat Brogdale passed away. Diane was crushed. Pat had been like a big sister. She taught Diane a lot about breadmaking, canning, and preserving food. She was also an influential teacher. How she lived her life was an example for many younger women in the community. We miss Pat to this day, but with great hope, we look forward to seeing her again one day.

With the help of so many friends and family, our lives were mending as we worked to overcome past tragedies.

Our friendship with the Meade family became a significant factor in our recovery. Shirley became another of Diane's friends and provided tremendous support and encouragement. Ron was my pastor, but more than that, he became my best friend.

We did develop a bad habit, however. Ron and Shirley loved to travel, and Diane and I were happy to join them.

In December 2005, we vacationed in Utah at Duck Creek Village. May 2006 found us in Sedona, Arizona, for an unforgettable adventure. In 2008, we traveled to Moab, Utah; Key West, Florida; and St. Augustine, Florida. In June 2012, we spent eight days in Maui, Hawaii, our destination.

All travel plans stalled in 2013. I will explain the reason at the end of this chapter. It was unbelievable.

2015 was Blowing Rock, NC. Our itinerary in September of 2016 included ten days in Alaska, with seven of those days cruising the inside passage. Many shared memories will become much more precious in 2022. I'll share more of that story a little later.

Late in 2016, I became very sick, and the reason was unclear. My ENT doctor could not explain the symptoms and referred me to a specialist at Shands Hospital in Gainesville, FL. From December 2016 until March 2017, I lost 60 pounds and developed headaches so painful that even the simplest of daily tasks were nearly impossible.

The wait to see the doctor in Gainesville was unbearable. Seeing my degrading condition, my good friend Ron Meade developed a plan. Out of concern for my survival, he insisted that I go along. He drove me to Gainesville to visit an emergency room in hopes that the doctors would see my condition and expedite my admission to the hospital. The doctor summarily dismissed the notion of early admission, and Ron was furious and did not spare his disdain for the doctor's judgment. At that moment, it became clear to Diane and me how dear friends Ron and Shirley had become.

In March 2017, I underwent surgery in Gainesville. I was subsequently diagnosed with Wegener's granulomatosis, an uncommon disorder that causes inflammation of the blood vessels in the nose, sinuses, throat, lungs, and kidneys. Without treatment, people with severe forms of this disease can die within a few months. With treatment, the outlook for most patients is good. Most people who receive corticosteroids and other medicines that slow the immune response get much better.

My condition has returned to near normal based on close management, including two Rituxan infusions per year. Without friends like Ron Meade and Diane's constant nurturing, I might not have survived.

Diane's Indomitable Spirit

Tragedy strikes again on 11/21/2018. Diane had become sick, and after examination, it was determined she needed to have exploratory surgery, but what the surgeon discovered horrified us. The diagnosis was colon cancer. The surgery resulted in a colostomy and a plan for chemotherapy, which included six months of treatment. Diane had been through a lot, but this was the biggest challenge yet. Her outlook and energy level plummeted. Daily activities were challenging.

Over the ensuing months, Diane's recovery began to take shape. After the chemotherapy, her energy started to improve. So did her outlook.

In November 2019, after several CT scans, it was determined that Diane was a candidate for colostomy reversal surgery. The successful completion of that surgery was a very happy day.

Subsequently, Diane has passed the 5-year mark with clear CT scans. Today, she engages in regular activity with some reduced mobility due to neuropathic damage caused by chemotherapy.

In December of 2021, we were invited to join Ron and Shirley on Ron's dream vacation. Ron had a lifelong love of trains. So, we were scheduled to depart New Orleans, LA, on Amtrak to Chicago, IL. Then to Emeryville, CA, by way of Omaha, NE, and Denver, CO. After a three-day stay in Emeryville, we took a quick trip to LA, CA, for two days and then home across New Mexico, Arizona, and Texas, then back to New Orleans.

This was Ron's lifelong dream.

In February 2022, Ron became the victim of COVID-19 and passed away. Becoming one of his closest friends, I was asked to preach at his funeral. It wasn't easy. Tragically, in June 2022, Shirley required surgery. It was not successful, and in September 2022, Shirley passed away. Again, I was asked to preach at her funeral—another tough day.

Our friendship with the Meade family was one of life's sweetest joys. Diane had leaned on Shirley through all the years of her medical challenges, and the loss of that friendship remained hurtful until this day.

The Browns' and Meades' long friendship was so impactful. As we entered the second Christmas season without them, with Diane's help, we wrote the following poem as a tribute to them. We hope that it will convey their unique place in our hearts. Our greatest hope is to see them again in the glorious resurrection.

A Tribute to Ron and Shirley

In '95, a friendship did begin.

Ron and Shirley, kin to kin.

Through thick and thin, through joy and strife,

We carved our memories, dear friends, for life.

Ron, my Pastor, a guiding light,

In his wisdom, finding paths is so right.

An older brother, in friendship strong,

Together, we stood, singing life's sweet song.

Shirley, a principal with grace,

A rock for many, a kind embrace.

In Lakewood's halls, her influence reigned.

A legacy of love is forever sustained.

Diane and Shirley, a friendship true,

Through shared vacations, the bond just grew.

From Duck Creek to the Alaskan Sea,

Our journeys are forged in unity.

Amidst the canyons, 'neath Hawaiian skies,

In Key West's warmth, laughter lies.

Moab's red rocks and Boone's embrace

Our adventures painted joy on life's vast canvas.

Stephine and Heather, like sisters dear,

In joy and sorrow, she is always near.

A wedding's joy, a funeral's pain,

In life's complex dance, forever intertwined.

But fate took its toll—a cruel decree,

In 2022, Ron was set free.

COVID's grasp, an untimely fate,

Left us mourning at heaven's gate.
Then Shirley, too, faced life's cruel twist.
The surgery's challenge, she could not resist.
In September's hush, a silent fall
An echo of sorrow, a tearful call.
I stand before you, Christmas 2023.
A heart heavy yet filled with glee.
For Ron and Shirley, now beyond our view,
In heaven's embrace, their spirits renew.
Ron, an older brother, I'll always miss.
In admiration, sealed with a parting kiss.
Shirley, the rock, is now a heavenly guide.
In memories, forever by our side.
Stephine, bear the weight with strength untold,
In your parents' footsteps, be brave and bold.
The principal's chair, now yours to fill,
May grace and wisdom guide you still.
As we face this Christmas, the first without cheer,
I feel their presence, ever near.
In the twinkle of lights, the warmth of a flame,
Ron and Shirley, in our hearts, eternally claim.
So, here's to the Meade family, our dear friends, true,
In life and in death, our bond has always grown.
In heaven's grand tapestry, we'll meet again,
Till then, dear friends, farewell, amen.

So, what of Diane's record-setting feat? In 2013, she faced her fourth heart surgery, a number unheard of in medical annals. This was no pursuit of glory; it was a testament to her indomitable spirit.

I'm struck by what we've shared as I type these words. Diane's journey isn't just a series of medical milestones; it's a story of unwavering love, support, and perseverance. Our partnership, spanning over four decades, is a tribute to her incredible strength. But beyond records and accolades, our story is one of love—a love that has endured the most harrowing storms and triumphed over every imaginable challenge. Diane, my devoted, loving wife, is the heart of this story—a heart that has beaten against all odds.

Summary of Chapter 36:

Chapter 36 discribes the remarkable journey of Diane, my beloved wife, whose life has been marked by extraordinary resilience and unwavering strength. It begins with the revelation of Diane's congenital heart defect, a ventral septal defect, which led to pioneering open-heart surgery at the tender age of six. This surgery, a rare and experimental procedure at the time, set the stage for Diane's lifelong battle against the odds.

Despite facing another major heart surgery shortly after our marriage, Diane's spirit remained unbroken. The chapter highlights her courage in navigating multiple heart surgeries, each accompanied by difficult decisions and uncertainties about the future. From choosing between valve types to managing the risks associated with anticoagulants, Diane's unwavering determination to embrace life's challenges shines through.

Amidst these trials, Diane's resilience is further illustrated by her role as a loving mother to our daughter, Lori Callista, and her ability to find joy and laughter even in the face of adversity. The chapter also explores the profound impact of friendships, particularly with the Brogdale and Meade families, whose unwavering support and faith provided solace during our darkest moments.

As Diane and I weathered the storms of life together, facing personal tragedies and health crises, our bond only grew stronger. Diane's fourth heart surgery in 2013, a feat unheard of in medical annals, serves as a testament to her indomitable spirit and unwavering determination to embrace life's challenges head-on.

In essence, Chapter 36 is a tribute to Diane's incredible strength and resilience, a testament to her unwavering love and support throughout our partnership spanning over four decades. Beyond medical milestones and records, Diane's journey is a story of love—a love that has endured the most harrowing storms and triumphed over every imaginable challenge. She is the heart of our story, beating against all odds and inspiring hope in the face of adversity.

Transition to Chapter 37:

As Diane's journey embodies resilience and love, the next chapter of our story introduces another remarkable individual whose dedication and service have left an indelible mark on my life and career. In the midst of challenges and triumphs, Brad Drake emerged as not only a trusted colleague but also a cherished friend and confidant.

Part 5

CONCLUDING REFLECTIONS AND TRIBUTES

CHAPTER 37

Brad Drake – My Righthand Man

I must pause here to share the story of Brad Drake, my indispensable legislative assistant. Brad stands out as a testament to commitment, vision, and service. Our collaboration began when ambition met opportunity, evolving into a partnership that went beyond the usual professional relationship to embody mentorship and shared goals.

When I announced my candidacy for the Florida House of Representative District 5 seat, Brad requested to join my campaign right after graduating from the University of Florida, showing a readiness to engage with our mission. I remembered Brad as the spirited second baseman from Little League, not just for his athletic prowess but for his infectious energy and relentless chattering—earning him the moniker "The Mouth of the South."

Brad had sent his resume, but I had "dropped the ball" (pun intended) and failed to respond for several days. Without me knowing, Brad was trying to decide whether to move home or look for a job in Gainesville, FL. My delayed response left him in a quandary.

Not knowing my intentions, he had agreed to sign a lease for a home in Gainesville at 4 pm the following day. As fate would have it, I called him the next day at about 2:30 pm to discuss his interest in my campaign. The good news was that he agreed to join the campaign. The bad news was that I had no money in the campaign to pay him. He decided to work for no pay, provided he would have the opportunity to work as my legislative assistant when I was elected.

In most business transactions, you get what you pay for. To my good fortune, Brad worked as if both his life and mine depended upon it. The days were long as we went from Esto to Bethlehem, Chipley to Wausau and Vernon, Darlington to Freeport, and Laurel Hill to Fort Walton Beach. After the primary election victory, campaign fundraising began to pick up, and Brad started to get paid for his hard work.

This was the start of a journey filled with challenges and achievements, where Brad's dedication shone brightly. We began to learn about each other and what motivated us both.

One day, as we took a break from the campaign trail, Brad shared part of his motivation.

Brad's grandfather, T. Troy Peacock, significantly shaped his path. The elder Peacock's principles and career in public service deeply inspired Brad. Mr. Peacock had served several terms in the Florida House of Representatives in the 1940s and 50s.

Brad's Grandfather lived in Marianna, FL, and Brad routinely visited him as he drove from Gainesville to his parents' house in DeFuniak Springs, FL. On one fateful weekend, Brad failed to stop in Marianna, going straight to DeFuniak

Springs instead. That Sunday evening, as Brad listened to the Pastor's sermon, he was overcome by the message: "Don't put off until tomorrow what should be done today." As the sermon ended, Brad knew what he had to do. He drove to Marianna, hoping his grandfather had not yet gone to bed. Fortunately for both, he was still awake and proud to see his grandson again.

After catching up with the latest news, the conversation took on a serious tone. "Brad, what do you intend to do with your life? What career do you plan to pursue?" Brad replied without hesitation, "I want to be elected to the Florida Legislature." "Why would you want to do that?" his grandfather asked. "Well, holding elected office is a prestigious thing to do. After all, I would like to follow in your footsteps and those of Pat Thomas," someone Brad also looked up to.

Brad was shocked to hear his grandfather's retort, "If that's the best reason you can find to run for the office, then you need to find another career." Brad didn't know what to say. He loved and looked up to his grandfather, but He didn't understand why he gave such blunt advice.

Brad drove home that night deflated as he pondered what he had heard. At the time, he could not have known that would be the last conversations with his grandfather. The following morning, at about 2:30 am, he got a call from the staff at the home where his grandfather lived, informing him that his beloved grandfather had passed away after midnight.

Years later, Brad realized that servant leadership was his grandfather's vision of public office. It became clear that public service was a duty to serve and uplift others rather than a route to personal prestige.

As Brad moved from an energetic campaign worker to a trusted legislative assistant and then to a respected position in the Florida House, his evolution showcased the impact of mentorship and a clear vision. Intertwined with his grandfather's legacy, his story serves as a beacon, highlighting that public service is a challenging yet rewarding path, rich with opportunities for personal growth and societal contribution.

Our partnership, characterized by shared ideals and a commitment to good governance, transcended a mere working relationship.

I am proud of Brad Drake and the opportunity to be a small part of his dream of being a public servant.

Summary of Chapter 37:

Chapter 37 shines a spotlight on Brad Drake, my indispensable legislative assistant, whose unwavering commitment and dedication have been instrumental in our shared journey of public service. Brad's story is one of ambition, mentorship, and service—a narrative that intertwines with his grandfather's legacy and embodies the ideals of servant leadership.

Our collaboration began amidst the fervor of a political campaign, where Brad's readiness to engage with our mission stood out. Despite initial challenges and uncertainties, Brad's dedication remained steadfast, even when financial constraints meant he initially volunteered his services. His tireless efforts and dedication to our cause soon became apparent as we traversed the campaign trail, from Esto to Bethlehem and beyond.

As our partnership evolved, Brad shared the profound influence of his grandfather, T. Troy Peacock, whose principles and career in public service deeply inspired him. Brad's journey was shaped by a pivotal moment when his grandfather's wisdom challenged his perception of public office, emphasizing the importance of servant leadership and a commitment to uplift others.

Through mentorship and a clear vision, Brad transitioned from a spirited campaign worker to a trusted legislative assistant, embodying the principles instilled by his grandfather. His evolution underscored the transformative power of mentorship and the enduring legacy of servant leadership in public service.

Beyond our professional collaboration, Brad's friendship and unwavering support enriched my life and career, serving as a constant source of inspiration and camaraderie. Together, we navigated the complexities of legislative work, driven by a shared commitment to good governance and the betterment of our community.

In retrospect, Brad's journey reflects the essence of servant leadership—a path marked by selflessness, dedication, and a steadfast commitment to serving others. I am proud to have played a small part in Brad's journey as he continues to uphold the ideals of public service, leaving an enduring legacy of integrity and compassion in his wake.

Transition to Chapter 38:

As we conclude our journey through the chapters of my life and career, we prepare to explore the broader implications of these experiences through op-eds and letters to the editor, reflecting on the lessons learned and the wisdom gained.

Part 6

Media Relations

Chapter 38

Introduction to Media Interactions

The following eight chapters describe my critical perspective on Florida's insurance reform and government intervention in the insurance market, particularly in the context of the passage of House Bill 1A (HB1A) in 2007.

HB1A was a comprehensive insurance reform package that aimed to address the state's property insurance crisis following the devastating hurricane seasons of 2004 and 2005. Key provisions of the bill included expanding the state-run Citizens Property Insurance Corporation, increasing the capacity of the Florida Hurricane Catastrophe Fund, and allowing Citizens to compete with private insurers.

A recurring theme throughout these chapters is my firm belief in market-driven solutions over government policies. This is evident in his opposition to HB1A and other legislative actions that sought to expand the government's role in the insurance industry. My stance is rooted in my understanding of the complex interplay between insurance, risk management, and environmental sustainability, as explored in the previous sections of this book.

The chapters are organized as follows:

Chapter 38: "Balancing Act - Op-Ed NWF Daily News 02.11.2007," - I discuss the unintended consequences of government subsidies for homeowners' insurance in high-risk areas, arguing that such policies distort the market and harm the environment. I likens the subsidies to an absurd scenario where electric car owners are taxed to make SUVs more affordable, illustrating how misguided government interventions can lead to perverse market outcomes.

Chapter 39: "Northwest Florida Daily News Guest Column" – Can Florida afford "affordable" insurance? I discusses the recent passage of House Bill 1A and bemoans the lack of engagement of the environmental community. Three citizen opinions are included.

Chapter 40: "The Walton Sun Editorial Opinion" and the "Northwest Florida Daily News Guest Column" echo my concerns about the reliance on state-run entities like Citizens Property Insurance Corporation and the expansion of the Hurricane Catastrophe Fund. These pieces also highlight my unique position as one of the few lawmakers opposing the prevailing insurance reform approach.

Chapter 41: "Principle Over Politics - The Story of Two Lawmakers Stand Against Insurance Reform" delves deeper into my legislative journey, detailing my opposition to the insurance reform bill and the subsequent political fallout. My hope it that this narrative reinforces my image as a principled leader willing to face political consequences for his beliefs.

Chapter 43: "Brown—Crist is a 'Classic Demagogue'" critiques Governor Crist's shifting political stances and the state's handling of the insurance crisis. My humorous and straightforward commentary sheds light on the political maneuvering and mischaracterization of the insurance industry's challenges in Florida.

Chapter 44: "Former Rep. Brown Speaks to State Farm Agents, Criticizes Gov. Crist" and "No Insurance Against Sore Winners" both reflect my critique of the insurance reform passed under Crist's administration, emphasizing its detrimental impacts on the industry and the state's economy. These chapters underscore my consistent stance against government overreach in the private market.

Chapter 45: "Don Brown - Unplugged Adapted," - Insights from my legislative service highlight my commitment to principles and fiscal conservatism. My tenure is marked by advocacy for market-based solutions and skepticism toward policies that I believed would burden taxpayers and hinder economic growth.

These chapters provide a comprehensive view of my interactions with the media and my unwavering critique of insurance policies in Florida. They underscore my advocacy for market-based solutions and my skepticism toward government intervention.

CHAPTER 39

Balancing Act: Navigating Insurance, Environment, and The Economy in Florida's High-Risk Waters

In the narrative that unfolds in this chapter, I delve into a topic very close to my heart and professional career, drawing upon a guest column I had the privilege to share with readers of the Northwest Florida Daily News on February 11, 2007.

Before we explore further, it's important to note that what follows is adapted from that piece and reflects a critical period in my journey as a public servant. At the time, I served as State Representative for Florida's 5th District. This role placed me at the heart of a contentious debate over insurance reform—a debate that culminated in a legislative package in January 2007, against which I was one of only two lawmakers to vote "No."

My opposition to these reforms was profound enough that I resigned from my position as chairman of the Jobs and Entrepreneurship Council, through which most of the House of Representatives insurance bills had passed, just a day before Governor Charlie Crist signed the reforms into law.

Now, let me explain the essence of my argument, which seems more relevant with each passing year.

Every attempt by elected officials to address Florida's insurance woes has been met with frustration and failure. Yet, amidst this turmoil, a critical voice has been conspicuously absent—the environmentalists.

These stewards of our coastlines, traditionally vocal against unchecked coastal development, have remained silent on how our state government's actions, particularly the subsidies for homeowners' insurance in high-risk areas, have distorted the market and inadvertently fueled the environmental risks they passionately fight against.

Consider this through a somewhat whimsical, albeit illuminating, analogy.

Consider a scenario where, to address concerns about high gasoline prices, the government subsidizes fuel for owners of large, fuel-inefficient vehicles like Hummers, while imposing taxes on those who opt for eco-friendly, battery-powered, or hybrid vehicles. The market distortion would be immediate and glaring: sales of gas-guzzling SUVs would surge, while more environmentally friendly vehicles would take a hit.

This hypothetical scenario contradicts market principles by penalizing those who make responsible choices while rewarding those who engage in wasteful practices. It also illustrates the unintended consequences of the resulting market distortions. Interestingly, a similar dynamic can be observed in Florida's insurance landscape.

Thankfully, such an absurd subsidy never came to pass with gasoline prices. Instead, the market operated as it should: as prices climbed, so did the appeal of fuel-efficient vehicles. This natural economic response underscores a simple yet often overlooked truth—that market prices when allowed to reflect real risks and costs, can guide consumer behavior in environmentally and economically healthy directions.

Yet, our state and federal governments have veered off this sensible path when insuring our homes against the ravages of nature, particularly in areas most vulnerable to hurricanes. Programs like the heavily subsidized national flood insurance and the state's Citizens Property Insurance Corporation have encouraged development in high-risk coastal areas by providing artificially low insurance rates. This approach not only exacerbates environmental risks but also undermines the financial sustainability of the insurance market.

Subsidies may seem like a benign helping hand, especially when disaster strikes. However, when these subsidies extend to vacation homes and investment properties, enabling development in areas that may be left to nature, we're forced to question the actual cost of 'affordable' insurance.

Congress's refusal to adjust flood insurance rates to reflect real risks and the Florida legislature's reluctance to remove subsidies for vacation homes highlight a disconnect between our environmental goals and economic policies.

As someone who has stood in the eye of this storm politically and philosophically, I've come to believe that we must redefine what we consider "affordable." True affordability isn't about short-term savings but long-term sustainability—for our wallets, homes, and planet. The path forward requires a delicate balance, ensuring that insurance remains accessible without encouraging irresponsible development that our environment, and ultimately, we, cannot afford.

Reflecting on my stance against the 2007 insurance reforms, my resignation from the council, and the broader implications of these policies, it's clear that the debate over insurance in Florida is about much more than premiums and policies.

It reflects our values, vision for the future, and commitment to our environment and economy.

Chapter 40

Northwest Florida Daily News
02.11.2007
Guest Column
By Don Brown
Can Florida afford "affordable" insurance?

(A lawmaker who opposed the legislature's 2007 insurance reform package argues that state government, by continuing to subsidize homeowners' insurance in high-risk areas, distorts the market and endangers the environment.)

"Every elected official who has tried to fix Florida's insurance problems has met with more frustration than success. One of my biggest frustrations is the silence of Florida's environmentalists.

The environmentalist community can always be counted on to support limits on coastal growth and oppose unwise or uncontrolled development. Today, we're learning that government actions that distort market forces - in particular, actions that subsidize insurance costs - create powerful incentives for unwise or uncontrolled growth.

It's time to consider whether accurate market pricing of insurance, where consumers pay the unsubsidized cost of living along our vulnerable coast, maybe the best way to protect the coast.

Let's try a thought experiment.

Let's say owners of Hummers and other big SUVs complain to the government that the high price of gasoline is making their vehicles unaffordable, and the businesses that depend on SUV sales complain that unaffordable SUVs will have devastating ripple effects through the economy. So, the government decided to provide affordable gasoline to SUV owners and tax owners of battery-powered and other hybrid vehicles to support the SUV subsidy.

Is there any doubt what would happen if electric cars were taxed to make Hummers and large SUVs more affordable? Inevitably, Hummers' and large SUV sales would go up, and battery-operated cars and Prius sales would go down.

Thankfully, the government did nothing that stupid back when gasoline topped $3 a gallon. Endearing the price surge (as any free-market conservative would have predicted), Hummer sales went down, and Prius sales went up.

Our state and federal governments have responded differently regarding affordable homeowners' insurance demands.

The federal government created the heavily subsidized national flood insurance program, and the state created the heavily subsidized Citizens Property Insurance Corporation (Citizens), which relies on broad base post-loss assessments of Citizens policyholders in addition to assessments on all other non-Citizens policyholders in the state to cover the deficits it accrues after future hurricanes.

As costly as insurance from Citizens is, Citizens premiums are far more affordable than they would be without the subsidy. To make matters worse, the subsidy goes to owners of vacation homes and investment properties.

Congress recently defeated proposals to force owners of vacation homes to pay the total actuarial cost of their flood insurance, and the Florida legislature has refused to adopt proposals to require citizens to charge an unsubsidized rate for vacation homes.

Everyone wants insurance to be affordable, but everyone has a different definition of affordability. Subsidies may make sense when they kick in only after a severe hurricane, and subsidies may make sense temporarily if that's what it takes to keep people from losing their homes.

But we need to determine what kind of affordability Florida can't afford.

For the people who care the most about our fragile environment, the immediate question is whether Florida can afford a coastal development policy that includes subsidized insurance for vacation homes.

(Below are three citizen opinions that appeared in the same publication in recent weeks)

"Congratulations to Don Brown for being one of only two lawmakers who understood the insurance problem in Florida. It's a shame that politics has taken precedence over sound economic practice. Let your representatives know that you do not want to subsidize coastal high-risk properties that the state is insuring."

"Rep. Brown nailed it in your Sunday story. Why should average Florida residents have to subsidize insurance premiums on rental properties and vacation homes of non-resident beach property owners?"

Brown's morality: "State Rep. Don Brown is right. The error he's fighting is the same government idiocy I've pointed out for a long time. It has every homeowner in Florida paying the costs of the insurance pool for the extremely expensive high-rises and homes built on the beaches where no one but an idiot would put a permanent structure."

"Of course, none of those high-rises and homes would be built without federal flood insurance, too, for which we all pay in taxes."

"Both the national and state governments are compounding this folly so parties can claim that the economy is booming with them in charge."

"We need a grass-roots Republican campaign to put Don Brown and his like in please of House Speaker Marco Rubio, the Bush/Crist governors, then similar Clinton/Bush presidents with Greenspan types in the Federal Reserve system. Maybe the United States could survive another 220 years with Don Brown's kind of morality back in fashion." F.H. - FWB

Chapter 41

The Walton Sun Editorial Opinion 02.2007
Don Brown voted correctly on the Florida Insurance Bill

Florida legislators could have addressed our insurance crisis in many ways, but putting a government-funded insurance company on equal footing with private companies makes no sense.

They could have removed all regulations and let the marketplace straighten itself out based on supply and demand.

They could have dissolved or phased out Citizens Insurance, the publicly funded company designed to be the insurer of last resort but currently the largest insurer in the state.

It could have allowed property owners to insure their property for its mortgage value plus the original down payment rather than replacement cost.

There is no doubt that Floridians need some relief from their doubling and tripling insurance rates, but increasing the government's participation in what should be a private enterprise is not a resolution.

Rep Don Brown, R-DeFuniak Springs, and Rep Dennis Ross, R-Lakeland, both of whom have strong ties to the insurance industry, were the only nay votes in the passage of bill 116-2, expressing concern about the way the plan relied on the state instead of the private market to address the rate increases. We agree with Rep.

Ronald Reagan, a Bradenton Republican who helped craft the bill and was quoted by the Miami Herald as saying, "What we're doing is we're gambling. We're doing that with all the people of Florida."

But we're not sure that the rest of his statement is accurate: "That's what insurance is- gambling.

Legislators are gambling on our future by promising to pay losses we know are coming, not if they are coming. We don't know what the answer is, but there should be plenty of insurance executives who could offer alternatives.

Government cannot be the end-all for all social and economic ills. It should be the business of governing its citizens, not insuring them.

Ultimately, the editorial argues that the state should regulate the insurance industry to ensure fair practices and consumer protection, not to provide coverage or subsidize rates directly. By stepping back from the market and allowing private insurers to price risk accurately, Florida could encourage more responsible development patterns, reduce its exposure to catastrophic losses, and foster a more stable and competitive insurance market in the long run.

While the editorial does not delve into the specific details of HB1A or explore the potential impacts of the suggested alternatives, it presents a clear perspective on the principles at stake in the debate over insurance reform. By siding with Don Brown's opposition to the bill, the editorial underscores the importance of considering the long-term consequences of government intervention in the insurance market and the need for solutions that prioritize fiscal responsibility and market stability.

CHAPTER 42

Principle Over Politics: The Story of Two Lawmakers Stand Against Insurance Reform

(This narrative is an adaption of a local newspaper article published in February 2007, after the passage of House Bill 1A)

In 2007, State Representative Don Brown, known for his principles and expertise in insurance, made a significant decision that led to his fall from grace within the Florida legislature.

He was positioned to spend his last two years in office among the legislature's elite as a House Speaker Marco Rubio's inner circle member.

During a special session in January, he voted against a bill aimed at reforming the state's insurance industry, a move that was in stark contrast to the overwhelming support the bill received.

The bill passed 116-2 in the House and unanimously in the 40-member Senate.

Brown's opposition stemmed from his belief that the bill was more of a gamble than a solution, particularly criticizing its reliance on expanding the state's Hurricane Catastrophe Fund and the Citizens Property Insurance Corporation.

"The bill that passed was more a scheme than a solution." "What the Legislature did was roll the dice and gamble against nature. If they are wrong, we will have a debt to pay."

This stance resulted in his resignation from key leadership positions, including the Jobs and Entrepreneurship Council chairmanship, and his removal from the House Rules and Calendar Council.

Despite the political consequences, Brown's decision to stand against the bill was rooted in his commitment to sound policy over politics. He was concerned about the potential long-term financial implications for Floridians, especially given the state's vulnerability to hurricanes and the increasing trend of building in high-risk areas.

Rubio had little to say about the demotions of Brown and State Rep. Dennis Ross of Lakeland, another council chair who voted against the insurance package. In a January 24 news release, he said that both men had offered their resignations and were accepted.

Brown agreed to some extent with Rubio's terse explanation. He said House leaders are expected to tow the party line on speaker-supported legislation.

But he also said the Speaker's willingness to allow politics to derail sound policy led him to resign his council chair.

Brown said he lobbied House leaders during the special session not to expand the state's Hurricane Catastrophe Fund from $16 billion to $32 billion. He also argued against increasing the size and potential market impact of the state-run Citizens Property Insurance Company.

"I was told we'd have to give on some policy, but at no point would we expand the Cat Fund on the upper end or expand Citizens."

"As the conference unfolded, we gave up on the principled positions. Then, late on Saturday night, we conceded on the two issues the Speaker told me we would never concede on."

"I was so upset by that, I went back to my office and drafted a letter of resignation," Brown said.

Brown said Rubio initially declined to accept his resignation but did accept it a few days later.

Following the vote and the resignation, there was much speculation that Brown, an insurance agent, had stood up in defense of the industry. However, several of his colleagues said Brown voted his conscience.

Senator Atwater, when asked, said: "Rep. Brown is a man of extremely high principles."

Senator Don Gaetz said too few legislators share Brown's conviction.

"I think he knew he would be virtually alone. His was an unpopular vote." Gaetz said. "But Don Brown is a man who stands up for his beliefs. In any legislative assembly, you need people like Don Brown."

The Governor and other state leaders say the new insurance legislation could cut homeowners' rates by up to 20%.

Brown agrees that could be true - as long as Florida has a few more hurricane seasons as quiet as 2006.

"If there are no hurricanes, they'll be the heroes," he said of his fellow lawmakers. "But the scientists are telling us we are in a multi-decadal cycle of increased hurricane frequency and severity that could last another 15 to 20 years. This bill was a foolish gamble on our constituent's premium dollars. I hope I'm wrong. To gamble with my money is one thing, but to gamble with someone else's money is another matter altogether."

In the months leading up to the special session, Brown worked on a committee appointed to formulate guidelines for developing insurance reform policies.[50] As early as last August, he was going against the grain by urging fellow lawmakers to look at the insurance crisis in Florida as a hurricane problem.

"Almost nothing in this bill addresses the real problem," he said.

"The only real problems are hurricanes and the insatiable appetite of people to build homes in high-risk areas, but we've got our heads in a hole when it comes to the real problem," he said.

In a paper he wrote well before the special session titled "Hurricane Crisis Reform Concepts,"[51] Brown outlined his opposition to raising the Cat Fund cap.

"A Cat Fund shifts the financial risk of catastrophic losses from private sector insurers to insurance buyers and taxpayers," he said.

"We piled the risk on Floridians," he said.

---

[50] The actual document titled "Hurricane Crisis Reform Guiding Principles" can be found as Exhibit A at the end of this book. These principles were initially agreed to but were abandoned before the passage of HB1A.

[51] "Hurricane Crisis Reform Concepts" can be found as Exhibit B at the end of this book. This is the document Brown tried to use in 2007 to frame the debate. He was ignored.

"One major hurricane or two moderate storms could exhaust Cat Fund revenues," said Brown.

"Expanding Citizens' Property Insurance and allowing it to compete with private firms borders on socialism," Brown said.

"(Crist) put the government in competition with the private sector," Brown said. "The government can outcompete the private sector, but it won't succeed because when the bill comes due, guess who has to pay for it?"

"If Citizens Insurance runs a deficit, as it did in 2004-05, all taxpayers, not just Citizens' policyholders, will pay off the deficit through insurance assessments," Brown said.

"That means added assessment statewide to automobile, general liability, boat, motorcycle, and business property policies," Brown said.

His efforts to highlight the real issues facing Florida's insurance crisis, backed by research and data, underscored his dedication to addressing the underlying problems rather than adopting short-term fixes.

This narrative underscore the challenges of navigating the complex interplay between politics and policy, especially concerning insurance reform. Brown's experience highlights the importance of principled leadership and the potential cost of adhering to one's convictions in the political arena.

While reasonable people may disagree on the specifics of insurance reform, Brown's experience raises important questions about the role of government in managing catastrophic risk, the balance between affordability and fiscal responsibility, and the long-term implications of subsidizing development in hazard-prone areas. As Florida continues to grapple with the challenges of insuring against hurricanes in a changing climate, policymakers must confront these issues head-on, guided by a commitment to evidence-based solutions and a vision for a more resilient future.

Footnote:

So, Let's discuss briefly what HB1A did:

Citizens Property Insurance Corp. Citizens was initially intended to be Florida's last resort property insurer. It was formed in 2002 by merging two state-created insurers, the FWUA and the FRPCRUA.

Citizens had been subject to strict requirements that limited eligibility to property owners who could not get coverage from admitted carriers at any price.

Citizens was also subject to ratemaking standards that required it to charge noncompetitive rates pegged to the highest rates in the market.

The thrust of HB 1A was to move toward lower rates for Citizens and to establish it as a competitor with the private sector rather than an insurer of last resort.

The most significant change for Citizens was the expansion of its assessment base. After HB1A, all property and casualty premiums except for workers' compensation and medical malpractice were subject to Citizens' deficit assessments; prior law applied assessments only to personal lines and commercial property premiums.

Florida Hurricane Catastrophe Fund ("Cat Fund") The Cat Fund was established in 1993 to provide a layer of reinsurance coverage for all Florida residential property insurers.

As constituted before the new law, the fund provided up to $16 billion in coverage for residential losses above an aggregate industry retention of $6 billion.

All residential property insurers are required to participate in the fund.

Cat Fund premiums are generally considered roughly 20 percent to 30 percent of the price that the insurer would otherwise pay for comparable private reinsurance.

The fund is exempt from federal taxation and has the power to issue tax-free bonds.

In a deficit, the fund issues bonds and levies assessments on all Florida property and casualty premiums except for workers' compensation premiums to provide a revenue stream to pay off the bonds.

HB 1A added several new layers of Cat Fund coverage, as follows:

1. New Optional coverage below the standard Cat Fund retention was authorized.

2. Optional coverage above the standard Cat Fund cap up to $28 Billion.

Cautionary Note: A catastrophe fund violates one of the fundamental tenets of insurance – spreading the risk. It also supplants private-sector reinsurance, which is fully paid for in advance. Private reinsurance spreads the risk globally, and the cost of that reinsurance is paid upfront. A state catastrophe fund concentrates that risk in one jurisdiction and shifts the financial risk of catastrophic losses from private sector insurers to insurance buyers and taxpayers.

On the other hand, private reinsurance promotes the spreading of risk and loss. Results from the 2005 hurricanes indicate that the losses were borne as follows: 41% in the private insurer market, 24% among Bermuda reinsurers, 11% for U.S. reinsurers, 13% among European reinsurers, 9% in Lloyds, and 1% for other. Risk spreading fosters a viable competitive market; risk concentration among a few insurers and state funds inhibits a competitive market.

In conclusion, high homeowner premiums are not the problem. Hurricanes and Florida's extraordinary vulnerability to the same and human behavior are the problems.

CHAPTER 43

DeFuniak Herald Breeze Editor's Comment 02.2007 No Insurance Against Sore Winners

The following is an adaptation of the DeFuniak Springs Herald Breeze Editor's comment in February 2007.

Imagine settling down for a cozy evening in DeFuniak Springs. In this place, folks' value straight talk and practical solutions, only to find the latest editorial from the "DeFuniak Herald Breeze" sparking a fire under the community pot.

The piece starts by spotlighting the first significant piece of legislation inked by Gov. Charlie Crist, hailed as insurance reform. This law promises to shield

Citizens customers from a daunting 56-percent rate hike by offering a modest 5-15 percent reduction, which sounds like a life preserver in a sea of high premiums.

But for the rest of us? It's more like being offered a Band-Aid after a shark bite.

You have options, like dropping your windstorm coverage, hiking your deductibles, or just saying goodbye to insuring your home's contents altogether.

The editorial astutely points out that when lawmakers admit, "Well, it's not perfect," it often signals a return to the usual political maneuvering. It brings to mind that old chestnut about the prescription drug plan - big promises, convoluted outcomes.

Then there's the tale of two holdouts, Reps. Dennis Ross and Don Brown dared to question the bandwagon, only to find themselves sidelined by House Speaker Marco Rubio from key leadership positions.

The editorial paints Ross as vocally defiant, regretting nothing despite the consequences, while Brown, the quintessential Southern gentleman, opts for dignified silence, his actions speaking volumes.

This story unfolds with all the drama of a Shakespearean tragedy, complete with political intrigue and whispers of dissent.

The punchline? If this is the nature of the reform being implemented, it raises questions about the effectiveness and intentions of the reformers themselves. It's a narrative that leaves readers chuckling ruefully, pondering the age-old wisdom that sometimes, the more things change, the more they stay the same.

Chapter 44

Brown: Crist is a 'Classic Demagogue'

The following is an adaptation of a news article in the Crestview News Bulletin 2008.

Let's unravel a narrative that intricately weaves together candid opinions, humorous analogies, and some good old-fashioned straight talk, all through the eyes of someone who's seen the ins and outs of insurance and politics up close.

Imagine stepping up to the Crestview Area Chamber of Commerce podium, ready to spill the tea on Florida's political and insurance landscape. You're not just anyone; you're someone with decades in the insurance game and a keen eye for political folly.

"Ever hear the one about the governor who flipped faster than a pancake at a Sunday breakfast?" you begin, drawing a few chuckles. Yep, that's our guy. He went from a staunch 'no drilling' stance to suddenly embracing oil exploration in the Gulf. Classic demagogues move, right? Webster's might as well have his picture next to the definition."

The crowd leans in as you shift gears, "But let's talk about the real elephant in the room – Florida's insurance circus.

After 30 years on that wild ride, I've seen it all. And here's the kicker: there's no 'insurance crisis.' Blaming the thermometer for the heat wave is like blaming the thermometer for the heat wave. Florida's sitting on 49% of the nation's wind risk, and what do we do? We play hot potato with insurance costs, spreading them around like a bad game of risk.

You pause, letting the absurdity sink in.

"And then there's the 2007 insurance reform. Oh, boy. If that was a solution, I'm a three-legged race champion. All it did was shuffle the deck chairs on the Titanic, passing the buck without fixing the leak."

As you wrap up, you lean in, "Here's the thing about government – it's like that friend who always orders the most expensive dish but forgets their wallet. Promising the moon when you're playing with someone else's money is easy. But it's time we called it out. Because if we keep letting big government pick the menu, we'll all end up washing dishes in the back."

With a nod to your roots and a tip of the hat to your audience, you conclude, "But here's to us, Crestview. We've got a knack for seeing through the nonsense. And if anyone's going to turn this ship around, it's folks who understand the value of a hard day's work and the importance of keeping our word."

There you have it: a blend of personal reflections, a dash of humor, and a call to action, all from someone in the trenches. It's not just about insurance or politics; it's about standing up for common sense and community values.

Chapter 45

Former Rep. Brown Speaks to State Farm Agents, Criticizes Gov. Crist

Former state Rep. Don Brown spoke to a group of Big Bend State Farm agents Thursday on how storms and politics have pummeled the insurance industry in Florida.

Most of the blame he put on Gov. Charlie Crist.

"The most damaging wind in Florida happened in 2006 – the wind of Charlie Crist," said Brown, a DeFuniak Springs Republican, insurance agent, and outspoken critic of insurance reform passed in Crist's first month in office in 2007. Brown was one of two votes against the legislation that more than doubled the risk assumed by consumers to back up companies against catastrophic storm losses.

Crist championed lower insurance rates when he took office. Earlier this year, State Farm was denied a rate increase, and the company decided to pull its property insurance policies out of the Florida market.

State Farm agent Eric Taylor was one of about a dozen agents who listened to Brown. He said it will be tough if the insurance company pulls its property policies.

"It could mean as much as 60 percent of my income," said Taylor, who works in Gadsden County. "There's no other company in Florida I would feel comfortable writing for."

Brown said legislation proposed this session to reduce the state's risk in the Hurricane Catastrophe Fund, which provides cheap backup coverage to insurance companies, which is good but not enough.

"It's a step in the right direction," Brown said, " but it doesn't come close to eliminating the danger."

The Cat Fund provides up to $28 billion in storm damage but only has $10 billion in assets. Because of the credit crisis, Brown said the state would not be able to make up the shortfall by selling bonds if a disaster were to happen and the Cat Fund was tapped out.

Brown said insurance companies usually take profits from years without storms to offset deficits when large storms occur. If insurance companies aren't allowed to make a profit, he said, it will be difficult to invite other insurers to the market.

Brown said that when a company like State Farm is not allowed to raise rates and leaves the market, it hurts Florida.

"The actions we're taking now is driving capital out of Florida," he said.

Real-estate broker Mark Trafton said Brown's presentation was revealing.

"I had no idea there's that much exposure," he said of the state's Cat Fund

Chapter 46

Don Brown: Unplugged
Adapted based on an Article Published in the
DeFuniak Springs Herald Breeze
June 19, 2008

Once asked about the essence of his legislative service, Don Brown, the unwavering District 5 Representative, shared insights reflecting a career built on conviction and principle. "It's not about the number of bills passed," he remarked, "but about the integrity and the fight for the values we hold dear."

In an era where politics often leaned towards expanding government and increased regulation, Brown firmly believed in the free market's power to solve complex issues.

He often said, "The best solutions come not from the government but from our people's ingenuity and hard work."

During his tenure, Brown was a vocal critic of policies he believed would burden the taxpayers or hinder economic growth. His opposition to HB1A in 2007, a bill aimed at expanding the government's role in the private insurance market, was a testament to his commitment to fiscal conservatism.

Brown warned, "Such expansion compromises the very principles of free enterprise that have driven our nation's success."

Brown's legislative achievements, particularly in insurance reform, underscored his expertise and dedication. He was instrumental in reforming state Workers' Compensation laws, efforts that were recognized by both the Florida Association of Insurance Agents and the Florida Association of Insurance and Financial Advisors.

Yet, his journey was not without challenges, especially in hurricane insurance reform, where his expectations for a more market-driven approach were not fully realized.

Reflecting on his journey, Brown advised future legislators: "Stay true to your principles, listen to your constituents, and remember, the allure of party politics should never overshadow the needs of the people you serve."

In conclusion, Don Brown's career is a narrative of principle over politics, a reminder of the enduring value of unwavering dedication to one's beliefs in the ever-evolving landscape of public service.

This narrative captures the essence of Don Brown's service and principles, integrating direct quotes and a summary of his legislative focus and achievements.

Section 7 - Appendix

Biographical Information
for
Donald D. Brown

P. O. Box 866

DeFuniak Springs, FL 32435

(850) 865-9280 Home

(850) 520-4677 Work

(850) 865-9280 Cell

info@donanddiane.com

don@donbrownflorida.com

www.donbrownflorida.com

Biographical Information:

Born: December 28, 1951,

Spouse: Glenda Diane Brown of DeFuniak Springs

City of Residence: DeFuniak Springs, FL

Children: Lori Callista, James C (deceased)

Occupation: Consultant/Retired Insurance Agent Religious

Affiliation: Protestant and Pastor Recreational Interest: fishing, woodworking, RC Airplanes and work

Photos:

Narrative:

Don Brown is a retired insurance agent from DeFuniak Springs, Florida. He has served on the Walton County Commission as a Republican State Committeeman, as Chairman of the Walton County Republican Executive Committee, and as a State Representative in the Florida House of Representatives.

Don is a veteran of numerous campaigns and served as a County Co-Chairman for Governor Jeb Bush and President George Bush.

Don Brown is best known for his work on insurance issues. In the back-to-back years of 2002 and 2003, he was recognized by both the Florida Association of Insurance Agents and the Florida Association of Insurance and Financial Advisors for his significant contribution to insurance reform. Most notably, in 2007, Don was one of only two legislators to vote "No" on HB1A, which significantly expanded the role of government into private markets. Since 2007, many of his objections to HB1A have proven correct.

Don Brown was known for being well-prepared and standing his ground during his tenure in the Florida House of Representatives. He was most vocal when advocating for smaller government, fewer taxes, the Free Enterprise System, and Market Solutions. He was widely regarded as one of the top orators in the House.

While serving in the Florida House of Representatives, Don was also known for his tireless work on such vital issues as Medical Malpractice Reform, Elections Reform, Workers' Compensation Reform, and Tort Reform. In 2004, the Emerald Coast Association of Realtors recognized him for his work on real estate issues. He was also recognized in 2004 by the Florida Pharmacy Association as their Most Outstanding Legislator. In 2005, the Florida Retail Federation named him the "House Legislator of the Year," and in 2006, the Florida Chamber of Commerce named him "Most Valuable Legislator" after the passage of his HB73, which repealed the doctrine of Joint and Several Liability.

Professional Experience:

2013 – Present	Florida Building Commission - Commissioner
2012 – Present	Florida Hurricane Advisory Council

Serve in an advisory capacity on numerous matters related to managing the Florida Hurricane Catastrophe Fund.

2012 – 2018	R Street Institute – Senior Fellow
2008 – Present	Market Based Solutions, LLC – Owner
2008 – Present	Donald Brown Consulting – Owner

Currently Representing in Florida:

Association of Bermuda Insurers and Reinsurers

Florida Insurance Council

2010 – 2012	Heartland Institute – Senior Fellow
10/1984 – Present	First National Insurance Agency, Inc. – DeFuniak Springs, FL

President and Owner

11/2000 – 11/2008	Florida House of Representatives – Tallahassee, FL

Representative

Served as Chair or Vice-Chair of many committees including:

Insurance Committee

State Administration Council

	Jobs and Entrepreneurship Council
	Select Committee on Workers' Compensation
	Select Committee on Florida's Economic Future
	Sub-Committee on Property & Casualty Insurance
1989 – 1992	Private Industry Council for Walton and Okaloosa County
	Board of Directors
12/1988 – 01/1991	Walton County Board of County Commissioners
	Commissioner

(Was appointed by Gov. Martinez to fill a vacant seat on the Walton County Board of County Commissioners.)

1989 – 1991	Walton County Airport Authority
	Chairman
1989 – 1990	Walton County Chamber of Commerce
	President
03/1983 – 10/1984	First National Insurance Agency of DeFuniak Springs, Inc.
	President and Manager

(In 1983, the First National Bank was purchased by Sun Bank, and the First National Insurance Agency of DeFuniak Springs, Inc. was moved out of the bank.)

08/1973 – 03/1983   First National Bank of DeFuniak Springs, Inc.

Insurance Agency Manager

(I worked for the First National Bank of DeFuniak Springs with banking responsibility in addition to managing the First National Insurance Agency of DeFuniak Springs, Inc., which was located in the bank.)

Publications:

Co-Authored

OMINOUS PARALLELS: The National Financial Crisis and Hurricane Insurance

Published in the James Madison Institute Journal

November 1, 2009

What happens when government policies trump sound business and economic judgment? The roots of the nation's current financial crisis and signs of the economic situation in Florida's future can be found in the answer to that question…

Education:

1973   University of West Florida   , Pensacola, FL: B.S. – Industrial Technology

1971   Okaloosa Walton Junior College, Niceville, FL: A.S. – Industrial Technology

1969   Freeport High School, Freeport, FL   : High School Diploma

Professional Licenses Previously Held:

Florida Department of Business and Professional Regulation

    Real Estate Broker

    Certified General Appraiser

National Association of Master Appraisers

    Master Farm and Land Appraiser

    Master Residential Appraiser

    Master Senior Appraiser

Florida Department of Financial Services

    Agent Licenses:

Life	0216
Life and Health	0218
Health	0240
General Lines Property & Casualty	0220
Legal Expense	0256

Major Accomplishments:

2008 Florida Association of Counties William "Doc" Myers Lifetime County Advocate Award

2008 Governor's Hurricane Conference Legislative Award

2008 Florida Chamber of Commerce Honor Roll

2007 National Association of Mutual Insurance Companies - Legislator of the Year

2007 Harry G. Landrum Outstanding Legislative Leadership and Distinguished Service Award

2007 Florida Chamber of Commerce Honor Roll

2007 Florida Chamber of Commerce Distinguished Advocate

2006 Passage of Property Insurance Reform (SB1980)

2006 Repeal of Joint and Several Liability (HB73)

2006 Florida Sheriffs Association Legislative Leadership Award

2006 Florida Chamber of Commerce Most Valuable Legislator

2006 Florida Chamber of Commerce Honor Roll

2006 Associated Industries of Florida Champion of Business

2005 Florida Chamber of Commerce Honor Roll

2005 Associated Industries of Florida Champion of Business

2005 Florida Retail Federation House Legislator of the Year

2005 Small County Coalition Chairman's Choice Award

2004 Florida Credit Union League Legislator of the Year

2004 Emerald Coast Association of Realtors Legislator of the Year

2004 Florida Funeral Directors Association Leadership Award

2004 Independent Funeral Directors Leadership Award

2004 Florida Pharmacy Association Most Outstanding Legislator Award

2004 Florida Monument Builders Legislator of the Year

2003 Passage of Workers' Compensation Reform (SB50A)

2003 Professional Insurance Agents Association Excellence in Government Award

2003 Florida Association of Insurance and Financial Advisors Legislator of the Year

2003 Florida Association of Insurance Agents Legislative Leadership Award

2002 Florida Association of Insurance and Financial Advisors Legislator of the Year

2002 Florida Association of Counties County Champion Award

2002 Florida Association of Technical Center Education Legislator of the Year

2002 North West Florida League of Cities Legislator of the Year

2002 Florida Association of Insurance Agents Legislative Leadership Award

2001 International Union of Police Associations Legislator of the Year

2001 Alliance of American Insurers Legislator of the Year

"Hurricane Crisis" Reform
Guiding Principles

Principle #1: It is better to pay for hurricane risk with private sector capital than to finance it with public debt.

Discussion: Paying for potential hurricane losses through premiums on the front end promotes homeowners' choices; taxing for actual hurricane losses through assessments on the back end restricts those freedoms. Accordingly, the use of private-sector resources to pay for hurricane damage to private property should be maximized.

Principle #2: Allowing the free market to operate and competition to work are the best ways to make property insurance more available and affordable.

Discussion: Insurance rates should be adequate to cover the risk. Premiums to protect a structure must be based on sound actuarial science (*the discipline that applies statistical and mathematical methods to assess risks and predict future claims*). Over regulation and artificial suppression of rates stifles competition and leads to unstable price fluctuations ultimately hurting property owners. Florida can no longer tolerate keeping rates artificially low simply because it's the most expedient thing to do.

Principle #3: If greater government intervention is necessary to make hurricane insurance available and affordable, it should be developed and evaluated under these goals:

A. The intervention should be the least intrusive possible to the private insurance market;

B. It should be limited in duration to the need;

C. It should be cautiously implemented and carefully regulated.

Principle #4: People have a right to live where they choose, but they do not have the right to expect that others will subsidize their choices.

Principle #5: The state responsibility to assure that coverage is available does not include the responsibility to provide subsidized coverage for investment and vacation properties. (Homestead vs. Non-Homestead; $1 Million Dollar Coastal Homes)

Principle #6: Subsidies for residential properties should be limited to primary residences and should not be permanent.

Discussion: This principle and the prior one are based upon the premise that if an obligation is owed to anyone, it is owed to helping Floridians insure the homes that provide shelter and the dwellings where they live with their families, rather than for properties that provide leisure or represent investment opportunities.

Principle #7: When necessary to protect the safety and security of its citizens, government must act. Government should promote the following objectives:

A. Fortifying one's home against potential hurricane damage is the single most direct measure to lower the cost of homeowners insurance. Government has a valid role in assisting homeowners who take personal responsibility to protect their homes.
B. Government also has a legitimate role in protecting its citizens by enforcing a uniform and appropriate building code.
C. In addition, direct taxpayer subsidies for fixed-income and low-income property owners who are at risk because of rising hurricane costs may be an appropriate short-term remedy.

Principle #8: Because changes to the structure and capacity of the Florida Hurricane Catastrophe Fund affect the private sector and have the very real potential to adversely impact Floridians through greater exposure to taxes (assessments), the Legislature should act cautiously, judiciously and in accordance with the following guideposts:

A. The FHCF should only be expanded when private market alternatives are not available or have failed, or a crisis in the marketplace has occurred.
B. Any expansion of coverage to the FHCF should be fair and available to all participating insurers. [Only providing the expanded coverage to selected groups of insurers will ultimately dilute benefits for all participants.]
C. If the FHCF is expanded to take care of a market crisis and the expanded coverage is available to all participating insurers, the additional coverage should be priced at "near" market pricing levels. [This will allow only those who need the extra capacity to purchase it from the FHCF. Also, private reinsurance will not be crowded out in the long run.]
D. Allow insurers to select just the additional capacity they need from the FHCF and what they need from the private reinsurance market. [If coverage is available in the private reinsurance market incentives should not be provided to motivate insurers to purchase FHCF coverage.]
E. Any expansion to the FHCF should be a temporary solution and should only be for 1 to 3 years. [At the end of this time, the expanded coverage should not be available unless re-enacted by the Legislature for another temporary time period.]

Principle #9: Policy solutions should come with a comprehensive and comprehendible plan for implementation that Floridians can understand and should include: (1) what their responsibilities are, (2) what the responsibilities of their insurance company are, and (3) what their government is going to do.

Discussion: There must be a sense of shared responsibility to solve the hurricane crisis. This means that policyholders, builders, insurance agents, insurance companies, Citizens, lenders, real estate professionals, governments at all levels, tourism officials and others must share in the solution.

Principle # 10: Reducing taxes for homeowners allows them, and not the government, to decide how to spend their money in insuring and protecting their homes. Non-insurance remedies, such as property tax relief, should be considered as alternatives that can reduce the cost of owning a home in Florida.

(The following document is provided for a historical perspective. The data contained in this document is stale but was reasonably current in 2007 when it was used during the debate over HB1A)

Hurricane Crisis Reform
Concepts

We have three related but different problems. They must all be addressed, but the solution for one may not necessarily be the correct solution for the other two. The three issues are:

1. The "<u>Political Crisis</u>" – must be addressed soon.
2. The "<u>Insurance Crisis</u>" – there is very little that can be done that will result in immediate relief. This is more of an intermediate-term issue.
3. The "<u>Hurricane Crisis</u>" – this is the BIG one. This crisis will require long-term solutions, but we MUST address it now.

Because several problems must be addressed and because they require very different solutions, I believe our proposal should be structured as follows:

Short Term Solutions

Consumer Protections

- Provide an opportunity for policyholders to decrease the amount of their hurricane deductible <u>as long as the policyholder implements hurricane mitigation measures</u>. This has been referred to as a "deductible buy-down" provision.
- Increase transparency and consumer awareness by requiring a "**Truth in Premium Billing**" statement provided by the insurer. This would clearly delineate the various components and prices of changes in premiums, including rate increases, coverage provisions, and recoupments.
- Require insurers to offer installment payment plans on homeowner policies based upon semi-annual and quarterly scheduling.

- For homeowners who have been an insurer's customer for at least three years and have not filed a claim, the insurance company to provide at least six months cancellation or non-renewal notice.

Mitigation

Also covered more fully in the "Long Term Solutions" section, mitigation would have short-term benefits as well, not the least of which is the message it sends to homeowners and the capital markets of its value in reducing future hurricane losses and increasing public safety.

The CAT Fund

- Offer coverage below the current CAT Fund retention level ($5.3 billion, subject to annual growth) voluntarily for all insurers. The offer of coverage for the lower coverage layer should be temporary/short-term, and the rate charged by the CAT Fund for this lower coverage layer should be near market rates. This change alone will A) reduce upward pressure on homeowner insurance rates and B) create additional capacity in the marketplace.
- Amend the State Constitution to limit the use of the assets of the CAT Fund (i.e., restrict legislative appropriations) to the purposes currently required by statute. Also require that any appropriation from the CAT Fund over $10 million be in a separate bill for that purpose only and be approved by a super-majority (e.g., three-fourths) of the membership of each house of the Legislature.

Cautionary Note: A catastrophe fund violates one of the fundamental tenets of insurance – spreading the risk. It also supplants private-sector reinsurance, which is fully paid for in advance. Private reinsurance spreads the risk globally, and the cost of that reinsurance is paid upfront. A state catastrophe fund concentrates that risk in one jurisdiction and shifts the financial risk of catastrophic losses from private sector insurers to insurance buyers and taxpayers.

Private reinsurance, on the other hand, promotes the spreading of risk and loss. Results from the 2005 hurricanes indicate that the losses were borne as follows: 41% in the private insurer market, 24% among Bermuda reinsurers, 11% for U.S. reinsurers, 13% among European reinsurers, 9% in Lloyds, and 1% for other. Risk spreading fosters a viable competitive market; risk concentration among a few insurers and state funds inhibits a competitive market.

Citizens Property Insurance Corporation

Require Citizens to create a separate, self-supporting account for non-homestead properties. This action would immediately reduce the potential for assessments. If the Citizens rate structure includes cross-subsidies (where the rates for less risky properties are somewhat higher than they need to be in order to make rates for the riskiest properties more affordable), the fourth account would also address that inequity. The fourth account would also substantially reduce the "Probable Maximum Loss" (PML) in at least the wind-only account, making it more likely that Citizens could afford reinsurance.

Note: Other changes for Citizens are proposed under "Intermediate Solutions". Of the Citizens proposed changes, the fourth account is the one that would have the most immediate impact. It could probably be implemented in early 2007, with a requirement that Citizens file new rates for all four accounts.

Intermediate Term Solutions:

(Solving the "Insurance Crisis") Intermediate solutions should focus on the Florida marketplace and "Citizens" Property Insurance Corporation. But before helpful changes are made, it is important that we understand a few basics:

Government-run insurers Lead to Poor Development Decisions

- Government-run insurers (markets of last resort) serve as a vital safety valve after significant market disruptions and as an enabler of unwise development…
- Government-run property insurers dilute market-based signals about relative risk.
- The consequence is runaway development in disaster-prone areas.
- Government-run insurers:
    - Generally, fail to charge actuarially sound rates.
    - Have weak underwriting standards.
    - They are thinly capitalized.
    - Can assess losses to policyholders other than their own.
    - Vulnerable to political pressure.
- Inadequate premiums, insufficient capital, and weak underwriting mean that most government plans, from Citizens Property Insurance Corporation to the National Flood Insurance Program, operate with frequent and large deficits.

Negative Outcomes from Flaws in Government-Run Insurers

- True risk associated with building on or owning a particular property is obscured.
- Subsidies are generated, leading to market distortions/inequities:
    - Many thousands of homes likely would not have been built (or built differently) if property owners were obligated to pay actuarially sound rates.

> CPIC assessments from Wilma will require grandmothers living in trailer parks on fixed incomes in Gainesville to subsidize million-dollar homes in Marco Island via assessment (surcharges).

> Is the best use of tax dollars to reduce deficit or LT investment in mitigation?

- Serial rebuilding in disaster-prone areas is the norm.
- Property owners come to assume that the government rate is the "fair" rate and object to moves to actuarially sound rates.
- Government-run insurers can't control their exposure.

> The legislature mandates that CPIC offers coverage in most cases if no private insurer will provide coverage due to high risk or near certainty of destruction.

> There are no restrictions on the value of property, so high-valued properties represent a disproportionate share of potential loss.

Therefore, our proposal for intermediate solutions should include, <u>but not necessarily be limited to,</u> the following issues:

The Florida Marketplace

- Allow insurers to include the cost of reinsurance in their rates with the burden of proof on OIR to prove the reinsurance costs added are excessive. Some insurers will not commit resources to Florida because they can not recoup their reinsurance costs.
- Allow insurers to renew homeowners' insurance if the homeowner had a specified hurricane deductible, i.e., 5% or 10%. The provision should be considered "consumer-friendly".

- Allow insurers to renew all homeowner policies with a 10% hurricane deductible, including the 10% hurricane deductible premium credit, provided: A) an insured would retain the option to reduce the deductible to the current 2% minimum hurricane deductible at the increased cost, and B) if the insured elected to keep the 10% hurricane deductible the insurer must provide a 3-year renewal guarantee except in case of material change in risk characteristics. This change alone would result in an immediate increase in insurance capacity, a decrease in upward pressure on homeowner insurance rates, and a direct incentive for homeowners to mitigate their homes for wind damage. When these larger deductibles are incurred, the State could provide a loan guarantee program to incentivize the private sector to provide loans for affected homeowners. The State would only be liable if: A) a hurricane deductible was incurred, B) the homeowner chose the option to borrow, and C) there was a default on the loan, in which case the State would be entitled to a lien on the property.

  ➢ Allow insurers greater flexibility in rate setting. For over 30 years, we have relied upon government control of rate setting, resulting in considerable measure in the current mess we are in. Market-regulated rates (competition) will produce fair and more realistic results in the long term. They will begin to provide the right incentives or disincentives for the future development of our Florida coastline.

  ➢ Pass a resolution requesting Congress to allow insurers to accumulate tax deferred catastrophic reserves to prepare for catastrophes and to reduce the necessity for reinsurance. (Please see the last graph in this document: "Estimated Cumulative New Insurance Capital Required to Support Growth in FL Homeownership, 2005-2015)

Citizens Property Insurance Corporation

- ➤ Provide authority for authorized insurers to write non-homestead Citizens' policies on an individual risk rate basis.

- ➤ Require a minimum 5% hurricane deductible for non-homestead Citizens' policies and a 10% hurricane deductible if the insured value is $250,000. or more

Note: The idea that Citizens is temporary probably includes an element of wishful thinking. It would be better to recognize that most of the million-plus properties in Citizens are, in effect, uninsurable at rates the private sector is allowed to charge. The rate increase that would make these high-risk properties insurable is probably so dramatic that we cannot realistically expect them, even if there are major changes in how rates are regulated. It may be that the focus on Citizens as a temporary entity, emphasizing depopulation, has taken attention away from the question of how to make Citizens work bett

Long Term Solutions:

(Solving the "Hurricane Crisis") This is the most difficult one to solve, but we must begin. First, we must recognize the magnitude of the problem. Florida is more exposed than any other state:

Total Value of Insured Coastal Exposure (2004, $ Billions). Source: Insurance Information Institute, PPP August 11, 2006, Slide 13.

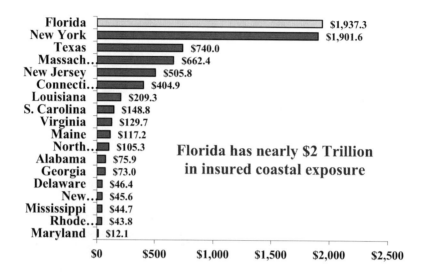

Insured Coastal Exposure as a % of Statewide Insured Exposure (2004, $ Billions).

Source: Insurance Information Institute, PPP August 11, 2006, Slide 14.

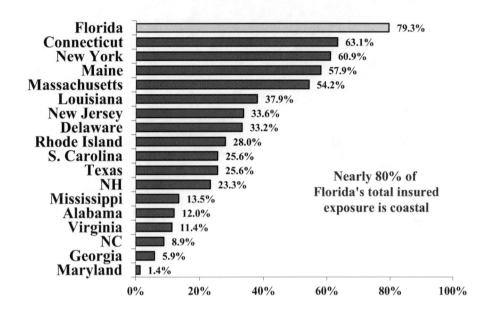

Value of Insured Residential Coastal Exposure (2004, $ Billions).
Source: Insurance Information Institute, PPP August 11, 2006, Slide 15.

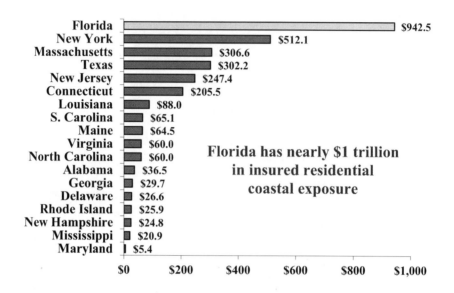

If we continue to develop our coast, we must acknowledge there will be a heavy price to pay. As a matter of fairness, the public policy question becomes: "Who should pay <u>and</u> how much should they pay, <u>and</u> should they pay before the catastrophe by way of insurance premiums or after the catastrophe by way of increased taxes?" The only way to reduce the cost of future disasters is to reduce the risk. In the context of long-term solutions, there are at least four ways to reduce the risk.

Therefore, our proposal for long-term solutions should advance policies that accomplish the following: A) Growth Management, i.e., beginning to develop our coastline in a more limited way, recognizing our vulnerability. Local communities should be forced to consider how their development decision will impact their catastrophe exposure. **B) <u>Improved Building Codes</u>.** If there is any lesson to be learned from the 2004-2005 storm season, it is that more robust building codes work. C) **Mitigation:** We should commit to the free wind inspection and matching grant mitigation program enacted in 2006. The program should be adequately funded so that within ten years or less, Florida's stock of over 2 million homes built to an inferior wind code can be inspected and hardened where practical. The effect of Growth Management, Improved Building Codes, and Mitigation will be huge. D) **Raise Public Awareness of Risk:** In addition to educational efforts on the part of the State, there should be mandatory risk disclosure in all residential real estate transactions. Also, signed waivers, including the right to any disaster aid, should be required if flood coverage is declined on property located in a FEMA-designated special flood hazard zone.

Some final thoughts

There is an appropriate role for the government in managing catastrophic risk. The government should seek to mitigate future losses through proper land use planning; risk-appropriate building codes and code enforcement; enabling coverage options, such as deductible alternatives; and appropriate rate regulations (to be sure insurers charge an adequate rate for the insured risk they assume so that policyholders are not put at risk by companies facing financial impairment or insolvency). Rational economic decisions regarding land use, building codes, disaster preparation, and loss reduction can only be made when there are no public subsidies and cross-subsidies or when such subsidies are transparent and independent of the insurance mechanism.

The facts should not be denied. Homeowner insurance rates had been suppressed before the 2004-2005 storm seasons. If we hope to attract private capital to the Florida market, we must recognize the contribution insurers and reinsurers have made and continue to make to cover Florida's risk.

(Please see the graphs on the remaining pages)

Insured Catastrophe Losses in Florida, 1980-2005. Source: Insurance Information Institute, PPP August 11, 2006, Slide 22.

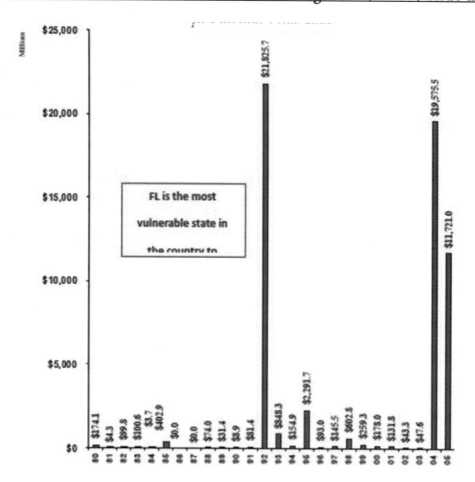

Underwriting Gain (Loss) in Florida Homeowners Insurance 1992-2005E*. Source: Insurance Information Institute, PPP August 11, 2006, Slide 23.

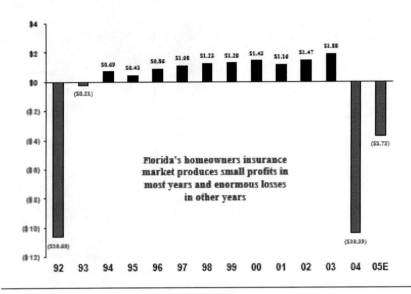

Cumulative Underwriting Gain (Loss) in Florida Homeowners Insurance, 1992-2005E*. Source: Insurance Information Institute, PPP August 11, 2006, Slide 24.

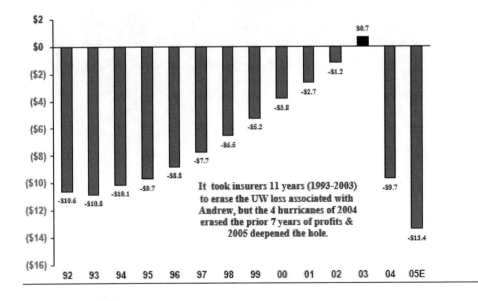

Estimated Cumulative New Insurance Capital Required to Support Growth in FL Homeownership, 2005-2015*

Florida may need to attract more than $9 billion in new capital over the next decade, assuming recent demographic trends continue.

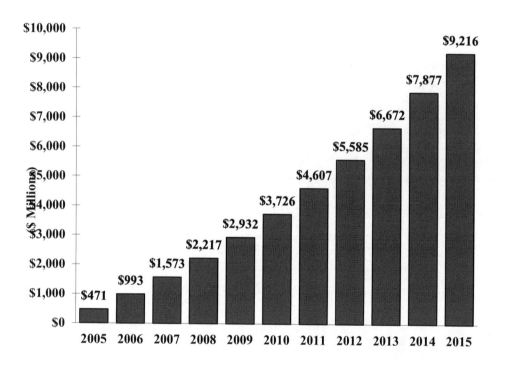

Summary of Academic Research

Journal of Insurance Regulation
Cassandra Cole and Kathleen McCullough, Co-Editors
Vol. 37, No. 3
The Florida Insurance Market: An Analysis of Vulnerabilities to Future Hurricane Losses
Jack E. Nicholson
Karen Clark
Glen Daraskevich
https://content.naic.org/sites/default/files/jir-za-37-03-el-florida-market-hurricane.pdf

A summary of this document, "The Florida Insurance Market: An Analysis of Vulnerabilities to Future Hurricane Losses," provides an in-depth examination of the vulnerabilities in Florida's insurance market in the face of hurricanes. Here is a summary of its main points:

1. Hurricane Exposure: Florida is a "peak zone" for hurricane risk, with an extensive history of severe hurricanes. The market has not faced a hurricane stronger than Andrew since 1992. Recent close calls like Hurricane Irma have highlighted the state's vulnerability.
2. Public Risk Entities: Florida's market relies heavily on three public risk financing entities: Citizens Property Insurance Corporation (Citizens), the Florida Hurricane Catastrophe Fund (FHCF), and the Florida Insurance Guaranty Association (FIGA). These entities, funded by taxpayer assessments, play key roles in market stability.
3. Market Changes Post-Andrew: The residential insurance market underwent substantial changes after Hurricane Andrew, including the establishment of the FHCF and the rise of smaller, more localized domestic insurers.
4. Catastrophe Models: Catastrophe models are now widely used to estimate probable maximum losses (PMLs). However, significant discrepancies in

models and their assumptions can lead to varying results in PMLs and stress tests.

5. Insurer Solvency Risks: A study conducted in this document evaluates 62 domestic insurers in Florida and identifies wide disparities in financial stability. Many insurers have negative normalized solvency ratios, making them susceptible to insolvency in a large hurricane event.

6. Impact on Public Entities: The study indicates that moderate hurricanes could overwhelm FIGA and FHCF, resulting in billions of dollars in debt. This would force Citizens to absorb a substantial number of policies from insolvent insurers.

Overall, the document emphasizes the urgent need to bolster financial resilience and transparency to handle future hurricanes. Without significant reform and improvements in risk management, Florida's insurance market remains vulnerable to massive losses and economic instability.

Regulation and Markets for Catastrophe Insurance
Paul R. Kleindorfer and Robert W. Klein
The Wharton School, University of Pennsylvania, Philadelphia
Georgia State University, Atlanta, Georgia

https://www.researchgate.net/publication/241125149_Regulation_and_Markets_for_Catastrophe_Insurance

The document, *Regulation and Markets for Catastrophe Insurance* by Paul R. Kleindorfer and Robert W. Klein, discusses the challenges of designing efficient markets for catastrophe insurance and managing the regulatory framework for private insurers.

Key Insights:

1. **Demand-Side Issues:**

- Consumers often struggle to evaluate the benefits of catastrophe insurance relative to other risk-mitigation strategies.
- Structural mitigation measures, such as reinforcing buildings, can significantly reduce potential losses from natural hazards.
- Regulatory policies like compulsory insurance or building codes can encourage people to adopt necessary coverage or mitigation measures.

2. **Supply-Side Issues**:

- Insurers face challenges in providing catastrophe insurance due to the correlated structure of natural hazard losses. This makes risk pooling difficult and requires substantial capital to cover potential catastrophic claims.
- Solvency constraints become vital in such markets because they ensure that insurers maintain sufficient capital to withstand major catastrophic events.

3. **Regulation**:

- Insurance regulation needs to balance protecting consumers from insolvency risk and encouraging insurers to maintain their capital structures and solvency.
- Rate caps, underwriting constraints, and entry/exit barriers can distort markets, making it difficult for insurers to operate profitably while serving high-risk areas.

Recommendations:

- Improve **public information** to help property owners understand the risks and benefits of insurance and mitigation strategies.
- Encourage **risk-based pricing** to align consumer behavior with actual risk exposure, promoting sound decision-making in high-risk zones.
- Allow **geographic diversification** for insurers to spread their risk portfolio effectively.

In summary, the document advocates for a balance between private insurance markets and regulatory frameworks, ensuring that insurers remain solvent while encouraging consumers to make informed decisions about coverage and mitigation..

The CATO Institute

The Unintended Effects of Government-Subsidized Weather Insurance

https://www.academia.edu/66634166/The_Unintended_Effects_of_Government_Subsidized_Weather_Insurance

Summary

The attached article, *The Unintended Effects of Government-Subsidized Weather Insurance*, by Omri Ben-Shahar and Kyle D. Logue, explores the consequences of government-subsidized weather insurance, specifically focusing on federal flood insurance through the National Flood Insurance Program (NFIP) and state-run wind insurance through Florida's Citizens Property Insurance Corporation.

Key Insights:

1. **Subsidized Insurance and Risk Behavior:**

- Government-subsidized insurance suppresses premiums, preventing market prices from reflecting the true risk. This distorts consumer behavior, leading people to build or remain in high-risk coastal areas.
- Coastal development in Florida has increased dramatically over the last few decades, with more property in storm-prone zones.

2. **Distribution of Subsidies:**

- Contrary to common belief, the beneficiaries of these subsidies are often affluent households rather than low-income families. Wealthier residents receive higher subsidies, particularly those who own more expensive properties or live in upscale neighborhoods.

3. **Negative Impact of Subsidies:**

- Subsidized insurance programs have led to regressive redistribution and increased the financial burden on taxpayers.
- Coastal development has surged due to artificially low insurance rates, resulting in higher property concentrations in disaster-prone areas.

4. **Policy Recommendations:**

- Reforming these programs to reflect actual risk and eliminating broad subsidies can reduce regressive redistribution and encourage responsible development.
- The government could mandate insurance in high-risk areas to prevent post-disaster relief dependency.
- A need-based subsidy system or a federal reinsurance role could help address coverage gaps without encouraging risky behavior.

These insights suggest that current subsidized insurance programs do not adequately incentivize risk mitigation or encourage responsible consumer behavior. Instead, they lead to inefficient resource allocation and increased taxpayer liabilities.

5 Trends to Watch in 2024 with Florida's Property Insurance Market

By Fred E. Karlinsky, Timothy F. Stanfield and Christian Brito

February 22, 2024

https://www.reuters.com/legal/legalindustry/5-trends-watch-2024-with-floridas-property-insurance-market-2024-02-22/

This document, titled "5 trends to watch in 2024 with Florida's property insurance market," is a commentary by attorneys Fred E. Karlinsky, Timothy F. Stanfield, and Christian Brito from the law firm Greenberg Traurig LLP. The article discusses the ongoing challenges and potential developments in Florida's property insurance market for the year 2024.

Key points from the article:

1. Despite the challenges faced by Florida's insurance market, the steps taken by lawmakers over the past 18 months have put the industry in a better position compared to the previous decade. However, consumers are only starting to see the positive impacts of the state's tort and insurance market reforms adopted in 2022 and 2023.
2. Continued inflation will provide upward pressure on insurance rates due to the high cost of rebuilding and labor, as well as losses from Hurricane Ian in 2022 and ongoing climate concerns.
3. Florida's continued population growth and development will strain the insurance market, as the state's growth likely means continued upward pressure on insurance rates for homeowners and reinsurance costs for insurers.
4. Climate change impact is real, and storms are becoming stronger, posing a significant risk for Florida insurers given the state's extensive coastline. Homeowners should be encouraged to strengthen their homes with improvements to better withstand future storms.
5. Capacity remains a constant challenge, with less traditional reinsurance available in Florida compared to a few years ago. The challenge will be to bring more insurers to Florida to provide coverage and help spread the risk.
6. Claims-related litigation is starting to trend downward due to legislative changes implemented in late 2022 and during the 2023 Florida Legislative session. However, resolving all existing litigation will be a drag on Florida insurers for years to come.
7. While it will take time to see the long-term impacts of the new laws and changes from 2023, the authors are optimistic that the property insurance market and rates will continue to stabilize in 2024.

In summary, the article highlights the ongoing challenges and potential trends in Florida's property insurance market for the year 2024, including the impact of inflation, population growth, climate change, capacity constraints, and claims-related litigation. Despite these challenges, the authors remain optimistic that the recent legislative reforms will help stabilize the market and rates in the coming year. They also note that the challenges faced by Florida may be a harbinger of things to come nationally.

Another Company Avoids Risky Florida Home Insurance Policies: Here's What Caused The Crisis

July 19, 2023

By Kinsey Crowley

USA TODAY

Contributing: Hannah Morse, Palm Beach Post; Brandon Girod, Pensacola News Journal

https://www.usatoday.com/story/money/personalfinance/2023/07/19/florida-home-insurance-aaa-farmers-policy-reduction/70427062007/

This news article from USA Today titled "Another company avoids risky Florida home insurance policies: Here's what caused the crisis." The article discusses the ongoing insurance crisis in Florida and its impact on homeowners.

Key points from the article:

1. AAA, a Florida-based insurer, recently announced that it will not renew certain homeowner insurance policies that combine home, automobile, and optional umbrella coverage. This decision comes shortly after Farmers Insurance announced its withdrawal from the state.
2. The insurance crisis in Florida is largely manmade, fueled by frivolous lawsuits and fraudulent insurance claims. A 2017 Florida Supreme Court ruling led to a surge in roofing scams and claim litigation, with Florida accounting for 80% of property claim lawsuits in the country over the past three years.

3. The high litigation costs have caused several local, residential-only insurers to become insolvent and prompted national insurers to raise premiums or reduce policy offerings.
4. Florida's hurricane risk has also contributed to the crisis, with Hurricane Ian in September 2022 causing the greatest insured loss after Hurricane Katrina.
5. The reduced supply of insurance options has driven up premiums, with Florida homeowners paying an average of $6,000 per year for homeowners' insurance, compared to the national average of $1,700.
6. In response to the crisis, nearly 15% of Florida homeowners are opting to go without insurance, while others are turning to the state-backed Citizens Property Insurance Corporation. However, Citizens' growing market share and lower premiums compared to private insurers raise concerns about its ability to fund payouts in the event of a major disaster.

In summary, the article highlights the ongoing insurance crisis in Florida, which is primarily driven by high litigation costs and exacerbated by the state's hurricane risk. The crisis has led to higher premiums, fewer insurance options, and an increasing number of homeowners either forgoing coverage or relying on the state-backed insurer. The situation underscores the need for reforms to address the **root causes** of the crisis and ensure a more stable and affordable insurance market for Florida residents.

Assessing Property Exposure to Cyclonic Winds Under Climate Change

(Published: 1 November 2023)

Evelyn G. Shu 1,*, Mariah Pope 1, Bradley Wilson 1, Mark Bauer 1, Mike Amodeo 1, Neil Freeman 1 and Jeremy R. Porter 1,2 1 First Street Foundation, Brooklyn, NY 11201, USA; mamodeo@firststreet.org (M.A.) 2 Department of Sociology and Demography, City University of New York, New York, NY 10017, USA * Correspondence: evelyn@firststreet.org

https://assets.firststreet.org/media/Wind_Peer_Review_FSF.pdf?_gl=1*1aq0oot*_gcl_au*NzkyNDc4MTA3LjE3MTUzODg0Njc.*_ga*MzA5ODAwNTk4LjE3MTUzODg0Njc.*_ga_NYKVC41QCL*MTcxNTM4ODQ2Ny4xLjEuMTcxNTM4ODkzNS4wLjAuMA..

This document is a research article titled "Assessing Property Exposure to Cyclonic Winds under Climate Change" by Evelyn G. Shu et al., published in the journal Climate in 2023. The article presents a wind exposure model that assesses the hyper-local climate tropical cyclone wind speed exposure across the contiguous United States (CONUS) due to Atlantic-formed cyclones.

Key points from the article:

1. The wind model combines open data, open science, and engineering expertise to create a high-resolution (30 m) tropical cyclone wind model that estimates wind exposure under current and future (30 years from now) climate conditions under the RCP 4.5 scenario.
2. The model uses approximately 50,000 synthetic hurricane tracks generated by computer models and based on historical storms, which are then downscaled using surface roughness corrections and projected into the future using CMIP6 climate models.
3. The results indicate extensive exposure to high winds along the Gulf and Southeastern Atlantic Coasts, with growing exposure in the Mid-Atlantic and Northeastern regions of the country, especially inland.
4. In the next 30 years, an additional 13.4 million properties are likely to face tropical cyclone-level winds that do not currently face such exposure, representing a 15.6% increase.
5. The number of properties exposed to Category 5 hurricane winds is expected to increase from 3.5 million in the current year to over 5.6 million in 30 years.
6. The counties expected to see the largest increase in maximum wind gust speeds in the 500-year return period are primarily in Virginia, South Carolina, Georgia, and North Carolina.

7. Areas with the highest probabilities of experiencing hurricane winds are focused along the Gulf Coast, with some areas exceeding a 27% likelihood in the current year. In 30 years, the spatial patterns remain similar, but some Gulf areas may see a slight decrease in their annual probabilities due to the northward shift of hurricanes.
8. The research highlights the importance of understanding changes in wind exposure over time to inform decisions about community resilience, resource allocation, and personal risk mitigation.

In summary, the article presents a high-resolution wind exposure model that demonstrates the increasing risk of property exposure to tropical cyclone winds under a changing climate, particularly in the Mid-Atlantic and Northeastern regions of the United States. **The findings emphasize the need for informed decision-making and adaptation strategies to mitigate the risks associated with hurricane winds.**

Can Lawmakers Save the Collapsing Florida Home Insurance Market?

By Cate Deventer

09/21/2023

https://www.nascus.org/2023/09/21/can-lawmakers-save-the-collapsing-florida-home-insurance-market/

This document, titled "Can lawmakers save the collapsing Florida home insurance market?," discusses the ongoing crisis in Florida's home insurance market and the legislative efforts to address the issues. The article, written by Cate Deventer and published on the NASCUS website, provides an in-depth look at the factors contributing to the crisis and the potential solutions.

Key points from the article:

1. The Florida home insurance market is facing a crisis due to a combination of factors, including insurance fraud, high litigation costs, and the risk of widespread weather-related damage.

2. Many insurance companies have gone insolvent, left the state, or drastically reduced their policy offerings, resulting in fewer options and higher premiums for homeowners.
3. Insurance fraud, particularly related to roofing claims, is a significant issue in Florida, with the state accounting for 79 percent of the country's home insurance lawsuits despite only having 9 percent of the claims.
4. Florida has lost over 30 insurance providers or some form of coverage from these providers in the past three years.
5. The Florida legislature has passed several bills in 2021, 2022, and 2023 to address the crisis, including measures to curb fraudulent claims, reduce litigation costs, and provide grants for home-hardening.
6. The December 2022 legislation, Senate Bill 2-A, focuses on eliminating one-way attorney fees and assignment of benefits scams, which could significantly reduce financial pressure on insurance companies.
7. Financial strength rating company Demotech announced it was considering downgrading the ratings of 27 property insurance companies, which could impact homeowners with federally-backed mortgages.
8. The Florida legislature approved a plan to search for a financial strength rating company to replace Demotech, aiming to find alternatives or create a state-backed rating agency.
9. While the legislative reforms are expected to help stabilize the market, it will likely take time for homeowners and insurers to feel the relief.

In summary, the Florida home insurance market is facing a severe crisis due to a combination of factors, including fraud, litigation costs, and weather-related risks. The state legislature has passed several bills to address these issues and stabilize the market, but the full effects of these measures have yet to be seen. As the situation continues to evolve, homeowners and insurers alike are hoping for relief from the ongoing challenges in the Florida insurance market.

Catastrophe Insurance, Capital Markets, and Uninsurable Risks

Dwight M. Jaffee Haas School of Business University of California Berkeley, CA 94720-1900 Tel: 510-642-1273 Email: jaffee@haas.berkeley.edu

Thomas Russell Department of Economics Santa Clara University Santa Clara, CA 95053 Tel: 408-554-6953 Email: trussell@scuacc.scu.edu

https://faculty.haas.berkeley.edu/jaffee/Papers/Jri697.PDF

The attached document, titled "Catastrophe Insurance, Capital Markets, and Uninsurable Risks," is a research paper by Dwight M. Jaffee and Thomas Russell. The paper examines the challenges faced by private insurance markets in providing coverage for catastrophic risks and explores potential solutions.

Key points from the paper:

1. Private insurance markets have struggled to provide adequate coverage for catastrophic risks such as hurricanes and earthquakes, often considering these risks "uninsurable."
2. The authors argue that the primary issue is not the size or unpredictability of the risks, but rather the mismatch between the annual premiums collected and the potentially large losses that could occur in a single year.
3. Historically, marine insurance markets have successfully dealt with catastrophic risks by either requiring the insured to pay the full premium upfront (with the loan forgiven if a loss occurs) or by arranging access to a large pool of capital to pay losses after the event.
4. Modern insurance companies face challenges in accumulating sufficient capital to cover catastrophic losses due to accounting rules, tax provisions, the risk of takeovers, and regulatory constraints.
5. Reinsurance markets and catastrophe-linked securities (such as Act of God bonds and catastrophe options) have emerged as potential solutions, but their effectiveness has been limited thus far.

6. The authors suggest that mortgage lenders could be an alternative source of capital for funding reconstruction following a catastrophe, as they are already at risk when disasters occur.
7. Government involvement in catastrophe insurance varies across countries, with some nations providing comprehensive coverage through public programs while others play a more limited role.
8. The authors conclude that for a private catastrophe insurance market to be viable, reforms are needed to allow insurance companies to accumulate and earmark capital for future catastrophe losses, and capital markets must continue to develop instruments that attract funding from investors.

In summary, the paper highlights the challenges faced by private insurance markets in covering catastrophic risks and discusses potential solutions, including the role of capital markets, government intervention, and alternative sources of capital such as mortgage lenders. The authors emphasize the need for reforms that enable insurance companies to build adequate capital reserves and for the continued development of innovative financial instruments to attract investment in catastrophe risk management.

The Coastline at Risk: 2016 Update to the Estimated Insured Value of U.S. Coastal Properties

AIR Worldwide

https://www.air-worldwide.com/SiteAssets/Publications/White-Papers/documents/The-Coastline-at-Risk-2016

This document, "The Coastline at Risk: 2016 Update to the Estimated Insured Value of U.S. Coastal Properties," is a report by AIR Worldwide that assesses the insured value of residential and commercial properties in coastal counties of the United States as of December 31, 2015.

Key points from the report:

1. The total insured value of properties located within the 100-year return period storm surge footprint exceeds USD 1.1 trillion.
2. In the past three years (2013-2015), the insured value of properties in coastal states increased at a compound annual growth rate (CAGR) of 5%, with a total increase of 15%.
3. The CAGR of the total insured value of properties in coastal counties was 4%, with a total increase of 13% over the same three-year period.
4. 38% of the total property replacement value in Gulf and East Coast states is located in coastal counties, accounting for nearly 16% of the total value of properties in the U.S.
5. The insured value of residential and commercial properties in coastal counties now exceeds USD 13 trillion. Florida and New York each have coastal county values exceeding USD 3 trillion.
6. New York has the highest coastal exposure at more than USD 5 trillion, followed closely by Florida. However, Florida has the largest proportion (79%) of its insured value in coastal counties.
7. The report highlights the growing risk of catastrophe losses from storm surge due to rising sea levels and severe weather events, which are expected to increase the portion of coastal areas at risk of flooding by 55% this century.
8. Maps are provided to illustrate the total insured value of commercial and residential properties in coastal counties for each state.

In summary, the report emphasizes the significant and growing insured value of properties in coastal areas of the United States, which are increasingly vulnerable to storm surge and flooding risks due to climate change and rising sea levels. The findings underscore the importance of catastrophe risk modeling and management for insurers, reinsurers, and other stakeholders in the coastal property market.

The Cost of Capital for Insurance Companies
By Walter Kielholz

The Geneva Papers on Risk and Insurance Vol. 25 No. 1 (January 2000) 4-24
https://link.springer.com/content/pdf/10.1111%2F1468-0440.00044.pdf

The this article, titled "The Cost of Capital for Insurance Companies" by Walter Kielholz, discusses the importance of the cost of capital for insurance companies, how to measure it, and strategies for managing it effectively.

Key points from the document:

1. The cost of capital is the expected rate of return insurers must pay for the capital they use. It is determined by capital markets, includes opportunity costs, and depends on risk.
2. Insurers need to supply their own capital to support their promise to pay claims, and this capital comes at a cost. Managing the trade-off between the costs and benefits of holding capital is crucial for insurers.
3. The author presents cost of capital estimates for the U.S., U.K., Switzerland, Germany, and France, showing a general decline in the cost of capital for insurers in these markets, largely due to the secular decline in nominal interest rates.
4. Five factors affect an insurer's capital efficiency: underwriting performance, investment performance, asset leverage, tax strategies, and solvency leverage. Current market conditions suggest that insurers may face challenges in improving their net after-tax income.
5. Insurers can incorporate the cost of capital into their daily business by using measures of economic profit to price risk and set incentives for management, aligning decision-making with shareholder interests.
6. Strategies for managing the cost of capital include diversification to reduce solvency risk, tax management, reducing transaction costs (agency costs), and managing regulatory capital requirements.
7. The globalization of capital markets, deregulation, and consolidation trends in the insurance industry have important implications for the cost of capital and its efficient use. Insurers who understand and manage their cost of capital effectively will have a competitive advantage.

8. Further research is needed to better understand the implications of global financial markets on insurers' cost of capital, the cost of capital for mutual insurers, and the effectiveness of newer risk management tools and strategies.

In summary, the document highlights the critical importance of understanding and managing the cost of capital for insurance companies, particularly in the context of changing market conditions, regulatory environments, and industry trends. Effective capital management, incorporating the cost of capital into decision-making, and adopting strategies to optimize capital efficiency are essential for insurers to remain competitive and create value for shareholders.

Introduction
Report of the Florida House Insurance Committee
To Speaker Marco Rubio

On January 22, 2007, the Florida Legislature passed House Bill 1A, a measure aimed at "reforming" the state's homeowners' insurance market. This bill significantly expanded the role of government in the market. However, in the wake of the 2008 national economic crisis, it became clear that Florida's decision to finance its catastrophe exposure with public debt rather than private capital was ill-timed. As the 2008 hurricane season approached, concerns arose about the potential for delayed claim payments and the imposition of post-storm assessments on policyholders, which could last up to 30 years.

In response to these concerns, the Speaker of the Florida House of Representatives requested that the House Insurance Committee convene a series of hearings to explore potential solutions. The Committee met on March 14 and March 24, 2008, to examine the issue of potential assessments and identify the root causes of Florida's dilemma. The Committee sought to quantify the amount policyholders could be required to pay and engage in an honest dialogue about the ability of the state's insurance mechanism to pay claims after a major hurricane or multiple storms. Additionally, the Committee explored the relationship between an insurer's ability to use actuarial adequate rates under current regulatory rules and interpretations and the likelihood of taxpayers being assessed due to these rates.

This report summarizes the findings of the House Insurance Committee following these hearings. For a detailed analysis of the Committee's work, video recordings of the hearings are available at the following addresses:

- March 14, 2008: https://thefloridachannel.org/videos/31408-house-insurance-committee/

- March 24, 2008: https://thefloridachannel.org/videos/3-24-08-house-insurance-committee/

The Florida House of Representatives

Jobs & Entrepreneurship Council

Committee on Insurance

Marco Rubio

Speaker

Donald D. "Don" Brown

Chair

April 2, 2008

Dear Speaker Rubio:

As you know, Florida's citizens have taken on an enormous financial burden since the Legislature convened in January 2007 for Special Session. As a result of the legislation passed during Special Session[52] and the 2007 Regular Session, our taxpayers are now responsible for billions of dollars more in potential insurance assessments. As you recently stated, these assessments will be the "**largest tax increase in Florida history.**"

A recent study by the Property and Casualty Insurer Association of America found that seventy-one percent of Floridians do not know that the recent legislative changes allow Citizens Property Insurance Corporation (Citizens) and the Florida

---

[52] HB 1A in 2007 Special Session A

308 House Office Building, 402 South Monroe Street, Tallahassee, Florida 32399-1300
(850) 414-7365 Fax: (850) 414-9632

Hurricane Catastrophe Fund (CAT Fund) to assess virtually all insurance policyholders in the state if there is a property insurance financial shortfall. It is deeply concerning that <u>the vast majority of Floridians are completely unaware that they face this potential assessment</u>. This suggests that Floridians are also unaware of the reason why these "**hurricane taxes**" exist. One major storm and the taxpayers of the state will be hit with assessment.

The House Committee on Insurance recently met on March 14th and March 24th to specifically explore the issue of potential assessments and to identify the root causes. The Committee wanted to quantify the amount policyholders could be required to pay. In addition, we sought an honest dialogue about the ability of our state's insurance mechanism to pay claims after a major hurricane or multiple storms. The Committee was also interested in the relationship between an insurers ability to use actuarial adequate rates under our current regulatory rules and interpretations and the likelihood of taxpayers being assessed because of these rates. It was the intent of this Committee to bring understanding and insight about the potential risk of assessment under our current system and to find ways to alleviate this risk. If levied, these assessments will pose a significant financial burden to our citizens.

During the March 14th meeting, the Committee heard testimony from officials with Citizens, and on March 24th, we heard testimony from the Office of Insurance Regulation (OIR). All the testimony received on these dates was taken under oath.

<u>During testimony from Citizens, officials from the organization revealed a sobering fact.</u> **Florida insurance policyholders would be liable for more than $10 billion in assessments from Citizens if a "1-in-100 year storm" struck**

our state this year.[53] This is despite the fact that Citizens consumes nearly 40% of the resources of the CAT Fund due to its massive, concentrated coastal exposure. Even a repeat of the 2004 and 2005 seasons, under today's exposure, would leave Citizens with a shortfall of over $4 billion.[54] This would result in assessments of hundreds of dollars per year on nearly every property, automobile, and small business policy in the state. In addition, the CAT Fund would be on the hook for roughly $25 billion in assessment potential for the same type of storm.[55]

Among those testifying before the Committee, were representatives of the CAT Fund, including their outside financial advisor John Forney (of Raymond James) who also serves as such for Citizens. During his testimony, Mr. Forney discussed the challenges the CAT Fund would face in meeting its financial obligations following major storm activity. The Committee learned from this testimony that even under ideal circumstances, that <u>it will be very difficult, if not impossible for the CAT Fund to raise the cash needed through bonding to reach its increased capacity of $28 billion</u>, which is nearly double its capacity before our recent legislation. In today's environment, the challenge would be significantly greater. For example, Mr. Forney described the CAT Fund's recent difficulties in bonding last fall when the sub-prime mortgage financial crisis adversely affected its ability to secure bond investors.

The question of whether or not the CAT Fund can meet its obligations affects all insurance companies and customers, not just Citizens policyholders. Private companies are forced to rely on this coverage because of a legislative mandate to

---

[53] Citizens presented detailed financial data underlying this conclusion to the House Committee on Insurance on December 13, 2007.
[54] Citizens presentation to House Insurance Committee, March 24, 2008.
[55] Florida Senate Interim Project Report 2008-104, "Options for Transferring Risk from the Florida Hurricane Catastrophe Fund," November 2007.

buy CAT Fund coverage. This means private companies operating in Florida are liable to their customers even if the CAT Fund defaults. To make matters worse, private insurers continue to meet with regulatory resistance when they try to buy reinsurance to cover the possibility of a CAT fund deficit.

For Citizens' policyholders, CAT Fund coverage is crucial to ensure their claims are paid. If the CAT Fund is unable to issue bonds, it is even more unlikely that Citizens will be able to bond in order to bridge the gap. **Simply stated, it is probable under our current system that hundreds of millions of dollars in storm claims will go unpaid for some time.**

Further, the Florida Insurance Guaranty Association (FIGA) undoubtedly would be financially strained following such a storm. Small domestic insurers would be struggling to recapitalize in a stressed reinsurance market after a catastrophic season. We saw the potential effects on this market segment with the insolvency of the Poe Financial Group in 2006, which resulted in over $740 million, and counting, in FIGA assessments for its unpaid claims.

In summary, <u>a severe but foreseeable storm season could cause $35 billion or more in assessments under current law</u>. These assessments would be charged primarily to repay the bonds issued to pay claims immediately after the storm. As such, the assessments could be in effect for up to thirty years. Worse still is the possibility of multiple years of storms causing assessments to compound. This would create perpetual assessments lasting for generations. We shudder to think that not only will our citizens be faced with this burden, but their children will face it as well.

The other side of the equation is premium rates, which allow for the buildup of financial resources to pay storm claims, and just as important, to inform the consumer of the cost of the risks they take. Citizens' officials acknowledge the reported disconnect between their financial resources and their obligations. **Citizens' outside actuary testified it is his belief that their rates have been**

actuarially inadequate since January of 2007 when they were rolled back by this Legislature. Moreover, Citizens' top financial executive agreed it is fiscally unsound to continue taking on new risks while rates are inadequate.

Testimony from OIR officials mainly focused on the process by which insurance rates are reviewed, especially Citizens' rates. In response to 2005 legislation requiring actuarially sound rates, Citizens filed such rates in 2006. This included a provision to reduce the reliance on assessments. A top Citizens executive testified that OIR's preference was that Citizens rely on post-event assessments rather than pre-event funding in its rates. OIR officials confirmed this was a major reason why the approved rates for Citizens' High Risk Account were significantly reduced from the requested amount. Even the approved rates were then rescinded in the 2007 Special Session thus leaving Citizens with a current rating plan which is not only well out of date, but not reflective of its obligations.

During the testimony, in a very enlightening development, OIR officials testified that when OIR's own actuaries recommend approval of a rate filing, managers not trained or certified in actuarial sciences (The discipline that applies statistical and mathematical methods to assess risks and predict future claims) can overrule these recommendations. Unfortunately, the committee received neither a clear response nor any documentation as to the reasons why their own actuarial recommendations are often rejected.

OIR officials were also unable to provide a coherent explanation of why they allow some insurance companies to charge twice as much (or even more) as other companies to cover identical risks in identical locations.

OIR also noted its frequent reliance in rate reviews on the public hurricane loss projection model developed with taxpayer dollars by Florida International University. As you know, the Florida Commission on Hurricane Loss Project Methodology (Commission) issued to you a recent report in which it notes the "low stability over time" and "insufficient geographic spread in loss projections" of the public model relative to the other accepted hurricane models. Yet OIR does not accept the results of the other Commission-accepted models in rate filings despite a statutory presumption of admissibility[56] and the fact that the models are used to set the rates for the CAT Fund.

OIR officials confirmed that the health of an insurance marketplace can be judged by the size of its residual market. Officials also confirmed markets generally can be considered healthy when a high degree of competition and a relatively small residual market exist. While it is common knowledge that Citizens is the largest property insurer in Florida, the committee's research further revealed it is also the largest property residual market entity in the world and based on the size of its Personal Lines Accounts alone, Citizens is the 10th largest property insurer of any kind in the United States. The diagnosis of our market's health is poor. Clearly, our current system of substituting regulatory and legislative fiat for actuarial science (The discipline that applies statistical and mathematical methods to assess risks and predict future claims), prudent financing, and economic signals is not working for our citizens, even those in the next generation.

In all, the committee heard more than ten hours of testimony from top officials at Citizens, the CAT Fund, FIGA, OIR, and the other insurance experts. After considering all of the testimony and documentary evidence, it is clear that action is needed to a) reduce the potential for **"hurricane taxes"** on Floridians, b) better educate our constituents on the financial burdens they currently face under today's property insurance structure, and c) attract private investment capital back to Florida. We believe there are several action items which are politically achievable in the short term and will begin to restore a healthy insurance market. Those

---

[56] 5 F.S. 627.0628(9).

action items will be covered in the "Recommendations" contained later in this report.

Summary of Committee Findings and Selected Quotes:

Committee

- If a 1-in-100 year storm hits Florida, assessments by Citizens would total over $10 billion and could be levied on Florida citizens and businesses for up to 30 years.
- Even a small storm (1-in-50 year storm) would lead to assessments being levied by Citizens.
- Since January 2007, insurance rates charted by Citizens have been actuarially inadequate.
- In the event of a hurricane or a series of hurricanes, the CAT Fund could have extreme difficulty paying its obligations.
- If the CAT Fund is unable to meet its financial obligations, many policyholders could experience delays or may not be paid for all their hurricane-related claims.
- OIR and Citizens disagree as to whether Citizens rates should include a rating factor to pre-fund a larger percent of hurricane exposure. OIR favors post-funding ("hurricane tax").
- Florida's property insurance market is not healthy as evidenced by the large size of the property insurance residual market (Citizens).

Selected Quotes

- "If the CAT Fund has difficulties, the whole thing breaks down and from a financial standpoint that would be a problem." *John Forney – Citizens and CAT Fund Financial Advisor.*
- In response to a question about the likelihood of a successful sell of bonds in excess of $14 billion to pay Citizens claims, "The CAT Fund would be bonding for about $25 billion and Citizens for about $2 billion, which is

clearly an unprecedented amount of money." *John Forney – Citizens and CAT Fund Financial Advisor.*

- **"The largest transaction that has ever been done in this market is for $10 billion. It is difficult to overestimate the difficulty of this challenge."** *John Forney – Citizens and CAT Fund Financial Advisor.*

- <u>Question</u>: "What happens if the CAT Fund could not get bonding and is only able to raise about half as much of what it needs to meet its obligations (if the CAT Fund owes you $12 and only pays you $6)?
  <u>Answer</u>: "Citizens has $10.5 billion to get through the mandatory CAT Fund layer. After that, Citizens would access other resources (policyholders, insurance companies, and ultimately policyholders around the state through the emergency mechanism). John Forney – Citizens and Cat Fund Financial Advisor.

- <u>Question</u>: "Is there any methodology in place under a worse-case scenario where you would have to pro-rate claims if you can't get the money?"
  <u>Answer</u>: I am not aware of this, <u>but if the worse of the worst occurs, it could ultimately happen</u>." *Sharon Binnun, CFO – Citizens.*

- <u>Question</u> by Representative Hays to John Forney. "Could you compare the sub-prime market conditions with what would be your perception of the market condition following a catastrophic storm?"
  <u>Response</u>: "There would be unprecedented market conditions. It would revolve around a "shadow banking" system, a broken-down system where short-term borrowing would be difficult, if not impossible. The CAT Fund is exceptionally fortunate to be able to access the money that it did this year on the terms that it did. The CAT Fund could not do that financing right now in this market if it wanted to."

- <u>Question</u>: "Was Citizens' decision to increase rates (as reflected in your 2005 rate filing) in the best interest of Citizens policyholders and the state's other insurance consumers?"
  <u>Response</u>: "Yes, and we do stand by the decision made in 2005." *Paul Erickson –*

Independent Actuary.

- Chairman Brown mentioned the Senate bill that freezes rates through 2009 and then asked the following questions of Paul Erickson, Independent Actuary.
    - <u>Question</u>: "What would the total impact be in terms of uncollected premium for what OIR determined should have begun in January 2007? <u>Answer</u>: "About $360 million given the assumption."
    - <u>Question</u>: "Are the rates for 2009 the same as those from 2005-2008?"
    <u>Answer</u>: "Not exactly because rates were changed in the beginning of 2006 and there was also a reduction in 2007."
    - <u>Question</u>: "What do you think of that?"
    <u>Answer</u>: "From an actuarial perspective, I would not think that is appropriate.
    - <u>Question</u>: "Are you basically charging the same rates that were approved in late 2005?"
    <u>Answer</u>: "Yes" o <u>Question</u>: "Would it be fair to say that the 2005 rates did not account for the 2005 storm season?"
    <u>Answer</u>: "That is correct." o <u>Question</u>: "**Is Citizens rate inadequate?**
    <u>Answer</u>: "**Yes, especially for the high-risk account.**

<u>Representative Ross – Summary of Citizens Findings</u>

"The facts that we saw today are rather compelling…":

- At the end of 2005, Citizens was required by statute to charge the highest premiums of anybody out there.
- At that time, Citizens had a policy count of 810,000.
- At the end of the year, Citizens had a $1.7 billion deficit.

- We used General Revenue to help alleviate that budget and amortized the net loss of $888,000 in assessments over 10 years.
- Citizens has grown as a result of HB1A (by 500,000 policies up to 1.3 million policies).
- Citizens may now compete in the insurance market.
- OIR determined that a 44% rate increase was excessive and approved a 25.9% increase instead.
- <u>The rates are woefully inadequate.</u>
- The private market has essentially left the industry except for in a few areas.
- We owe it to the consumer to have competition; and
- Citizens could not bond if there were a catastrophe.

"We cannot keep telling ourselves that this is a good situation," said Representative Ross.

Jack Nichoson, Senior Officer – Florida Hurricane Catastrophe Fund Summary of Testimony

- FHCF may have market access problems due to unforeseen costs and substantial uncertainty in financial markets.
- Funding to capacity equals dire consequences.
- The CAT Fund provides the backbone of the residential insurance market.
- <u>Question</u> by Chairman Brown: "What is the difference between financing risk with capital as opposed to debt?"
  <u>Answer</u>: **"Funding with cash is good and funding with debt is bad."**
- <u>Question</u> by Chairman Brown: "I am feeling like the original CAT Fund mission has been distorted. Have we tortured it to the end where we are now on risky ground?"
  Answer: "There are limitations on what one can rely on or do. This is a concern of the Advisory Council, and the CFO is concerned about bonding issues."

- Question by Representative Hays (referring to recent testimony about potential CAT Fund assessments per policy that may be in the range of $11K to $32 K). Has there been any more refinement of those numbers and is the characterization adequate?
  Answer: "As an example, a category 3 hurricane that causes damages of $40 to $50 billion would max out the CAT Fund."
- 10% is the maximum of the assessment base (at 6% per year).
- The average assessable policy in Florida costs $6,000 per year.
- The calculations are as follows – 6% of $6,000 is $360.00 and 10% is $600. $600 x 30 years equals $18,000 per household on average, which would be the maximum assessment for about 6.2 million households (however, if should be noted that this includes multiple policies for some individuals).

Dr. David Leston, Associate Professor of Economic – University of Miami
Summary of Testimony

- Dr. Leston was asked to look at the economic impact of a $15 billion assessment.
- Under this scenario, there would be sizeable loss in jobs, taxes, and revenues. Job losses would amount to about 29,000 and there would be lost revenues of $300 million per year.
- For a 100-year storm, the amount is $25.8 billion, which is amortized over 30 years at a 4% rate. The annual assessment is $1.8 billion. For Citizens, the assessment is $1.6 billion. This would result in substantial losses in earnings, jobs to the state and to local governments.
- Preserve incentives concept: assessments are not just a tax, but also a tax on capital. This could create the potential of distorting incentives.

Recommendations

<u>Citizens Recommendations:</u>

1) Rewrite the Citizens rate freeze to allow a modernized rating plan and actuarially sound rates to be filed as soon as possible and effective in 2009, while protecting consumers by phasing in any rate increases for existing individual policies from current levels at a reasonable pace.[57] This will signal consumers to make responsible insurance choices and put Citizens on the path to funding its obligations while easing the transition effects on consumer and business budgets.

2) Revisit Citizens' charter as a true residual market entity. Property owners offered private insurance at approved rates should be ineligible for Citizens, especially for commercial policies such as coastal builders' risks. This will ensure Citizens is a safety net and not a subsidized alternative to willing, regulated providers.

3) Specify that actuarially sound rates for Citizens include a provision for pre-funding of its obligations via reinsurance. Such funding should cover the same loss scenarios as required by OIR of all private market insurers: the "1-in-100 year" probable maximum loss.[58] It has been recently reported that only the High Risk Account would see significant rate increases as a result, and consumers now have a choice to buy a multi-

---

[57] HB1A imposed the freeze by forcing Citizens to reinstate the rates from an old rate filing effective 03/01/2006 based on market rates charged during late 2005. It wiped out not only rate increased, but the significant rating plan modernizations made in Citizens' approved rate filings effective 01/01/2007.

[58] A form of this provision, requiring rates to be set assuming eventual pre-funding of severe events over time, was included in Senate Bill 1980 and repealed in HB1A.

peril Citizens policy to forestall that effect anyway. Finally, with the provisions above any rate increase would be phased in over time.[59]

Rate Regulation Recommendations:

4) Increase the transparency of regulatory activities by requiring OIR to maintain a public, web-accessible database of overall rate level requests filed, the amount recommended by OIR actuaries, and the amount approved by the Commissioner. Given that private actuaries must swear under penalty of perjury that their indications are fair, not misleading and reflect all legislative enactments[60], require a similar statement from OIR actuaries with respect to their published recommendations. In the public filing documentation, require OIR actuaries to disclose their major assumptions, and whether those deviate from the professional standards of the American Academy of Actuaries. Additionally, when any proposed action on a rate filing is reviewed by OIR, require those meetings to be open to the affected parties (including the public) and in the sunshine.

5) Increase the efficiency of rate regulation by restoring a provision allowing expedited approval of rates and rating plan adjustments not exceeding a certain level[61], but with new consumer safeguards: a phase-in of individual policy premium increases exceeding an annual limit, and a requirement that annual filings be up-to-date before and after the expedited adjustment for a period of one year. This would speed competitive rates to market, free OIR to focus on significant pricing and coverage issues, and force insurers to continuously maintain fair rates.

---

[59] Christine Turner, Palm Beach Post editorial, March 31, 2008.
[60] See form OIR-B1-1790, based on the language in HB1A.
[61] SB1980 in 2006 regular session contained such a provision; it was repealed in HB1A.

6) Allow the temporary prohibition on "use and file" rate filings, whereby rates are changed and full filings made within 30 days to sunset. This will let insurers respond to changing market conditions – including offering competitive rate decreases – in the future, as well as lessening the regulatory burden on OIR. This would not prevent Citizens takeouts from still being regulated to allow depopulations only at approved rates.

7) If the temporary prohibition on property rate arbitrations is not allowed to sunset then replace it with provisions installing an expedited judiciary process at the Division of Administrative Hearing (DOAH) so that insurers and OIR may have fast, final decisions on rate and rule disputes.

8) Allow the unfettered use of information from hurricane risk models accepted by the Commission as actuarial support for rate filings. Rates are already regulated, and filing actuaries are already bound by law and standards regarding supporting information. However, OIR continues to stonewall the use of accepted models by insisting on the ability to disclose proprietary documentation already reviewed by the Commission under a process which assures public accountability while protecting trade secrets.

9) Allow insurers direct access to the Public Hurricane Model and its detailed loss results prior to OIR's decisions based on those results.

10) Prohibit OIR from mandating territorial rate caps which force low risk homeowners to subsidize the insurance costs of high risk homeowners.

Other Public Policy Recommendations:

11) Increase consumer awareness of the potential for "hurricane taxes" or assessments by requiring Citizens and the FHCF to annually calculate

and publish an estimated percentage assessment, levied over a defined period, for a 1-in-100 year storm that strikes in the upcoming season. Require all insurance policy declarations pages to contain a notice specifying this estimated annual assessment in dollars and the period over which it would be levied.

12) Continue to encourage responsible and affordable wind mitigation by funding the My Safe Florida Home program and requiring wind loss mitigation rating plans for insurers. Allow insurers to develop these plans using the results of any and all hurricane models accepted by the Commission, but including discounts for all features enumerated in the current rule.[62]

13) Develop a long-term growth management plan for the State of Florida that does not encourage inappropriate development by forcing Floridians to provide below market insurance coverage for coastal development.

We know these proposals will not result in an overnight fix to Florida's property insurance crisis. However, we must begin to take steps in the right direction if we are to rebuild a stable and competitive marketplace. Although the storms we face are the ultimate cause of this crisis, we have worsened our situation by creating a legal and regulatory environment in which the private market cannot function, coupled with a public insurance market that will collapse after a single major storm. Our constituents deserve a Legislature which will take the fiscally responsible path and ensure a bright economic future for the State of Florida.

Sincerely,   Sincerely,

---

[62] See rule 690-170-017, which mandates discounts from a particular hurricane model which is not commonly used by insurers and which produces generally higher losses than other models.

Donald D. Brown, Chairman   Dennis A. Ross, Chairman
Committee on Insurance   Committee on Courts
cc: Chairman Ray Sansom
cc: Chairman Dean Cannon

Insurance Terms 101

Why do buildings stand tall and unyielding? It's not just about the bricks and mortar; it's about the foundation. Similarly, the strength of an insurance agent lies not just in their ability to sell but in their understanding of the foundational terms of their industry. These terms are the bedrock on which the complex insurance world is built. But what are these terms, and why are they crucial for every policyholder and legislator to know?

Actual Cash Value (ACV)

Definition: The replacement cost of property minus depreciation, representing its value at the time of loss after accounting for wear and tear.

Example: If a 5-year-old roof is damaged and needs replacement, the insurance company may pay the ACV, which is the cost of a new roof minus depreciation for the 5 years of use.

Case Study: In 2018, a homeowner in Florida filed a claim for roof damage caused by a hurricane. The insurance company determined the ACV of the 8-year-old roof to be $12,000, while the replacement cost value (RCV) was $18,000. The homeowner had to pay the difference of $6,000 out of pocket to replace the roof with a new one of like kind and quality.

Actuarial Risk

Definition: "Actuarial risk" refers to the process by which actuaries evaluate and manage the financial risks associated with uncertain future events. This evaluation primarily uses mathematical and statistical methods. Actuaries play a crucial role in the insurance industry, where they use their skills to assess the likelihood and potential costs of various events, from natural disasters to changes in life expectancy.

By analyzing past data and forecasting future trends, actuaries help insurance companies determine the premiums they should charge to cover the risks they insure. They also ensure that these companies maintain sufficient reserves to pay out claims while still being financially stable. This balance is vital for the insurer's solvency and for protecting the interests of policyholders.

Example: Actuaries frequently assess risks associated with natural disasters, such as hurricanes or earthquakes. They analyze historical data on these events, including frequency, location, and cost of damages. Using this data, they create models to predict future occurrences and their potential financial impact. This information is crucial for insurance companies in setting premium rates for policies covering such disasters. If an actuary predicts a high likelihood of hurricanes in a particular region, insurers may increase premiums for policies in that area to cover the increased risk.

Actuarial Soundness

Definition: The financial principles ensuring that an insurance or pension system has sufficient funds to cover present and future liabilities, often mandated by regulations.

Example: The Affordable Care Act (ACA) requires that premium rates for health insurance plans be actuarially sound, meaning they must be adequate to cover expected claims and administrative expenses while maintaining a reasonable reserve.

Case Study: In 2015, the Centers for Medicare & Medicaid Services (CMS) found that some insurers participating in the ACA marketplaces had set premium rates that were not actuarially sound, leading to financial losses. CMS issued guidance to improve the rate-setting process and ensure actuarial soundness.

Adjustable-Rate Mortgage (ARM)

Definition: A mortgage loan where the interest rate can fluctuate over the loan term, causing the monthly payment amount to change periodically based on market interest rates.

Example: An ARM may start with a fixed rate for the first 5 years, after which the rate becomes adjustable annually based on market conditions, impacting the monthly mortgage payment.

Adverse Selection

Definition: Adverse selection refers to a situation in the insurance industry where individuals who are more likely to make a claim are more inclined to buy insurance, or purchase more of it, than those who are less likely to make claims. This scenario occurs when there is an asymmetry of information between the insurer and the insured. The insurer might price its products based on an average risk, not knowing that higher-risk individuals are more likely to take up the offer, potentially leading to financial losses for the insurer.

Example: In health insurance, individuals who know they have health issues are more likely to purchase or opt for more comprehensive health insurance compared to healthier individuals. If insurers do not accurately adjust the premiums to account for this higher risk, they may end up paying out more in claims than they receive in premiums, leading to losses.

Agreed Value Policy

Definition: An insurance policy where the insurer and policyholder agree on the value of the insured property at the inception of the policy, waiving the coinsurance clause.

Example: A business owner may opt for an agreed value policy for their commercial property, ensuring that in the event of a total loss, the insurer will pay the agreed-upon value rather than applying a coinsurance penalty.

Appraisal

Definition: A professional estimation of a property's market value based on its condition, features, location, and recent sale prices of comparable properties.

Example: Before approving a mortgage loan, lenders typically require an appraisal to ensure the home's value provides sufficient collateral for the loan amount.

Case Study: In a hot real estate market, some homes may appraise higher than the agreed purchase price, giving buyers equity immediately after closing.

Binder

Definition: A temporary insurance contract that provides coverage until a formal, permanent policy is issued, ensuring the policyholder has coverage in place during the interim.

Example: When purchasing a new home, the lender may require a binder to be in place before closing, providing temporary coverage until the homeowner's insurance policy is issued.

Claim

Definition: A request made by the policyholder to the insurance company to pay for a covered loss under the policy.

Example: After a car accident, the policyholder files a claim with their auto insurance company, initiating the process of evaluating the damage and determining the payout amount.

Case Study: In 2021, a series of severe thunderstorms in Texas led to a significant increase in homeowner insurance claims for roof and window damage. Some insurers faced challenges in promptly processing the high volume of claims, leading to delays and customer dissatisfaction.

Coinsurance

Definition: Coinsurance refers to the percentage of the cost of a claim that an insured person is responsible for paying, after the deductible (*the amount of money a policyholder must pay out-of-pocket before an insurance company begins to cover the remaining costs*) is met. This term is commonly used in health insurance and property insurance. In a typical coinsurance scenario, the insurance policy specifies that the insurer and the insured will share the cost of covered claims at a certain ratio, such as 70/30 or 80/20, where the insurer pays the larger percentage.

Example: Let's say you own a building worth $500,000, and your property insurance policy has an 80% coinsurance clause. This means you need to insure the building for at least $400,000 (80% of $500,000) to avoid a coinsurance penalty in the event of a claim.

Now, if you insure the building for only $300,000 and then experience a loss of $250,000, the insurance payout would be calculated using the coinsurance formula:

- Insured amount ($300,000) / Required insurance amount (80% of $500,000 = $400,000) x Loss amount ($250,000) = Insurance payout
- $300,000 / $400,000 x $250,000 = $187,500

So, instead of receiving the full $250,000 for the claim, you would only receive $187,500 due to underinsuring the property. The remaining $62,500 would be your responsibility to cover, illustrating the impact of the coinsurance clause in property insurance.

Deductible

Definition: The amount the policyholder must pay out-of-pocket before the insurance coverage kicks in.

Example: A homeowner's insurance policy may have a $1,000 deductible, meaning the homeowner must pay the first $1,000 of a covered claim, and the insurer covers the remaining amount up to the policy limits.

Deep Pocket Syndrome

Definition: "Deep Pocket Syndrome" refers to the tendency in litigation to target or sue individuals or entities not because they are the most at fault, but because they have the most financial resources. In legal contexts, this phenomenon is often observed when plaintiffs choose to pursue the party that is most able to pay a significant judgment or settlement, regardless of their actual level of responsibility for the incident in question.

Example: In a case where multiple parties are involved in an accident, a plaintiff might focus their lawsuit on a large corporation involved rather than a smaller business or individual, even if the latter were more culpable. The rationale is that the large corporation, with its substantial assets, can afford to pay a large settlement, whereas the smaller entities might not be able to pay at all.

Case Study: In a maritime accident case, a charterer with deep pockets faced claims despite seeking indemnity, i.e. financial compensation or reimbursement provided to cover a loss or damage as stated in an insurance policy, from the shipowner based on their contract terms, as the plaintiff targeted the party with more financial resources.

Depreciation

Definition: The decrease in the value of property over time due to wear and tear or obsolescence, often factored into determining a property's actual cash value.

Example: When calculating the ACV of a 10-year-old roof, the insurer will consider the depreciation due to age and weather conditions to determine the appropriate payout amount.

Endorsement

Definition: An addition to a standard insurance policy that provides extra protection or coverage for specific items or events not covered under the base policy.

Example: A homeowner may add an endorsement to their policy to cover expensive jewelry or artwork, as these items may have limited coverage or be excluded from the standard homeowner's policy.

Equity

Definition: In the context of property insurance, "equity" refers to the financial interest or value that an owner has in their property. It's calculated as the difference between the property's market value and any outstanding debts or liens against the property, such as a mortgage. Equity can increase over time as the property owner pays down the mortgage and as the property value appreciates.

Example: If someone owns a home valued at $300,000 and they owe $200,000 on their mortgage, their equity in the home is $100,000. This equity represents the homeowner's actual stake in the property's value and can be affected by changes in the market value of the property, as well as by the amount of debt against it.

Escrow

Definition: A neutral third-party account where funds or documents are held until specific conditions are met, commonly used in real estate transactions.

Example: During a home purchase, the buyer's down payment and closing costs are held in an escrow account until the sale is finalized, at which point the funds are released to the appropriate parties.

Excess Insurance

Definition: A type of insurance that provides coverage above the underlying policy limits, offering additional protection against large claims.

Example: A business owner may purchase excess liability insurance to extend coverage beyond the limits of their standard liability policy, protecting against potentially catastrophic claims.

Exclusions

Definition: Specific circumstances, events, or risks that are explicitly not covered by an insurance policy.

Example: Standard homeowners insurance policies typically exclude damage from floods, earthquakes, and acts of war or terrorism from coverage.

Flood Insurance

Definition: A separate insurance policy that covers damage caused by flooding, as standard homeowner's insurance policies typically exclude flood-related losses.

Case Study: During Hurricane Harvey in 2017, many homeowners in Houston who did not have flood insurance faced significant financial losses, as their standard policies did not cover the widespread flooding caused by the storm.

Frequency Distribution

Definition: A statistical measure that helps insurers understand the regularity of certain events, like claims, within a given time frame, which is crucial for premium pricing and risk management.

Example: An insurance company analyzes its data over the past year and creates a frequency distribution of property claims. They find that theft claims are the most frequent, followed by water damage and then fire damage. This information helps the company adjust its premium rates and underwriting (*the process of evaluating the risks involved in insuring a person or asset and determining appropriate premium rates*) practices to better reflect the risks associated with insuring properties.

Fixed-Rate Mortgage

Definition: A mortgage loan where the interest rate remains constant throughout the loan term, providing predictable monthly payments.

Example: A 30-year fixed-rate mortgage with a 4% interest rate will have the same monthly payment amount for the entire 30-year term, regardless of market fluctuations.

Home Inspection

Definition: A comprehensive evaluation of a home's condition, systems, and structure by a professional inspector, typically conducted before a purchase or sale.

Example: Before buying a home, potential buyers often hire a home inspector to identify any issues or defects that may need to be addressed or factored into the purchase price.

Home Warranty

Definition: A service contract that covers the repair or replacement of major home systems and appliances, such as HVAC, plumbing, or refrigerators, for a specified period.

Example: New homeowners may purchase a home warranty to provide protection against costly repairs or replacements of key systems and appliances during the first year of ownership.

Homeowners Insurance (HO-3)

Definition: A standard homeowner's insurance policy that covers the dwelling, personal belongings, liability protection, and additional living expenses if the home is uninhabitable due to a covered peril.

Example: An HO-3 policy may cover damage caused by fire, wind, or theft, but typically excludes perils like floods or earthquakes, which require separate coverage.

Case Study: After a severe thunderstorm caused a tree to fall onto a homeowner's roof, their HO-3 policy covered the cost of repairs to the roof and any damaged personal belongings, as well as temporary living expenses while the home was being repaired.

Indemnity

Definition: The principle that an insurance policy should provide compensation for losses in such a way that the insured party is returned to the financial position they were in prior to the loss. It's a fundamental concept in insurance that ensures policyholders are neither profited nor disadvantaged by a claim but are restored to their pre-loss state.

Example: If a homeowner suffers a fire that causes $100,000 worth of damage to their home, and they have an indemnity-based insurance policy, the insurance company would compensate them up to $100,000 to repair or rebuild the damaged property, minus any applicable deductible. This payment allows the homeowner to restore their property to its original condition before the fire occurred.

Inflation Guard

Definition: A feature in some insurance policies that automatically adjusts the coverage limit to keep pace with inflation, helping ensure policyholders maintain adequate coverage levels over time.

Example: A homeowner's insurance policy with an inflation guard may increase the dwelling coverage limit by a few percentage points each year to account for rising construction costs.

Insurance To Value (ITV)

Definition: The principle that a property should be insured for its total value, not just a portion, often contrasted with coinsurance requirements.

Example: An ITV policy would insure a commercial building for its full replacement cost value, without requiring the property owner to meet a coinsurance clause percentage.

Liability Coverage

Definition: Protection against claims or lawsuits arising from bodily injury or property damage caused by the policyholder, covering legal fees and potential settlements or judgments.

Example: If a homeowner's tree falls and damages a neighbor's property, their liability coverage would pay for repairs to the neighbor's property and any associated legal costs.

Case Study: In 2019, a homeowner in California faced a multi-million dollar lawsuit after their outdoor firepit caused a wildfire that damaged several neighboring properties. Their liability coverage helped cover the legal expenses and eventual settlement.

Loss of Use

Definition: Coverage that pays for additional living expenses, such as hotel bills or meals, if the policyholder's home becomes uninhabitable due to a covered peril.

Example: If a homeowner's house is severely damaged by a fire and they need to temporarily relocate, their loss of use coverage would reimburse them for the cost of a hotel or rental during the repair or rebuilding process.

Moral Hazard

Definition: The situation where an insured individual or entity is incentivized to take on more risk because they are shielded from the consequences of that risk due to insurance coverage.

Example: A person with comprehensive auto insurance may be less cautious about locking their car or driving carefully, knowing that any theft or damage would be covered by their policy.

Case Study: After implementing deductibles and exclusions for intentional neglect, an insurer noticed a reduction in claims related to moral hazard, as policyholders had a financial stake in avoiding risky behavior.

Mortgage

Definition: A loan used to purchase a home or property, where the borrower makes regular payments over a set period, including principal and interest, until the loan is fully repaid.

Example: A couple may take out a 30-year fixed-rate mortgage to finance the purchase of their first home, making monthly payments to the lender until the mortgage is paid off.

Ordinance or Law Coverage

Definition: Insurance coverage that helps pay for the cost of rebuilding or repairing a home to comply with current building codes and regulations, which may have changed since the home was initially constructed.

Example: If a home built in the 1980s is severely damaged and requires significant reconstruction, ordinance or law coverage would cover the additional costs of meeting modern building codes for electrical, plumbing, or accessibility requirements.

Peril

Definition: The specific cause of loss or damage covered by an insurance policy, such as fire, theft, or natural disasters.

Example: A standard homeowner's policy may cover perils like windstorms, hail, and lightning, but exclude perils like earthquakes or floods, which require separate coverage.

Policy Limit

Definition: The maximum amount an insurance company will pay for a covered loss under a policy, often specified as a per occurrence or annual limit.

Example: A homeowner's insurance policy may have a $500,000 policy limit for dwelling coverage, meaning the insurer will not pay more than that amount for repairs or rebuilding, regardless of the actual cost.

Premium

Definition: The amount paid by the policyholder to the insurance company for coverage, often calculated based on the perceived risk, coverage limits, deductibles, and other factors.

Example: A homeowner in a high-risk area for natural disasters may pay a higher annual premium for their homeowner's insurance policy compared to someone in a lower-risk area.

Property Tax

Definition: A tax levied by local governments on real estate properties, based on the assessed value of the property, which helps fund public services and infrastructure.

Example: A homeowner living in an area with high property taxes may have to pay several thousand dollars annually in taxes, in addition to their mortgage and insurance payments.

Refinancing

Definition: The process of obtaining a new mortgage loan with different terms, typically to take advantage of lower interest rates or adjust the loan term or amount.

Example: A homeowner with a 30-year mortgage at a 6% interest rate may choose to refinance to a lower 4% rate, potentially saving thousands of dollars in interest over the life of the loan.

Reinsurance

Definition: A practice where an insurance company transfers a portion of its risk to another insurer, known as a reinsurer, to spread the risk and maintain financial stability.

Case Study: After a devastating hurricane season in Florida, several insurers turned to reinsurance to help cover the high volume of claims and ensure they had enough reserves to remain solvent.

Replacement Cost

Definition: The amount it would cost to rebuild or repair a property with materials of similar kind and quality, without deducting for depreciation.

Example: If a 10-year-old home is destroyed by fire, the replacement cost would be the amount required to construct an entirely new home with comparable features and specifications, regardless of the existing home's age or condition.

Subrogation

Definition: The process by which an insurance company, after paying a claim, seeks to recover the amount paid from the party legally responsible for the loss or damage.

Example: If a homeowner's property is damaged due to a negligent contractor, the insurance company may pay the claim upfront and then pursue subrogation against the contractor to recover the payout amount.

Title Insurance

Definition: Insurance that protects the policyholder against defects or issues with the property's title or ownership history, which could potentially lead to legal disputes or financial losses.

Example: When purchasing a home, buyers often obtain title insurance to protect against any undiscovered liens, encumbrances, or ownership claims that could jeopardize their rights to the property.

Case Study: In 2020, a homeowner in Texas faced a legal battle after it was discovered that a previous owner had fraudulently obtained the property's title. The homeowner's title insurance policy covered the legal costs and eventual settlement, protecting their ownership rights.

Umbrella Insurance

Definition: A type of personal liability insurance that provides additional coverage above the limits of other policies, such as homeowner's or auto insurance, offering extra protection against significant claims or lawsuits.

Example: A high-net-worth individual may purchase an umbrella insurance policy to extend their liability coverage beyond the limits of their homeowner's and auto policies, safeguarding their assets in the event of a substantial legal judgment or settlement.

Underinsurance

Definition: The situation where a policyholder does not have enough insurance coverage, leading to significant out-of-pocket expenses in the event of a claim.

Example: If a homeowner insures their $500,000 home for only $300,000, they are underinsured and may have to pay a significant portion of the rebuilding costs out-of-pocket if the home is completely destroyed.

Underwriting

Definition: The process by which insurers evaluate the risk of insuring a property, individual, or entity, determining the appropriate premium and scope of coverage based on various factors.

Example: When applying for homeowner's insurance, the underwriting process may consider factors such as the home's age, construction type, location, and the applicant's claims history to assess the level of risk and set the premium rate accordingly.

Emerging Trends in the Insurance Industry

The insurance sector is continuously evolving, with advancements in technology and changes in consumer expectations shaping the future. Understanding trends like the increasing use of artificial intelligence in risk assessment and the growing importance of cybersecurity insurance can provide a forward-looking perspective on the industry.

In conclusion, just as a carpenter needs to know his hammer and nails, policymakers and policyholders should master these terms. It is not just about enhancing one's vocabulary; it's about deepening one's comprehension of the insurance landscape. This knowledge empowers us to make informed decisions, advocate for necessary coverage, and navigate the complexities of the insurance world with confidence.

In future discussions, we can delve deeper into how these terms apply to different insurance sectors, explore advanced concepts, and examine the interplay of emerging technologies with traditional insurance practices. By continuing our education, we remain adept at facing the ever-evolving challenges of the insurance industry.

Suggested Reading List

Introduction to Selected Works on Conservative and Libertarian Political Thought

The following is a curated reading list of seminal works that have shaped conservative and libertarian thought over the past three centuries. These texts explore fundamental questions about the nature of individual liberty, the proper role of government, the mechanisms of economic organization, and the moral underpinnings of a free society.

Spanning treatises on political economy, works of moral philosophy, historical analyses, and even fiction, this diverse collection provides an accessible introduction to many of the key ideas and debates that have defined these overlapping intellectual traditions. From the classical liberalism of Adam Smith and Frederic Bastiat to the 20th century contributions of thinkers like F.A. Hayek, Milton Friedman, and Russell Kirk, to contemporary voices like Thomas Sowell, these authors grapple with timeless questions about how to organize society in a way that promotes human flourishing.

While not an exhaustive list, these titles offer a representative sampling of the rich literature that has developed around conservative and libertarian approaches to social, political, and economic issues. Whether addressing the dangers of centralized state power, the importance of free markets and private property, or the central role of individual rights and responsibilities, these works reflect a deep commitment to human freedom and a wariness of concentrated authority.

Included are foundational texts of economics like Smith's "The Wealth of Nations" and Hazlitt's "Economics in One Lesson," which illuminate the dynamics of free markets and the unintended consequences of government interventions. Works by Hayek and Friedman build on these insights to champion economic and political liberty as essential for human progress.

Another strain of thought emphasizes traditionalist conservatism, with writers like Kirk and Buckley seeking to preserve cultural continuity and moral order against the perceived dangers of rapid change and untethered individualism. Reflecting the fusionist project of post-war conservatism, many titles draw on both free market principles and cultural traditionalism.

Distinctively libertarian perspectives are represented in works by thinkers like Rand, Rothbard, and Nozick, who advocate for a minimal state and robust individual rights. Running throughout is a concern for the dangers of overreaching state power and the importance of constitutional constraints, perhaps best exemplified by Hayek's warnings in "The Road to Serfdom."

Of course, not everyone will agree with all the arguments advanced in these pages. But engaging with them offers an opportunity to grapple with fundamental questions about the relationship between the individual and the state, the mechanisms of social coordination, and the requirements of a free and humane social order. Only by wrestling with these ideas can citizens equip themselves for the great task of self-government.

As Thomas Jefferson wrote, "Wherever the people are well informed they can be trusted with their own government." By exploring this literature and critically examining the key ideas that have shaped conservative and libertarian thought, readers can take part in the ongoing conversation about how best to secure the blessings of liberty.

Resources like this reading list offer a starting point for developing the knowledge and habits of mind essential for an engaged citizenry. After all, as James Madison put it, "Knowledge will forever govern ignorance; and a people who mean to be their own governors must arm themselves with the power which knowledge gives." It is in that spirit that these works are offered for the reader's consideration.

Selected Works on Conservative and Libertarian Political Thought:

Foundational Economic Principles

1. **"The Wealth of Nations" by Adam Smith (1776)** - Often considered the bible of capitalism, Smith's extensive work on economics lays the groundwork for the free market system. It discusses the importance of self-interest, division of labor, and the invisible hand in economic theory.
2. **"Capitalism and Freedom" by Milton Friedman (1962)** - This seminal work by Nobel laureate Milton Friedman advocates for the freedom of the individual and the proper role of government in a free society, emphasizing the importance of a capitalist economic system as the best way to achieve economic and social prosperity.
3. **"Economics in One Lesson" by Henry Hazlitt (1946)** - A straightforward, easy-to-understand introduction to economic principles that reveals the often-overlooked consequences of government intervention.
4. **"Risk, Uncertainty and Profit" by Frank H. Knight (1921)** - This book, published in 1921, explores the distinction between risk (which can be measured and thus priced) and genuine uncertainty (which cannot be quantified). Knight's analysis laid the groundwork for much of modern economic theory on the role of uncertainty in economics, particularly in the behavior of entrepreneurs. He argues that profit is the reward for assuming uncertainty, and this insight has profound implications for understanding the functioning of economies and the role of entrepreneurship within them.

5. **"Basic Economics" by Thomas Sowell (2000)** - An accessible, comprehensive overview of economic principles, free from jargon and equations. Sowell's work provides clear examples and explanations of how economies function, government's role, and policies' impact on economic outcomes.
6. **"Free to Choose" by Milton and Rose Friedman (1980)** - Expanding on the themes of "Capitalism and Freedom," the Friedmans offer a passionate argument for the freedom of choice as a means to economic and societal health.

Political Philosophy and Governance

7. **"The Road to Serfdom" by F.A. Hayek (1944)** - First published in 1944, "The Road to Serfdom" is a seminal work in political philosophy and economics. Hayek critically examines the dangers of centralized planning and the tyranny resulting from government control over economic decisions. He argues that socialism and excessive government control inevitably lead to the loss of freedom and tyranny, drawing from the examples of Nazi Germany and the Soviet Union. Hayek champions the importance of individual liberty and the free market as the best means of creating a prosperous and just society.
8. **"Democracy in America" by Alexis de Tocqueville (1835)** - A classic exploration of the American political system, society, and culture. Tocqueville's observations on the democratic process and the balance of liberty and equality remain relevant today.
9. **"The Federalist Papers" by Alexander Hamilton, James Madison, and John Jay (1788)** - A collection of essays that argued for the ratification of the United States Constitution. These papers offer deep insights into the founders' thoughts on federalism, checks and balances, and the protection of individual rights.
10. **"The Constitution of Liberty" by F.A. Hayek (1960)** - Furthering the discussion initiated in "The Road to Serfdom," Hayek delves

deeper into the concept of liberty, the rule of law, and the individual's role in a free society, offering a robust defense of democratic liberalism.

11. **"Anarchy, State, and Utopia" by Robert Nozick (1974)** - Nozick's landmark work presents a libertarian perspective on the nature of the state and individual rights. He argues for a minimal "night-watchman" state and explores the idea of a utopian society based on voluntary association.

12. **"The Law" by Frédéric Bastiat (1850) - Published in 1850**, "The Law" is a passionate defense and explanation of what Bastiat considered the proper role of the law and government. He argues that the law should protect individual rights and property and ensure liberty rather than be used as a tool for plunder or to grant special privileges to specific groups. Bastiat emphasizes the principles of freedom, property, and individual responsibility, critiquing socialist policies that were becoming popular in his time. "The Law" remains a foundational text in libertarian and conservative thought for its clear exposition of the relationship between law and liberty.

13. **"The Quest for Cosmic Justice" by Thomas Sowell (1999)** - This book challenges the modern conception of social justice, arguing that the quest for 'cosmic justice' often leads to unintended consequences that undermine the very goals it seeks to achieve.

14. **"The Road to Serfdom: Text and Documents" by F.A. Hayek, edited by Bruce Caldwell (2007)** - While you've already delved into Hayek's "The Road to Serfdom," this edition includes extensive introductory material and a collection of relevant documents that enrich Hayek's original arguments. Caldwell's edition provides deeper insight into Hayek's work and its historical context.

Cultural and Moral Foundations

15. **"The Conservative Mind" by Russell Kirk (1953)** - This book traces the development of conservative thought from Edmund Burke to the 20th century, offering insights into the intellectual underpinnings of conservatism in the United States and the United Kingdom. Kirk's work is pivotal for understanding modern conservatism's philosophical and cultural foundations.

16. **"The Quest for Community" by Robert Nisbet (1953)** - Nisbet's work challenges the increasing power of the state over individual lives and communities, arguing for a return to the social structures and communities that provide individuals with a sense of belonging and identity.

17. **"Mere Christianity" by C.S. Lewis (1952)** - In this theological work, Lewis argues for the rationality of belief in God and the fundamental truths of the Christian faith. His arguments have been influential among Christian conservatives, who often emphasize the importance of faith and morality in public life.

18. **"The Light and the Glory" by Peter Marshall and David Manuel (1977) - Published in 1977**, "The Light and the Glory" explores the history of the United States from a Christian perspective, arguing that America was founded on Christian principles and has a unique role in God's plan. The authors use historical narratives to suggest that many of America's pivotal events and founding fathers were guided by divine providence. This book is part of a series that seeks to provide an interpretation of American history that emphasizes the role of faith and Christian values in the nation's founding and development.

19. **"God and Man at Yale" by William F. Buckley Jr. (1951)** - Buckley's critique of his alma mater provides insight into the conservative critique of higher education and the perceived liberal biases within academia. This book is seminal for understanding the

conservative movement's stance on education and academic freedom.

20. **"The Virtue of Selfishness" by Ayn Rand (1964)** - A collection of essays that further details Rand's Objectivist philosophy, focusing on why she believes that rational self-interest is the key to a thriving society.

21. **"Atlas Shrugged" by Ayn Rand (1957)** - While more philosophical and controversial, Rand's magnum opus presents a dramatized version of her Objectivist philosophy, emphasizing the moral right of individuals to live for their own sake and the dangers of collectivist thought.

Contemporary Voices and Perspectives

22. **"The Vision of the Anointed" by Thomas Sowell (1999)** Thomas Sowell critiques the mindset of self-appointed experts or "anointed" who propose social policies believing they know what's best for society. He examines the consequences of such policies in areas like education and crime, demonstrating how they can worsen the issues they aim to solve. Sowell advocates for more empirical evidence-based approaches, emphasizing the limits of government intervention and the value of individual and market-driven solutions.

23. **"The Righteous Mind" by Jonathan Haidt (2012)** In this thought-provoking book, social psychologist Jonathan Haidt explores the psychological underpinnings of our moral beliefs and how they shape our politics and religion. Haidt delves into why people are divided by politics, presenting his research on moral foundations theory. He suggests that individuals across the political spectrum rely on different sets of moral intuitions, which influence their worldview. "The Righteous Mind" offers insights into understanding and bridging the ideological divides, advocating for more empathy and understanding in political and social discourse.

24. **"The Conservative Sensibility" by George F. Will (2019)** This book by renowned columnist and political commentator George F. Will is a comprehensive exploration of conservative philosophy and its implications for contemporary American politics. Will argues for a conservatism based on the principles of limited government, individual liberty, and the rule of law, drawing on the nation's founding ideals. He critiques modern political developments that deviate from these principles, offering a vision for a grounded and principled conservatism.

25. **"Liberty Defined" by Ron Paul (2011)** In "Liberty Defined," former Congressman and presidential candidate Ron Paul presents his views on fifty key issues facing America, from taxation to education, foreign policy to healthcare. Each chapter tackles a different topic, offering Paul's libertarian perspective on how liberty should be understood and applied in these areas. The book serves as a manifesto of Paul's beliefs, advocating for a government that is smaller, less intrusive, and more in tune with the principles of individual freedom.

26. **"Coming Apart" by Charles Murray (2012)** Sociologist Charles Murray examines the growing divide in American society in "Coming Apart." Focusing on white Americans to avoid the confounding factor of race, Murray analyzes how the upper and lower classes have diverged significantly since the mid-20th century in terms of culture, values, marriage, education, and work ethic. The book provides a detailed and data-driven look at the fragmentation of American communities and offers insights into the social and economic factors contributing to this divide.

27. **"Witness" by Whittaker Chambers (1952)** - "Witness" is the autobiographical account of Whittaker Chambers, a former communist spy who became a key figure in the Alger Hiss case during the early years of the Cold War. Chambers' narrative goes beyond espionage, offering a deeply personal and philosophical look

at his journey from communism to faith in freedom and Christianity. The book is not only a compelling spy story but also a reflection on the ideological struggle between communism and capitalism, making it a significant work in conservative literature.

28. "The Closing of the American Mind" by Allan Bloom (1987) - Bloom's book is a critique of what he sees as the intellectual and moral decline of American higher education. He argues that relativism and a lack of grounding in the Western canon have led to a crisis in American culture and education.

29. "The Fatal Conceit" by F.A. Hayek (1988) - In this work, Hayek critiques socialist economic planning and argues for the superiority of market economies. He emphasizes the importance of evolved cultural traditions and the limits of human reason in designing social institutions.

30. "Man, Economy, and State" by Murray Rothbard (1962) - Rothbard's treatise on economics combines the principles of Austrian economics with libertarian political philosophy, offering a comprehensive look at the relationship between the state and the economy.

31. "The Tragedy of American Compassion" by Marvin Olasky (1992) - Olasky critiques modern welfare policies and argues for a return to the principles of private charity and personal responsibility, drawing on historical examples to suggest a conservative approach to social welfare.

32. "The Conscience of a Conservative" by Barry Goldwater (1960) - In this influential work, Senator Goldwater articulates the core principles of conservatism, emphasizing limited government, individual liberty, and the importance of the Constitution. Goldwater's book played a significant role in shaping the modern conservative movement in the United States.

33. "The Law of Nations" by Emer de Vattel (1758) - This 18th-century work on international law emphasizes the principles of

national sovereignty, justice, and the rights and duties of nations, offering a foundational perspective on the conservative view of international relations and law.

34. **"Reflections on the Revolution in France" by Edmund Burke (1790)** - Burke's reflections critically examine the principles behind the French Revolution and lay the groundwork for conservative thought, highlighting the importance of tradition, social cohesion, and the dangers of rapid societal change.

Each of these works offers a distinct perspective on law, economics, political philosophy, and history, reflecting the authors' deep engagements with the challenges of governance, economic organization, and society's moral and ethical underpinnings. They continue to be widely read and influential in discussions of freedom, the role of government, and the moral foundations of economic and political systems.

Made in the USA
Middletown, DE
27 July 2024

58082755R00320